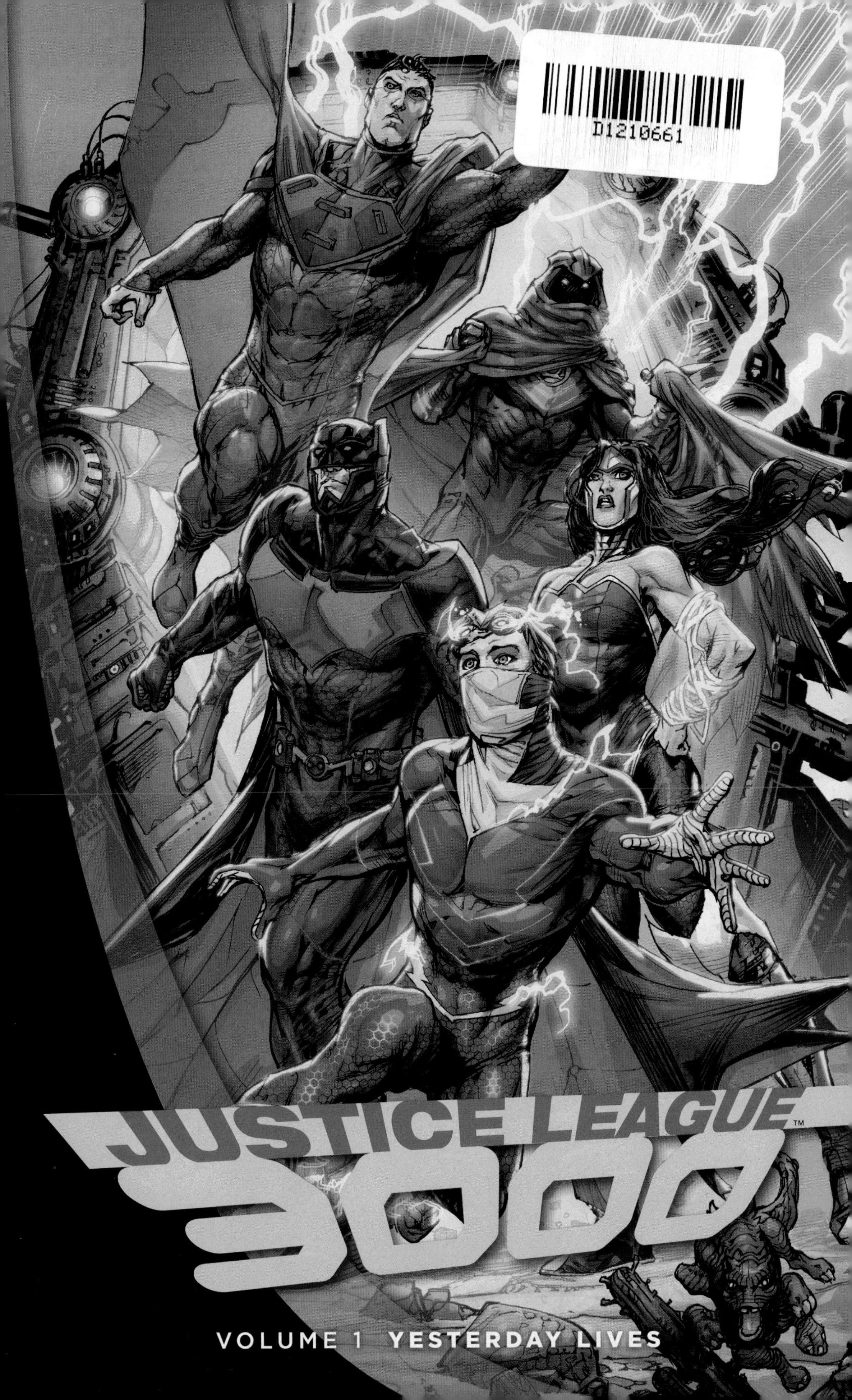

JUSTICE LEAGUE™ 3000

VOLUME 1 YESTERDAY LIVES

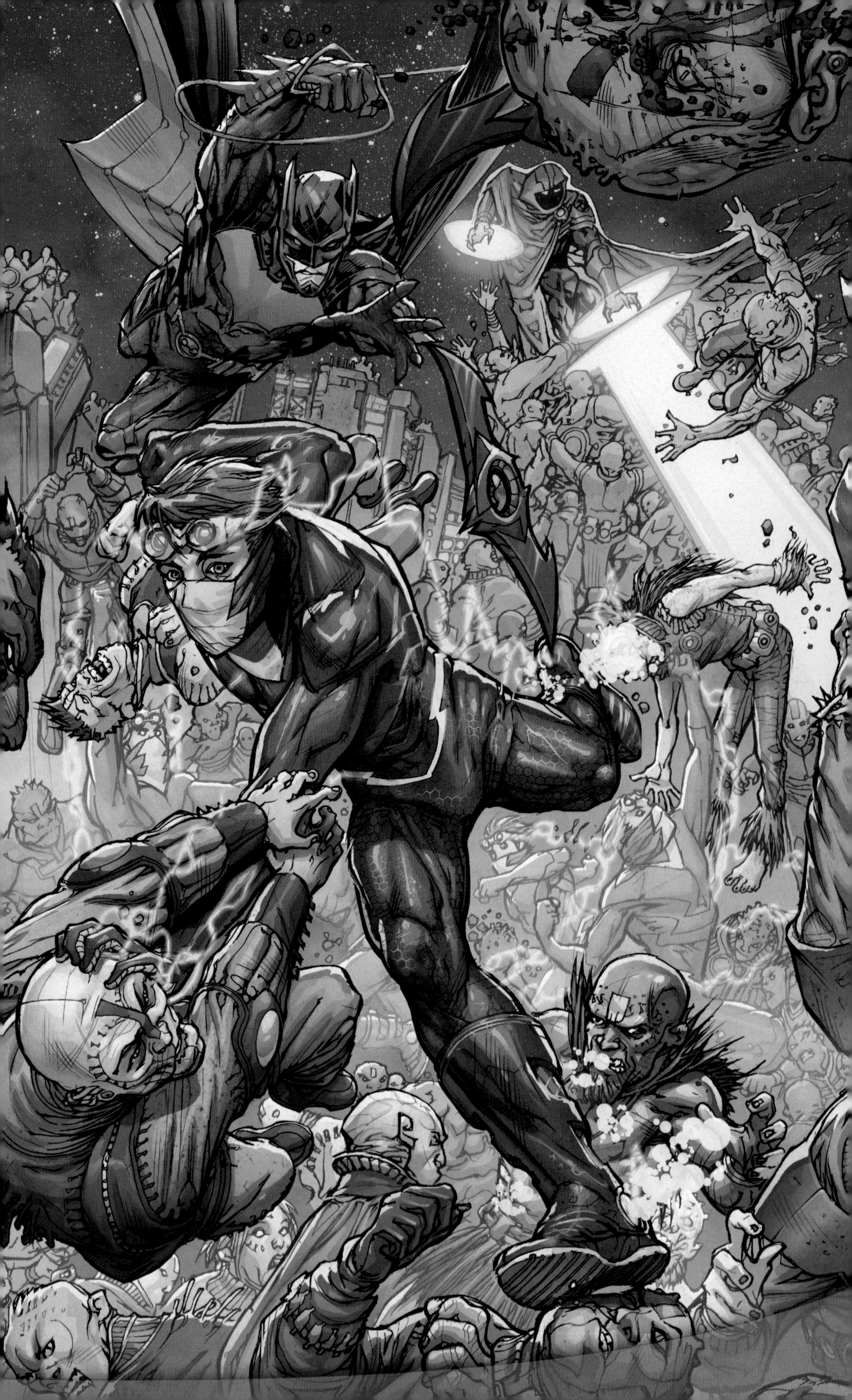

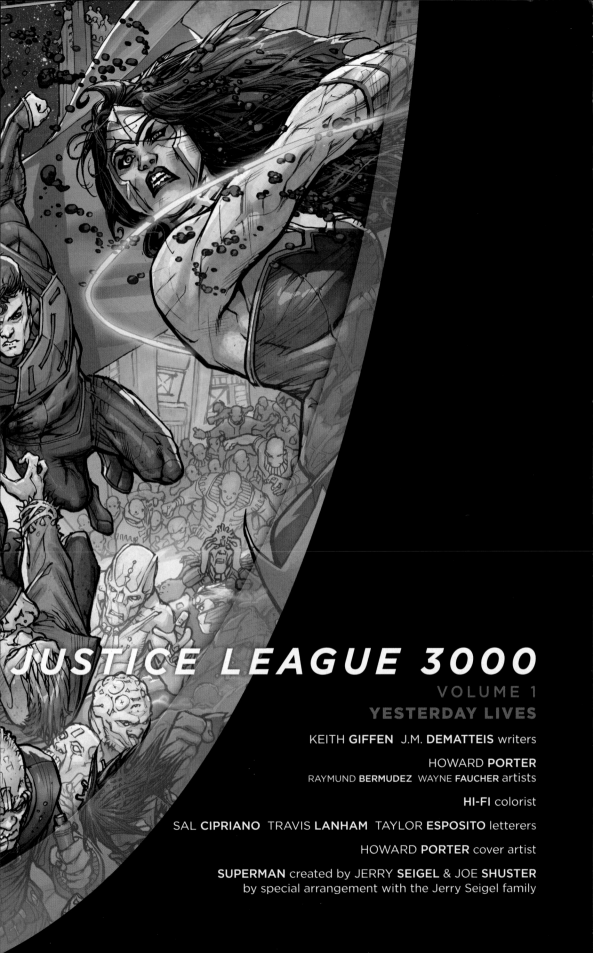

JUSTICE LEAGUE 3000

VOLUME 1
YESTERDAY LIVES

KEITH **GIFFEN** J.M. **DEMATTEIS** writers

HOWARD **PORTER**
RAYMUND **BERMUDEZ** WAYNE **FAUCHER** artists

HI-FI colorist

SAL **CIPRIANO** TRAVIS **LANHAM** TAYLOR **ESPOSITO** letterers

HOWARD **PORTER** cover artist

SUPERMAN created by JERRY **SEIGEL** & JOE **SHUSTER**
by special arrangement with the Jerry Seigel family

JOEY CAVALIERI HARVEY RICHARDS Editors – Original Series KYLE ANDRUKIEWICZ Assistant Editor – Original Series
JEREMY BENT Editor ROBBIN BROSTERMAN Design Director – Books ROBBIE BIEDERMAN – Publication Design

BOB HARRAS Senior VP – Editor-in-Chief, DC Comics

DIANE NELSON President DAN DIDIO & JIM LEE Co-Publishers
GEOFF JOHNS Chief Creative Officer
AMIT DESAI Senior VP – Marketing & Franchise Management
AMY GENKINS Senior VP – Business & Legal Affairs NAIRI GARDINER Senior VP – Finance
JEFF BOISON VP – Publishing Planning MARK CHIARELLO VP – Art Direction & Design
JOHN CUNNINGHAM VP – Marketing TERRI CUNNINGHAM VP – Editorial Administration
LARRY GANEM VP – Talent Relations & Services ALISON GILL Senior VP – Manufacturing & Operations
HANK KANALZ Senior VP – Vertigo & Integrated Publishing
JAY KOGAN VP – Business & Legal Affairs, Publishing JACK MAHAN VP – Business Affairs, Talent
NICK NAPOLITANO VP – Manufacturing Administration SUE POHJA VP – Book Sales
FRED RUIZ VP – Manufacturing Operations COURTNEY SIMMONS Senior VP – Publicity BOB WAYNE Senior VP – Sales

JUSTICE LEAGUE 3000 VOLUME 1: YESTERDAY LIVES

Published by DC Comics. Copyright © 2014 DC Comics. All Rights Reserved.

Originally published in single magazine form in JUSTICE LEAGUE 3000 1-7 © 2013, 2014 DC Comics. All Rights Reserved. All characters, their
distinctive likenesses and related elements featured in this publication are trademarks of DC Comics. The stories, characters and incidents
featured in this publication are entirely fictional. DC Comics does not read or accept unsolicited ideas, stories or artwork.

DC Comics, 1700 Broadway, New York, NY 10019
A Warner Bros. Entertainment Company.
Printed by RR Donnelley, Salem, VA, USA. 2/24/15. Second Printing.

ISBN: 978-1-4012-5046-1

Library of Congress Cataloging-in-Publication Data

Giffen, Keith, author.
Justice League 3000. Volume 1, Yesterday Lives / Keith Giffen, J.M. Dematteis, Howard Porter.
pages cm
ISBN 978-1-4012-5046-1 (paperback)
1. Graphic novels. I. DeMatteis, J. M., author. II. Porter, Howard, illustrator. III. Title. IV. Title: Yesterday Lives.
PN6728.J87G536 2014
741.5'973—dc23
2014014891

SUSTAINABLE
FORESTRY
INITIATIVE
Certified Chain of Custody
20% Certified Forest Content,
80% Certified Sourcing
www.sfiprogram.org
SFI-01042

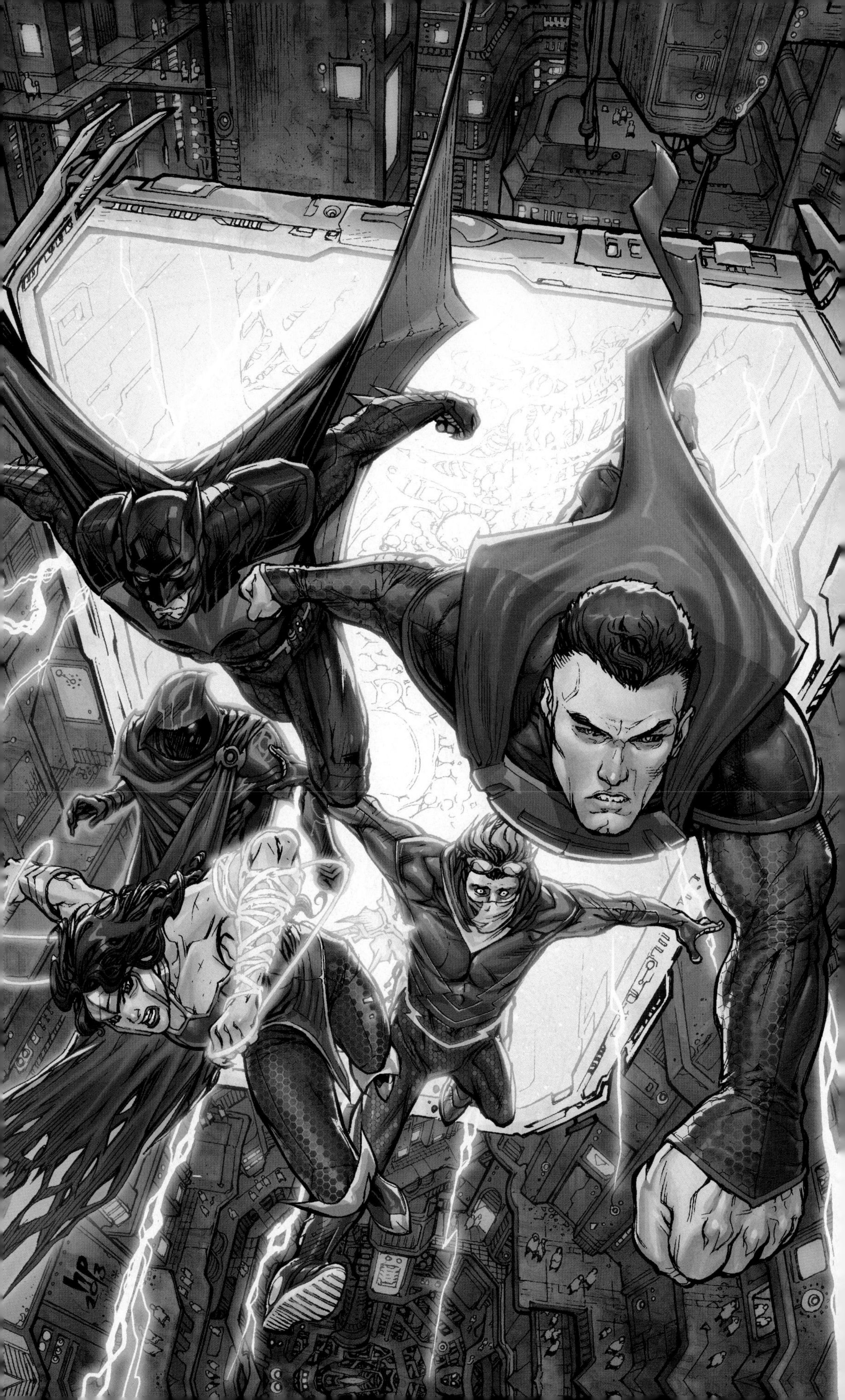

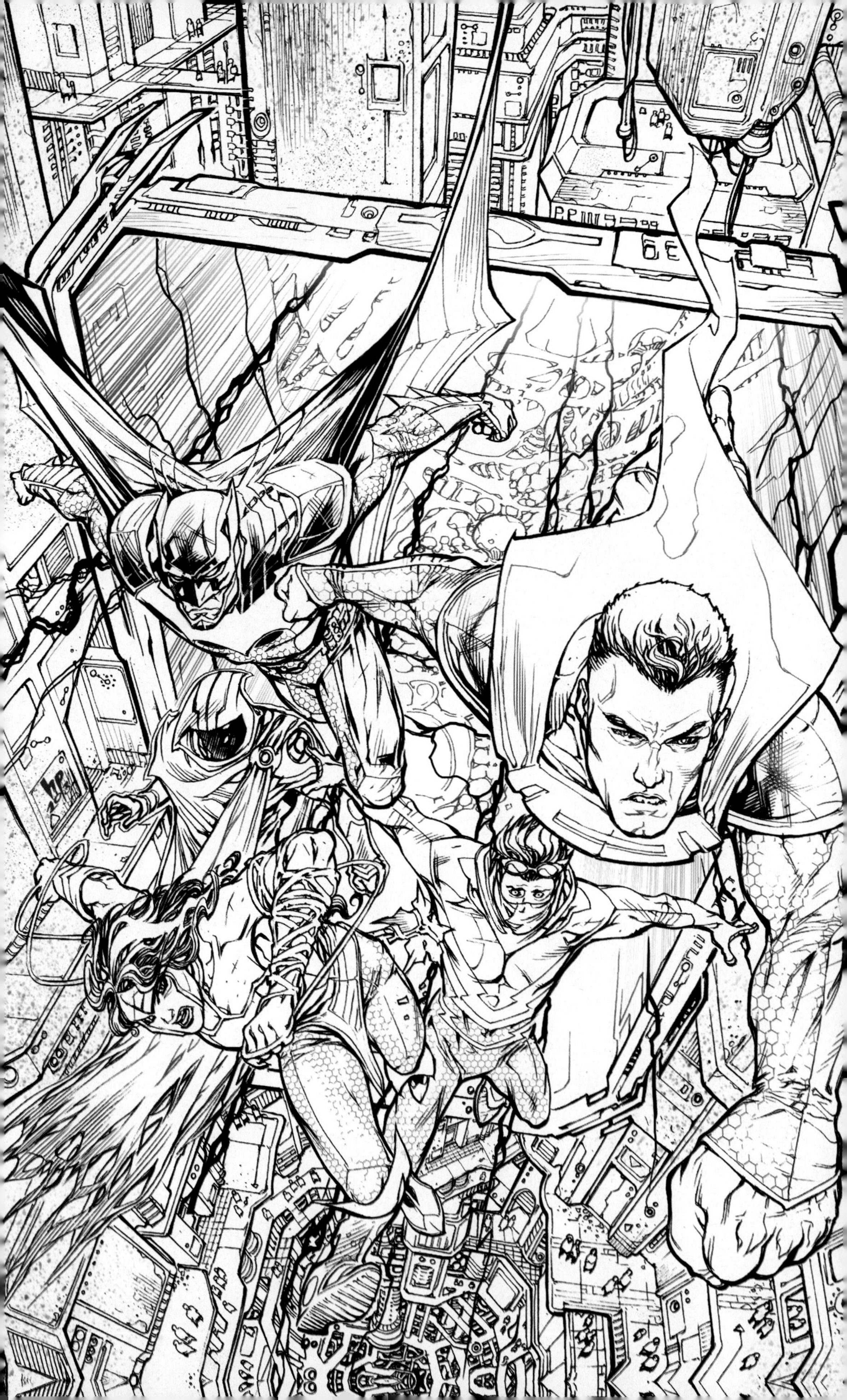

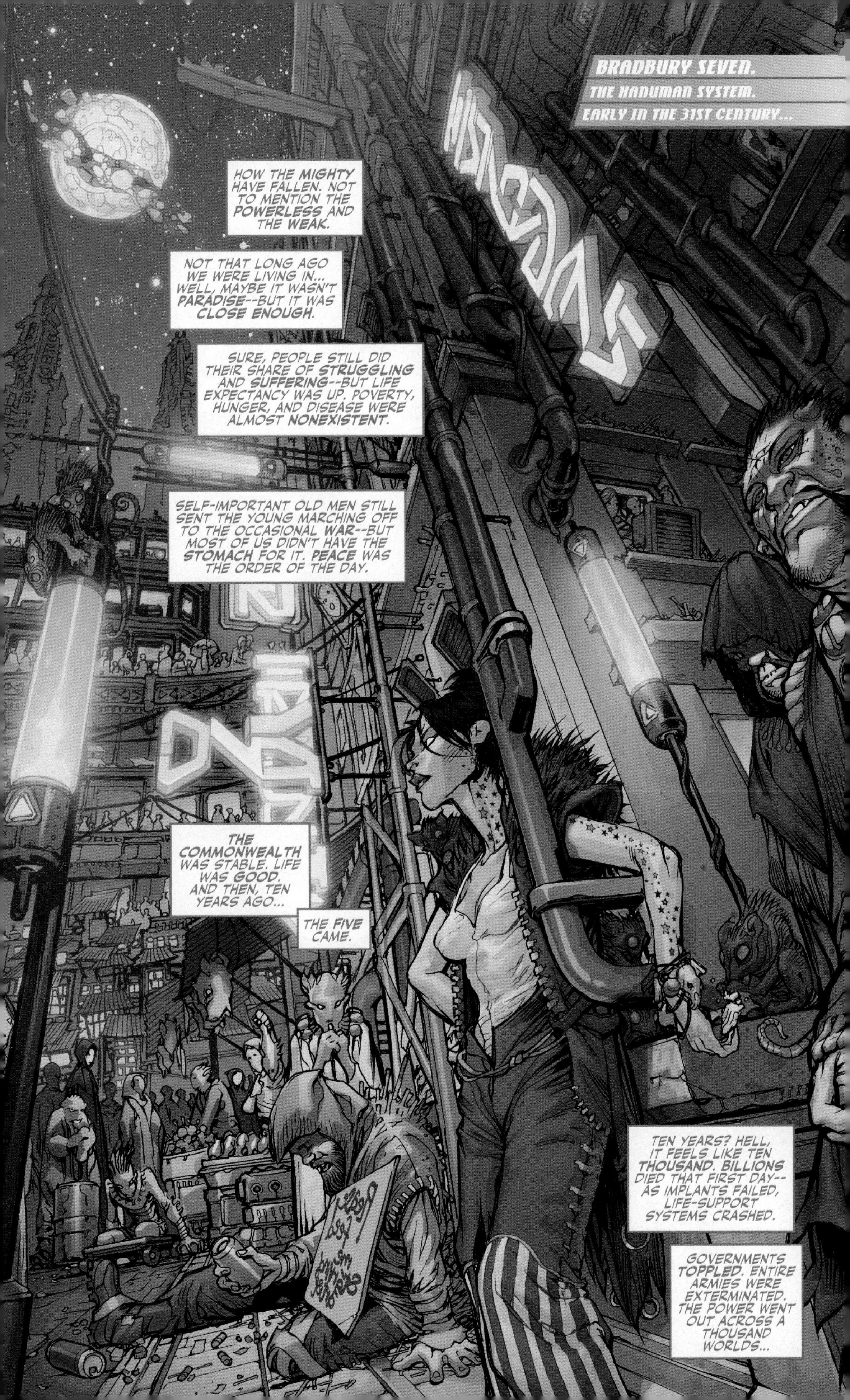
BRADBURY SEVEN.
THE HANUMAN SYSTEM.
EARLY IN THE 31ST CENTURY...
HOW THE MIGHTY HAVE FALLEN. NOT TO MENTION THE POWERLESS AND THE WEAK.
NOT THAT LONG AGO WE WERE LIVING IN... WELL, MAYBE IT WASN'T PARADISE--BUT IT WAS CLOSE ENOUGH.
SURE, PEOPLE STILL DID THEIR SHARE OF STRUGGLING AND SUFFERING--BUT LIFE EXPECTANCY WAS UP. POVERTY, HUNGER, AND DISEASE WERE ALMOST NONEXISTENT.
SELF-IMPORTANT OLD MEN STILL SENT THE YOUNG MARCHING OFF TO THE OCCASIONAL WAR--BUT MOST OF US DIDN'T HAVE THE STOMACH FOR IT. PEACE WAS THE ORDER OF THE DAY.
THE COMMONWEALTH WAS STABLE. LIFE WAS GOOD. AND THEN, TEN YEARS AGO...
THE FIVE CAME.
TEN YEARS? HELL, IT FEELS LIKE TEN THOUSAND. BILLIONS DIED THAT FIRST DAY--AS IMPLANTS FAILED, LIFE-SUPPORT SYSTEMS CRASHED.
GOVERNMENTS TOPPLED. ENTIRE ARMIES WERE EXTERMINATED. THE POWER WENT OUT ACROSS A THOUSAND WORLDS...

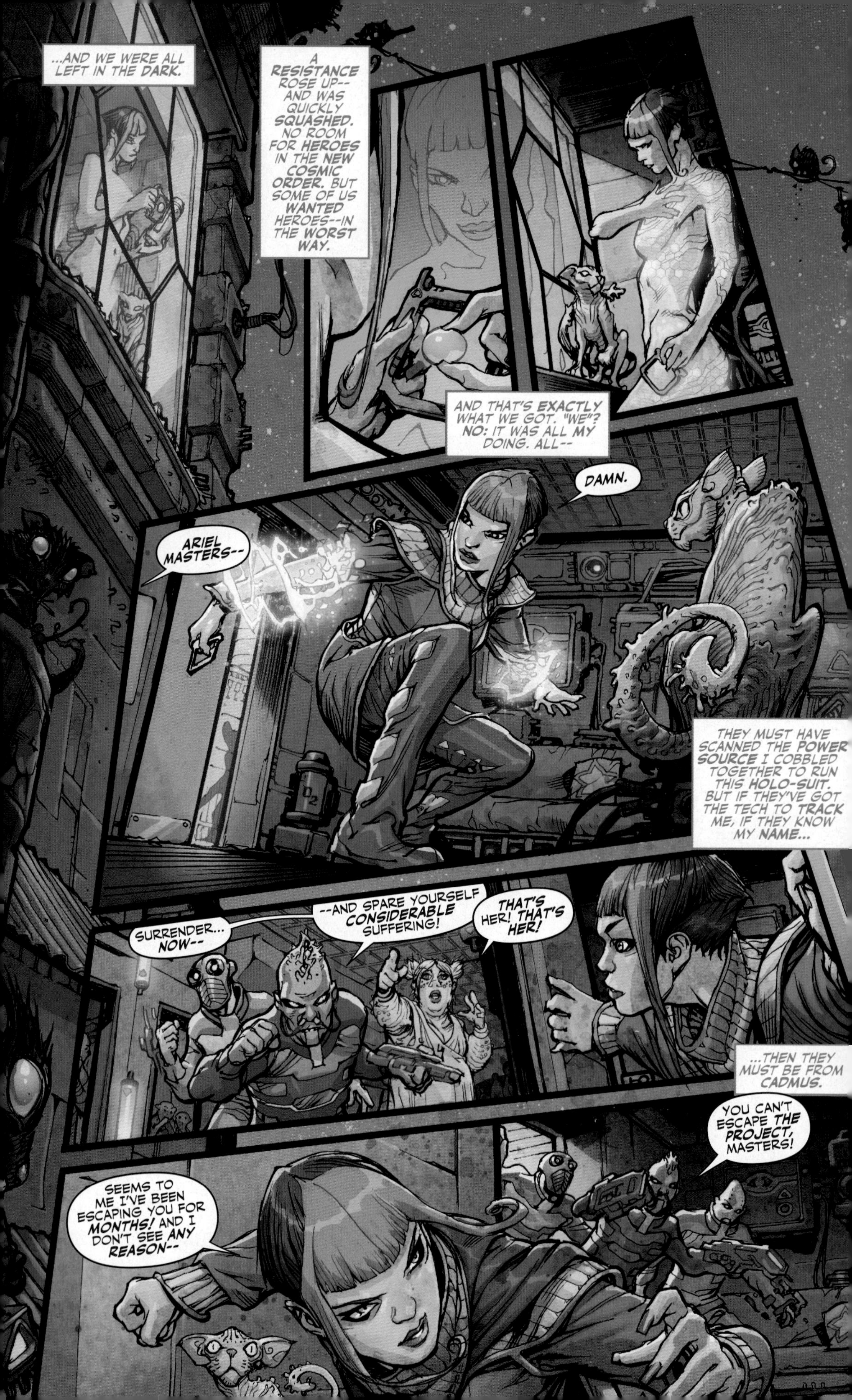
...AND WE WERE ALL LEFT IN THE DARK.
A RESISTANCE ROSE UP-- AND WAS QUICKLY SQUASHED. NO ROOM FOR HEROES IN THE NEW COSMIC ORDER. BUT SOME OF US WANTED HEROES--IN THE WORST WAY.
AND THAT'S EXACTLY WHAT WE GOT. "WE"? NO: IT WAS ALL MY DOING. ALL--
DAMN.
ARIEL MASTERS--
THEY MUST HAVE SCANNED THE POWER SOURCE I COBBLED TOGETHER TO RUN THIS HOLO-SUIT. BUT IF THEY'VE GOT THE TECH TO TRACK ME, IF THEY KNOW MY NAME...
SURRENDER... NOW--
--AND SPARE YOURSELF CONSIDERABLE SUFFERING!
THAT'S HER! THAT'S HER!
...THEN THEY MUST BE FROM CADMUS.
YOU CAN'T ESCAPE THE PROJECT, MASTERS!
SEEMS TO ME I'VE BEEN ESCAPING YOU FOR MONTHS! AND I DON'T SEE ANY REASON--

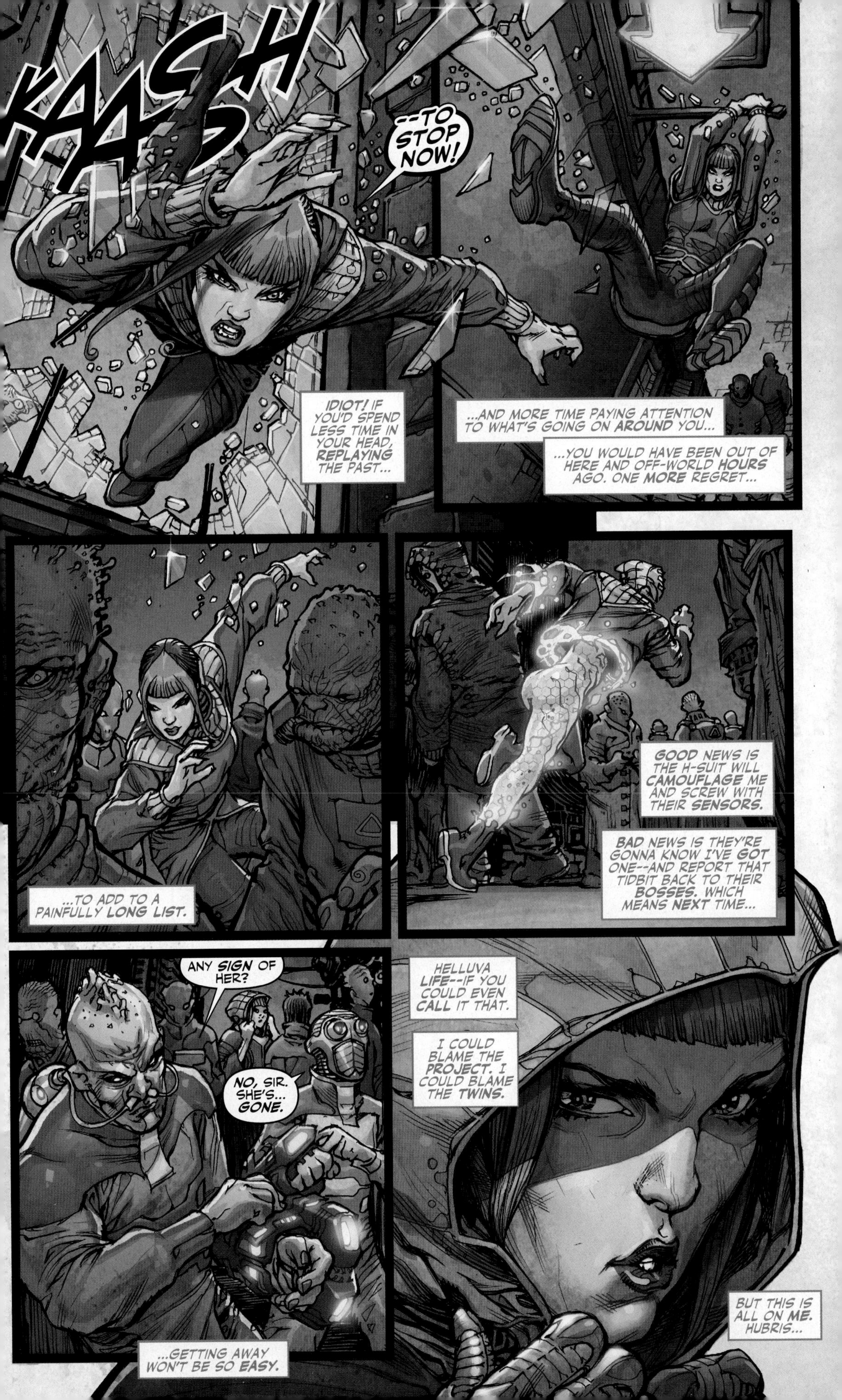
KAASH
--TO STOP NOW!
IDIOT! IF YOU'D SPEND LESS TIME IN YOUR HEAD, REPLAYING THE PAST...
...AND MORE TIME PAYING ATTENTION TO WHAT'S GOING ON AROUND YOU...
...YOU WOULD HAVE BEEN OUT OF HERE AND OFF-WORLD HOURS AGO. ONE MORE REGRET...
...TO ADD TO A PAINFULLY LONG LIST.
GOOD NEWS IS THE H-SUIT WILL CAMOUFLAGE ME AND SCREW WITH THEIR SENSORS.
BAD NEWS IS THEY'RE GONNA KNOW I'VE GOT ONE--AND REPORT THAT TIDBIT BACK TO THEIR BOSSES. WHICH MEANS NEXT TIME...
ANY SIGN OF HER?
NO, SIR. SHE'S... GONE.
...GETTING AWAY WON'T BE SO EASY.
HELLUVA LIFE--IF YOU COULD EVEN CALL IT THAT.
I COULD BLAME THE PROJECT. I COULD BLAME THE TWINS.
BUT THIS IS ALL ON ME. HUBRIS...

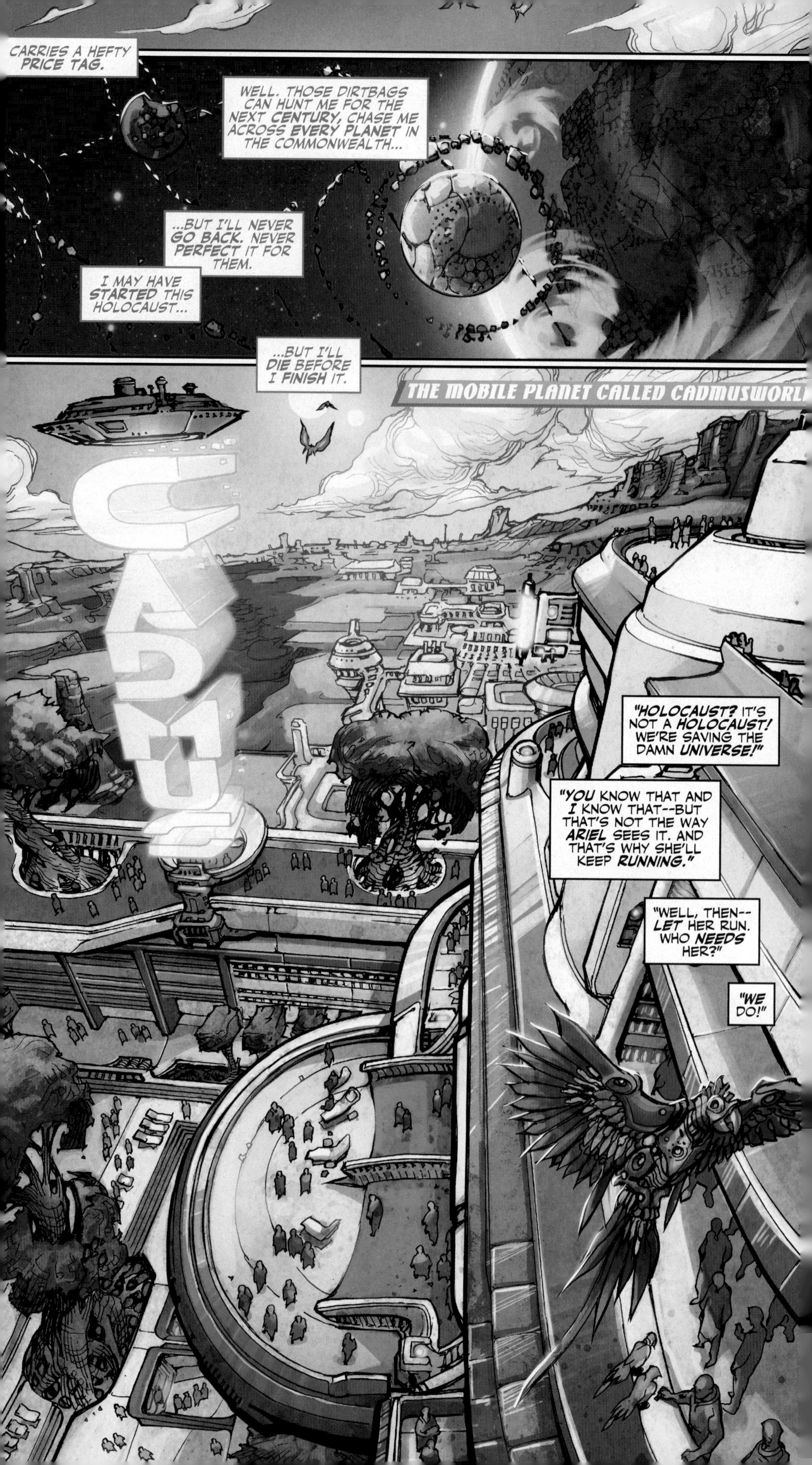

CARRIES A HEFTY PRICE TAG.
WELL. THOSE DIRTBAGS CAN HUNT ME FOR THE NEXT CENTURY, CHASE ME ACROSS EVERY PLANET IN THE COMMONWEALTH...
...BUT I'LL NEVER GO BACK. NEVER PERFECT IT FOR THEM.
I MAY HAVE STARTED THIS HOLOCAUST...
...BUT I'LL DIE BEFORE I FINISH IT.
THE MOBILE PLANET CALLED CADMUSWORLD
CADMUS
"HOLOCAUST? IT'S NOT A HOLOCAUST! WE'RE SAVING THE DAMN UNIVERSE!"
"YOU KNOW THAT AND I KNOW THAT--BUT THAT'S NOT THE WAY ARIEL SEES IT. AND THAT'S WHY SHE'LL KEEP RUNNING."
"WELL, THEN-- LET HER RUN. WHO NEEDS HER?"
"WE DO!"

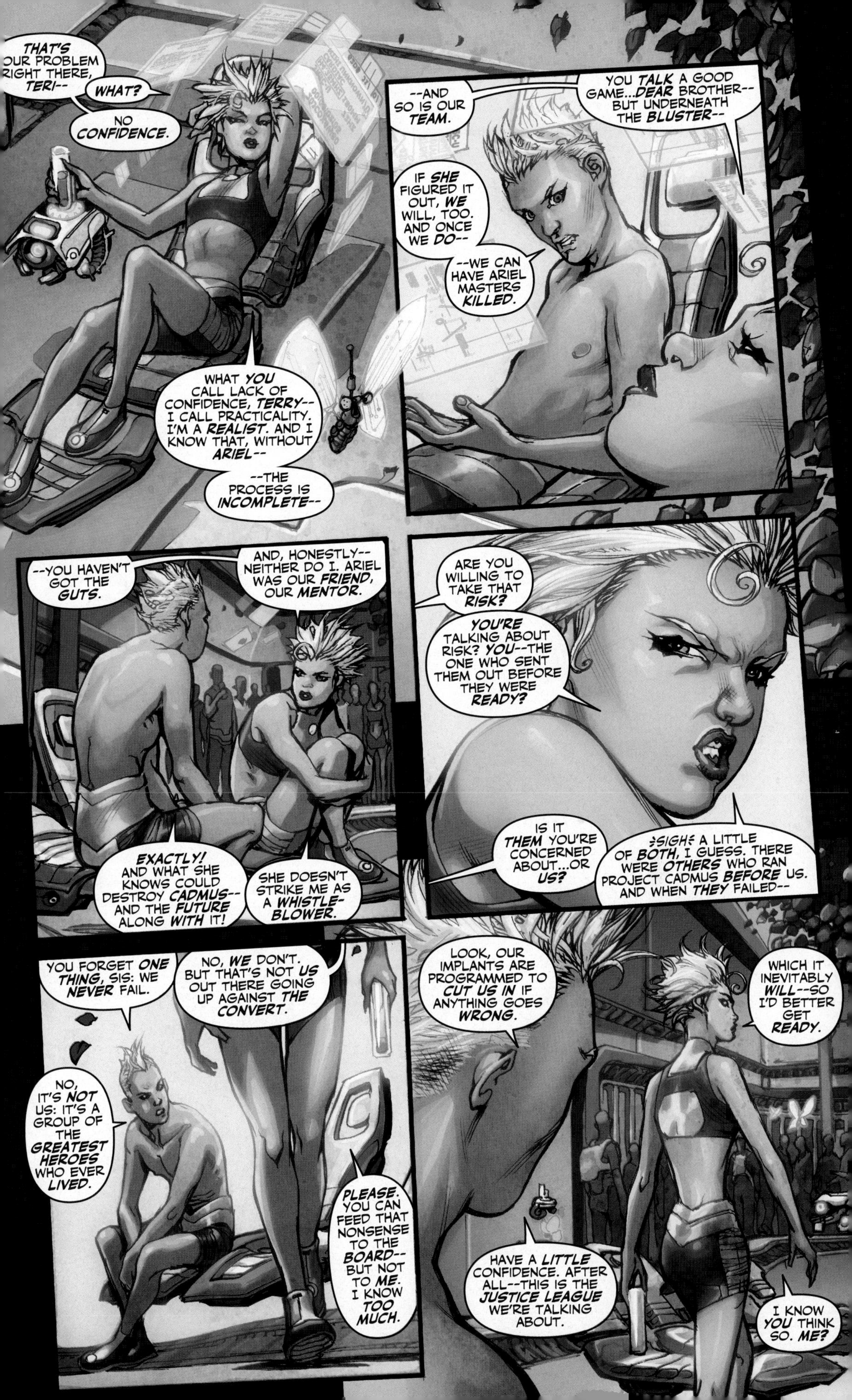
THAT'S OUR PROBLEM RIGHT THERE, TERI--
WHAT?
NO CONFIDENCE.
WHAT YOU CALL LACK OF CONFIDENCE, TERRY--I CALL PRACTICALITY. I'M A REALIST. AND I KNOW THAT, WITHOUT ARIEL--
--THE PROCESS IS INCOMPLETE--
--AND SO IS OUR TEAM.
YOU TALK A GOOD GAME...DEAR BROTHER--BUT UNDERNEATH THE BLUSTER--
IF SHE FIGURED IT OUT, WE WILL, TOO. AND ONCE WE DO--
--WE CAN HAVE ARIEL MASTERS KILLED.
--YOU HAVEN'T GOT THE GUTS.
AND, HONESTLY--NEITHER DO I. ARIEL WAS OUR FRIEND, OUR MENTOR.
EXACTLY! AND WHAT SHE KNOWS COULD DESTROY CADMUS--AND THE FUTURE ALONG WITH IT!
SHE DOESN'T STRIKE ME AS A WHISTLE-BLOWER.
ARE YOU WILLING TO TAKE THAT RISK?
YOU'RE TALKING ABOUT RISK? YOU--THE ONE WHO SENT THEM OUT BEFORE THEY WERE READY?
IS IT THEM YOU'RE CONCERNED ABOUT...OR US?
SIGH A LITTLE OF BOTH, I GUESS. THERE WERE OTHERS WHO RAN PROJECT CADMUS BEFORE US. AND WHEN THEY FAILED--
YOU FORGET ONE THING, SIS: WE NEVER FAIL.
NO, WE DON'T. BUT THAT'S NOT US OUT THERE GOING UP AGAINST THE CONVERT.
NO, IT'S NOT US: IT'S A GROUP OF THE GREATEST HEROES WHO EVER LIVED.
PLEASE. YOU CAN FEED THAT NONSENSE TO THE BOARD--BUT NOT TO ME. I KNOW TOO MUCH.
LOOK, OUR IMPLANTS ARE PROGRAMMED TO CUT US IN IF ANYTHING GOES WRONG.
WHICH IT INEVITABLY WILL--SO I'D BETTER GET READY.
HAVE A LITTLE CONFIDENCE. AFTER ALL--THIS IS THE JUSTICE LEAGUE WE'RE TALKING ABOUT.
I KNOW YOU THINK SO. ME?

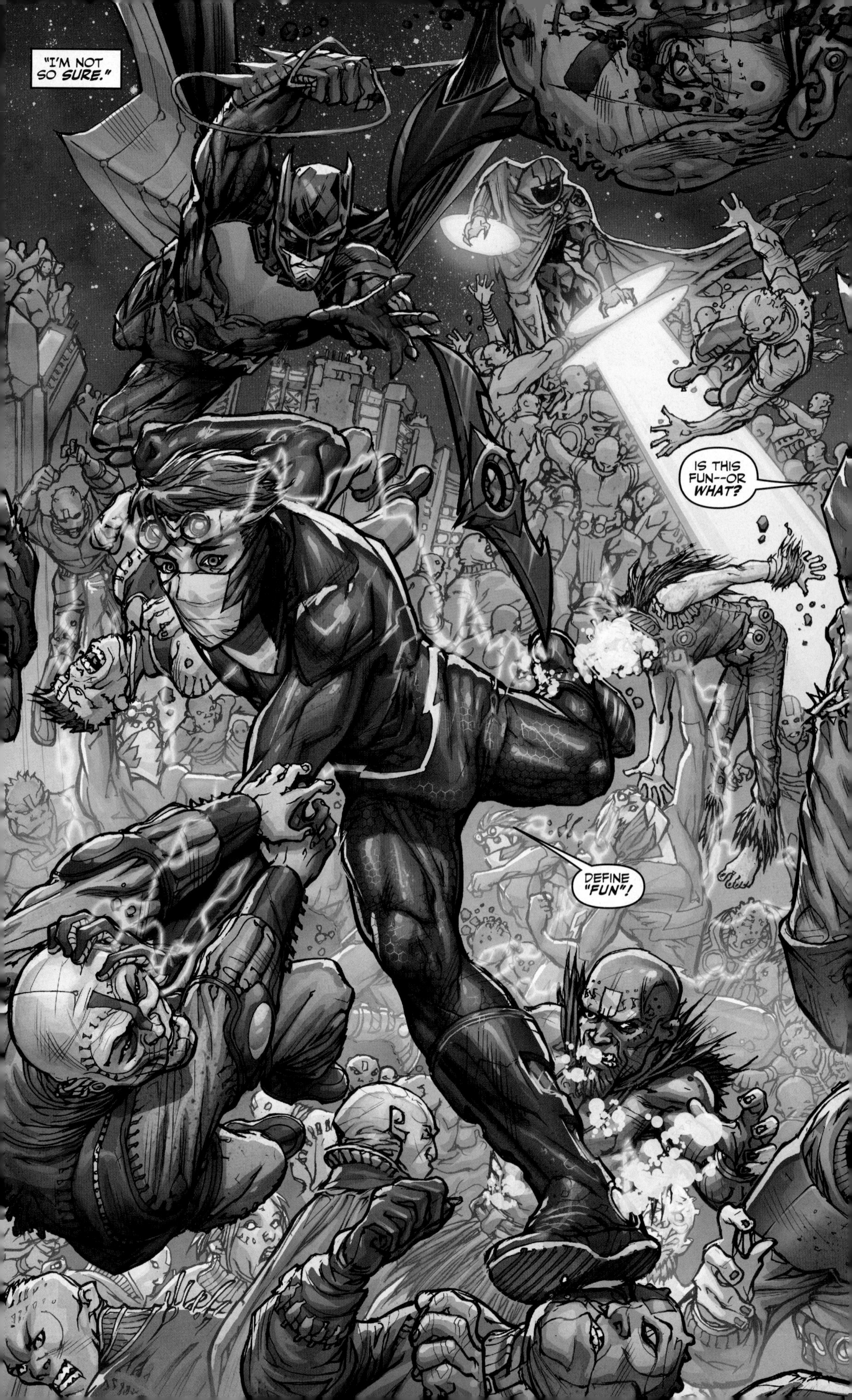
"I'M NOT SO SURE."
IS THIS FUN--OR WHAT?
DEFINE "FUN"!

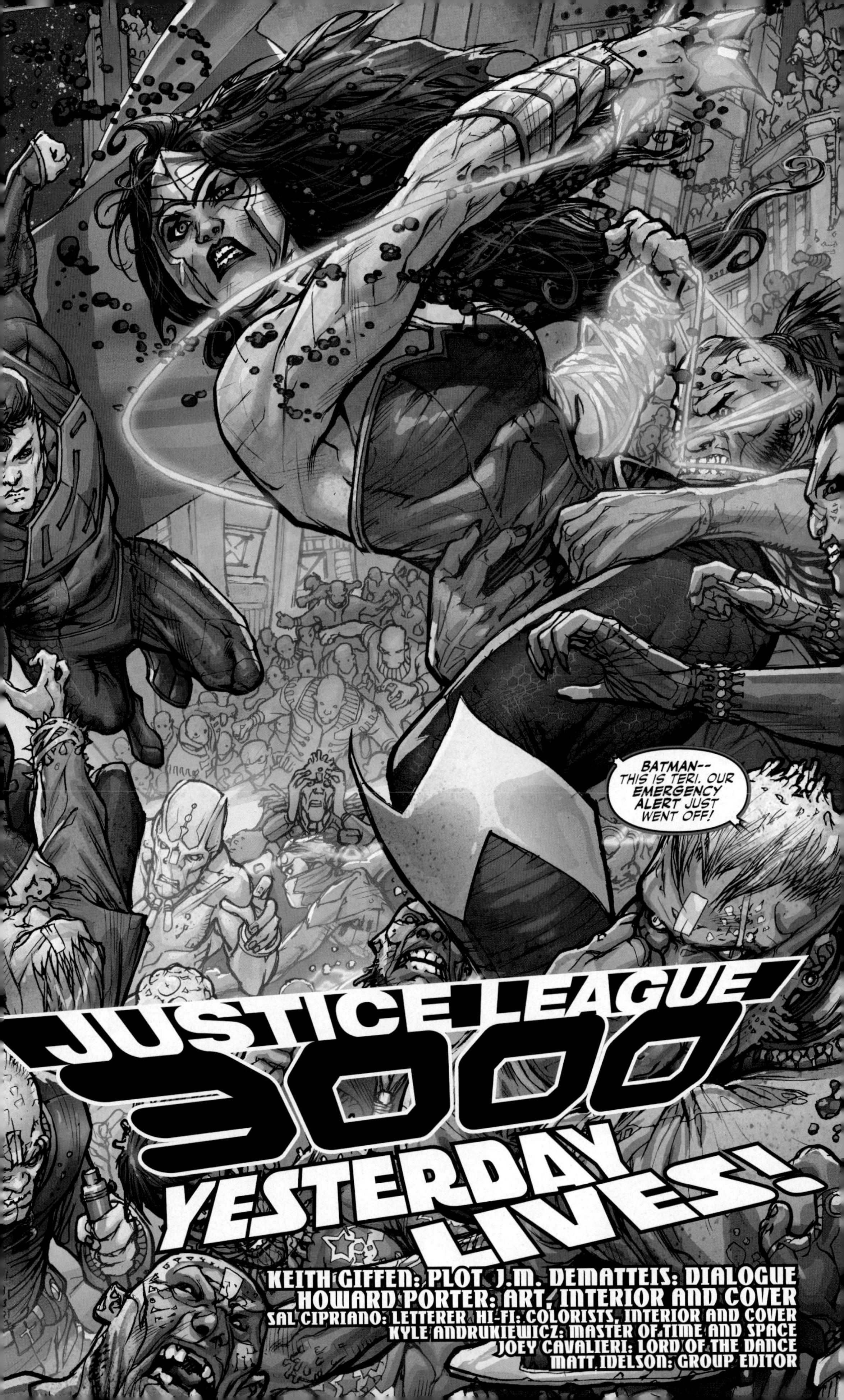
BATMAN-- THIS IS TERI. OUR EMERGENCY ALERT JUST WENT OFF!
JUSTICE LEAGUE 3000
YESTERDAY LIVES!!
KEITH GIFFEN: PLOT J.M. DEMATTEIS: DIALOGUE
HOWARD PORTER: ART, INTERIOR AND COVER
SAL CIPRIANO: LETTERER HI-FI: COLORISTS, INTERIOR AND COVER
KYLE ANDRUKIEWICZ: MASTER OF TIME AND SPACE
JOEY CAVALIERI: LORD OF THE DANCE
MATT IDELSON: GROUP EDITOR

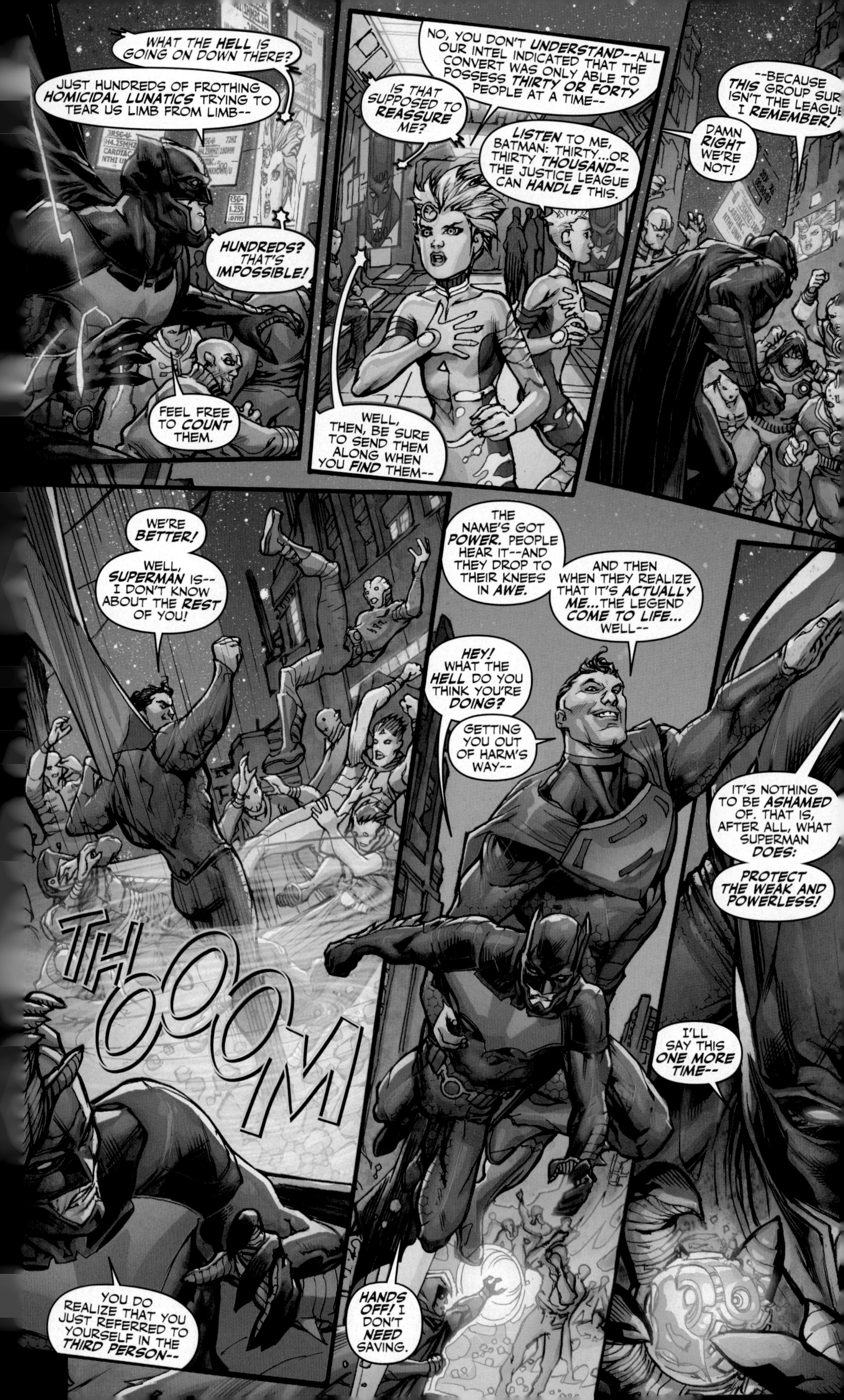
WHAT THE HELL IS GOING ON DOWN THERE?
JUST HUNDREDS OF FROTHING HOMICIDAL LUNATICS TRYING TO TEAR US LIMB FROM LIMB--
HUNDREDS? THAT'S IMPOSSIBLE!
FEEL FREE TO COUNT THEM.
NO, YOU DON'T UNDERSTAND--ALL OUR INTEL INDICATED THAT THE CONVERT WAS ONLY ABLE TO POSSESS THIRTY OR FORTY PEOPLE AT A TIME--
IS THAT SUPPOSED TO REASSURE ME?
LISTEN TO ME, BATMAN: THIRTY...OR THIRTY THOUSAND--THE JUSTICE LEAGUE CAN HANDLE THIS.
WELL, THEN, BE SURE TO SEND THEM ALONG WHEN YOU FIND THEM--
--BECAUSE THIS GROUP SURE ISN'T THE LEAGUE I REMEMBER!
DAMN RIGHT WE'RE NOT!
WE'RE BETTER!
WELL, SUPERMAN IS--I DON'T KNOW ABOUT THE REST OF YOU!
THE NAME'S GOT POWER. PEOPLE HEAR IT--AND THEY DROP TO THEIR KNEES IN AWE.
AND THEN WHEN THEY REALIZE THAT IT'S ACTUALLY ME...THE LEGEND COME TO LIFE... WELL--
HEY! WHAT THE HELL DO YOU THINK YOU'RE DOING?
GETTING YOU OUT OF HARM'S WAY--
IT'S NOTHING TO BE ASHAMED OF. THAT IS, AFTER ALL, WHAT SUPERMAN DOES:
PROTECT THE WEAK AND POWERLESS!
THOOOOM
I'LL SAY THIS ONE MORE TIME--
YOU DO REALIZE THAT YOU JUST REFERRED TO YOURSELF IN THE THIRD PERSON--
HANDS OFF! I DON'T NEED SAVING.

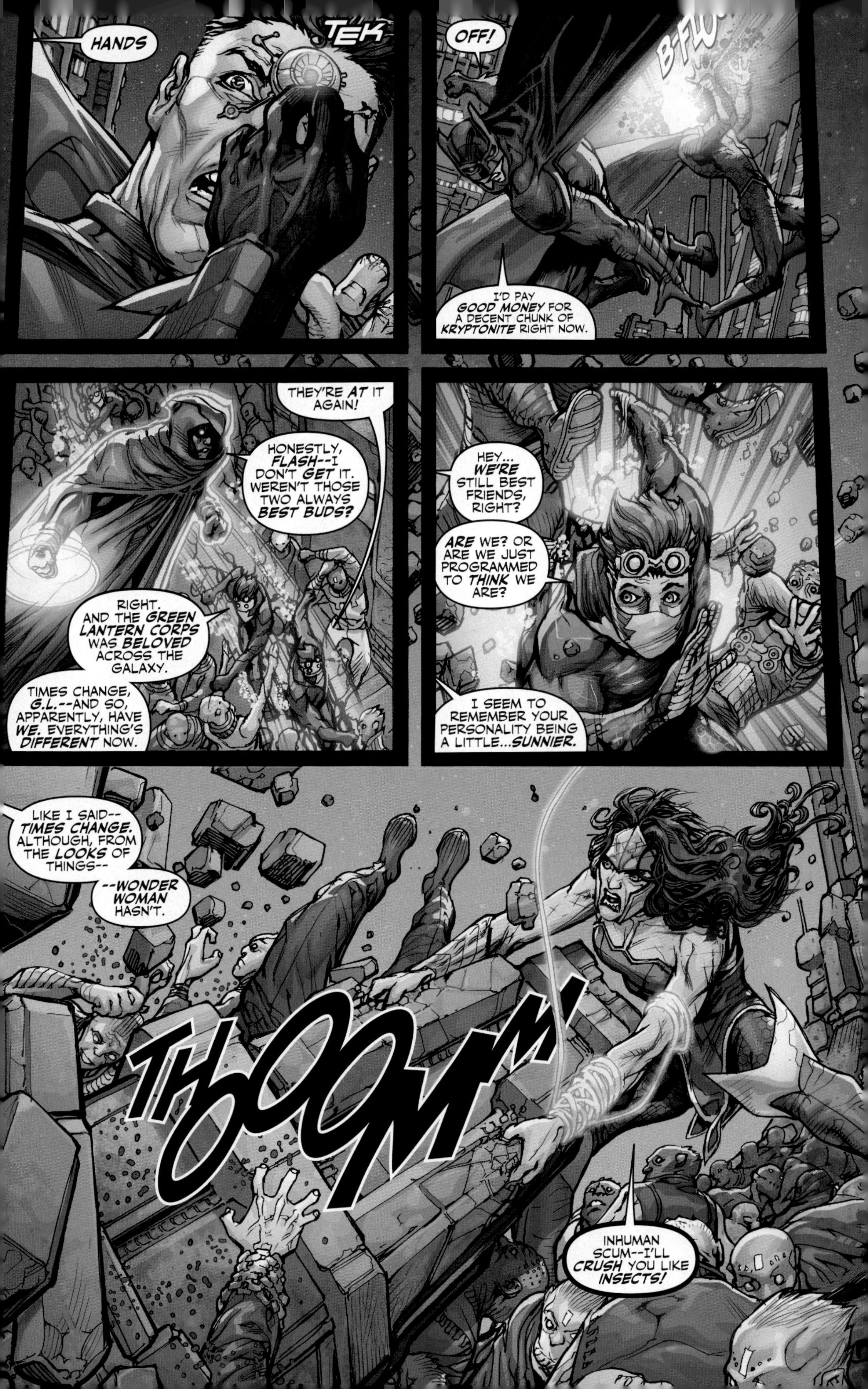
HANDS
TEK
OFF!
B-FLU
I'D PAY GOOD MONEY FOR A DECENT CHUNK OF KRYPTONITE RIGHT NOW.
THEY'RE AT IT AGAIN!
HONESTLY, FLASH--I DON'T GET IT. WEREN'T THOSE TWO ALWAYS BEST BUDS?
RIGHT. AND THE GREEN LANTERN CORPS WAS BELOVED ACROSS THE GALAXY.
TIMES CHANGE, G.L.--AND SO, APPARENTLY, HAVE WE. EVERYTHING'S DIFFERENT NOW.
HEY... WE'RE STILL BEST FRIENDS, RIGHT?
ARE WE? OR ARE WE JUST PROGRAMMED TO THINK WE ARE?
I SEEM TO REMEMBER YOUR PERSONALITY BEING A LITTLE...SUNNIER.
LIKE I SAID--TIMES CHANGE. ALTHOUGH, FROM THE LOOKS OF THINGS--
--WONDER WOMAN HASN'T.
THOOOM
INHUMAN SCUM--I'LL CRUSH YOU LIKE INSECTS!

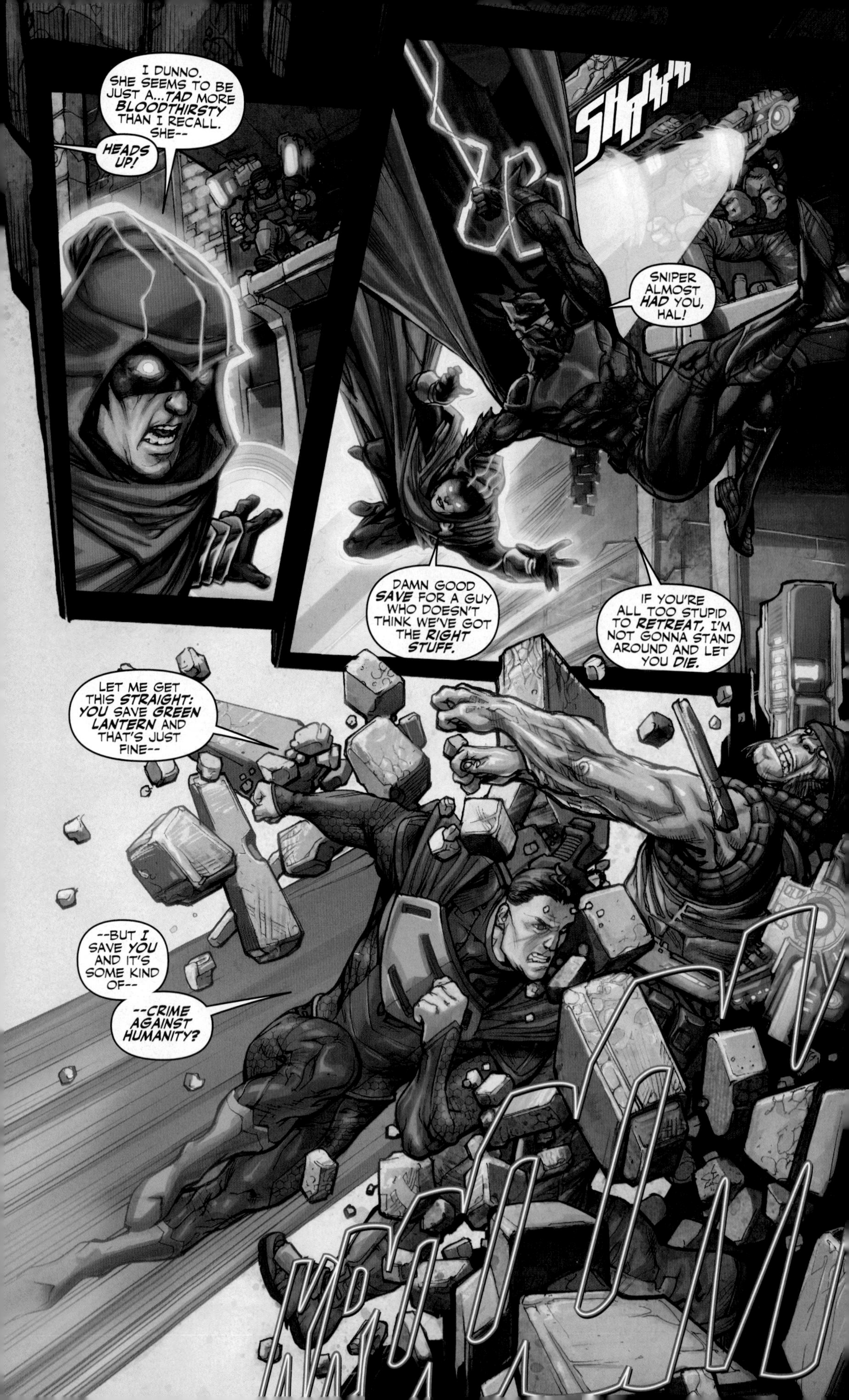
I DUNNO. SHE SEEMS TO BE JUST A...TAD MORE BLOODTHIRSTY THAN I RECALL. SHE--
HEADS UP!
SNIPER ALMOST HAD YOU, HAL!
DAMN GOOD SAVE FOR A GUY WHO DOESN'T THINK WE'VE GOT THE RIGHT STUFF.
IF YOU'RE ALL TOO STUPID TO RETREAT, I'M NOT GONNA STAND AROUND AND LET YOU DIE.
LET ME GET THIS STRAIGHT: YOU SAVE GREEN LANTERN AND THAT'S JUST FINE--
--BUT I SAVE YOU AND IT'S SOME KIND OF--
--CRIME AGAINST HUMANITY?

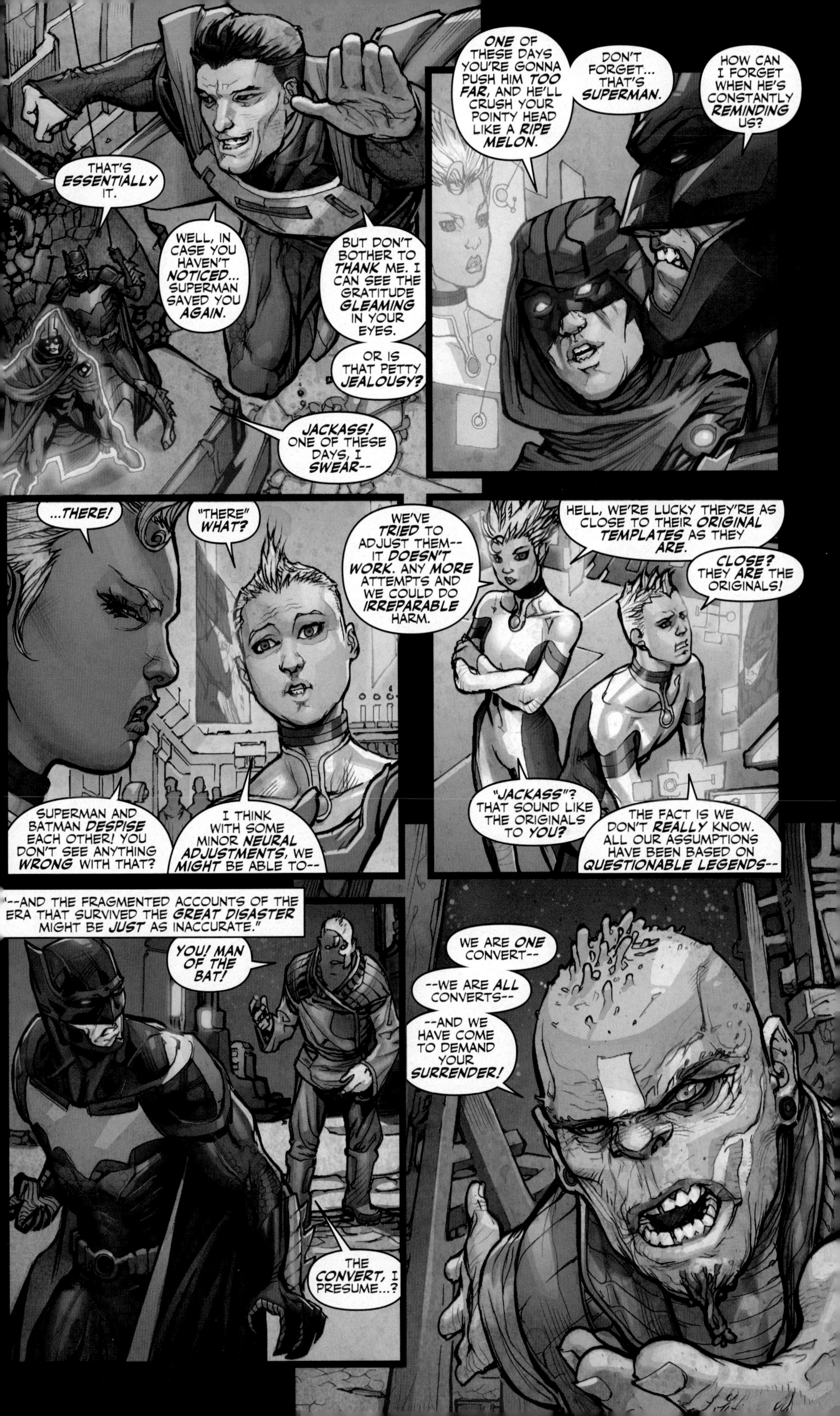
THAT'S ESSENTIALLY IT.
WELL, IN CASE YOU HAVEN'T NOTICED... SUPERMAN SAVED YOU AGAIN.
BUT DON'T BOTHER TO THANK ME. I CAN SEE THE GRATITUDE GLEAMING IN YOUR EYES.
OR IS THAT PETTY JEALOUSY?
JACKASS! ONE OF THESE DAYS, I SWEAR--
ONE OF THESE DAYS YOU'RE GONNA PUSH HIM TOO FAR, AND HE'LL CRUSH YOUR POINTY HEAD LIKE A RIPE MELON.
DON'T FORGET... THAT'S SUPERMAN.
HOW CAN I FORGET WHEN HE'S CONSTANTLY REMINDING US?
...THERE!
"THERE" WHAT?
SUPERMAN AND BATMAN DESPISE EACH OTHER! YOU DON'T SEE ANYTHING WRONG WITH THAT?
I THINK WITH SOME MINOR NEURAL ADJUSTMENTS, WE MIGHT BE ABLE TO--
WE'VE TRIED TO ADJUST THEM-- IT DOESN'T WORK. ANY MORE ATTEMPTS AND WE COULD DO IRREPARABLE HARM.
HELL, WE'RE LUCKY THEY'RE AS CLOSE TO THEIR ORIGINAL TEMPLATES AS THEY ARE.
CLOSE? THEY ARE THE ORIGINALS!
"JACKASS"? THAT SOUND LIKE THE ORIGINALS TO YOU?
THE FACT IS WE DON'T REALLY KNOW. ALL OUR ASSUMPTIONS HAVE BEEN BASED ON QUESTIONABLE LEGENDS--
"--AND THE FRAGMENTED ACCOUNTS OF THE ERA THAT SURVIVED THE GREAT DISASTER MIGHT BE JUST AS INACCURATE."
YOU! MAN OF THE BAT!
THE CONVERT, I PRESUME...?
WE ARE ONE CONVERT--
--WE ARE ALL CONVERTS--
--AND WE HAVE COME TO DEMAND YOUR SURRENDER!

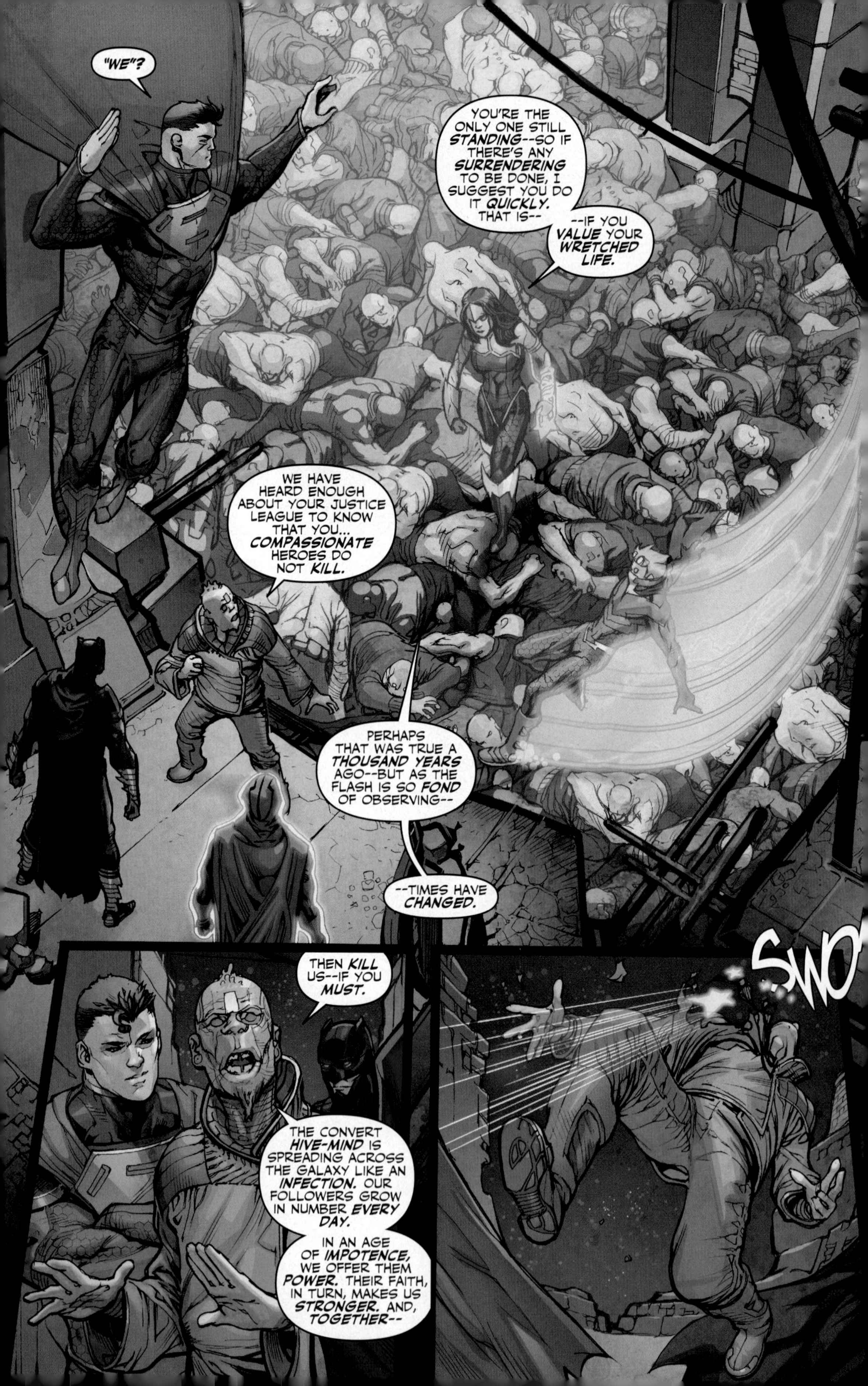
"WE"?
YOU'RE THE ONLY ONE STILL STANDING--SO IF THERE'S ANY SURRENDERING TO BE DONE, I SUGGEST YOU DO IT QUICKLY. THAT IS--
--IF YOU VALUE YOUR WRETCHED LIFE.
WE HAVE HEARD ENOUGH ABOUT YOUR JUSTICE LEAGUE TO KNOW THAT YOU... COMPASSIONATE HEROES DO NOT KILL.
PERHAPS THAT WAS TRUE A THOUSAND YEARS AGO--BUT AS THE FLASH IS SO FOND OF OBSERVING--
--TIMES HAVE CHANGED.
THEN KILL US--IF YOU MUST.
THE CONVERT HIVE-MIND IS SPREADING ACROSS THE GALAXY LIKE AN INFECTION. OUR FOLLOWERS GROW IN NUMBER EVERY DAY.
IN AN AGE OF IMPOTENCE, WE OFFER THEM POWER. THEIR FAITH, IN TURN, MAKES US STRONGER. AND, TOGETHER--
SWO

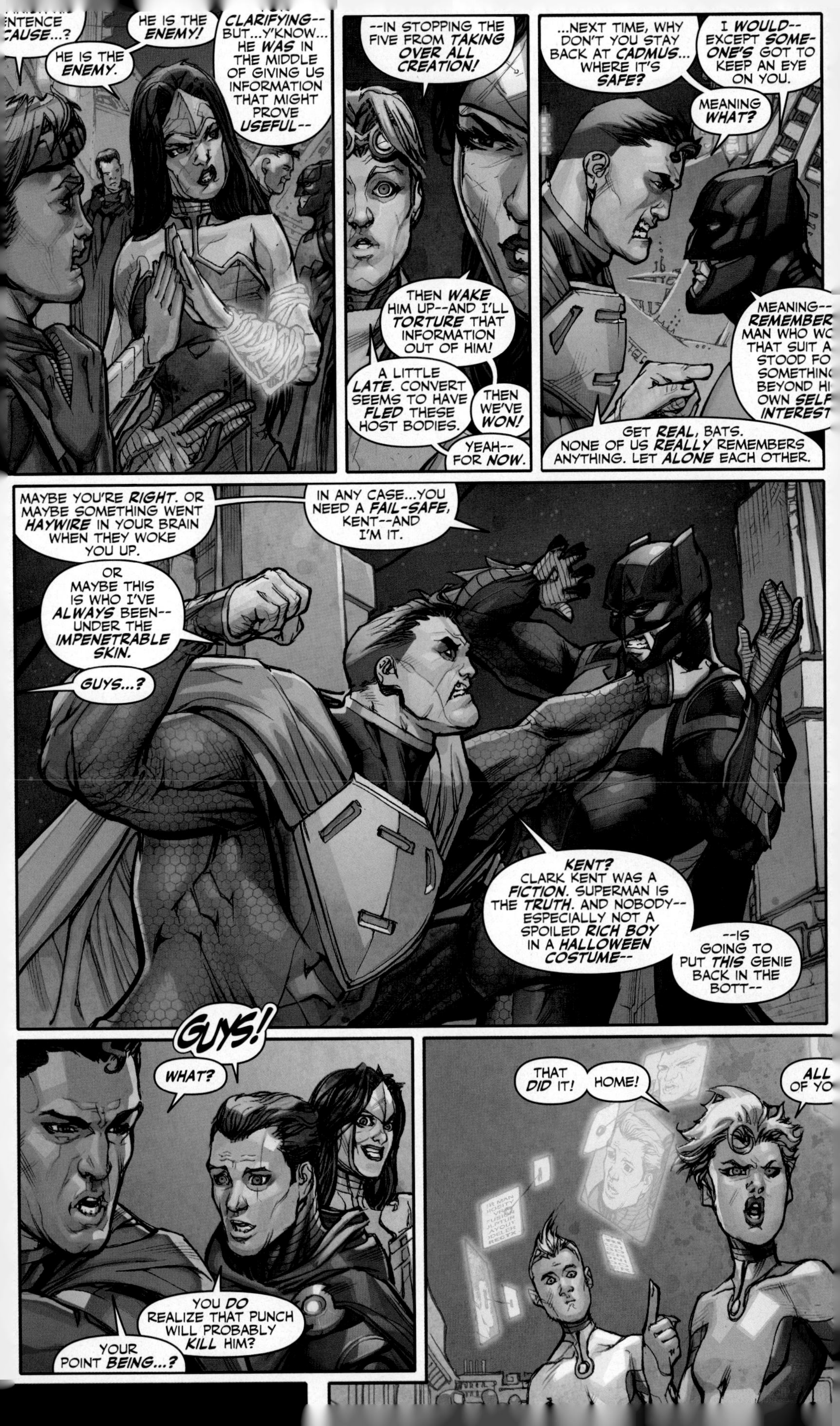
ENTENCE CAUSE...?
HE IS THE ENEMY!
HE IS THE ENEMY.
CLARIFYING-- BUT...Y'KNOW... HE WAS IN THE MIDDLE OF GIVING US INFORMATION THAT MIGHT PROVE USEFUL--
--IN STOPPING THE FIVE FROM TAKING OVER ALL CREATION!
THEN WAKE HIM UP--AND I'LL TORTURE THAT INFORMATION OUT OF HIM!
A LITTLE LATE. CONVERT SEEMS TO HAVE FLED THESE HOST BODIES.
THEN WE'VE WON!
YEAH-- FOR NOW.
...NEXT TIME, WHY DON'T YOU STAY BACK AT CADMUS... WHERE IT'S SAFE?
I WOULD-- EXCEPT SOME-ONE'S GOT TO KEEP AN EYE ON YOU.
MEANING WHAT?
MEANING-- REMEMBER MAN WHO WO THAT SUIT A STOOD FO SOMETHING BEYOND HI OWN SELF INTEREST
GET REAL, BATS. NONE OF US REALLY REMEMBERS ANYTHING. LET ALONE EACH OTHER.
MAYBE YOU'RE RIGHT. OR MAYBE SOMETHING WENT HAYWIRE IN YOUR BRAIN WHEN THEY WOKE YOU UP.
IN ANY CASE...YOU NEED A FAIL-SAFE, KENT--AND I'M IT.
OR MAYBE THIS IS WHO I'VE ALWAYS BEEN-- UNDER THE IMPENETRABLE SKIN.
GUYS...?
KENT? CLARK KENT WAS A FICTION. SUPERMAN IS THE TRUTH. AND NOBODY-- ESPECIALLY NOT A SPOILED RICH BOY IN A HALLOWEEN COSTUME--
--IS GOING TO PUT THIS GENIE BACK IN THE BOTT--
GUYS!
WHAT?
YOU DO REALIZE THAT PUNCH WILL PROBABLY KILL HIM?
YOUR POINT BEING...?
THAT DID IT!
HOME!
ALL OF YO

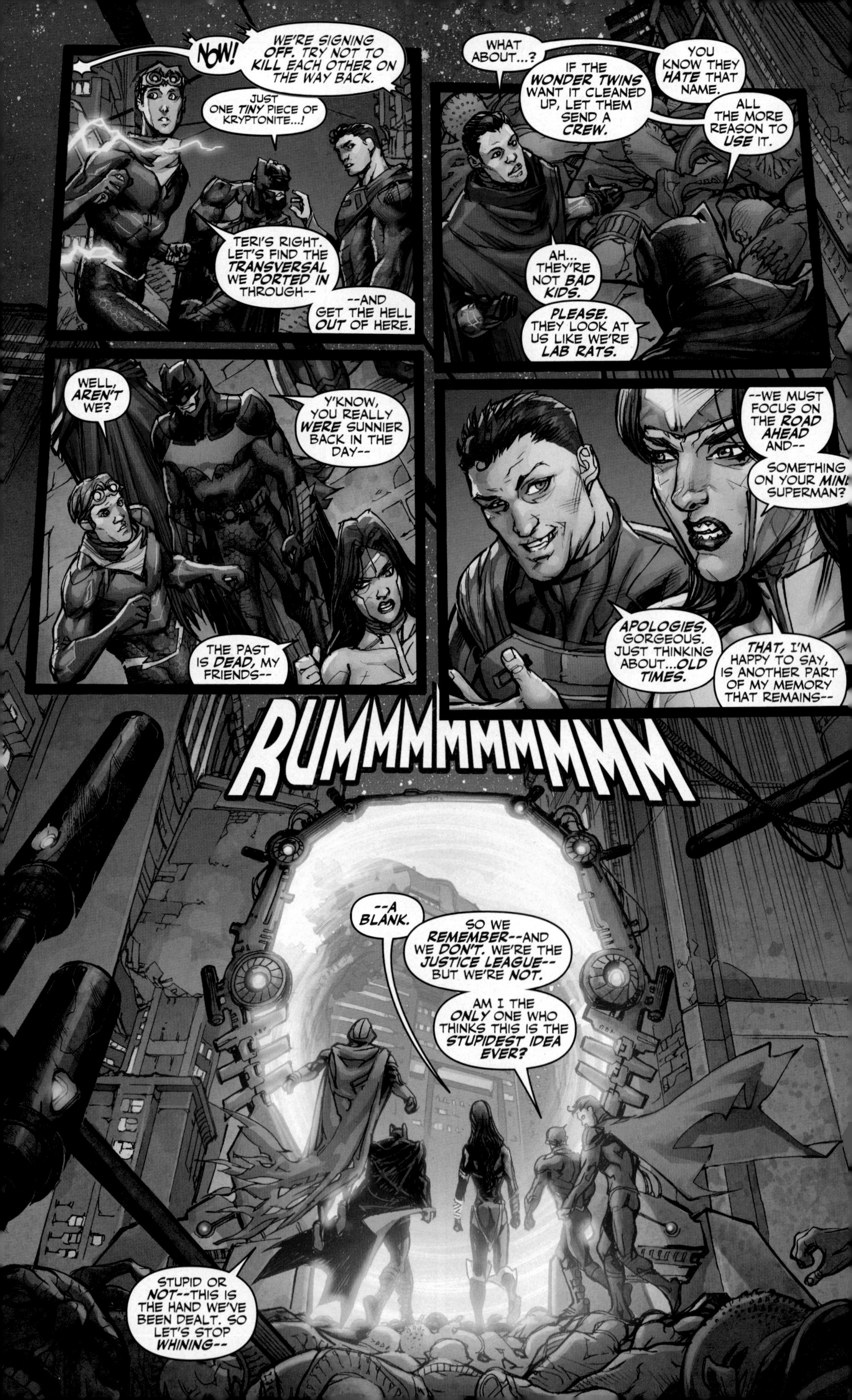
NOW!
WE'RE SIGNING OFF. TRY NOT TO KILL EACH OTHER ON THE WAY BACK.
JUST ONE TINY PIECE OF KRYPTONITE...!
TERI'S RIGHT. LET'S FIND THE TRANSVERSAL WE PORTED IN THROUGH--
--AND GET THE HELL OUT OF HERE.
WHAT ABOUT...?
IF THE WONDER TWINS WANT IT CLEANED UP, LET THEM SEND A CREW.
YOU KNOW THEY HATE THAT NAME.
ALL THE MORE REASON TO USE IT.
AH... THEY'RE NOT BAD KIDS.
PLEASE. THEY LOOK AT US LIKE WE'RE LAB RATS.
WELL, AREN'T WE?
Y'KNOW, YOU REALLY WERE SUNNIER BACK IN THE DAY--
THE PAST IS DEAD, MY FRIENDS--
--WE MUST FOCUS ON THE ROAD AHEAD AND--
SOMETHING ON YOUR MIND, SUPERMAN?
APOLOGIES, GORGEOUS. JUST THINKING ABOUT...OLD TIMES.
THAT, I'M HAPPY TO SAY, IS ANOTHER PART OF MY MEMORY THAT REMAINS--
RUMMMMMMMMMM
--A BLANK.
SO WE REMEMBER--AND WE DON'T. WE'RE THE JUSTICE LEAGUE--BUT WE'RE NOT.
AM I THE ONLY ONE WHO THINKS THIS IS THE STUPIDEST IDEA EVER?
STUPID OR NOT--THIS IS THE HAND WE'VE BEEN DEALT. SO LET'S STOP WHINING--

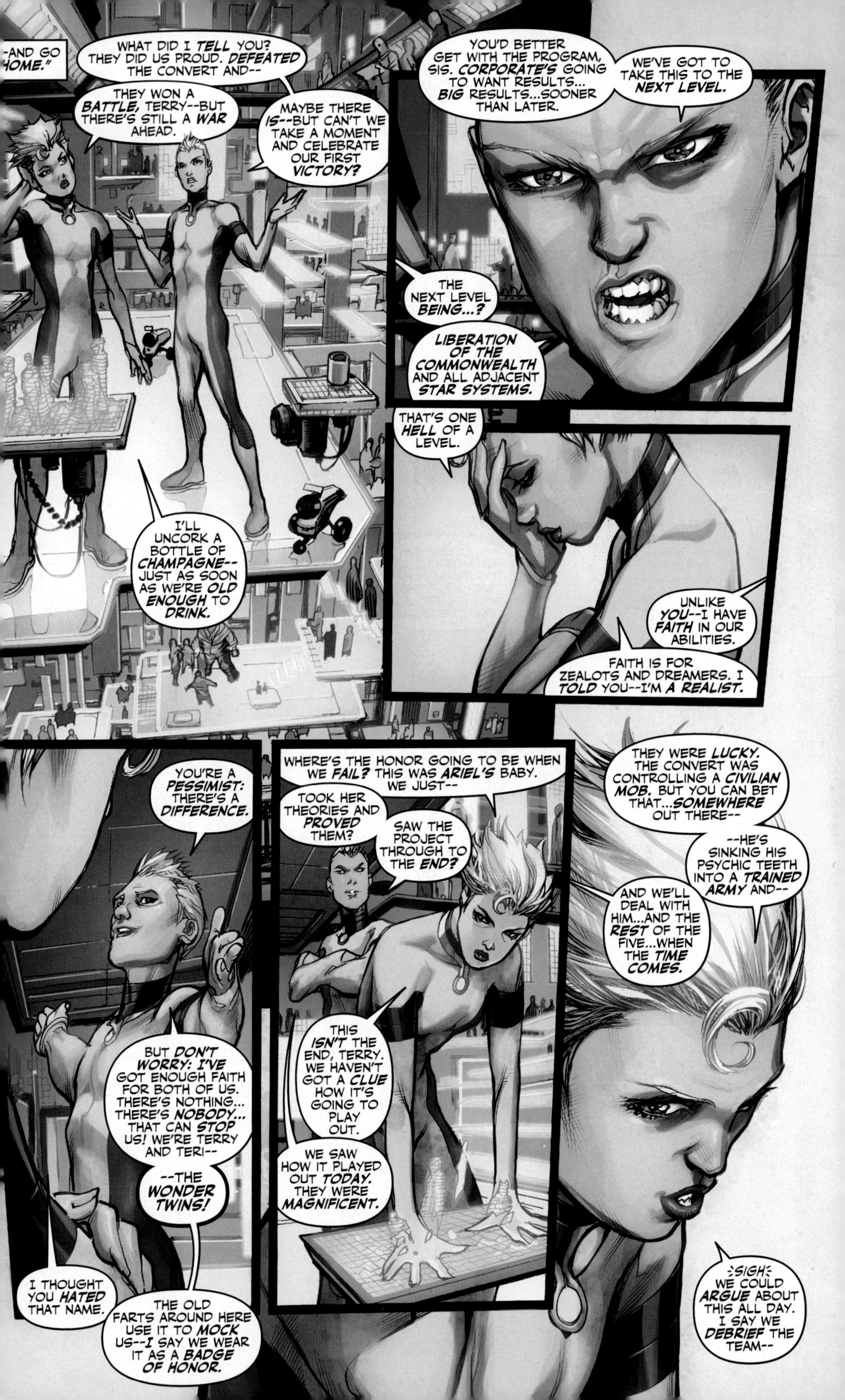
-AND GO
HOME."
WHAT DID I TELL YOU? THEY DID US PROUD. DEFEATED THE CONVERT AND--
THEY WON A BATTLE, TERRY--BUT THERE'S STILL A WAR AHEAD.
MAYBE THERE IS--BUT CAN'T WE TAKE A MOMENT AND CELEBRATE OUR FIRST VICTORY?
I'LL UNCORK A BOTTLE OF CHAMPAGNE--JUST AS SOON AS WE'RE OLD ENOUGH TO DRINK.
YOU'D BETTER GET WITH THE PROGRAM, SIS. CORPORATE'S GOING TO WANT RESULTS... BIG RESULTS...SOONER THAN LATER.
WE'VE GOT TO TAKE THIS TO THE NEXT LEVEL.
THE NEXT LEVEL BEING...?
LIBERATION OF THE COMMONWEALTH AND ALL ADJACENT STAR SYSTEMS.
THAT'S ONE HELL OF A LEVEL.
UNLIKE YOU--I HAVE FAITH IN OUR ABILITIES.
FAITH IS FOR ZEALOTS AND DREAMERS. I TOLD YOU--I'M A REALIST.
YOU'RE A PESSIMIST: THERE'S A DIFFERENCE.
BUT DON'T WORRY: I'VE GOT ENOUGH FAITH FOR BOTH OF US. THERE'S NOTHING... THERE'S NOBODY... THAT CAN STOP US! WE'RE TERRY AND TERI--
--THE WONDER TWINS!
I THOUGHT YOU HATED THAT NAME.
THE OLD FARTS AROUND HERE USE IT TO MOCK US--I SAY WE WEAR IT AS A BADGE OF HONOR.
WHERE'S THE HONOR GOING TO BE WHEN WE FAIL? THIS WAS ARIEL'S BABY. WE JUST--
TOOK HER THEORIES AND PROVED THEM?
SAW THE PROJECT THROUGH TO THE END?
THIS ISN'T THE END, TERRY. WE HAVEN'T GOT A CLUE HOW IT'S GOING TO PLAY OUT.
WE SAW HOW IT PLAYED OUT TODAY. THEY WERE MAGNIFICENT.
THEY WERE LUCKY. THE CONVERT WAS CONTROLLING A CIVILIAN MOB. BUT YOU CAN BET THAT...SOMEWHERE OUT THERE--
--HE'S SINKING HIS PSYCHIC TEETH INTO A TRAINED ARMY AND--
AND WE'LL DEAL WITH HIM...AND THE REST OF THE FIVE...WHEN THE TIME COMES.
SIGH WE COULD ARGUE ABOUT THIS ALL DAY. I SAY WE DEBRIEF THE TEAM--

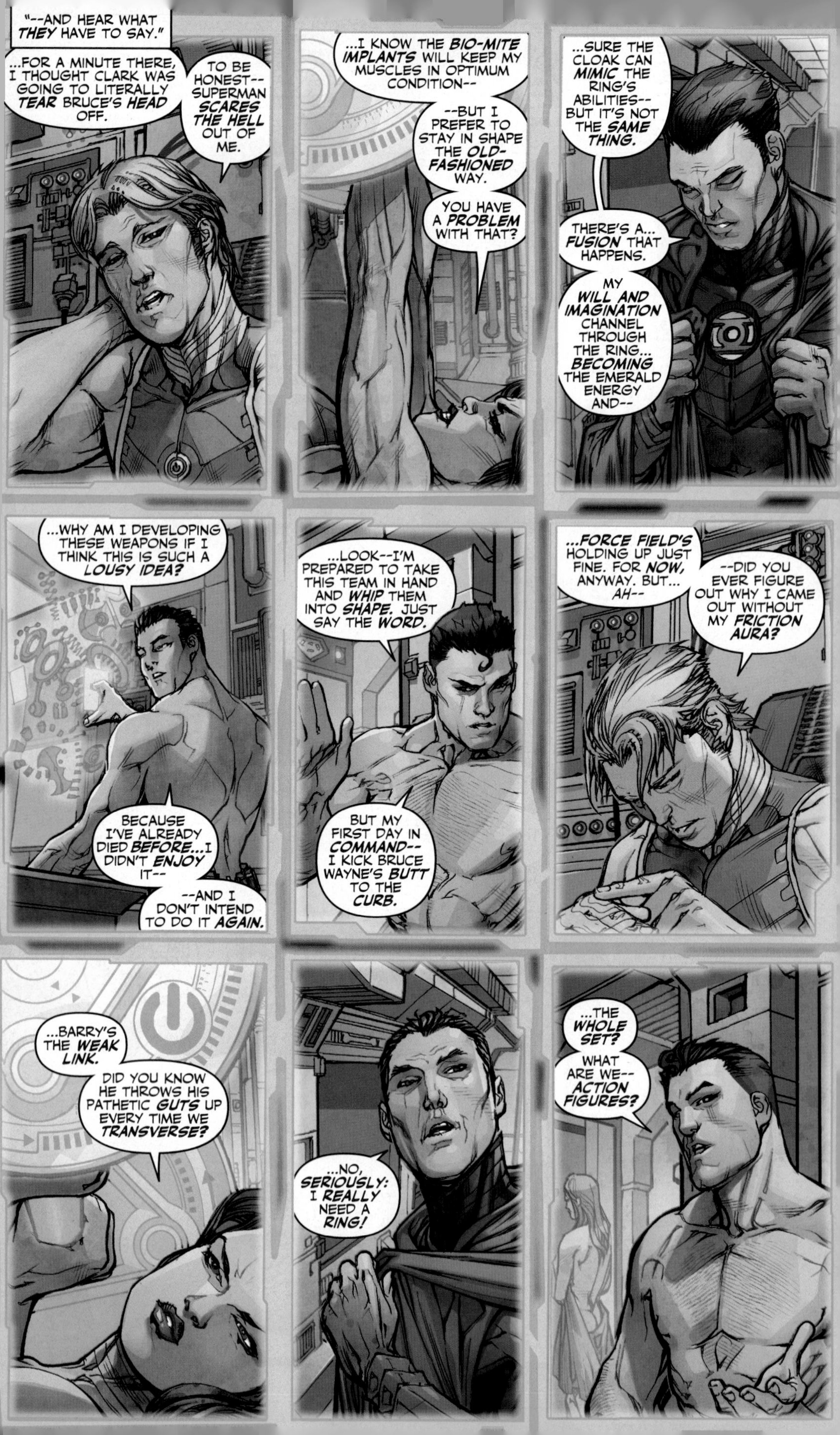
"--AND HEAR WHAT THEY HAVE TO SAY."
...FOR A MINUTE THERE, I THOUGHT CLARK WAS GOING TO LITERALLY TEAR BRUCE'S HEAD OFF.
TO BE HONEST--SUPERMAN SCARES THE HELL OUT OF ME.
...I KNOW THE BIO-MITE IMPLANTS WILL KEEP MY MUSCLES IN OPTIMUM CONDITION--
--BUT I PREFER TO STAY IN SHAPE THE OLD-FASHIONED WAY.
YOU HAVE A PROBLEM WITH THAT?
...SURE THE CLOAK CAN MIMIC THE RING'S ABILITIES--BUT IT'S NOT THE SAME THING.
THERE'S A... FUSION THAT HAPPENS.
MY WILL AND IMAGINATION CHANNEL THROUGH THE RING... BECOMING THE EMERALD ENERGY AND--
...WHY AM I DEVELOPING THESE WEAPONS IF I THINK THIS IS SUCH A LOUSY IDEA?
BECAUSE I'VE ALREADY DIED BEFORE...I DIDN'T ENJOY IT--
--AND I DON'T INTEND TO DO IT AGAIN.
...LOOK--I'M PREPARED TO TAKE THIS TEAM IN HAND AND WHIP THEM INTO SHAPE. JUST SAY THE WORD.
BUT MY FIRST DAY IN COMMAND--I KICK BRUCE WAYNE'S BUTT TO THE CURB.
...FORCE FIELD'S HOLDING UP JUST FINE. FOR NOW, ANYWAY. BUT... AH--
--DID YOU EVER FIGURE OUT WHY I CAME OUT WITHOUT MY FRICTION AURA?
...BARRY'S THE WEAK LINK.
DID YOU KNOW HE THROWS HIS PATHETIC GUTS UP EVERY TIME WE TRANSVERSE?
...NO, SERIOUSLY: I REALLY NEED A RING!
...THE WHOLE SET?
WHAT ARE WE--ACTION FIGURES?

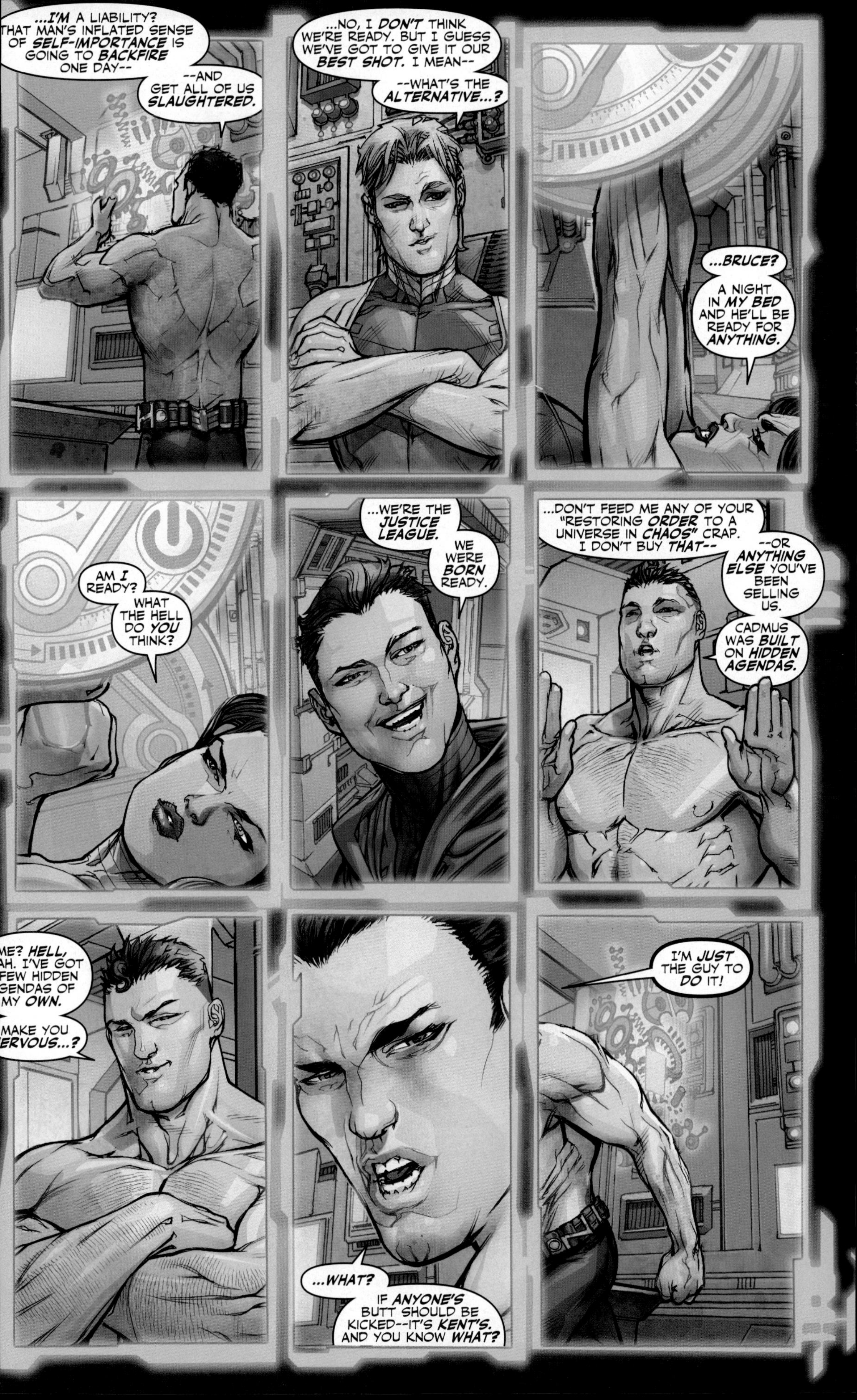
...I'M A LIABILITY? THAT MAN'S INFLATED SENSE OF SELF-IMPORTANCE IS GOING TO BACKFIRE ONE DAY--
--AND GET ALL OF US SLAUGHTERED.
...NO, I DON'T THINK WE'RE READY. BUT I GUESS WE'VE GOT TO GIVE IT OUR BEST SHOT. I MEAN--
--WHAT'S THE ALTERNATIVE...?
...BRUCE?
A NIGHT IN MY BED AND HE'LL BE READY FOR ANYTHING.
AM I READY?
WHAT THE HELL DO YOU THINK?
...WE'RE THE JUSTICE LEAGUE.
WE WERE BORN READY.
...DON'T FEED ME ANY OF YOUR "RESTORING ORDER TO A UNIVERSE IN CHAOS" CRAP. I DON'T BUY THAT--
--OR ANYTHING ELSE YOU'VE BEEN SELLING US.
CADMUS WAS BUILT ON HIDDEN AGENDAS.
ME? HELL, AH. I'VE GOT FEW HIDDEN GENDAS OF MY OWN.
MAKE YOU ERVOUS...?
...WHAT?
IF ANYONE'S BUTT SHOULD BE KICKED--IT'S KENT'S. AND YOU KNOW WHAT?
I'M JUST THE GUY TO DO IT!

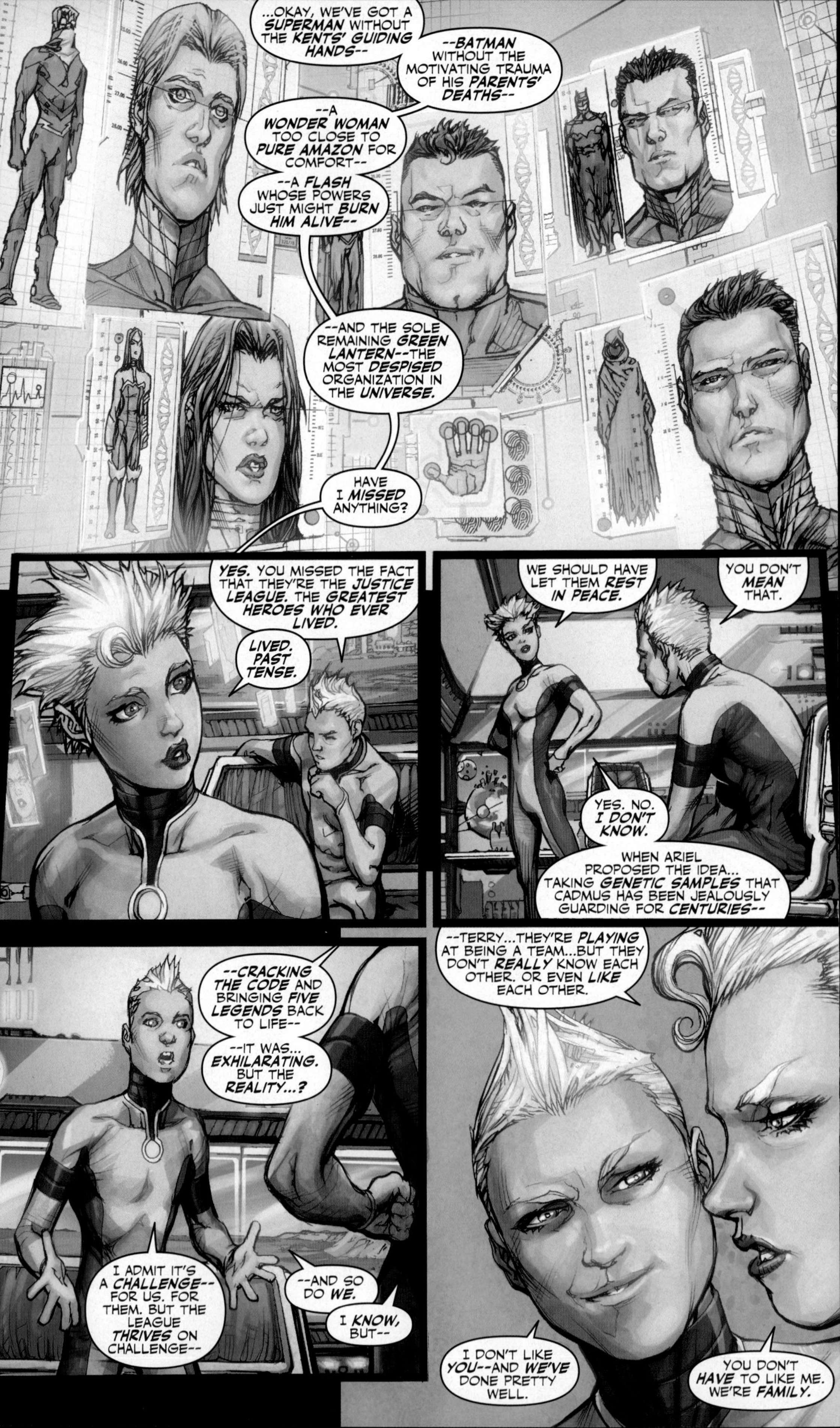
...OKAY, WE'VE GOT A SUPERMAN WITHOUT THE KENTS' GUIDING HANDS--
--BATMAN WITHOUT THE MOTIVATING TRAUMA OF HIS PARENTS' DEATHS--
--A WONDER WOMAN TOO CLOSE TO PURE AMAZON FOR COMFORT--
--A FLASH WHOSE POWERS JUST MIGHT BURN HIM ALIVE--
--AND THE SOLE REMAINING GREEN LANTERN--THE MOST DESPISED ORGANIZATION IN THE UNIVERSE.
HAVE I MISSED ANYTHING?
YES. YOU MISSED THE FACT THAT THEY'RE THE JUSTICE LEAGUE. THE GREATEST HEROES WHO EVER LIVED.
LIVED. PAST TENSE.
WE SHOULD HAVE LET THEM REST IN PEACE.
YOU DON'T MEAN THAT.
YES. NO. I DON'T KNOW.
WHEN ARIEL PROPOSED THE IDEA... TAKING GENETIC SAMPLES THAT CADMUS HAS BEEN JEALOUSLY GUARDING FOR CENTURIES--
--CRACKING THE CODE AND BRINGING FIVE LEGENDS BACK TO LIFE--
--IT WAS... EXHILARATING. BUT THE REALITY...?
I ADMIT IT'S A CHALLENGE--FOR US. FOR THEM. BUT THE LEAGUE THRIVES ON CHALLENGE--
--AND SO DO WE.
I KNOW, BUT--
--TERRY...THEY'RE PLAYING AT BEING A TEAM...BUT THEY DON'T REALLY KNOW EACH OTHER. OR EVEN LIKE EACH OTHER.
I DON'T LIKE YOU--AND WE'VE DONE PRETTY WELL.
YOU DON'T HAVE TO LIKE ME. WE'RE FAMILY.

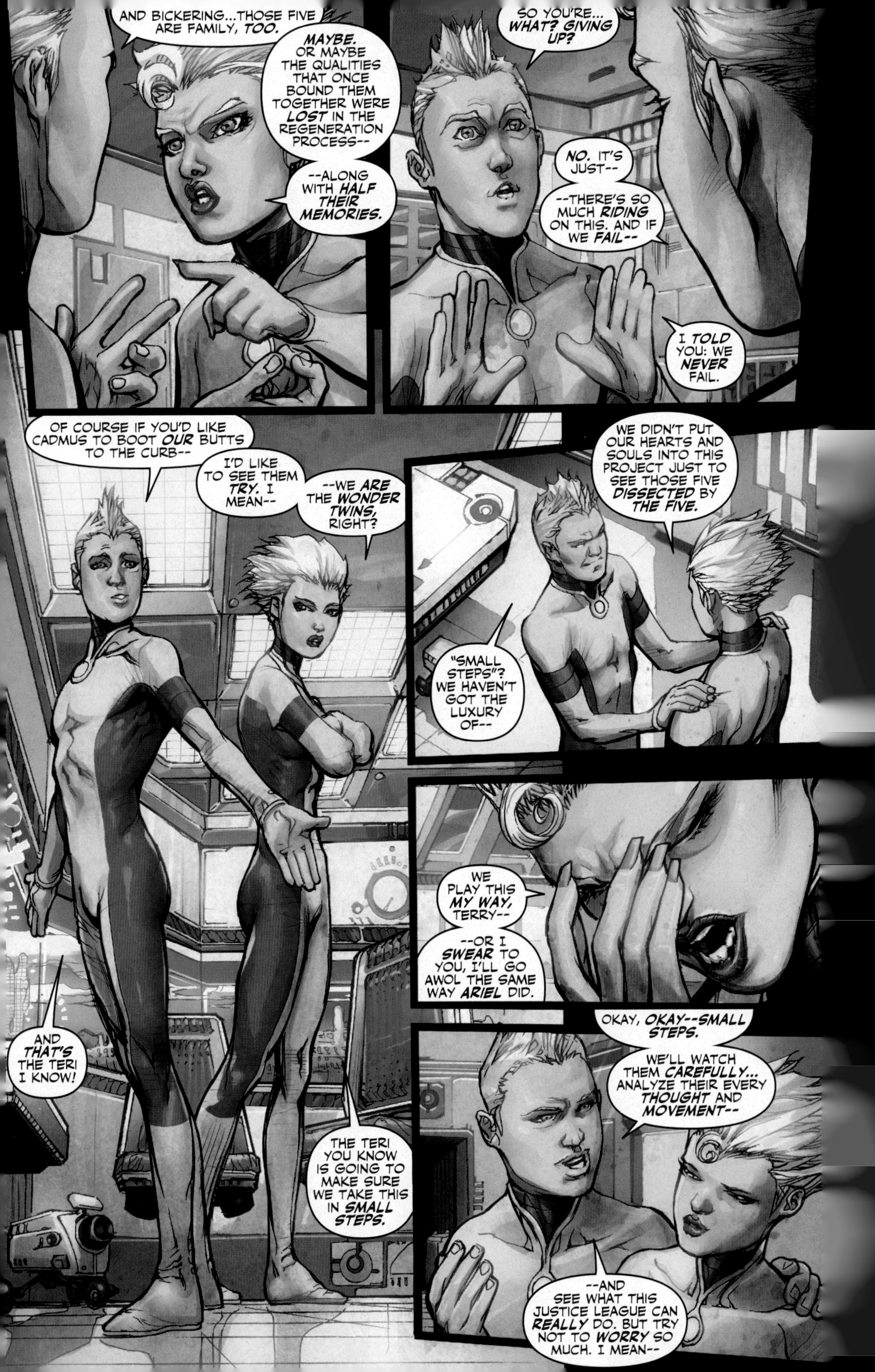
AND BICKERING...THOSE FIVE ARE FAMILY, TOO.
MAYBE. OR MAYBE THE QUALITIES THAT ONCE BOUND THEM TOGETHER WERE LOST IN THE REGENERATION PROCESS--
--ALONG WITH HALF THEIR MEMORIES.
SO YOU'RE... WHAT? GIVING UP?
NO. IT'S JUST--
--THERE'S SO MUCH RIDING ON THIS. AND IF WE FAIL--
I TOLD YOU: WE NEVER FAIL.
OF COURSE IF YOU'D LIKE CADMUS TO BOOT OUR BUTTS TO THE CURB--
I'D LIKE TO SEE THEM TRY. I MEAN--
--WE ARE THE WONDER TWINS, RIGHT?
AND THAT'S THE TERI I KNOW!
THE TERI YOU KNOW IS GOING TO MAKE SURE WE TAKE THIS IN SMALL STEPS.
WE DIDN'T PUT OUR HEARTS AND SOULS INTO THIS PROJECT JUST TO SEE THOSE FIVE DISSECTED BY THE FIVE.
"SMALL STEPS"? WE HAVEN'T GOT THE LUXURY OF--
WE PLAY THIS MY WAY, TERRY--
--OR I SWEAR TO YOU, I'LL GO AWOL THE SAME WAY ARIEL DID.
OKAY, OKAY--SMALL STEPS.
WE'LL WATCH THEM CAREFULLY... ANALYZE THEIR EVERY THOUGHT AND MOVEMENT--
--AND SEE WHAT THIS JUSTICE LEAGUE CAN REALLY DO. BUT TRY NOT TO WORRY SO MUCH. I MEAN--

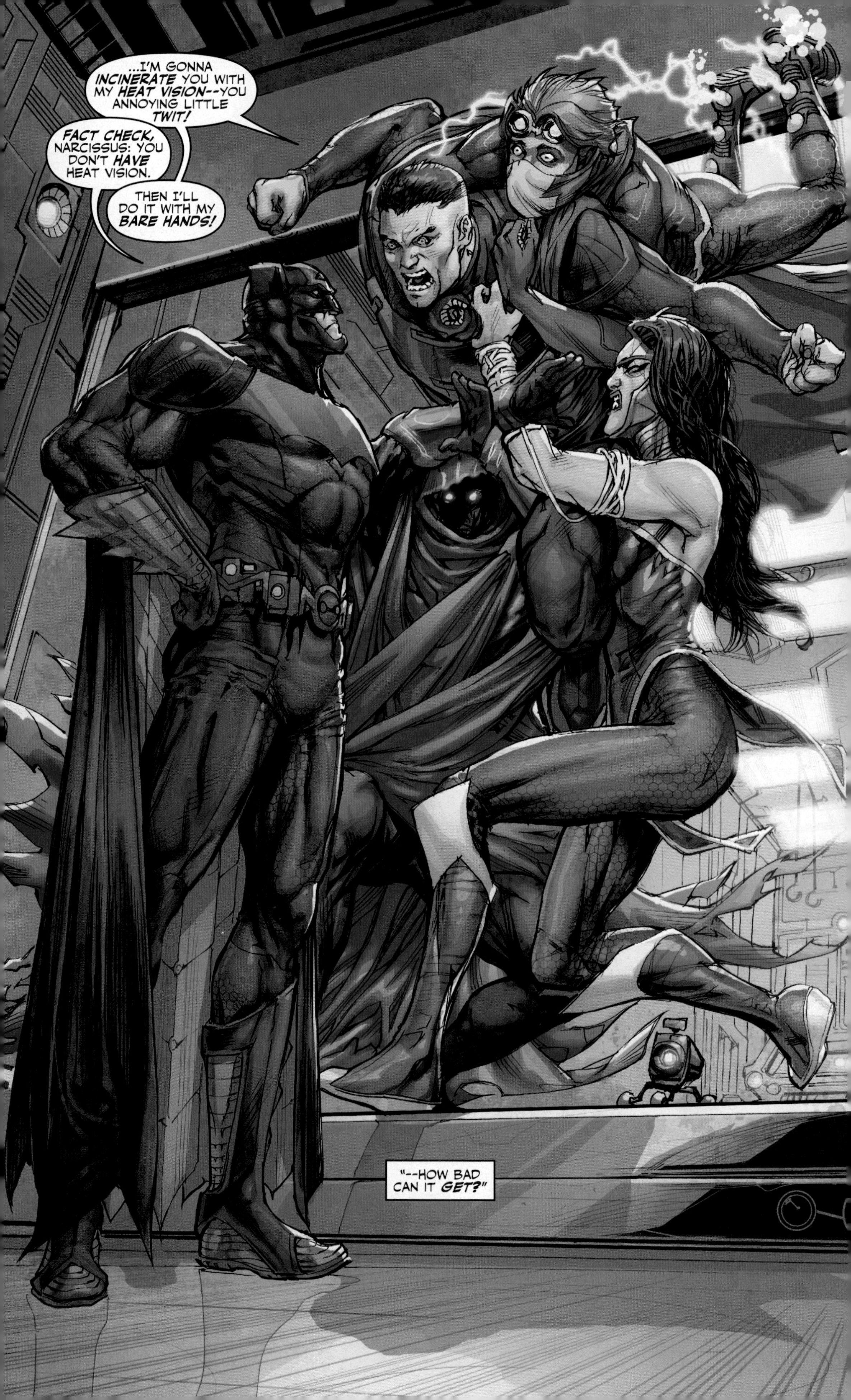
...I'M GONNA INCINERATE YOU WITH MY HEAT VISION--YOU ANNOYING LITTLE TWIT!
FACT CHECK, NARCISSUS: YOU DON'T HAVE HEAT VISION.
THEN I'LL DO IT WITH MY BARE HANDS!
"--HOW BAD CAN IT GET?"

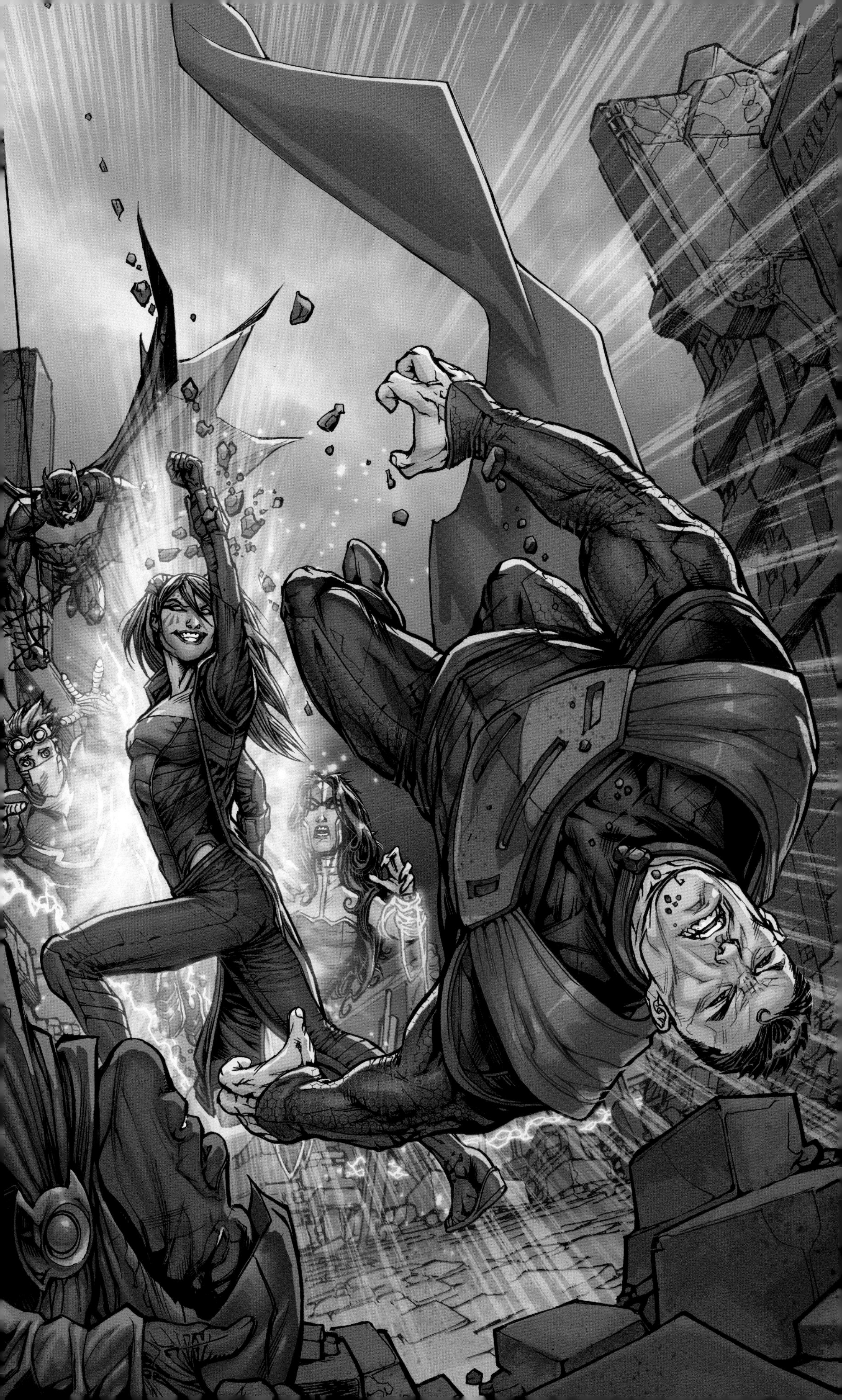

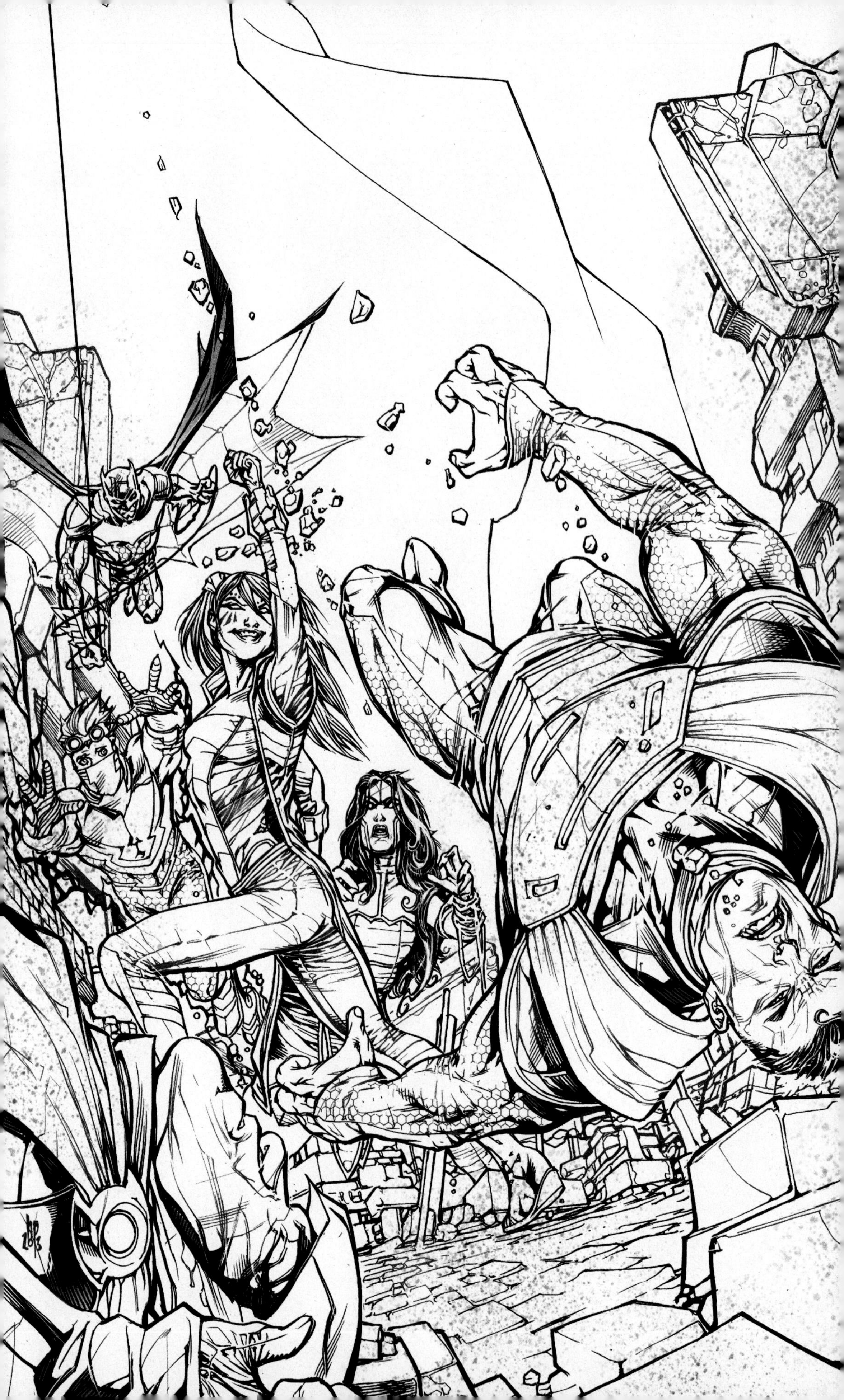

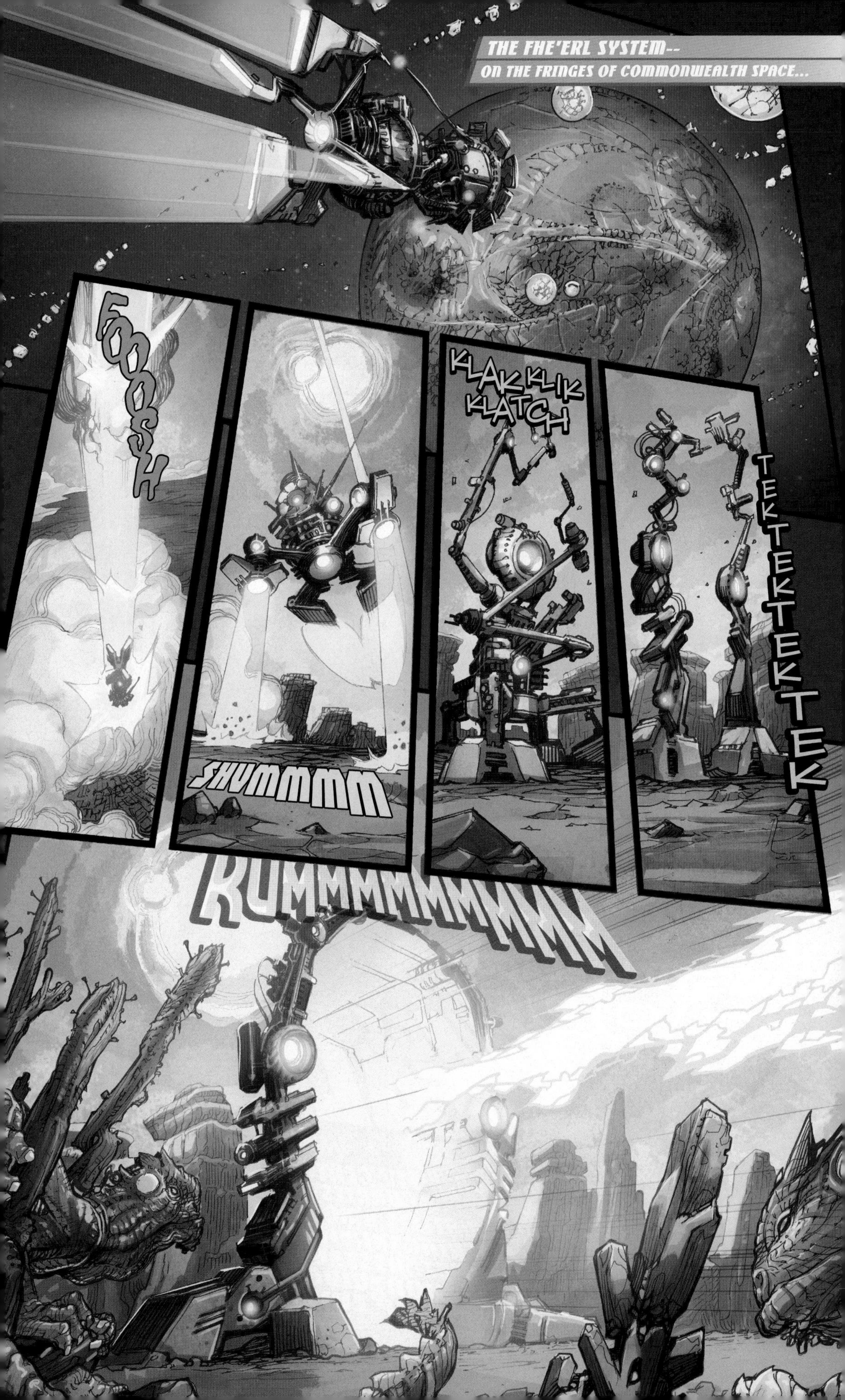

THE FHE'ERL SYSTEM--
ON THE FRINGES OF COMMONWEALTH SPACE...
FOOOSH
SHUMMMM
KLAK KLIK KLATCH
TEKTEKTEK
RUMMMMMMMM

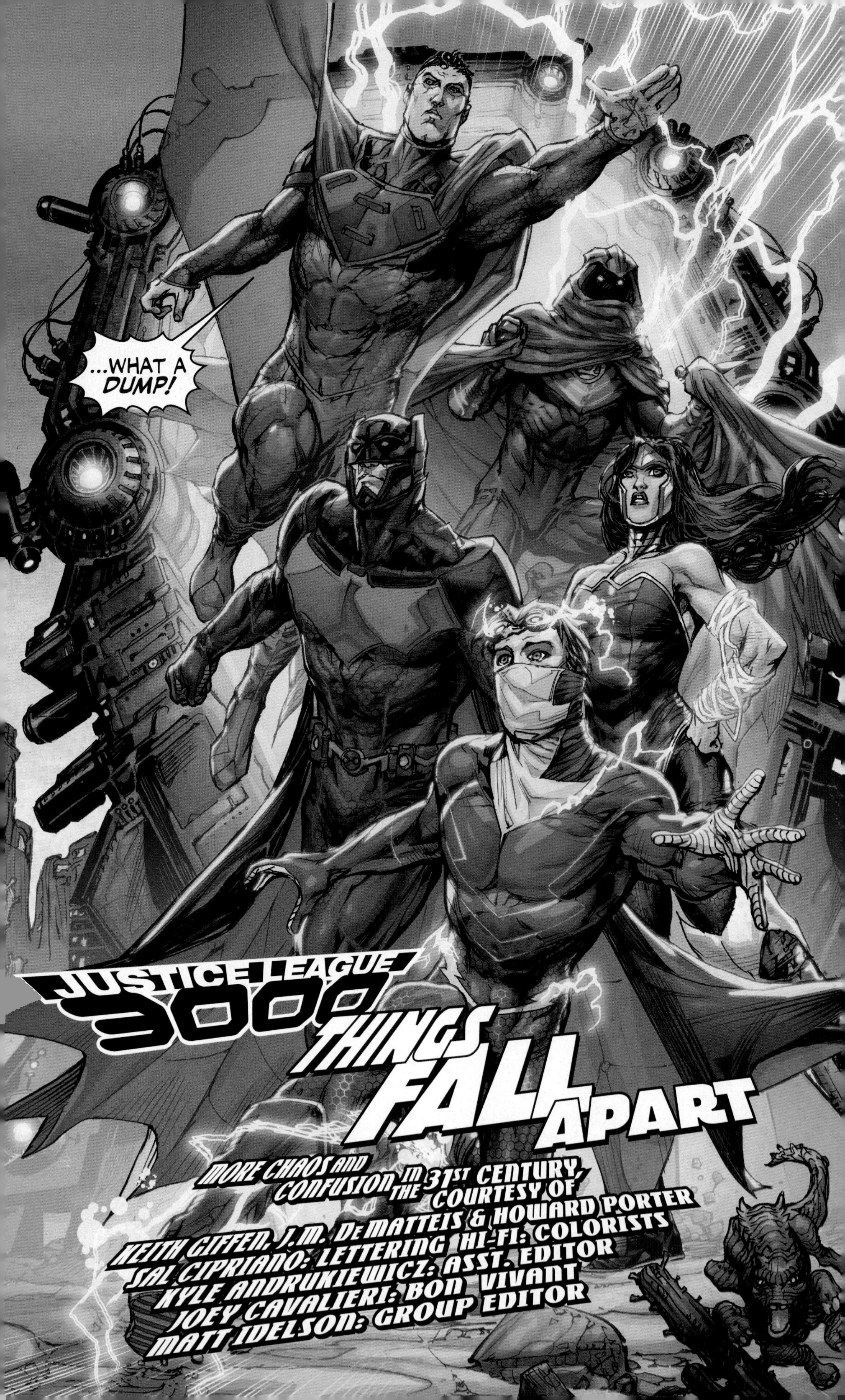
...WHAT A DUMP!
JUSTICE LEAGUE 3000
THINGS FALL APART
MORE CHAOS AND CONFUSION IN THE 31ST CENTURY, COURTESY OF
KEITH GIFFEN, J.M. DeMATTEIS & HOWARD PORTER
SAL CIPRIANO: LETTERING HI-FI: COLORISTS
KYLE ANDRUKIEWICZ: ASST. EDITOR
JOEY CAVALIERI: BON VIVANT
MATT IDELSON: GROUP EDITOR

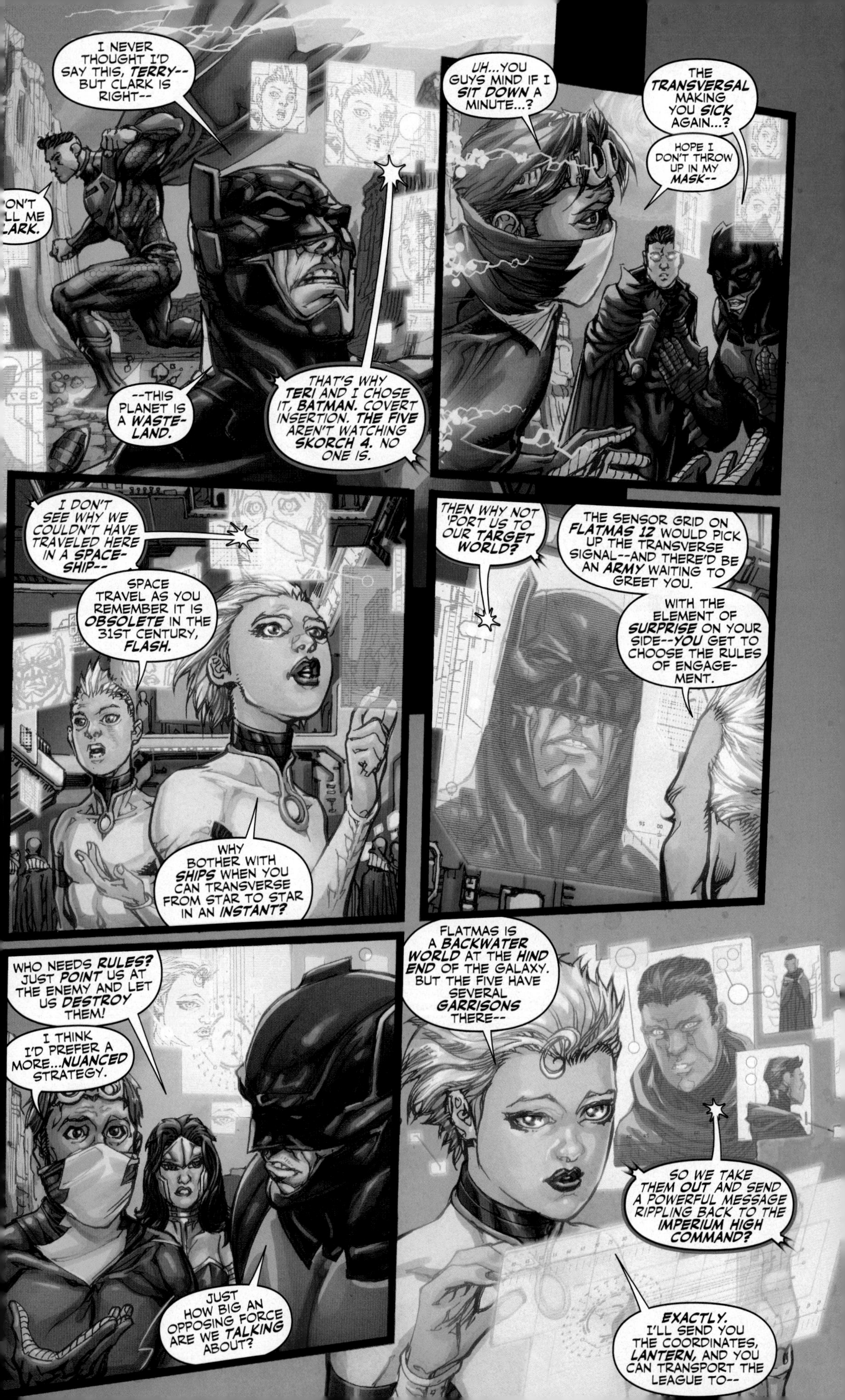
I NEVER THOUGHT I'D SAY THIS, TERRY-- BUT CLARK IS RIGHT--
ON'T LL ME LARK.
--THIS PLANET IS A WASTELAND.
THAT'S WHY TERI AND I CHOSE IT, BATMAN. COVERT INSERTION. THE FIVE AREN'T WATCHING SKORCH 4. NO ONE IS.
UH...YOU GUYS MIND IF I SIT DOWN A MINUTE...?
THE TRANSVERSAL MAKING YOU SICK AGAIN...?
HOPE I DON'T THROW UP IN MY MASK--
I DON'T SEE WHY WE COULDN'T HAVE TRAVELED HERE IN A SPACESHIP--
SPACE TRAVEL AS YOU REMEMBER IT IS OBSOLETE IN THE 31ST CENTURY, FLASH.
WHY BOTHER WITH SHIPS WHEN YOU CAN TRANSVERSE FROM STAR TO STAR IN AN INSTANT?
THEN WHY NOT 'PORT US TO OUR TARGET WORLD?
THE SENSOR GRID ON FLATMAS 12 WOULD PICK UP THE TRANSVERSE SIGNAL--AND THERE'D BE AN ARMY WAITING TO GREET YOU.
WITH THE ELEMENT OF SURPRISE ON YOUR SIDE--YOU GET TO CHOOSE THE RULES OF ENGAGEMENT.
WHO NEEDS RULES? JUST POINT US AT THE ENEMY AND LET US DESTROY THEM!
I THINK I'D PREFER A MORE...NUANCED STRATEGY.
JUST HOW BIG AN OPPOSING FORCE ARE WE TALKING ABOUT?
FLATMAS IS A BACKWATER WORLD AT THE HIND END OF THE GALAXY. BUT THE FIVE HAVE SEVERAL GARRISONS THERE--
SO WE TAKE THEM OUT AND SEND A POWERFUL MESSAGE RIPPLING BACK TO THE IMPERIUM HIGH COMMAND?
EXACTLY. I'LL SEND YOU THE COORDINATES, LANTERN, AND YOU CAN TRANSPORT THE LEAGUE TO--

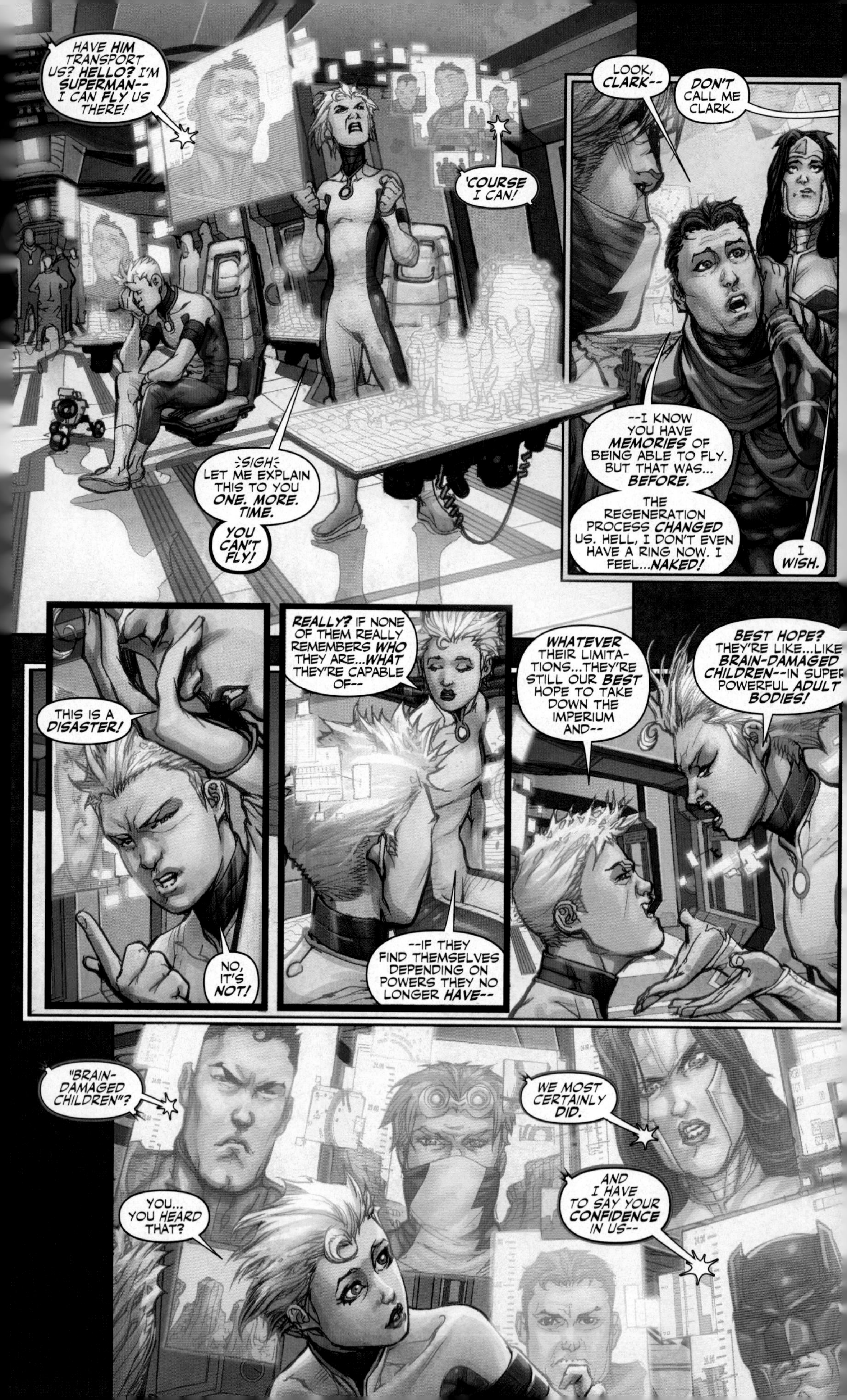
HAVE HIM TRANSPORT US? HELLO? I'M SUPERMAN-- I CAN FLY US THERE!
'COURSE I CAN!
SIGH LET ME EXPLAIN THIS TO YOU ONE. MORE. TIME.
YOU CAN'T FLY!
LOOK, CLARK--
DON'T CALL ME CLARK.
--I KNOW YOU HAVE MEMORIES OF BEING ABLE TO FLY. BUT THAT WAS... BEFORE.
THE REGENERATION PROCESS CHANGED US. HELL, I DON'T EVEN HAVE A RING NOW. I FEEL...NAKED!
I WISH.
THIS IS A DISASTER!
NO, IT'S NOT!
REALLY? IF NONE OF THEM REALLY REMEMBERS WHO THEY ARE...WHAT THEY'RE CAPABLE OF--
--IF THEY FIND THEMSELVES DEPENDING ON POWERS THEY NO LONGER HAVE--
WHATEVER THEIR LIMITATIONS...THEY'RE STILL OUR BEST HOPE TO TAKE DOWN THE IMPERIUM AND--
BEST HOPE? THEY'RE LIKE...LIKE BRAIN-DAMAGED CHILDREN--IN SUPER POWERFUL ADULT BODIES!
"BRAIN-DAMAGED CHILDREN"?
YOU... YOU HEARD THAT?
WE MOST CERTAINLY DID.
AND I HAVE TO SAY YOUR CONFIDENCE IN US--

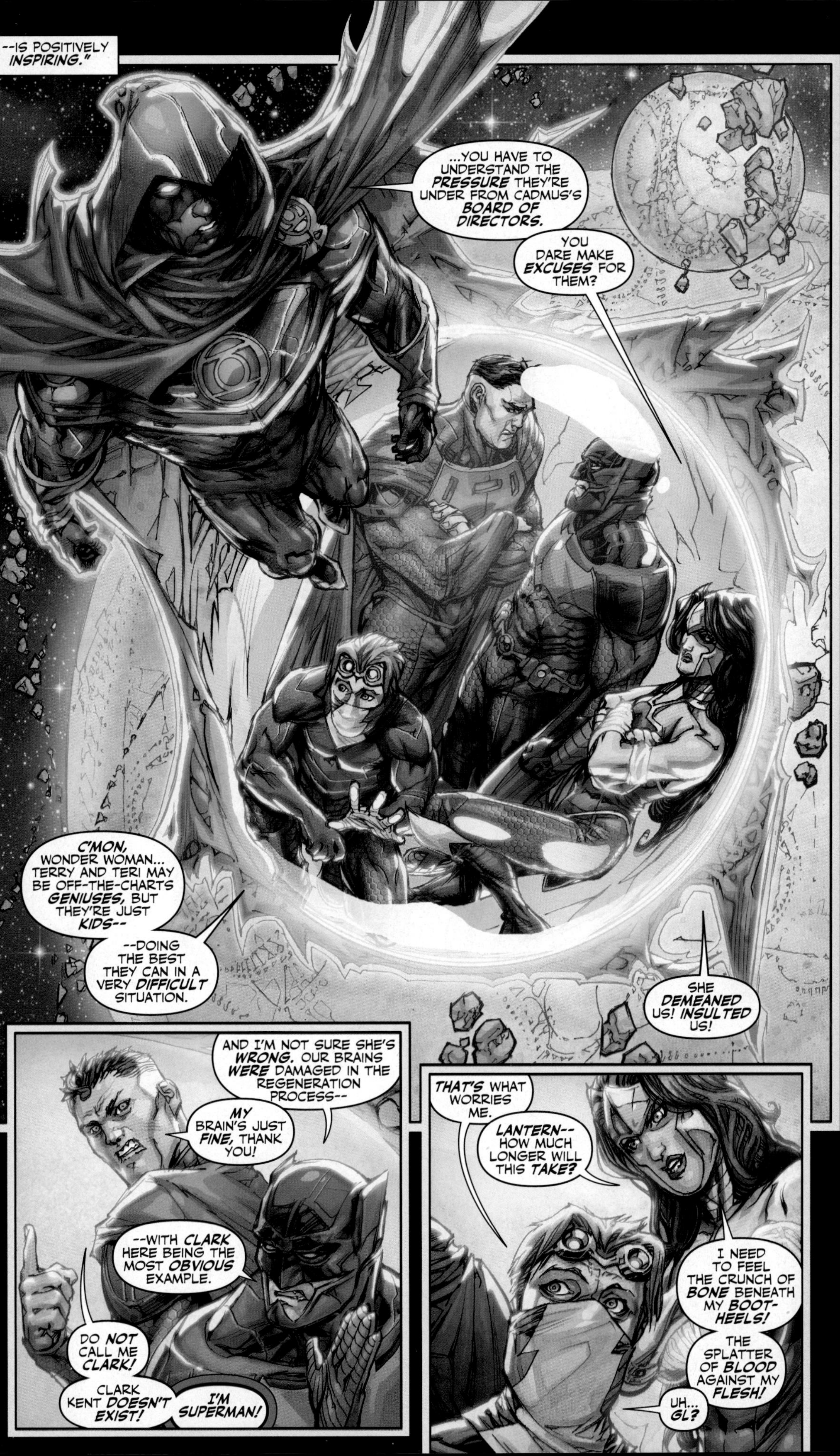
--IS POSITIVELY INSPIRING."
...YOU HAVE TO UNDERSTAND THE PRESSURE THEY'RE UNDER FROM CADMUS'S BOARD OF DIRECTORS.
YOU DARE MAKE EXCUSES FOR THEM?
C'MON, WONDER WOMAN... TERRY AND TERI MAY BE OFF-THE-CHARTS GENIUSES, BUT THEY'RE JUST KIDS--
--DOING THE BEST THEY CAN IN A VERY DIFFICULT SITUATION.
SHE DEMEANED US! INSULTED US!
AND I'M NOT SURE SHE'S WRONG. OUR BRAINS WERE DAMAGED IN THE REGENERATION PROCESS--
MY BRAIN'S JUST FINE, THANK YOU!
--WITH CLARK HERE BEING THE MOST OBVIOUS EXAMPLE.
DO NOT CALL ME CLARK!
CLARK KENT DOESN'T EXIST!
I'M SUPERMAN!
THAT'S WHAT WORRIES ME.
LANTERN-- HOW MUCH LONGER WILL THIS TAKE?
I NEED TO FEEL THE CRUNCH OF BONE BENEATH MY BOOT-HEELS!
THE SPLATTER OF BLOOD AGAINST MY FLESH!
UH... GL?

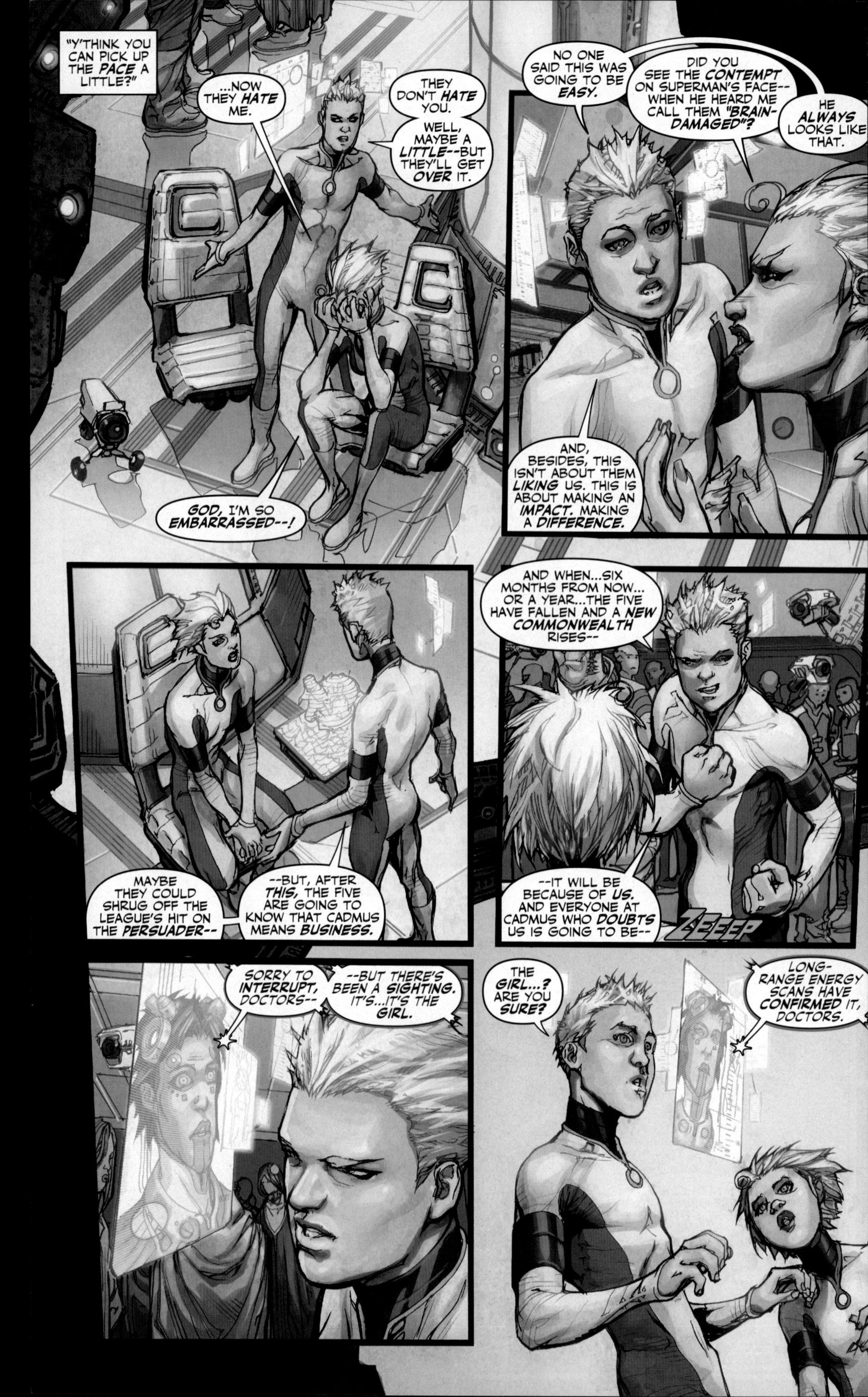

"Y'THINK YOU CAN PICK UP THE PACE A LITTLE?"
...NOW THEY HATE ME.
THEY DON'T HATE YOU.
WELL, MAYBE A LITTLE--BUT THEY'LL GET OVER IT.
GOD, I'M SO EMBARRASSED--!
NO ONE SAID THIS WAS GOING TO BE EASY.
DID YOU SEE THE CONTEMPT ON SUPERMAN'S FACE--WHEN HE HEARD ME CALL THEM "BRAIN-DAMAGED"?
HE ALWAYS LOOKS LIKE THAT.
AND, BESIDES, THIS ISN'T ABOUT THEM LIKING US. THIS IS ABOUT MAKING AN IMPACT. MAKING A DIFFERENCE.
MAYBE THEY COULD SHRUG OFF THE LEAGUE'S HIT ON THE PERSUADER--
--BUT, AFTER THIS, THE FIVE ARE GOING TO KNOW THAT CADMUS MEANS BUSINESS.
AND WHEN...SIX MONTHS FROM NOW... OR A YEAR...THE FIVE HAVE FALLEN AND A NEW COMMONWEALTH RISES--
--IT WILL BE BECAUSE OF US. AND EVERYONE AT CADMUS WHO DOUBTS US IS GOING TO BE--
ZEEEP
SORRY TO INTERRUPT, DOCTORS--
--BUT THERE'S BEEN A SIGHTING. IT'S...IT'S THE GIRL.
THE GIRL...? ARE YOU SURE?
LONG-RANGE ENERGY SCANS HAVE CONFIRMED IT, DOCTORS.

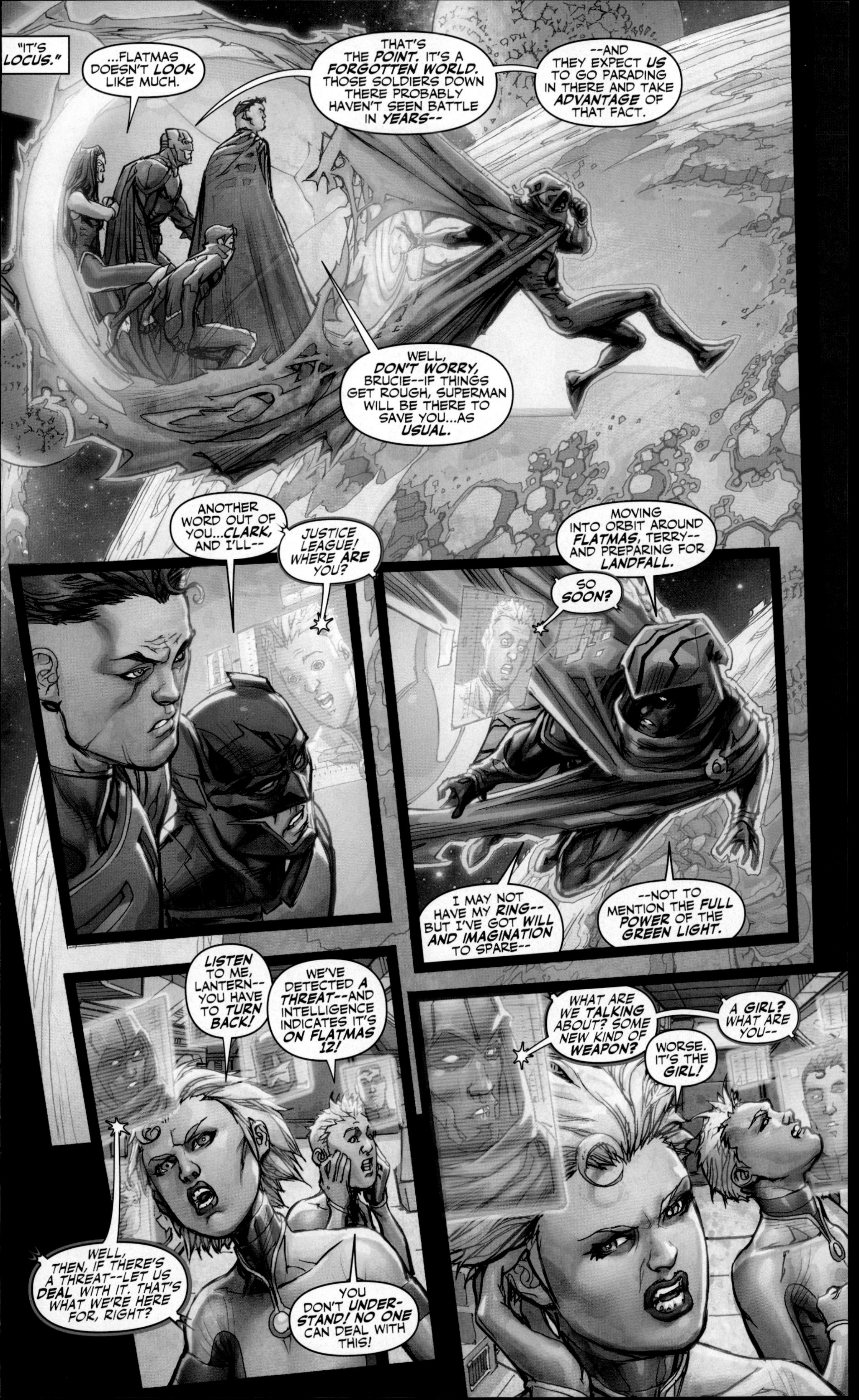
"IT'S LOCUS."
...FLATMAS DOESN'T LOOK LIKE MUCH.
THAT'S THE POINT. IT'S A FORGOTTEN WORLD. THOSE SOLDIERS DOWN THERE PROBABLY HAVEN'T SEEN BATTLE IN YEARS--
--AND THEY EXPECT US TO GO PARADING IN THERE AND TAKE ADVANTAGE OF THAT FACT.
WELL, DON'T WORRY, BRUCIE--IF THINGS GET ROUGH, SUPERMAN WILL BE THERE TO SAVE YOU...AS USUAL.
ANOTHER WORD OUT OF YOU...CLARK, AND I'LL--
JUSTICE LEAGUE! WHERE ARE YOU?
MOVING INTO ORBIT AROUND FLATMAS, TERRY--AND PREPARING FOR LANDFALL.
SO SOON?
I MAY NOT HAVE MY RING--BUT I'VE GOT WILL AND IMAGINATION TO SPARE--
--NOT TO MENTION THE FULL POWER OF THE GREEN LIGHT.
LISTEN TO ME, LANTERN--YOU HAVE TO TURN BACK!
WE'VE DETECTED A THREAT--AND INTELLIGENCE INDICATES IT'S ON FLATMAS 12!
WELL, THEN, IF THERE'S A THREAT--LET US DEAL WITH IT. THAT'S WHAT WE'RE HERE FOR, RIGHT?
YOU DON'T UNDERSTAND! NO ONE CAN DEAL WITH THIS!
WHAT ARE WE TALKING ABOUT? SOME NEW KIND OF WEAPON?
A GIRL? WHAT ARE YOU--
WORSE. IT'S THE GIRL!

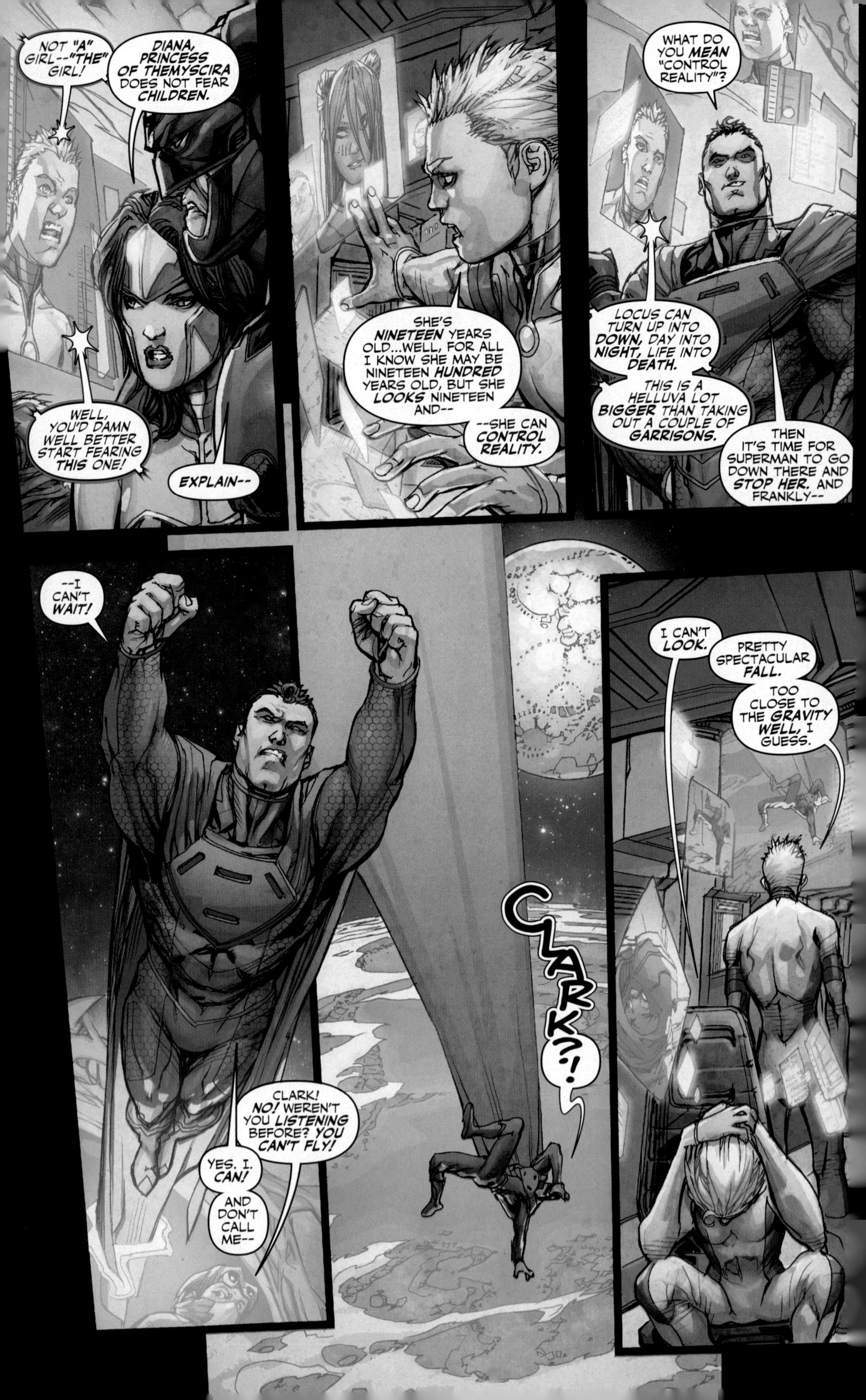

NOT "A" GIRL--"THE" GIRL!
DIANA, PRINCESS OF THEMYSCIRA DOES NOT FEAR CHILDREN.
WELL, YOU'D DAMN WELL BETTER START FEARING THIS ONE!
EXPLAIN--
SHE'S NINETEEN YEARS OLD...WELL, FOR ALL I KNOW SHE MAY BE NINETEEN HUNDRED YEARS OLD, BUT SHE LOOKS NINETEEN AND--
--SHE CAN CONTROL REALITY.
WHAT DO YOU MEAN "CONTROL REALITY"?
LOCUS CAN TURN UP INTO DOWN, DAY INTO NIGHT, LIFE INTO DEATH.
THIS IS A HELLUVA LOT BIGGER THAN TAKING OUT A COUPLE OF GARRISONS.
THEN IT'S TIME FOR SUPERMAN TO GO DOWN THERE AND STOP HER. AND FRANKLY--
--I CAN'T WAIT!
CLARK! NO! WEREN'T YOU LISTENING BEFORE? YOU CAN'T FLY!
YES. I. CAN!
AND DON'T CALL ME--
CLARK?!
I CAN'T LOOK.
PRETTY SPECTACULAR FALL.
TOO CLOSE TO THE GRAVITY WELL, I GUESS.

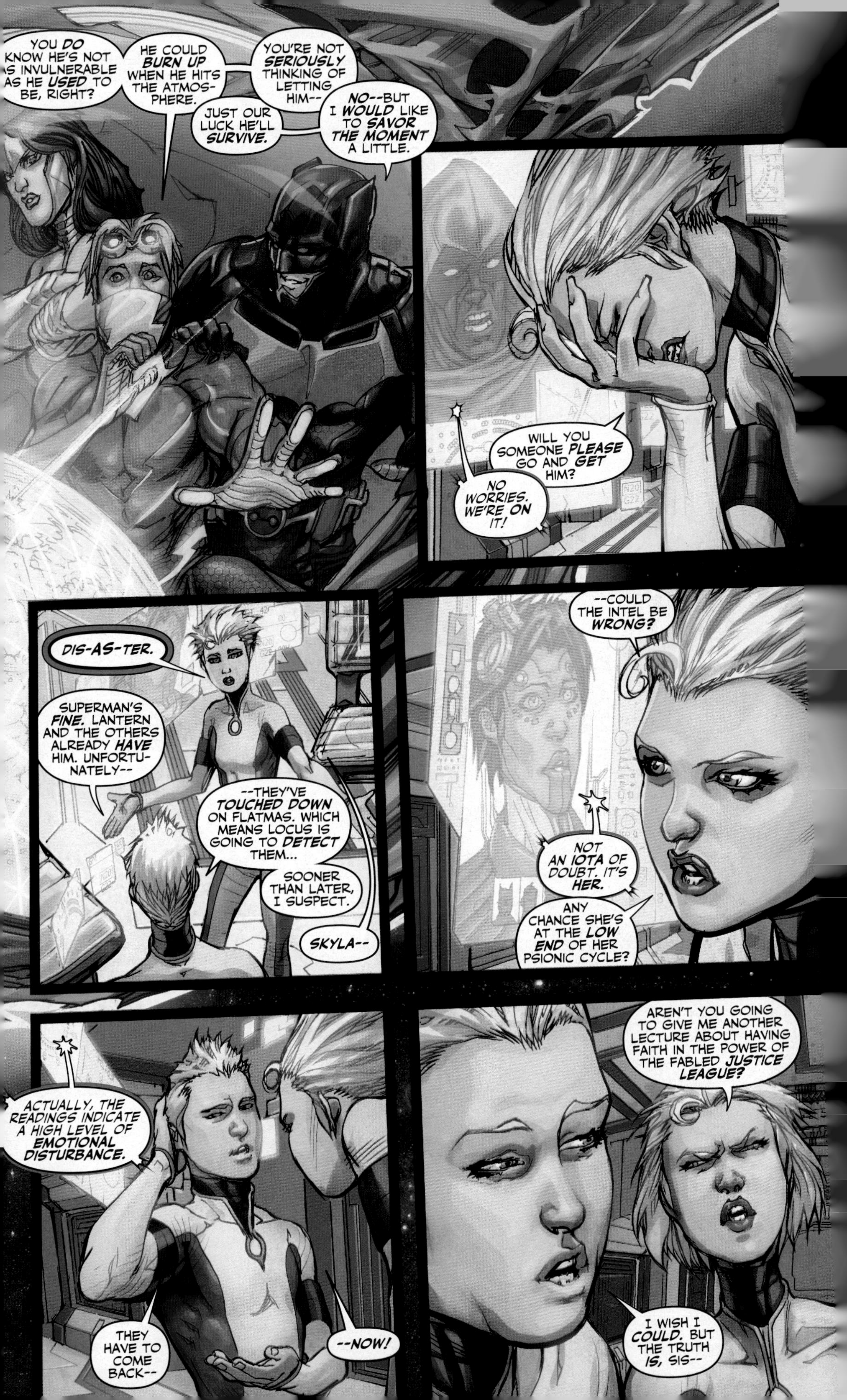
YOU DO KNOW HE'S NOT AS INVULNERABLE AS HE USED TO BE, RIGHT?
HE COULD BURN UP WHEN HE HITS THE ATMOSPHERE.
YOU'RE NOT SERIOUSLY THINKING OF LETTING HIM--
JUST OUR LUCK HE'LL SURVIVE.
NO--BUT I WOULD LIKE TO SAVOR THE MOMENT A LITTLE.
WILL YOU SOMEONE PLEASE GO AND GET HIM?
NO WORRIES. WE'RE ON IT!
DIS-AS-TER.
SUPERMAN'S FINE. LANTERN AND THE OTHERS ALREADY HAVE HIM. UNFORTUNATELY--
--THEY'VE TOUCHED DOWN ON FLATMAS. WHICH MEANS LOCUS IS GOING TO DETECT THEM...
SOONER THAN LATER, I SUSPECT.
SKYLA--
--COULD THE INTEL BE WRONG?
NOT AN IOTA OF DOUBT. IT'S HER.
ANY CHANCE SHE'S AT THE LOW END OF HER PSIONIC CYCLE?
ACTUALLY, THE READINGS INDICATE A HIGH LEVEL OF EMOTIONAL DISTURBANCE.
THEY HAVE TO COME BACK--
--NOW!
AREN'T YOU GOING TO GIVE ME ANOTHER LECTURE ABOUT HAVING FAITH IN THE POWER OF THE FABLED JUSTICE LEAGUE?
I WISH I COULD. BUT THE TRUTH IS, SIS--

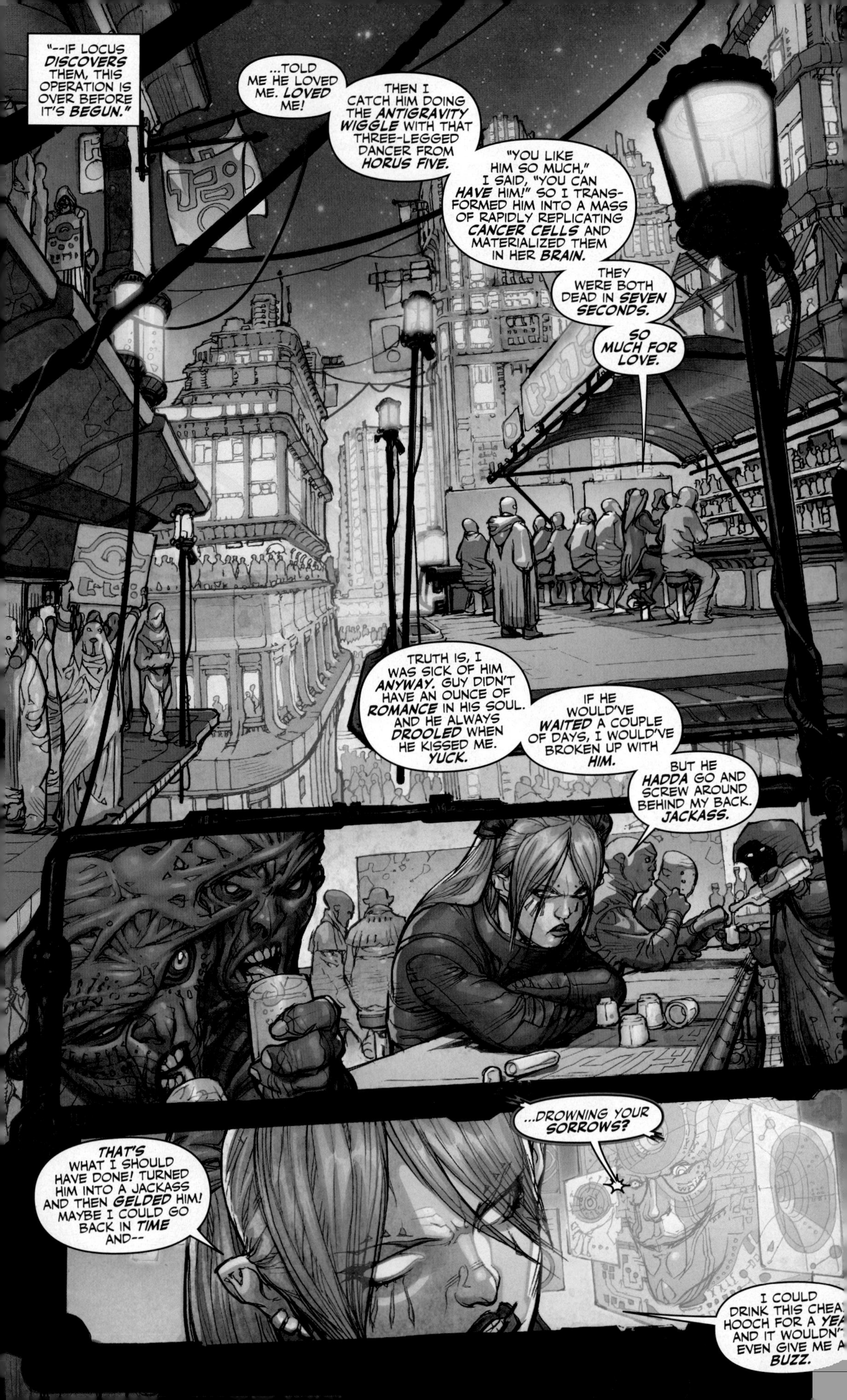
"--IF LOCUS DISCOVERS THEM, THIS OPERATION IS OVER BEFORE IT'S BEGUN."
...TOLD ME HE LOVED ME. LOVED ME!
THEN I CATCH HIM DOING THE ANTIGRAVITY WIGGLE WITH THAT THREE-LEGGED DANCER FROM HORUS FIVE.
"YOU LIKE HIM SO MUCH," I SAID, "YOU CAN HAVE HIM!" SO I TRANSFORMED HIM INTO A MASS OF RAPIDLY REPLICATING CANCER CELLS AND MATERIALIZED THEM IN HER BRAIN.
THEY WERE BOTH DEAD IN SEVEN SECONDS.
SO MUCH FOR LOVE.
TRUTH IS, I WAS SICK OF HIM ANYWAY. GUY DIDN'T HAVE AN OUNCE OF ROMANCE IN HIS SOUL. AND HE ALWAYS DROOLED WHEN HE KISSED ME. YUCK.
IF HE WOULD'VE WAITED A COUPLE OF DAYS, I WOULD'VE BROKEN UP WITH HIM.
BUT HE HADDA GO AND SCREW AROUND BEHIND MY BACK. JACKASS.
...DROWNING YOUR SORROWS?
THAT'S WHAT I SHOULD HAVE DONE! TURNED HIM INTO A JACKASS AND THEN GELDED HIM! MAYBE I COULD GO BACK IN TIME AND--
I COULD DRINK THIS CHEA HOOCH FOR A YEA AND IT WOULDN' EVEN GIVE ME A BUZZ.

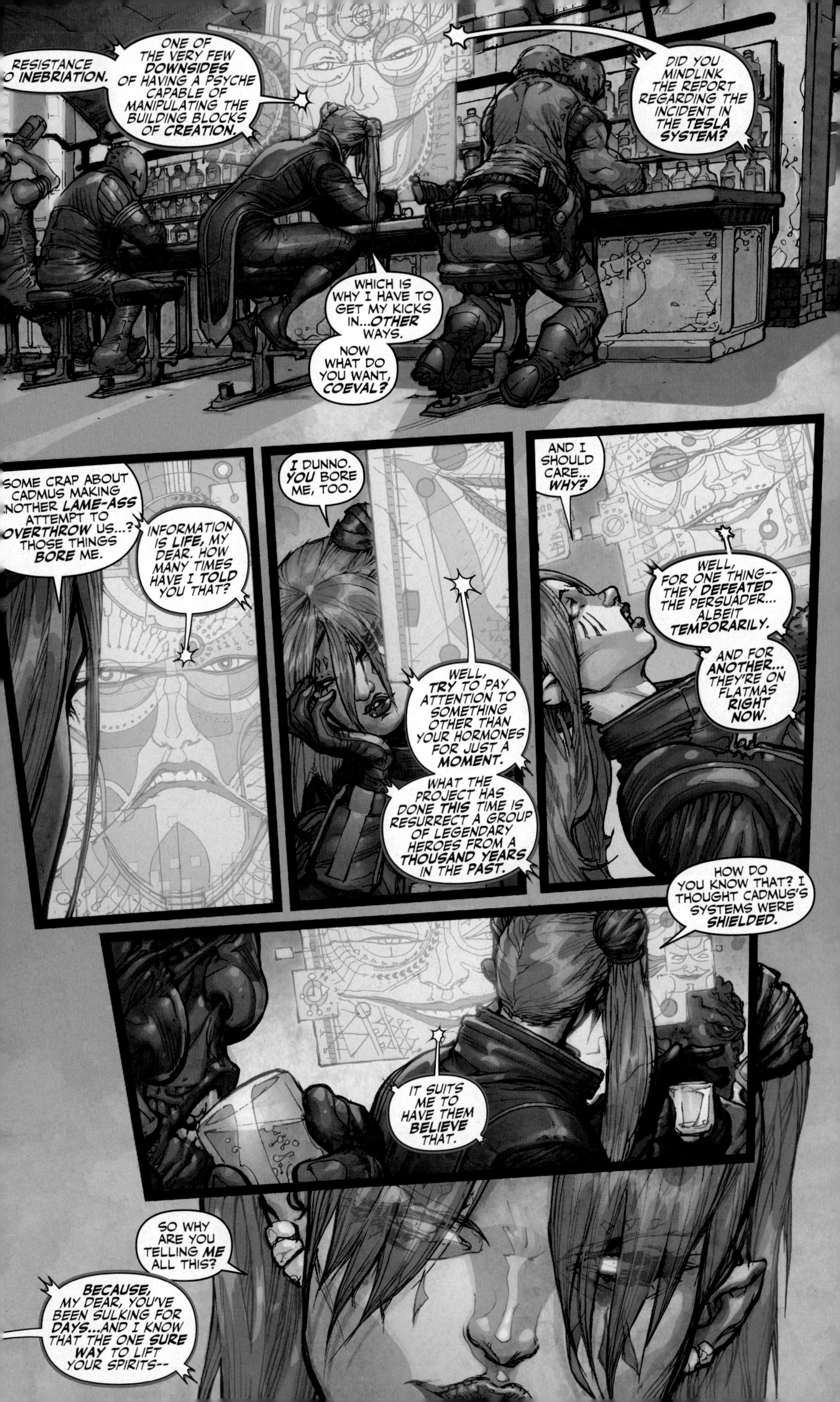
RESISTANCE TO INEBRIATION.
ONE OF THE VERY FEW DOWNSIDES OF HAVING A PSYCHE CAPABLE OF MANIPULATING THE BUILDING BLOCKS OF CREATION.
DID YOU MINDLINK THE REPORT REGARDING THE INCIDENT IN THE TESLA SYSTEM?
WHICH IS WHY I HAVE TO GET MY KICKS IN...OTHER WAYS.
NOW WHAT DO YOU WANT, COEVAL?
SOME CRAP ABOUT CADMUS MAKING ANOTHER LAME-ASS ATTEMPT TO OVERTHROW US...? THOSE THINGS BORE ME.
INFORMATION IS LIFE, MY DEAR. HOW MANY TIMES HAVE I TOLD YOU THAT?
I DUNNO. YOU BORE ME, TOO.
WELL, TRY TO PAY ATTENTION TO SOMETHING OTHER THAN YOUR HORMONES FOR JUST A MOMENT.
WHAT THE PROJECT HAS DONE THIS TIME IS RESURRECT A GROUP OF LEGENDARY HEROES FROM A THOUSAND YEARS IN THE PAST.
AND I SHOULD CARE... WHY?
WELL, FOR ONE THING-- THEY DEFEATED THE PERSUADER... ALBEIT TEMPORARILY.
AND FOR ANOTHER... THEY'RE ON FLATMAS RIGHT NOW.
HOW DO YOU KNOW THAT? I THOUGHT CADMUS'S SYSTEMS WERE SHIELDED.
IT SUITS ME TO HAVE THEM BELIEVE THAT.
SO WHY ARE YOU TELLING ME ALL THIS?
BECAUSE, MY DEAR, YOU'VE BEEN SULKING FOR DAYS...AND I KNOW THAT THE ONE SURE WAY TO LIFT YOUR SPIRITS--

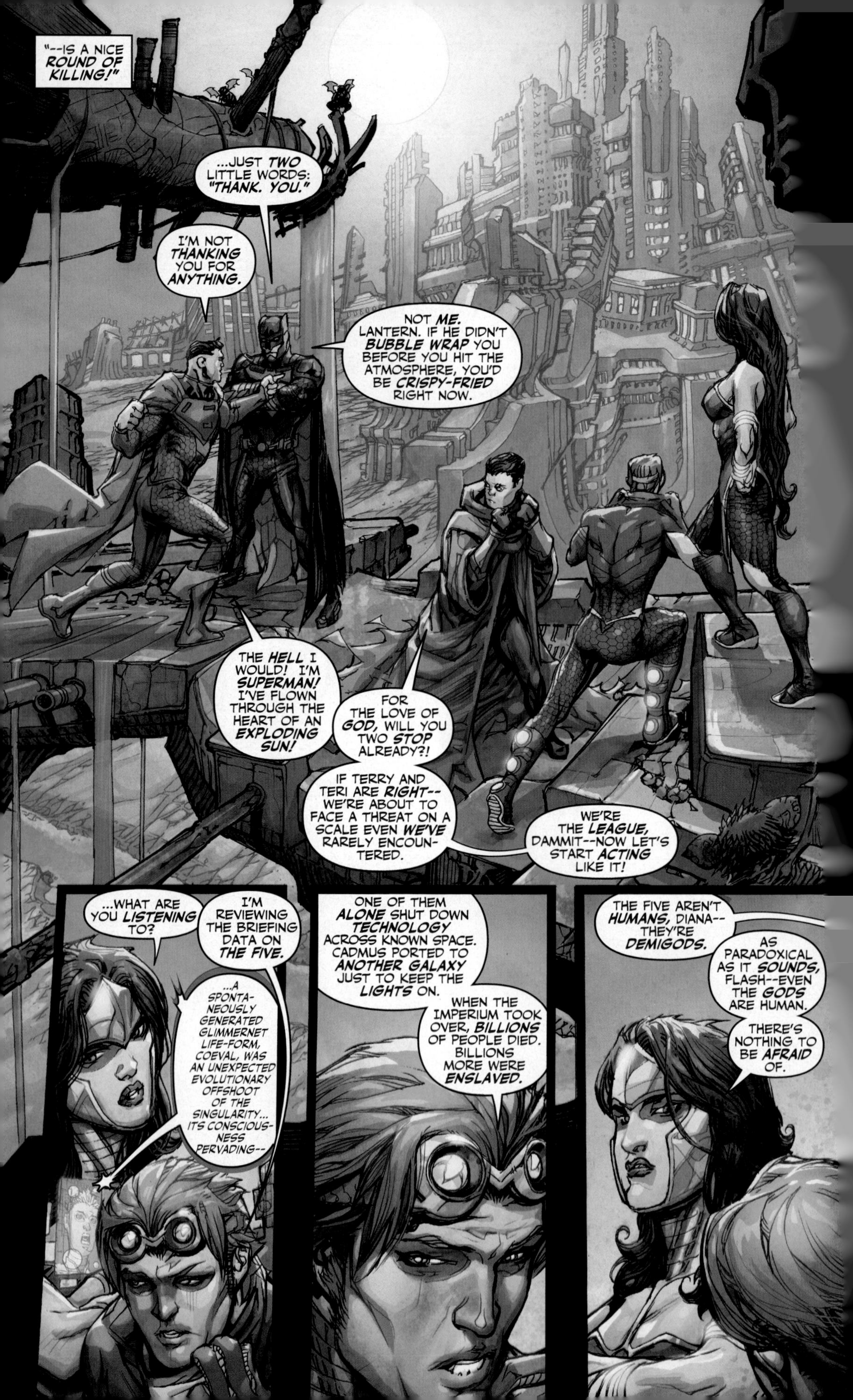
"--IS A NICE ROUND OF KILLING!"
...JUST TWO LITTLE WORDS: "THANK. YOU."
I'M NOT THANKING YOU FOR ANYTHING.
NOT ME. LANTERN. IF HE DIDN'T BUBBLE WRAP YOU BEFORE YOU HIT THE ATMOSPHERE, YOU'D BE CRISPY-FRIED RIGHT NOW.
THE HELL I WOULD! I'M SUPERMAN! I'VE FLOWN THROUGH THE HEART OF AN EXPLODING SUN!
FOR THE LOVE OF GOD, WILL YOU TWO STOP ALREADY?!
IF TERRY AND TERI ARE RIGHT--WE'RE ABOUT TO FACE A THREAT ON A SCALE EVEN WE'VE RARELY ENCOUNTERED.
WE'RE THE LEAGUE, DAMMIT--NOW LET'S START ACTING LIKE IT!
...WHAT ARE YOU LISTENING TO?
I'M REVIEWING THE BRIEFING DATA ON THE FIVE.
...A SPONTANEOUSLY GENERATED GLIMMERNET LIFE-FORM, COEVAL, WAS AN UNEXPECTED EVOLUTIONARY OFFSHOOT OF THE SINGULARITY... ITS CONSCIOUSNESS PERVADING--
ONE OF THEM ALONE SHUT DOWN TECHNOLOGY ACROSS KNOWN SPACE. CADMUS PORTED TO ANOTHER GALAXY JUST TO KEEP THE LIGHTS ON.
WHEN THE IMPERIUM TOOK OVER, BILLIONS OF PEOPLE DIED. BILLIONS MORE WERE ENSLAVED.
THE FIVE AREN'T HUMANS, DIANA--THEY'RE DEMIGODS.
AS PARADOXICAL AS IT SOUNDS, FLASH--EVEN THE GODS ARE HUMAN.
THERE'S NOTHING TO BE AFRAID OF.

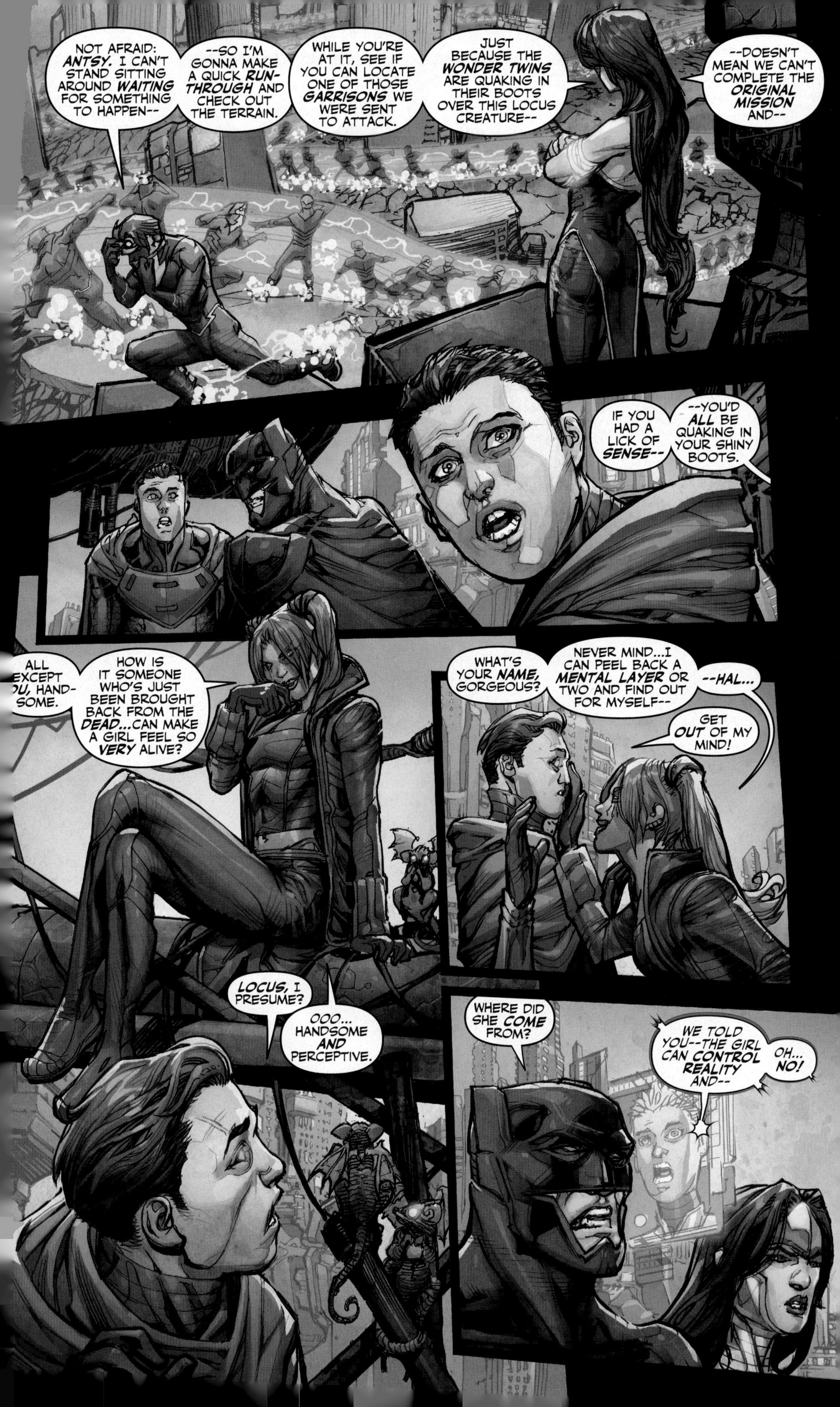

NOT AFRAID: ANTSY. I CAN'T STAND SITTING AROUND WAITING FOR SOMETHING TO HAPPEN--
--SO I'M GONNA MAKE A QUICK RUN-THROUGH AND CHECK OUT THE TERRAIN.
WHILE YOU'RE AT IT, SEE IF YOU CAN LOCATE ONE OF THOSE GARRISONS WE WERE SENT TO ATTACK.
JUST BECAUSE THE WONDER TWINS ARE QUAKING IN THEIR BOOTS OVER THIS LOCUS CREATURE--
--DOESN'T MEAN WE CAN'T COMPLETE THE ORIGINAL MISSION AND--
IF YOU HAD A LICK OF SENSE--
--YOU'D ALL BE QUAKING IN YOUR SHINY BOOTS.
ALL EXCEPT OU, HAND-SOME.
HOW IS IT SOMEONE WHO'S JUST BEEN BROUGHT BACK FROM THE DEAD...CAN MAKE A GIRL FEEL SO VERY ALIVE?
WHAT'S YOUR NAME, GORGEOUS?
NEVER MIND...I CAN PEEL BACK A MENTAL LAYER OR TWO AND FIND OUT FOR MYSELF--
--HAL...
GET OUT OF MY MIND!
LOCUS, I PRESUME?
OOO... HANDSOME AND PERCEPTIVE.
WHERE DID SHE COME FROM?
WE TOLD YOU--THE GIRL CAN CONTROL REALITY AND--
OH... NO!

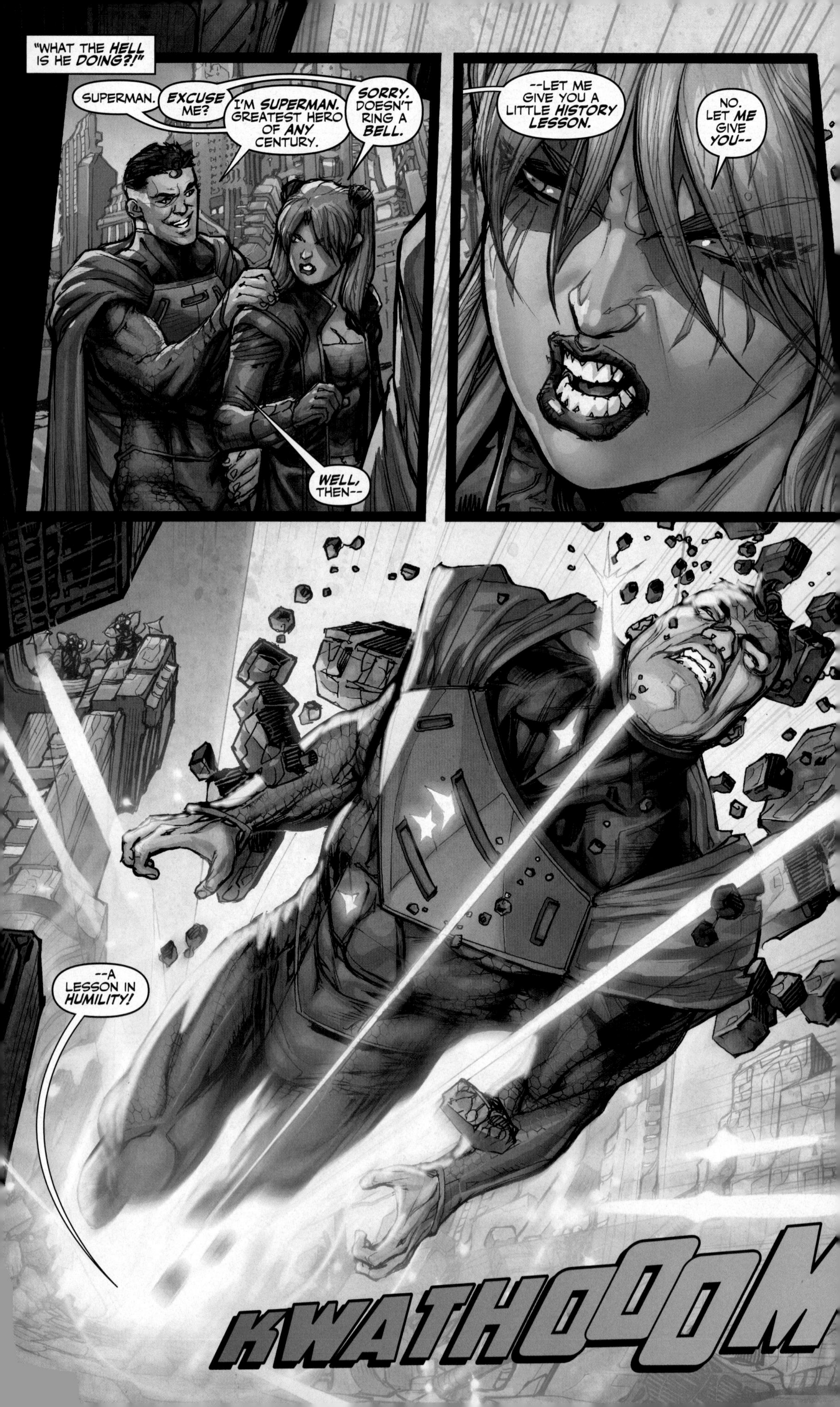
"WHAT THE HELL IS HE DOING?!"
SUPERMAN.
EXCUSE ME?
I'M SUPERMAN. GREATEST HERO OF ANY CENTURY.
SORRY. DOESN'T RING A BELL.
WELL, THEN--
--LET ME GIVE YOU A LITTLE HISTORY LESSON.
NO. LET ME GIVE YOU--
--A LESSON IN HUMILITY!
KWATHOOOOM

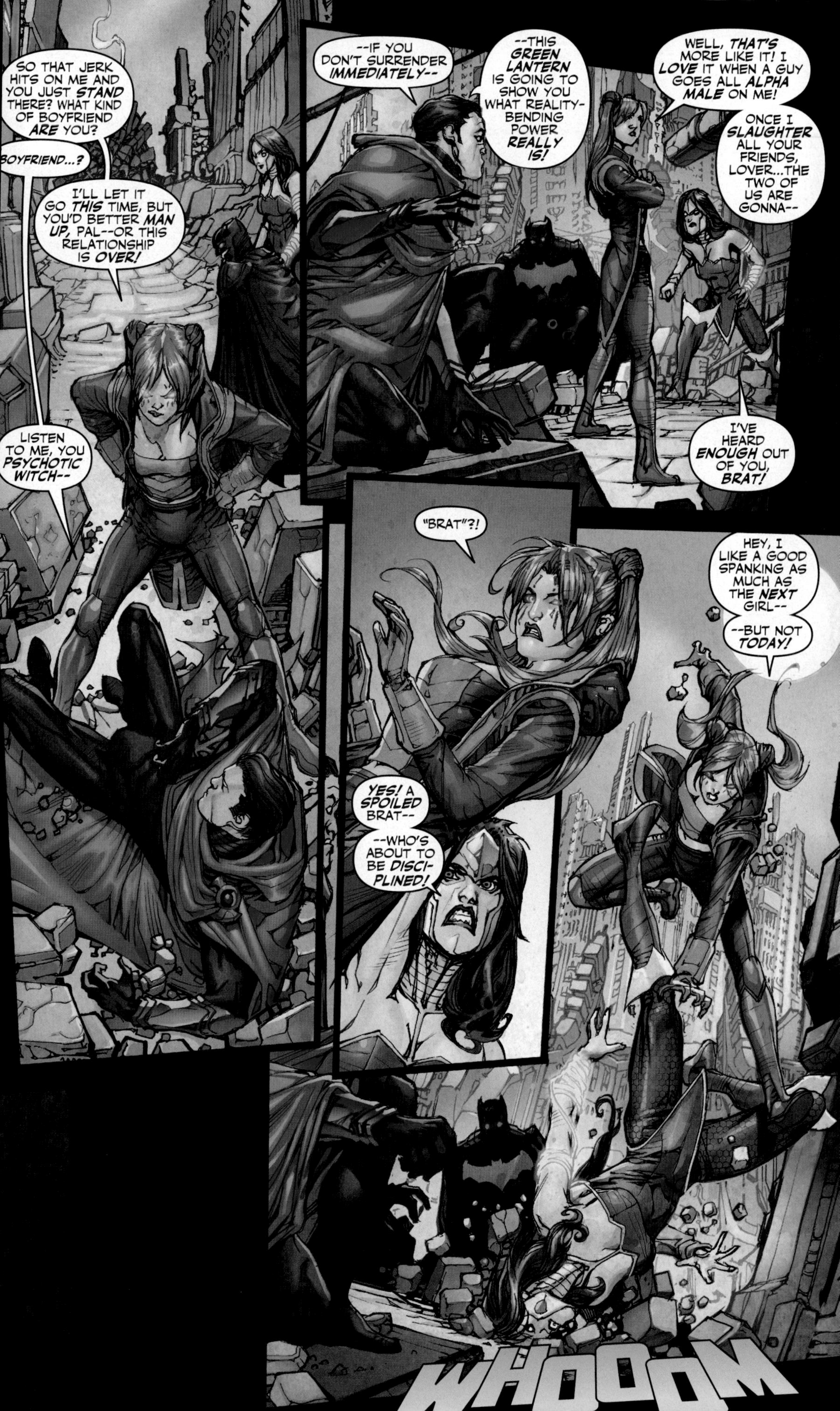
SO THAT JERK HITS ON ME AND YOU JUST STAND THERE? WHAT KIND OF BOYFRIEND ARE YOU?
BOYFRIEND...?
I'LL LET IT GO THIS TIME, BUT YOU'D BETTER MAN UP, PAL--OR THIS RELATIONSHIP IS OVER!
LISTEN TO ME, YOU PSYCHOTIC WITCH--
--IF YOU DON'T SURRENDER IMMEDIATELY--
--THIS GREEN LANTERN IS GOING TO SHOW YOU WHAT REALITY-BENDING POWER REALLY IS!
WELL, THAT'S MORE LIKE IT! I LOVE IT WHEN A GUY GOES ALL ALPHA MALE ON ME!
ONCE I SLAUGHTER ALL YOUR FRIENDS, LOVER...THE TWO OF US ARE GONNA--
I'VE HEARD ENOUGH OUT OF YOU, BRAT!
"BRAT"?!
YES! A SPOILED BRAT--
--WHO'S ABOUT TO BE DISCI-PLINED!
HEY, I LIKE A GOOD SPANKING AS MUCH AS THE NEXT GIRL--
--BUT NOT TODAY!
WHOOOM

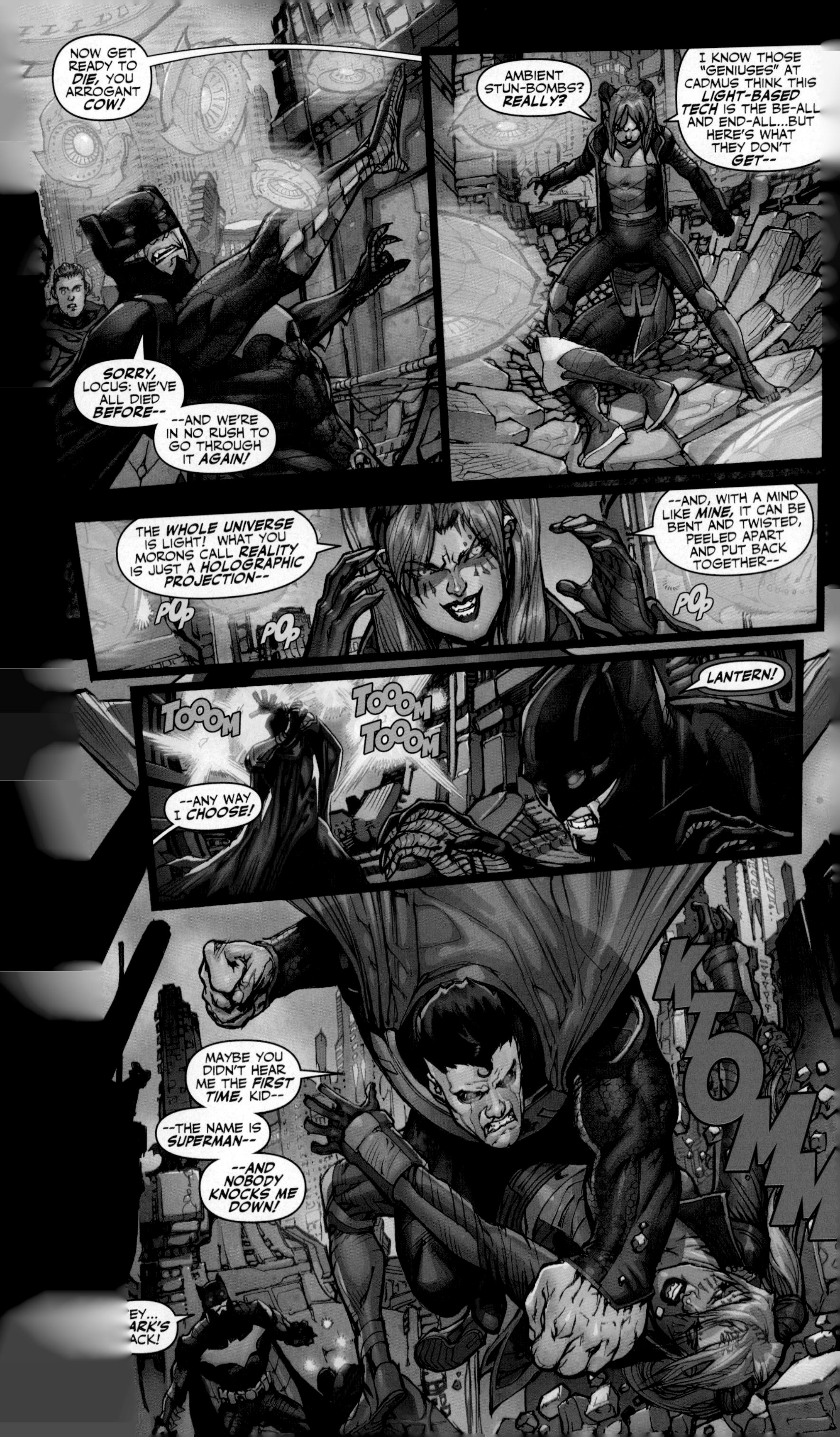
NOW GET READY TO DIE, YOU ARROGANT COW!
AMBIENT STUN-BOMBS? REALLY?
I KNOW THOSE "GENIUSES" AT CADMUS THINK THIS LIGHT-BASED TECH IS THE BE-ALL AND END-ALL...BUT HERE'S WHAT THEY DON'T GET--
SORRY, LOCUS: WE'VE ALL DIED BEFORE--
--AND WE'RE IN NO RUSH TO GO THROUGH IT AGAIN!
THE WHOLE UNIVERSE IS LIGHT! WHAT YOU MORONS CALL REALITY IS JUST A HOLOGRAPHIC PROJECTION--
--AND, WITH A MIND LIKE MINE, IT CAN BE BENT AND TWISTED, PEELED APART AND PUT BACK TOGETHER--
POP
POP
POP
TOOOM
TOOOM
TOOOM
--ANY WAY I CHOOSE!
LANTERN!
KTOOM
MAYBE YOU DIDN'T HEAR ME THE FIRST TIME, KID--
--THE NAME IS SUPERMAN--
--AND NOBODY KNOCKS ME DOWN!
EY... ARK'S ACK!

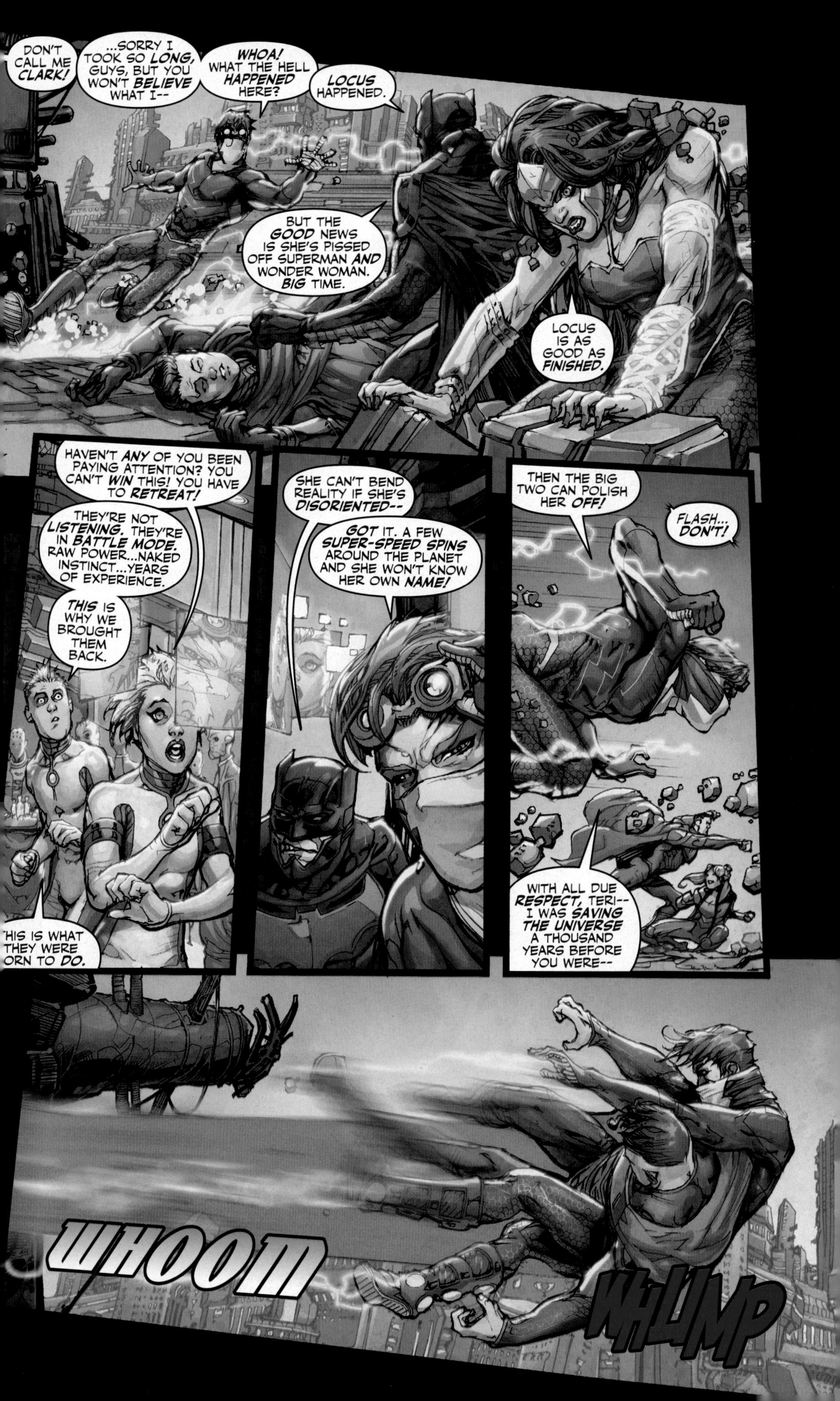
DON'T CALL ME CLARK!
...SORRY I TOOK SO LONG, GUYS, BUT YOU WON'T BELIEVE WHAT I--
WHOA! WHAT THE HELL HAPPENED HERE?
LOCUS HAPPENED.
BUT THE GOOD NEWS IS SHE'S PISSED OFF SUPERMAN AND WONDER WOMAN. BIG TIME.
LOCUS IS AS GOOD AS FINISHED.
HAVEN'T ANY OF YOU BEEN PAYING ATTENTION? YOU CAN'T WIN THIS! YOU HAVE TO RETREAT!
THEY'RE NOT LISTENING. THEY'RE IN BATTLE MODE. RAW POWER...NAKED INSTINCT...YEARS OF EXPERIENCE.
THIS IS WHY WE BROUGHT THEM BACK.
THIS IS WHAT THEY WERE ORN TO DO.
SHE CAN'T BEND REALITY IF SHE'S DISORIENTED--
GOT IT. A FEW SUPER-SPEED SPINS AROUND THE PLANET AND SHE WON'T KNOW HER OWN NAME!
THEN THE BIG TWO CAN POLISH HER OFF!
FLASH... DON'T!
WITH ALL DUE RESPECT, TERI-- I WAS SAVING THE UNIVERSE A THOUSAND YEARS BEFORE YOU WERE--
WHOOM
WHUMP

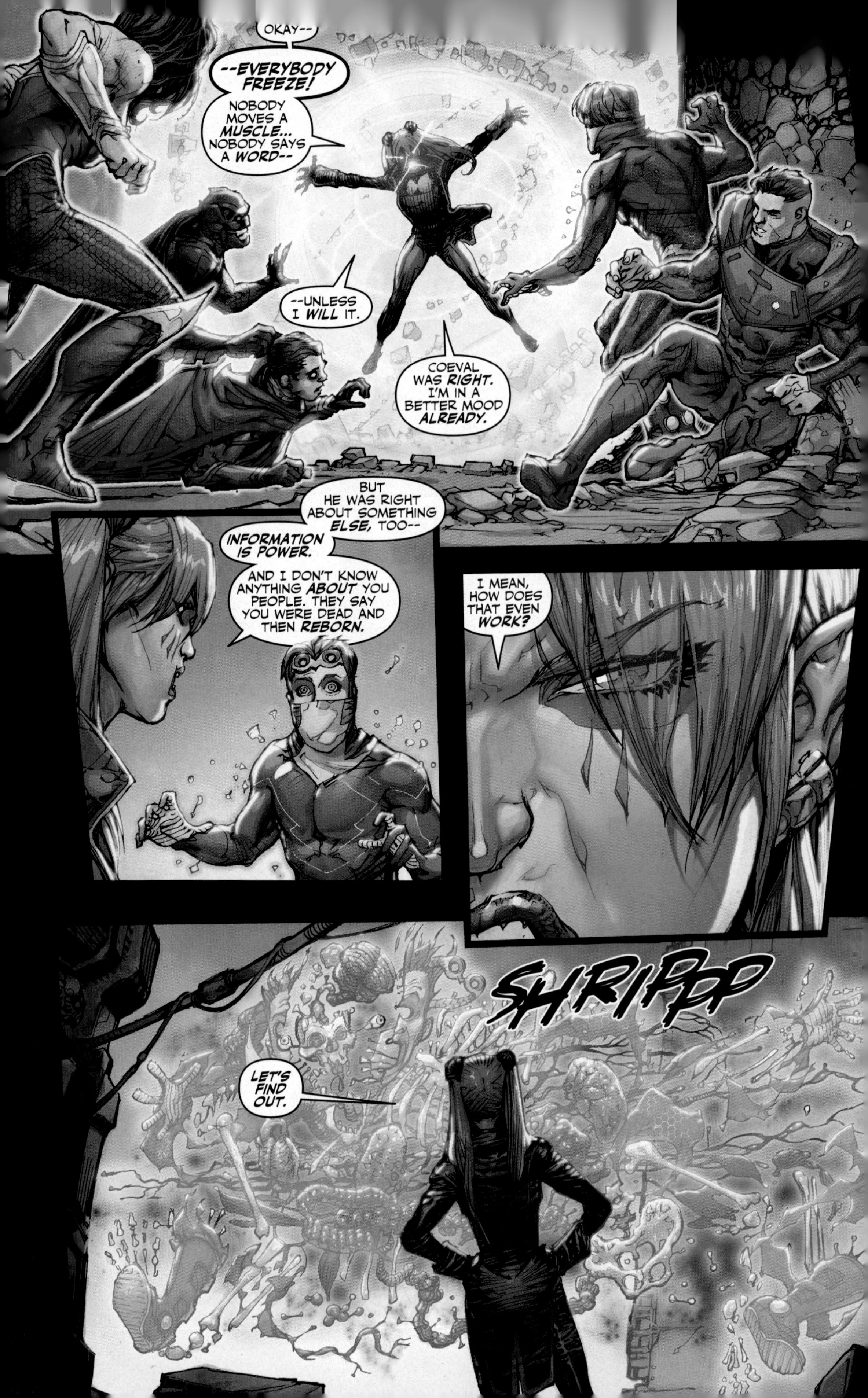
OKAY--
--EVERYBODY FREEZE!
NOBODY MOVES A MUSCLE... NOBODY SAYS A WORD--
--UNLESS I WILL IT.
COEVAL WAS RIGHT. I'M IN A BETTER MOOD ALREADY.
BUT HE WAS RIGHT ABOUT SOMETHING ELSE, TOO--
INFORMATION IS POWER.
AND I DON'T KNOW ANYTHING ABOUT YOU PEOPLE. THEY SAY YOU WERE DEAD AND THEN REBORN.
I MEAN, HOW DOES THAT EVEN WORK?
SHRIPP
LET'S FIND OUT.

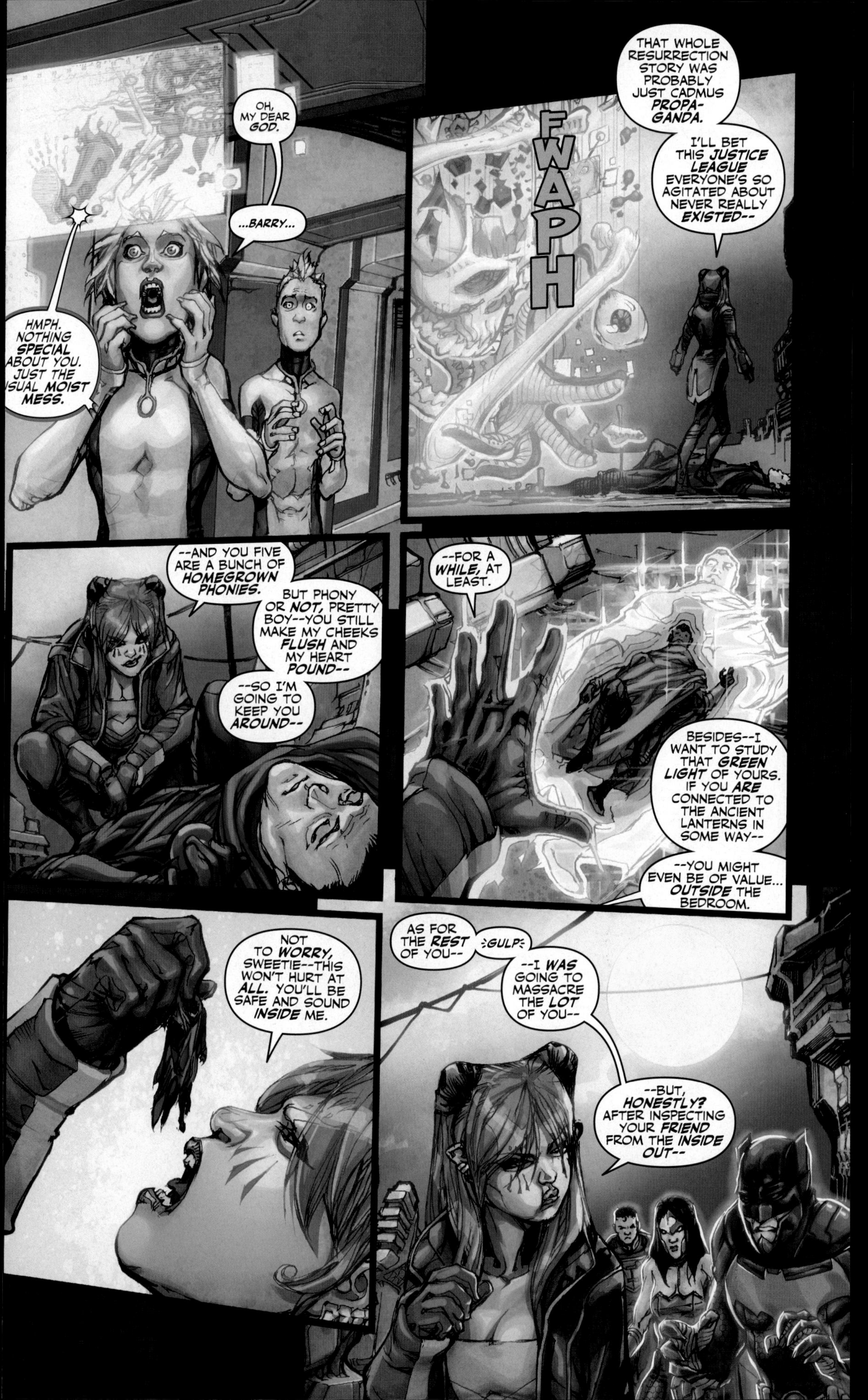
OH, MY DEAR GOD.
...BARRY...
HMPH. NOTHING SPECIAL ABOUT YOU. JUST THE USUAL MOIST MESS.
FWAPH
THAT WHOLE RESURRECTION STORY WAS PROBABLY JUST CADMUS PROPAGANDA.
I'LL BET THIS JUSTICE LEAGUE EVERYONE'S SO AGITATED ABOUT NEVER REALLY EXISTED--
--AND YOU FIVE ARE A BUNCH OF HOMEGROWN PHONIES.
BUT PHONY OR NOT, PRETTY BOY--YOU STILL MAKE MY CHEEKS FLUSH AND MY HEART POUND--
--SO I'M GOING TO KEEP YOU AROUND--
--FOR A WHILE, AT LEAST.
BESIDES--I WANT TO STUDY THAT GREEN LIGHT OF YOURS. IF YOU ARE CONNECTED TO THE ANCIENT LANTERNS IN SOME WAY--
--YOU MIGHT EVEN BE OF VALUE... OUTSIDE THE BEDROOM.
NOT TO WORRY, SWEETIE--THIS WON'T HURT AT ALL. YOU'LL BE SAFE AND SOUND INSIDE ME.
AS FOR THE REST OF YOU--
GULP
--I WAS GOING TO MASSACRE THE LOT OF YOU--
--BUT, HONESTLY? AFTER INSPECTING YOUR FRIEND FROM THE INSIDE OUT--

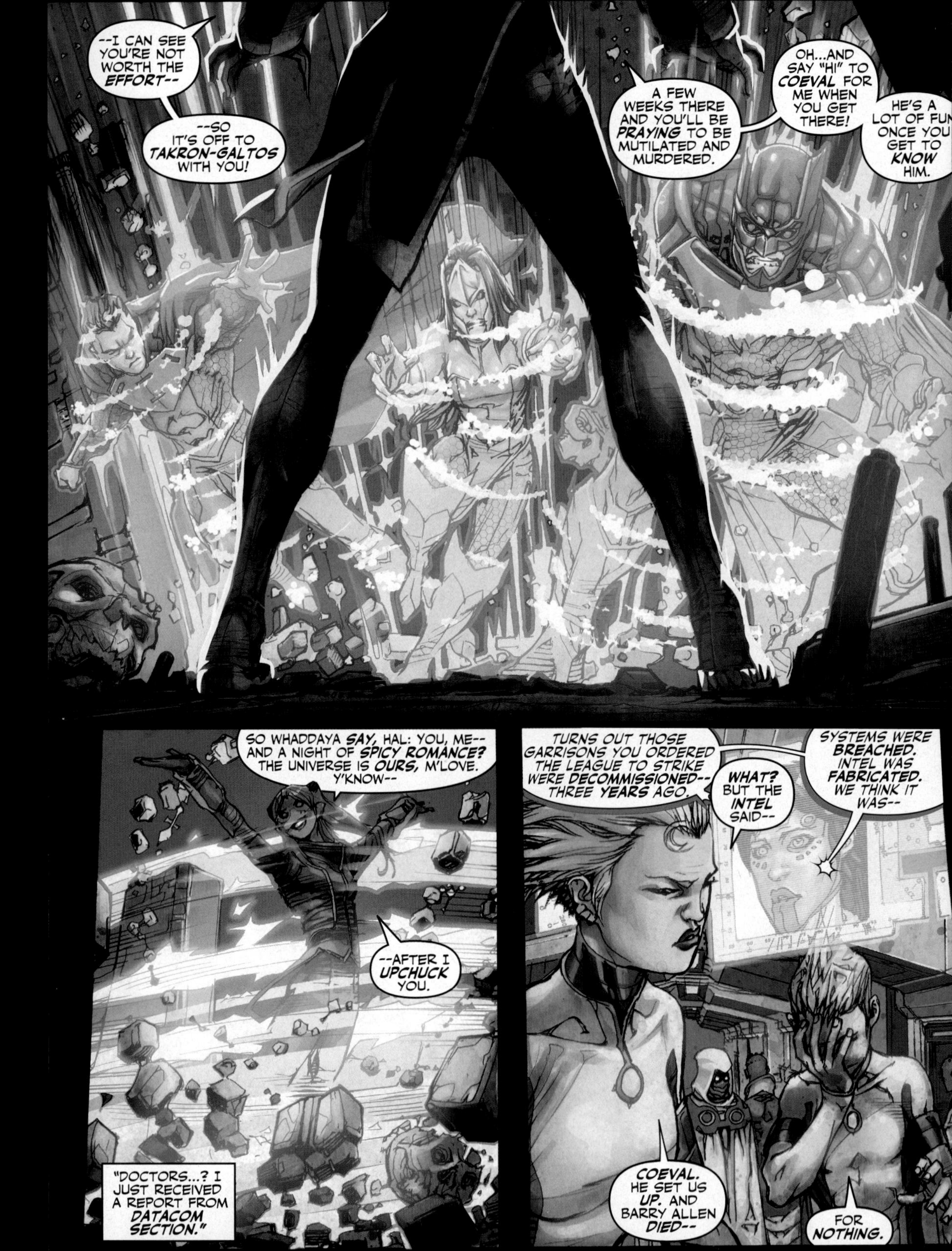
--I CAN SEE YOU'RE NOT WORTH THE EFFORT--
--SO IT'S OFF TO TAKRON-GALTOS WITH YOU!
A FEW WEEKS THERE AND YOU'LL BE PRAYING TO BE MUTILATED AND MURDERED.
OH...AND SAY "HI" TO COEVAL FOR ME WHEN YOU GET THERE!
HE'S A LOT OF FUN ONCE YOU GET TO KNOW HIM.
SO WHADDAYA SAY, HAL: YOU, ME--AND A NIGHT OF SPICY ROMANCE? THE UNIVERSE IS OURS, M'LOVE. Y'KNOW--
--AFTER I UPCHUCK YOU.
"DOCTORS...? I JUST RECEIVED A REPORT FROM DATACOM SECTION."
TURNS OUT THOSE GARRISONS YOU ORDERED THE LEAGUE TO STRIKE WERE DECOMMISSIONED--THREE YEARS AGO.
WHAT? BUT THE INTEL SAID--
SYSTEMS WERE BREACHED. INTEL WAS FABRICATED. WE THINK IT WAS--
COEVAL. HE SET US UP. AND BARRY ALLEN DIED--
FOR NOTHING.

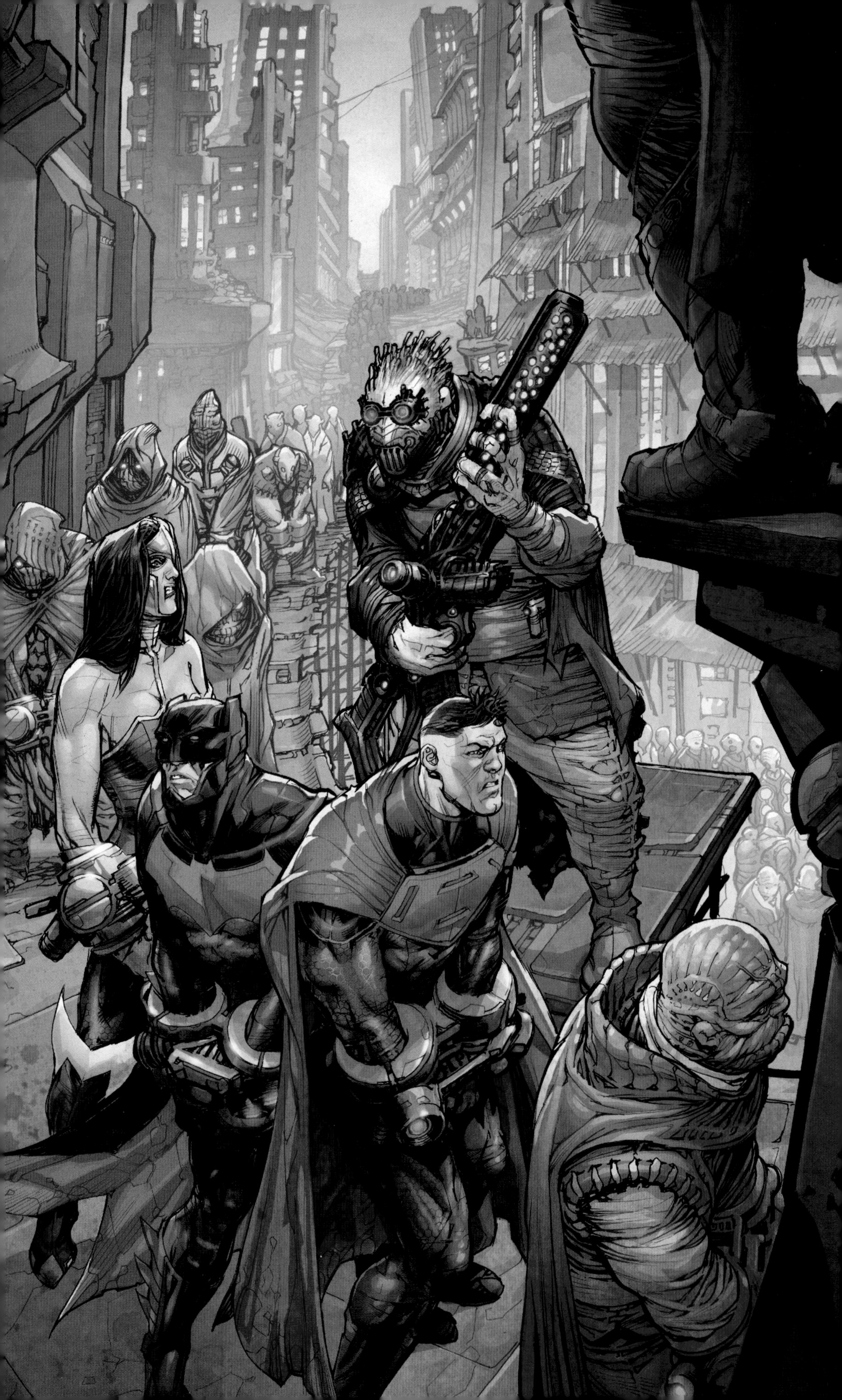

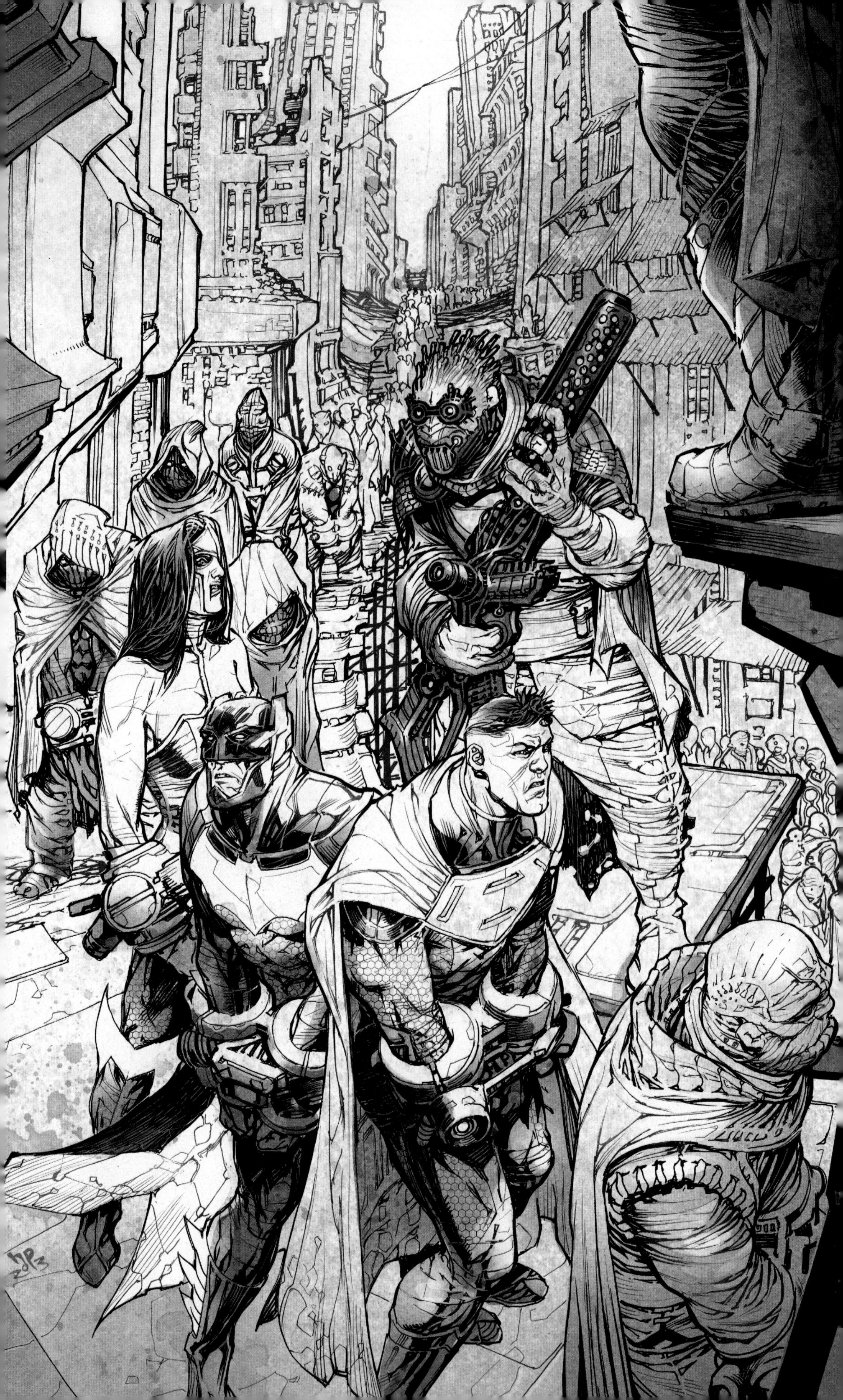

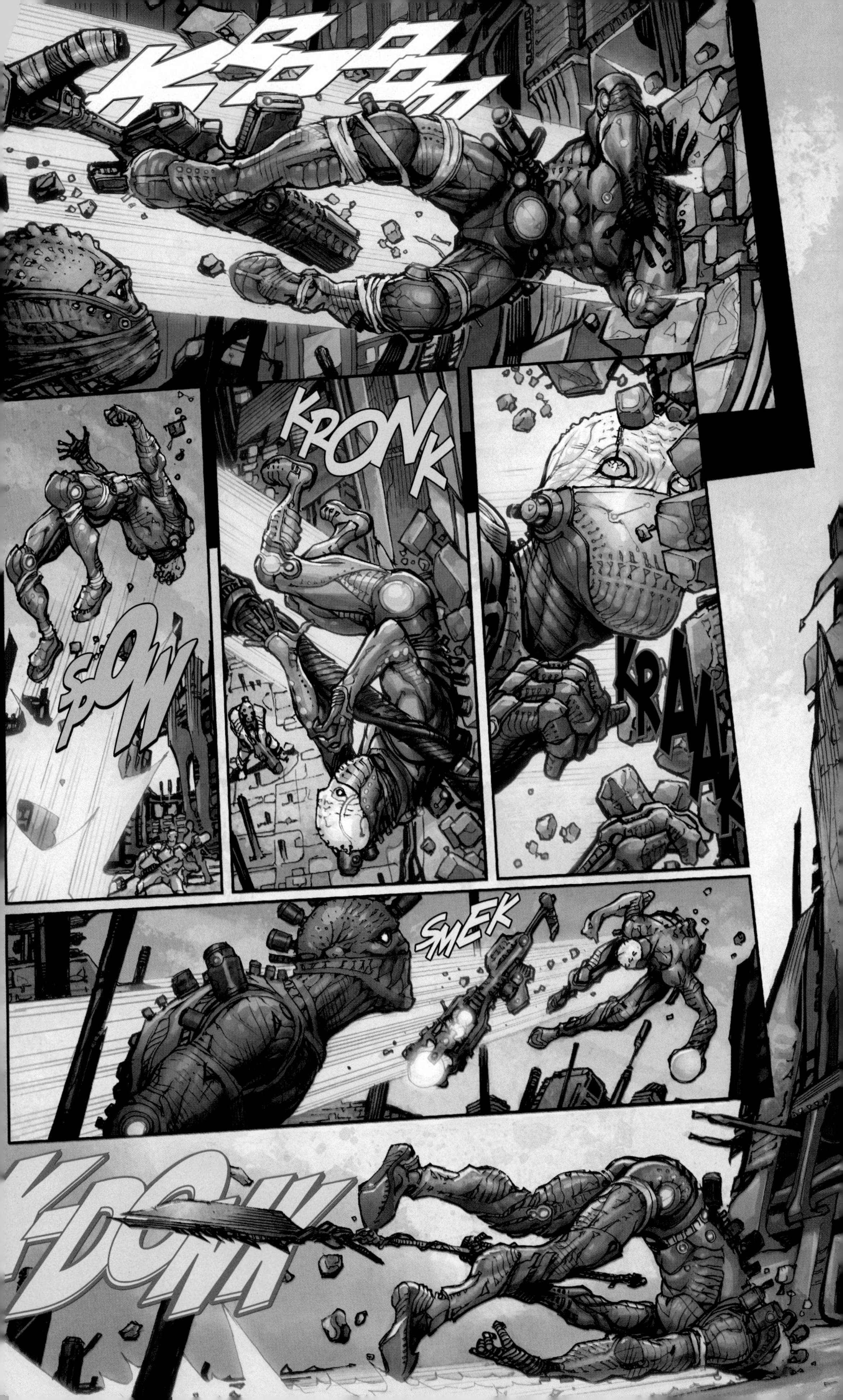
KRONK
SMEK

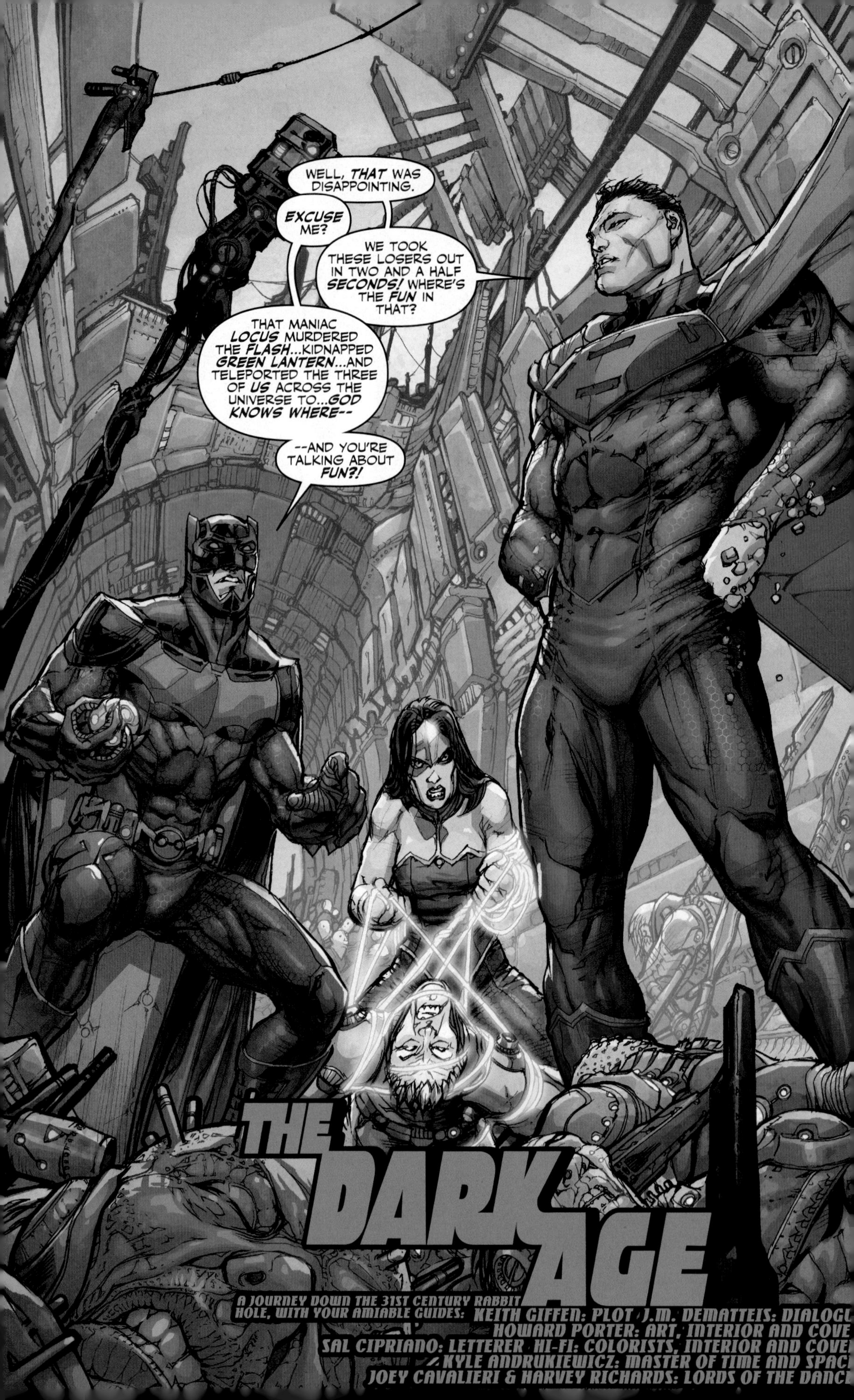

WELL, THAT WAS DISAPPOINTING.
EXCUSE ME?
WE TOOK THESE LOSERS OUT IN TWO AND A HALF SECONDS! WHERE'S THE FUN IN THAT?
THAT MANIAC LOCUS MURDERED THE FLASH...KIDNAPPED GREEN LANTERN...AND TELEPORTED THE THREE OF US ACROSS THE UNIVERSE TO...GOD KNOWS WHERE--
--AND YOU'RE TALKING ABOUT FUN?!
THE DARK AGE
A JOURNEY DOWN THE 31ST CENTURY RABBIT HOLE, WITH YOUR AMIABLE GUIDES: KEITH GIFFEN: PLOT J.M. DEMATTEIS: DIALOGU
HOWARD PORTER: ART, INTERIOR AND COVE
SAL CIPRIANO: LETTERER HI-FI: COLORISTS, INTERIOR AND COVE
KYLE ANDRUKIEWICZ: MASTER OF TIME AND SPAC
JOEY CAVALIERI & HARVEY RICHARDS: LORDS OF THE DANC

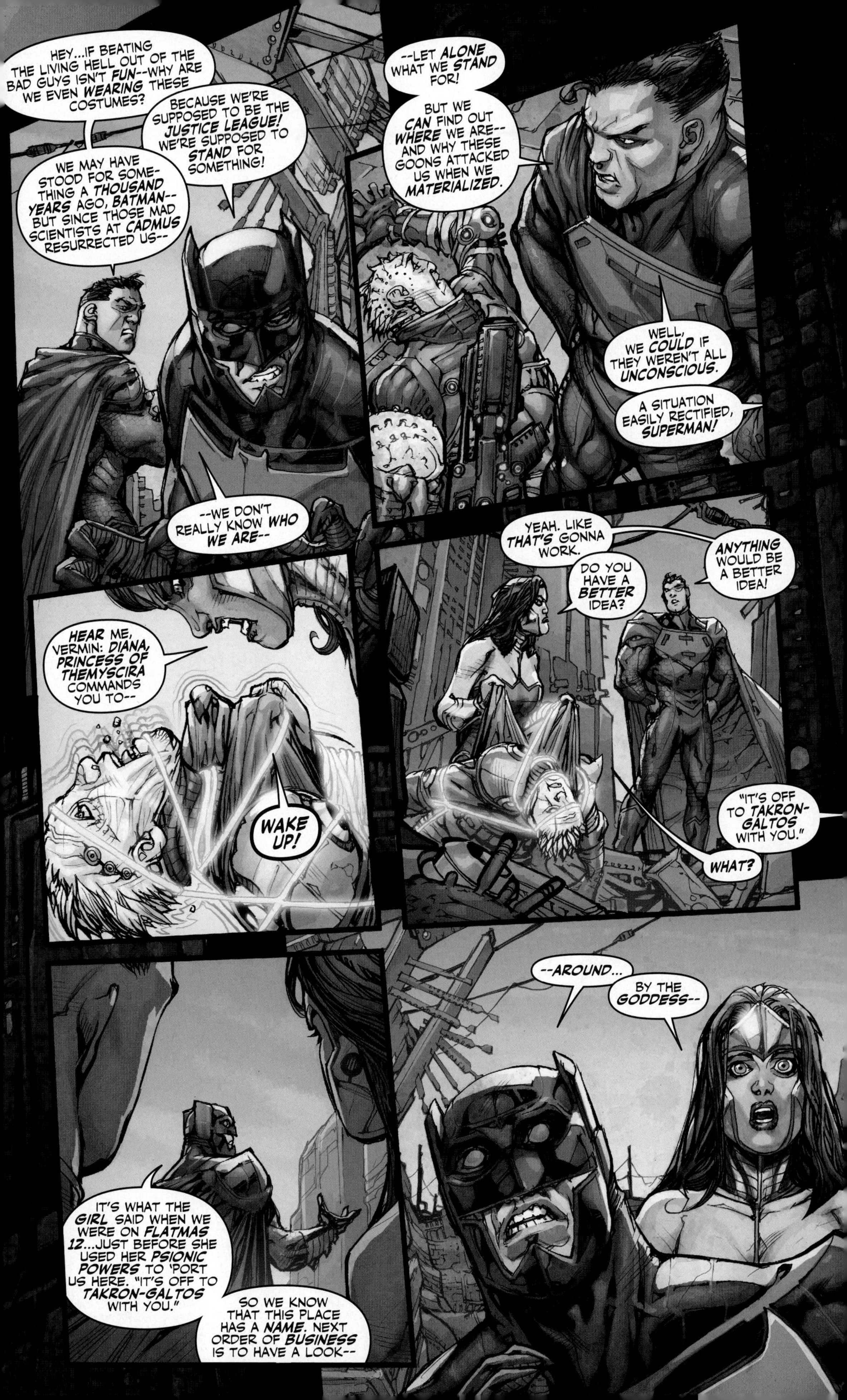
HEY...IF BEATING THE LIVING HELL OUT OF THE BAD GUYS ISN'T FUN--WHY ARE WE EVEN WEARING THESE COSTUMES?
BECAUSE WE'RE SUPPOSED TO BE THE JUSTICE LEAGUE! WE'RE SUPPOSED TO STAND FOR SOMETHING!
WE MAY HAVE STOOD FOR SOME-THING A THOUSAND YEARS AGO, BATMAN--BUT SINCE THOSE MAD SCIENTISTS AT CADMUS RESURRECTED US--
--WE DON'T REALLY KNOW WHO WE ARE--
--LET ALONE WHAT WE STAND FOR!
BUT WE CAN FIND OUT WHERE WE ARE--AND WHY THESE GOONS ATTACKED US WHEN WE MATERIALIZED.
WELL, WE COULD IF THEY WEREN'T ALL UNCONSCIOUS.
A SITUATION EASILY RECTIFIED, SUPERMAN!
HEAR ME, VERMIN: DIANA, PRINCESS OF THEMYSCIRA COMMANDS YOU TO--
WAKE UP!
YEAH. LIKE THAT'S GONNA WORK.
DO YOU HAVE A BETTER IDEA?
ANYTHING WOULD BE A BETTER IDEA!
"IT'S OFF TO TAKRON-GALTOS WITH YOU."
WHAT?
IT'S WHAT THE GIRL SAID WHEN WE WERE ON FLATMAS 12...JUST BEFORE SHE USED HER PSIONIC POWERS TO 'PORT US HERE. "IT'S OFF TO TAKRON-GALTOS WITH YOU."
SO WE KNOW THAT THIS PLACE HAS A NAME. NEXT ORDER OF BUSINESS IS TO HAVE A LOOK--
--AROUND...
BY THE GODDESS--

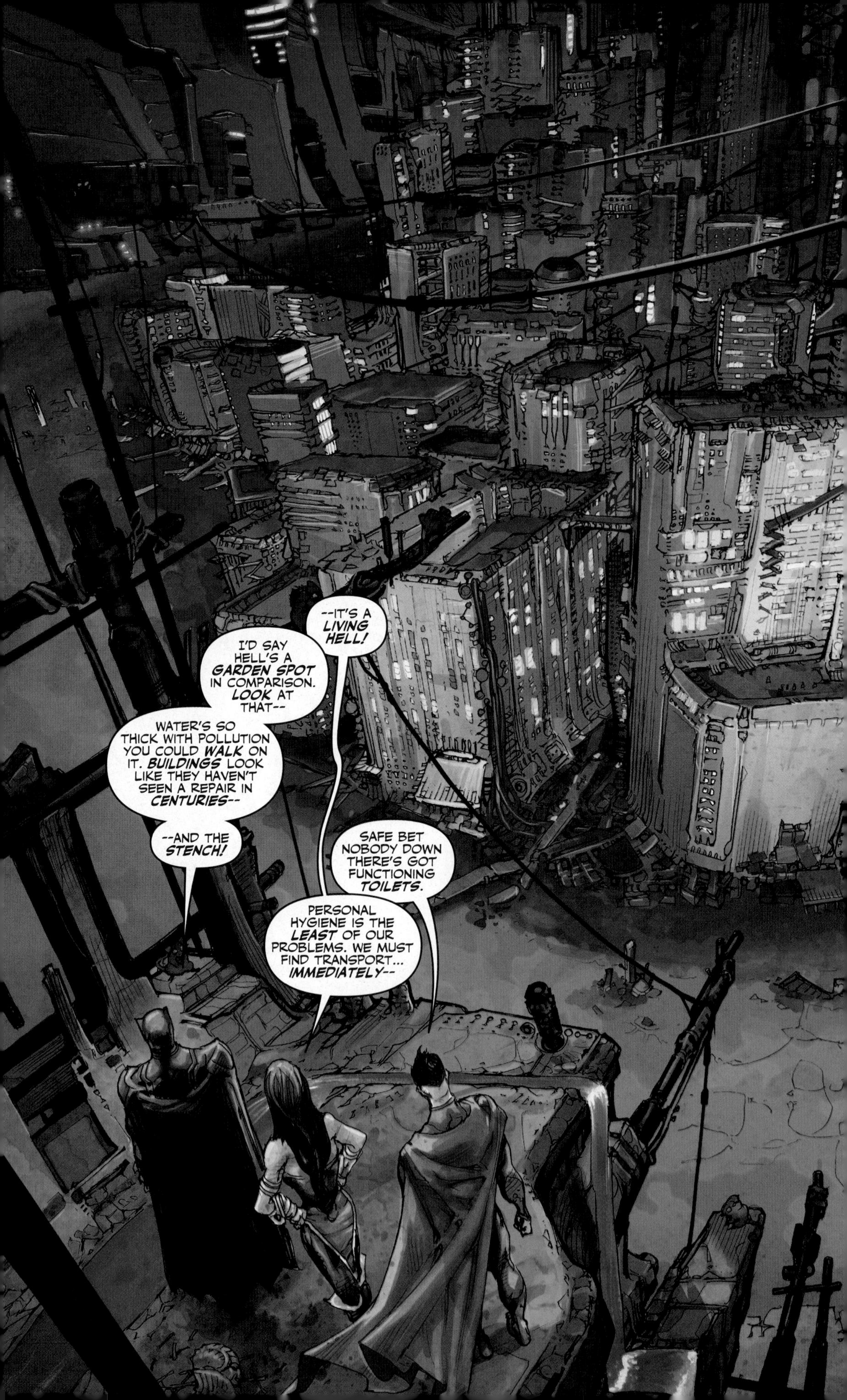

I'D SAY HELL'S A GARDEN SPOT IN COMPARISON. LOOK AT THAT--
--IT'S A LIVING HELL!
WATER'S SO THICK WITH POLLUTION YOU COULD WALK ON IT. BUILDINGS LOOK LIKE THEY HAVEN'T SEEN A REPAIR IN CENTURIES--
--AND THE STENCH!
SAFE BET NOBODY DOWN THERE'S GOT FUNCTIONING TOILETS.
PERSONAL HYGIENE IS THE LEAST OF OUR PROBLEMS. WE MUST FIND TRANSPORT... IMMEDIATELY--

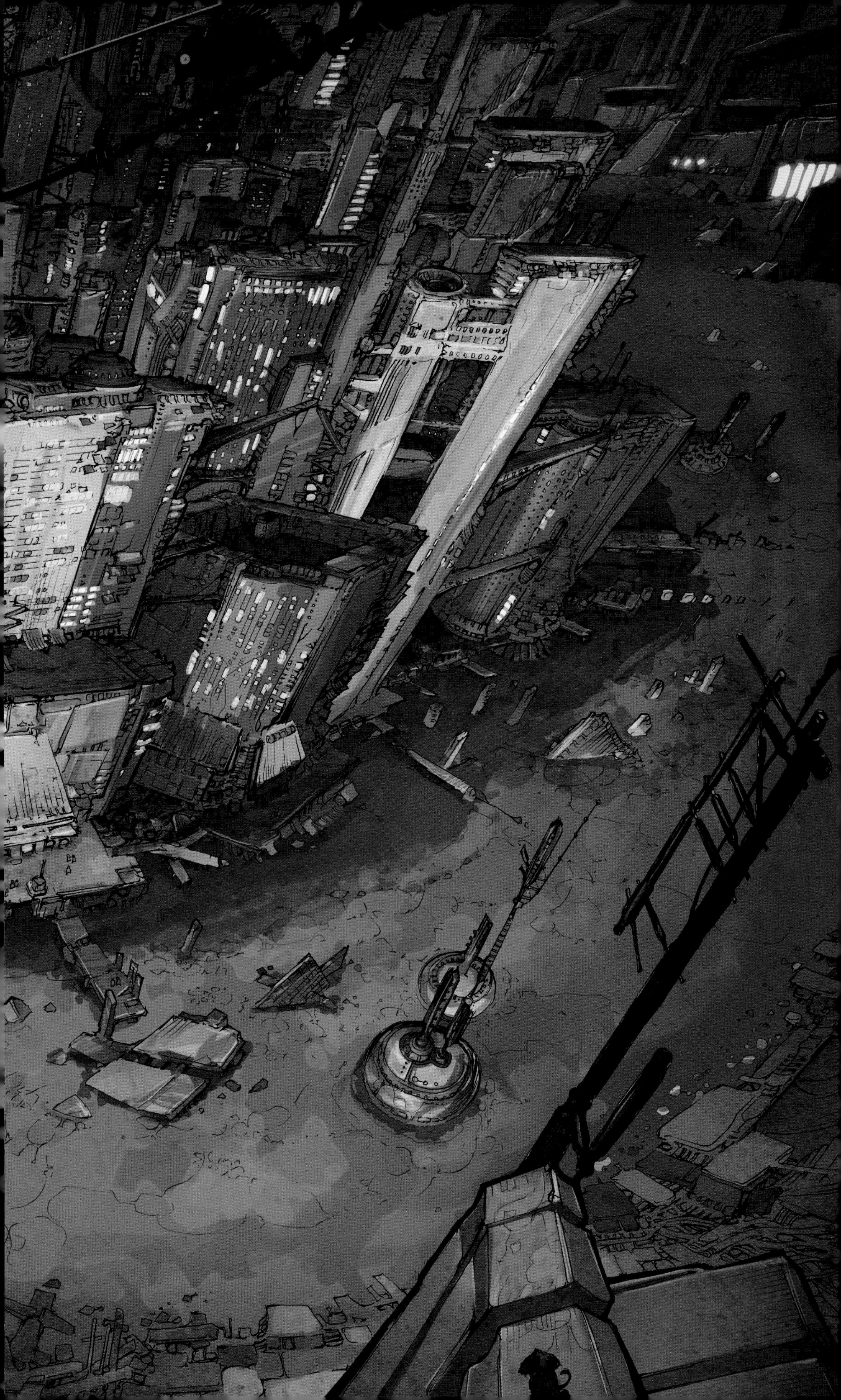

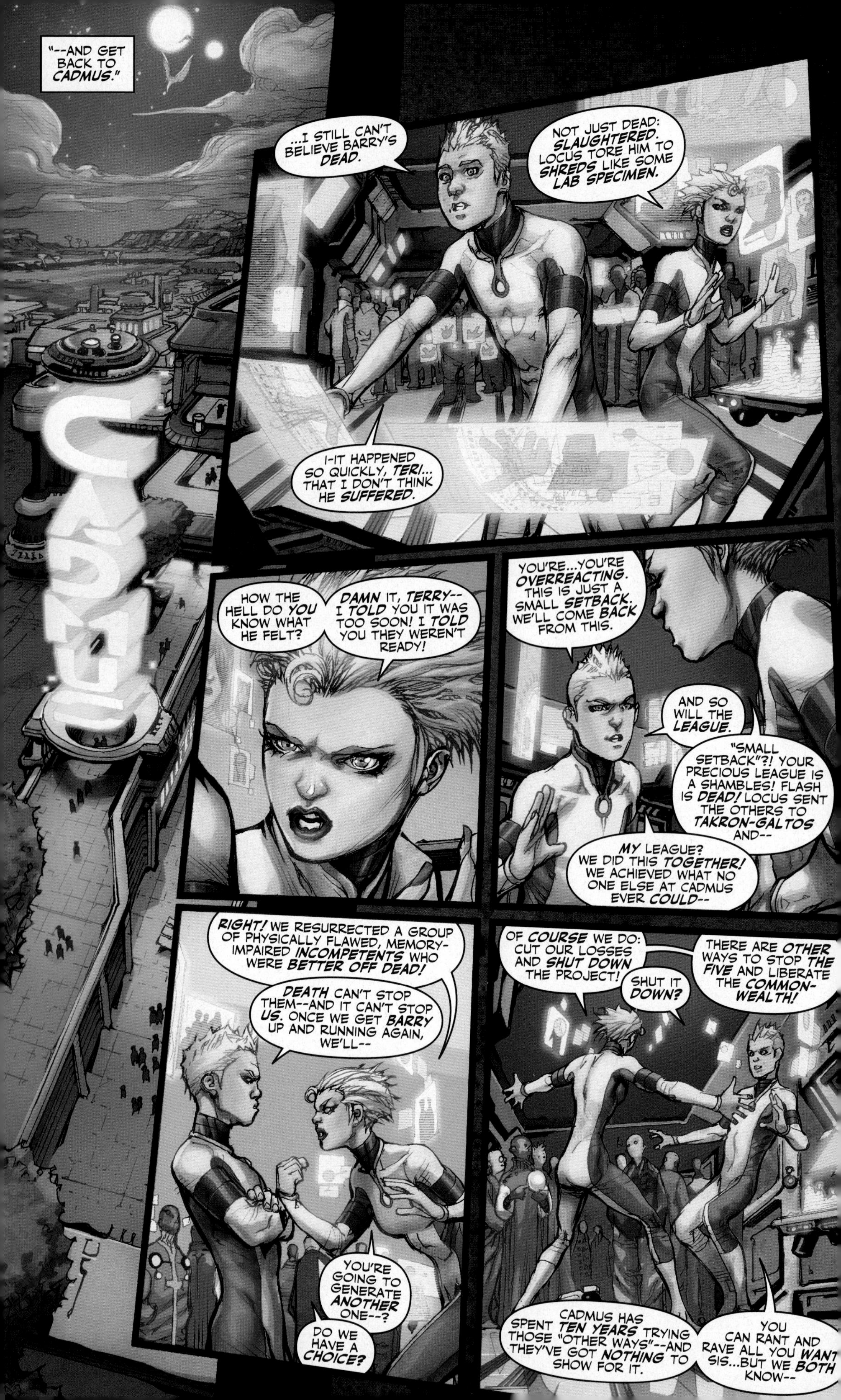
"--AND GET BACK TO CADMUS."
...I STILL CAN'T BELIEVE BARRY'S DEAD.
NOT JUST DEAD: SLAUGHTERED. LOCUS TORE HIM TO SHREDS LIKE SOME LAB SPECIMEN.
I-IT HAPPENED SO QUICKLY, TERI... THAT I DON'T THINK HE SUFFERED.
HOW THE HELL DO YOU KNOW WHAT HE FELT?
DAMN IT, TERRY-- I TOLD YOU IT WAS TOO SOON! I TOLD YOU THEY WEREN'T READY!
YOU'RE...YOU'RE OVERREACTING. THIS IS JUST A SMALL SETBACK. WE'LL COME BACK FROM THIS.
AND SO WILL THE LEAGUE.
"SMALL SETBACK"?! YOUR PRECIOUS LEAGUE IS A SHAMBLES! FLASH IS DEAD! LOCUS SENT THE OTHERS TO TAKRON-GALTOS AND--
MY LEAGUE? WE DID THIS TOGETHER! WE ACHIEVED WHAT NO ONE ELSE AT CADMUS EVER COULD--
RIGHT! WE RESURRECTED A GROUP OF PHYSICALLY FLAWED, MEMORY-IMPAIRED INCOMPETENTS WHO WERE BETTER OFF DEAD!
DEATH CAN'T STOP THEM--AND IT CAN'T STOP US. ONCE WE GET BARRY UP AND RUNNING AGAIN, WE'LL--
YOU'RE GOING TO GENERATE ANOTHER ONE--?
DO WE HAVE A CHOICE?
OF COURSE WE DO: CUT OUR LOSSES AND SHUT DOWN THE PROJECT!
SHUT IT DOWN?
THERE ARE OTHER WAYS TO STOP THE FIVE AND LIBERATE THE COMMON-WEALTH!
CADMUS HAS SPENT TEN YEARS TRYING THOSE "OTHER WAYS"--AND THEY'VE GOT NOTHING TO SHOW FOR IT.
YOU CAN RANT AND RAVE ALL YOU WANT, SIS...BUT WE BOTH KNOW--

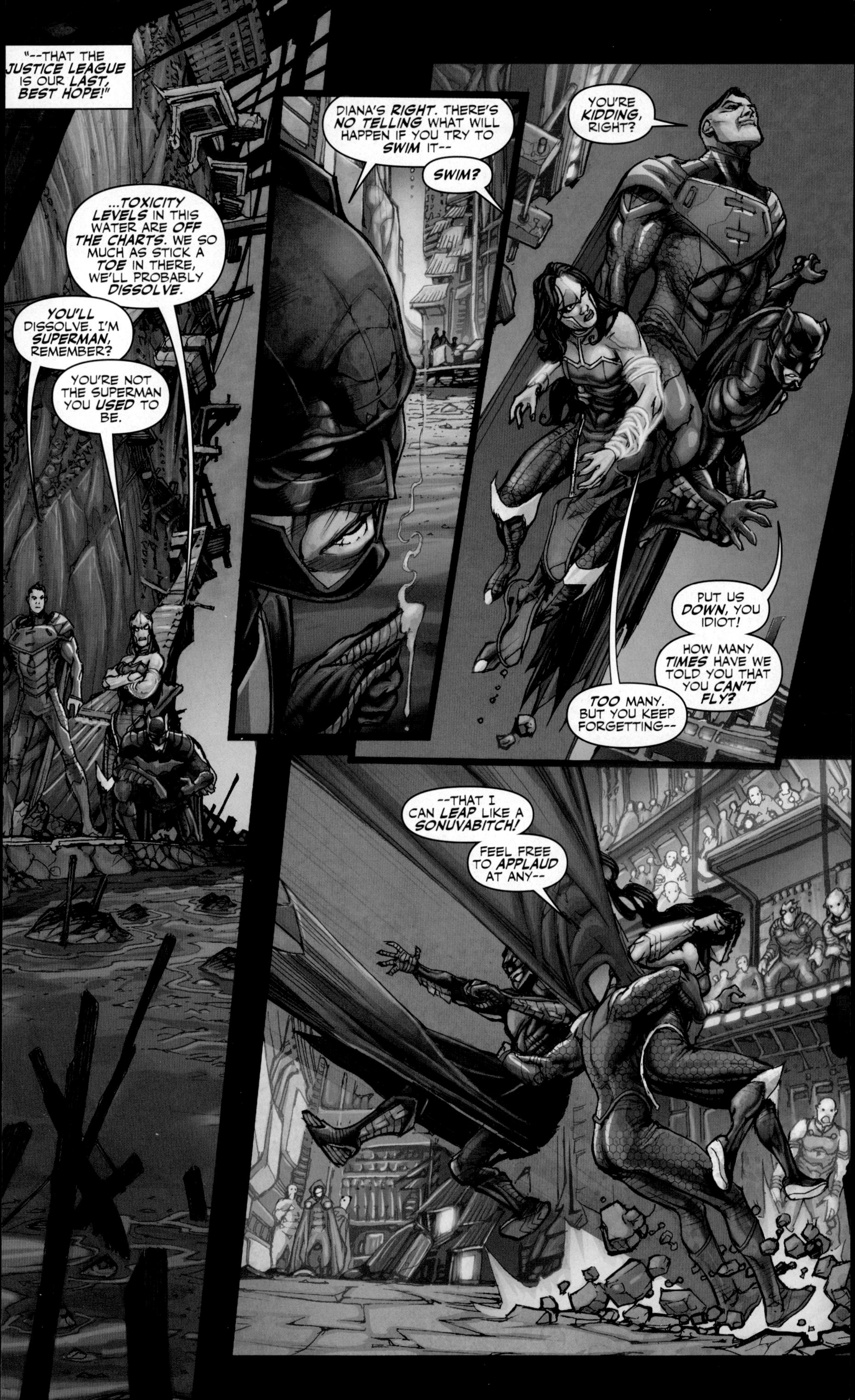
"--THAT THE JUSTICE LEAGUE IS OUR LAST, BEST HOPE!"
...TOXICITY LEVELS IN THIS WATER ARE OFF THE CHARTS. WE SO MUCH AS STICK A TOE IN THERE, WE'LL PROBABLY DISSOLVE.
YOU'LL DISSOLVE. I'M SUPERMAN, REMEMBER?
YOU'RE NOT THE SUPERMAN YOU USED TO BE.
DIANA'S RIGHT. THERE'S NO TELLING WHAT WILL HAPPEN IF YOU TRY TO SWIM IT--
SWIM?
YOU'RE KIDDING, RIGHT?
PUT US DOWN, YOU IDIOT!
HOW MANY TIMES HAVE WE TOLD YOU THAT YOU CAN'T FLY?
TOO MANY. BUT YOU KEEP FORGETTING--
--THAT I CAN LEAP LIKE A SONUVABITCH!
FEEL FREE TO APPLAUD AT ANY--

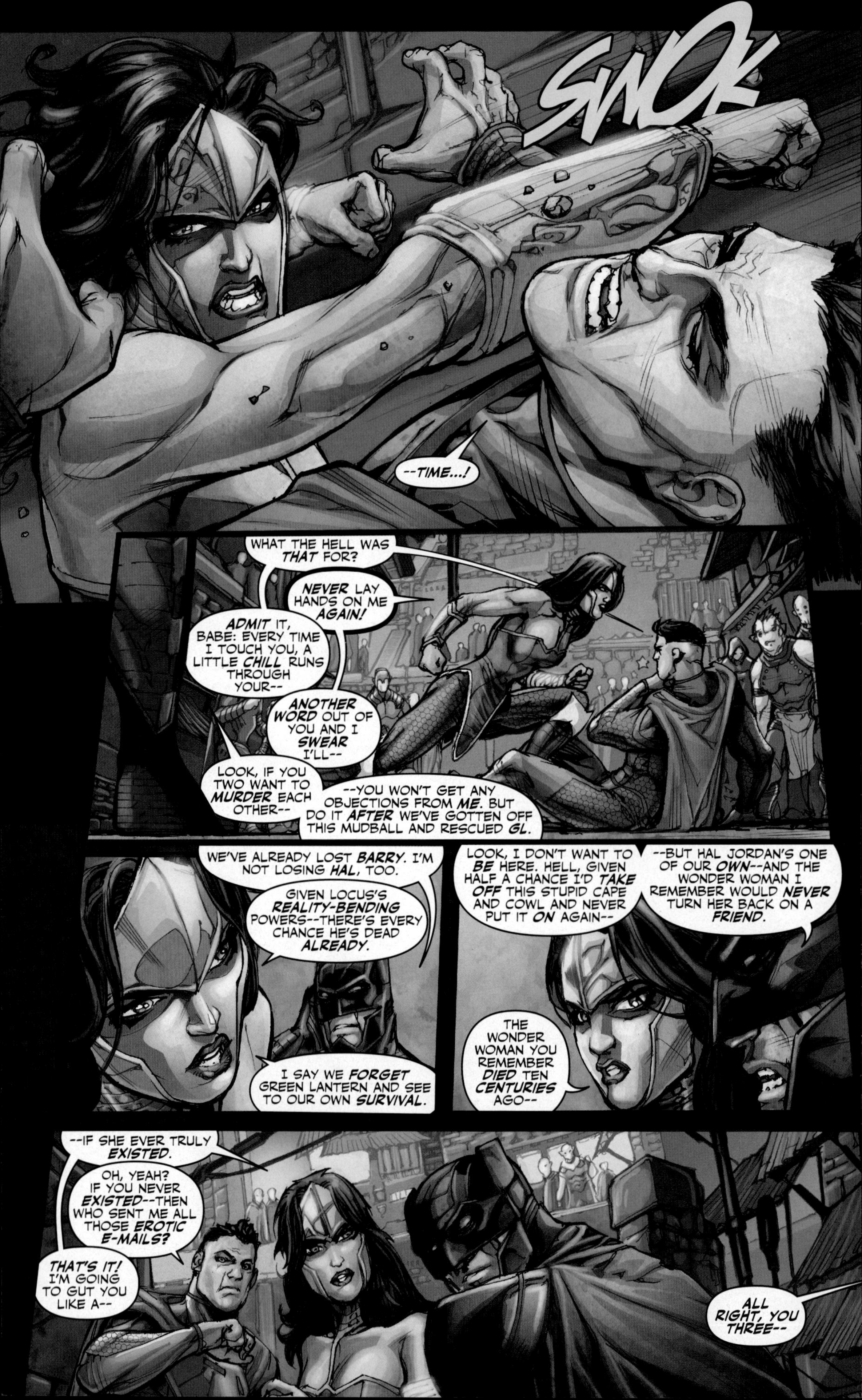
SWOK
--TIME...!
WHAT THE HELL WAS THAT FOR?
NEVER LAY HANDS ON ME AGAIN!
ADMIT IT, BABE: EVERY TIME I TOUCH YOU, A LITTLE CHILL RUNS THROUGH YOUR--
ANOTHER WORD OUT OF YOU AND I SWEAR I'LL--
LOOK, IF YOU TWO WANT TO MURDER EACH OTHER--
--YOU WON'T GET ANY OBJECTIONS FROM ME. BUT DO IT AFTER WE'VE GOTTEN OFF THIS MUDBALL AND RESCUED GL.
WE'VE ALREADY LOST BARRY. I'M NOT LOSING HAL, TOO.
GIVEN LOCUS'S REALITY-BENDING POWERS--THERE'S EVERY CHANCE HE'S DEAD ALREADY.
I SAY WE FORGET GREEN LANTERN AND SEE TO OUR OWN SURVIVAL.
LOOK, I DON'T WANT TO BE HERE. HELL, GIVEN HALF A CHANCE I'D TAKE OFF THIS STUPID CAPE AND COWL AND NEVER PUT IT ON AGAIN--
--BUT HAL JORDAN'S ONE OF OUR OWN--AND THE WONDER WOMAN I REMEMBER WOULD NEVER TURN HER BACK ON A FRIEND.
THE WONDER WOMAN YOU REMEMBER DIED TEN CENTURIES AGO--
--IF SHE EVER TRULY EXISTED.
OH, YEAH? IF YOU NEVER EXISTED--THEN WHO SENT ME ALL THOSE EROTIC E-MAILS?
THAT'S IT! I'M GOING TO GUT YOU LIKE A--
ALL RIGHT, YOU THREE--

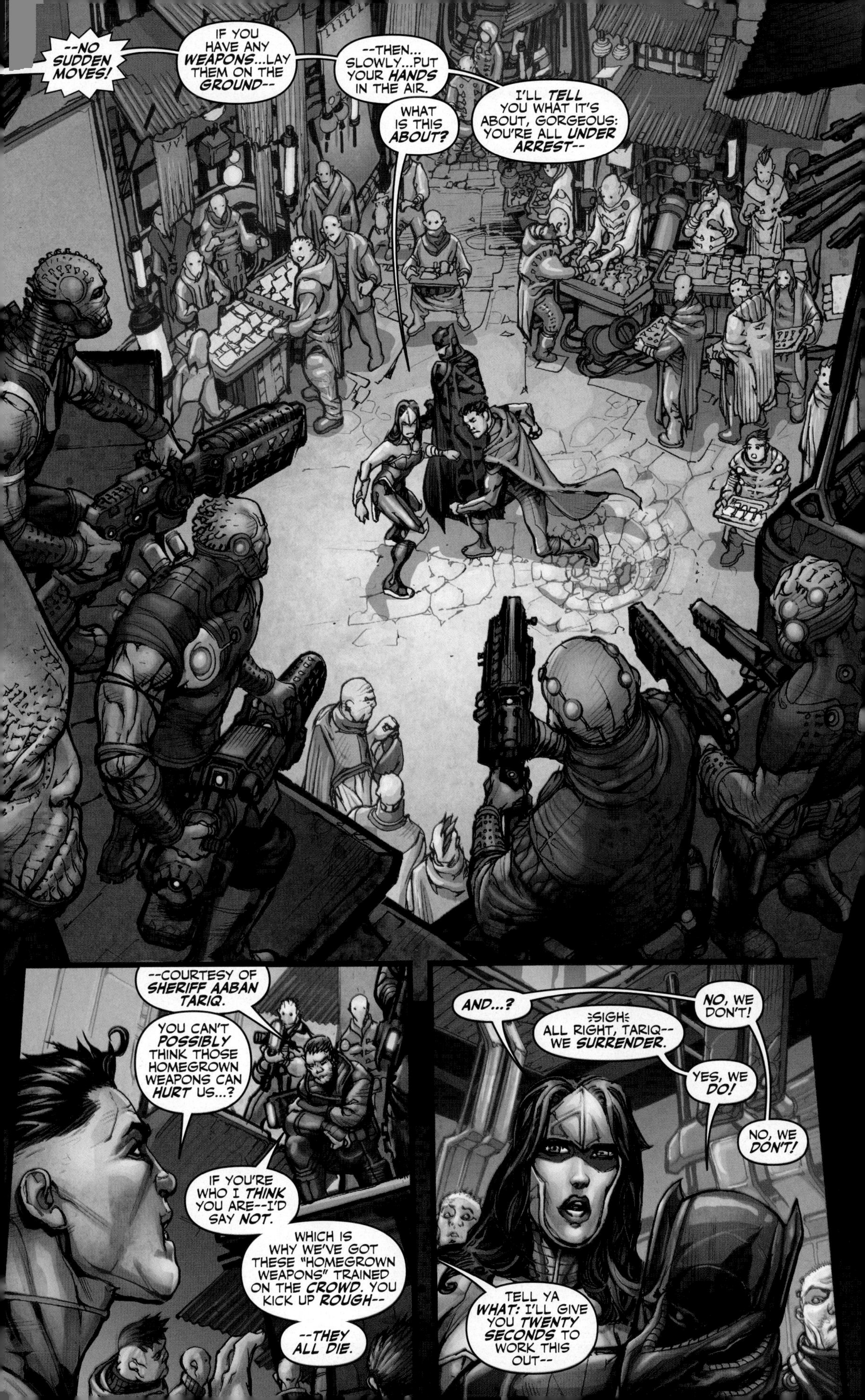
--NO SUDDEN MOVES!
IF YOU HAVE ANY WEAPONS...LAY THEM ON THE GROUND--
--THEN... SLOWLY...PUT YOUR HANDS IN THE AIR.
WHAT IS THIS ABOUT?
I'LL TELL YOU WHAT IT'S ABOUT, GORGEOUS: YOU'RE ALL UNDER ARREST--
--COURTESY OF SHERIFF AABAN TARIQ.
YOU CAN'T POSSIBLY THINK THOSE HOMEGROWN WEAPONS CAN HURT US...?
IF YOU'RE WHO I THINK YOU ARE--I'D SAY NOT.
WHICH IS WHY WE'VE GOT THESE "HOMEGROWN WEAPONS" TRAINED ON THE CROWD. YOU KICK UP ROUGH--
--THEY ALL DIE.
AND...?
NO, WE DON'T!
SIGH ALL RIGHT, TARIQ-- WE SURRENDER.
YES, WE DO!
NO, WE DON'T!
TELL YA WHAT: I'LL GIVE YOU TWENTY SECONDS TO WORK THIS OUT--

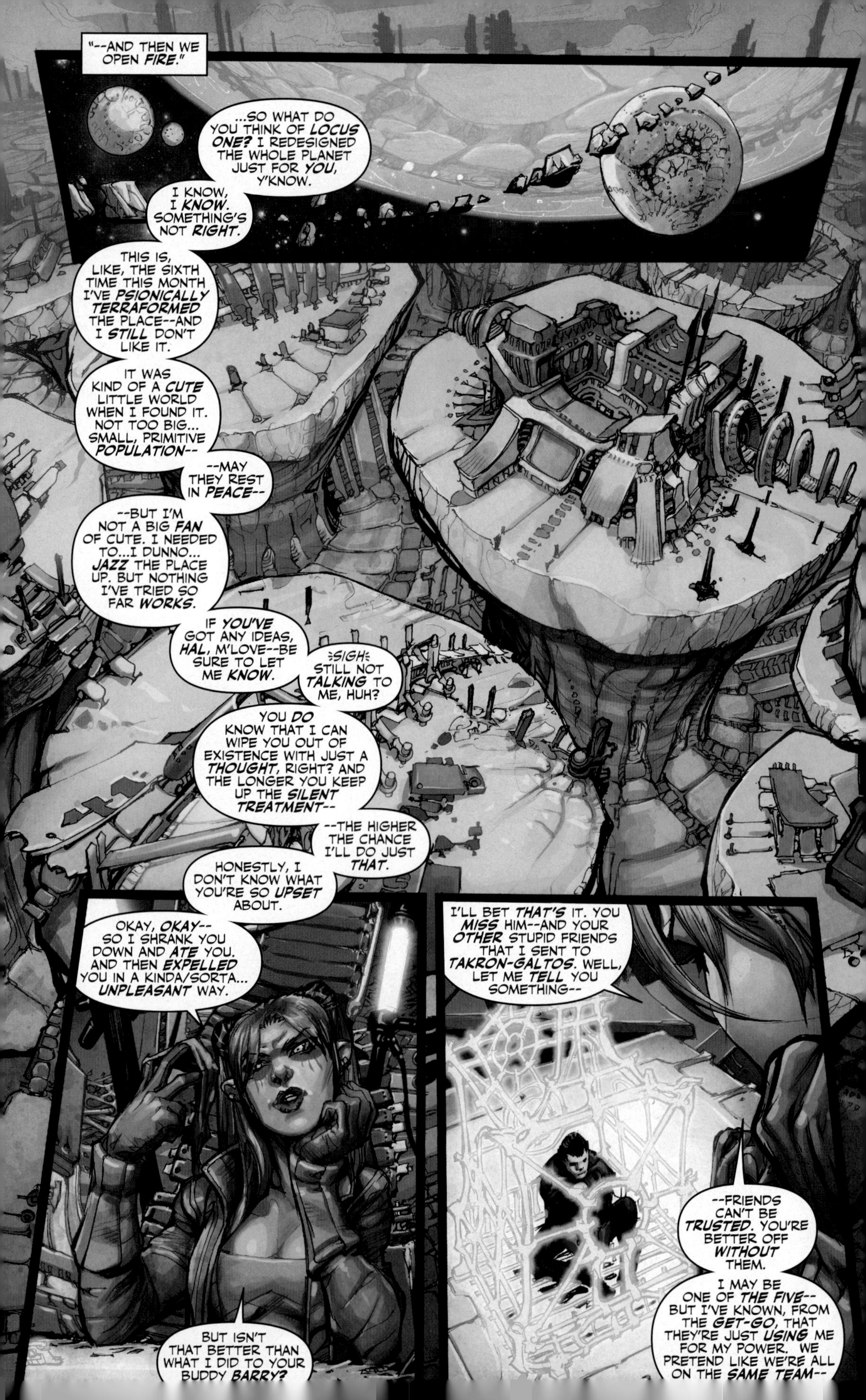
"--AND THEN WE OPEN FIRE."
...SO WHAT DO YOU THINK OF LOCUS ONE? I REDESIGNED THE WHOLE PLANET JUST FOR YOU, Y'KNOW.
I KNOW, I KNOW. SOMETHING'S NOT RIGHT.
THIS IS, LIKE, THE SIXTH TIME THIS MONTH I'VE PSIONICALLY TERRAFORMED THE PLACE--AND I STILL DON'T LIKE IT.
IT WAS KIND OF A CUTE LITTLE WORLD WHEN I FOUND IT. NOT TOO BIG... SMALL, PRIMITIVE POPULATION--
--MAY THEY REST IN PEACE--
--BUT I'M NOT A BIG FAN OF CUTE. I NEEDED TO...I DUNNO... JAZZ THE PLACE UP. BUT NOTHING I'VE TRIED SO FAR WORKS.
IF YOU'VE GOT ANY IDEAS, HAL, M'LOVE--BE SURE TO LET ME KNOW.
SIGH
STILL NOT TALKING TO ME, HUH?
YOU DO KNOW THAT I CAN WIPE YOU OUT OF EXISTENCE WITH JUST A THOUGHT, RIGHT? AND THE LONGER YOU KEEP UP THE SILENT TREATMENT--
--THE HIGHER THE CHANCE I'LL DO JUST THAT.
HONESTLY, I DON'T KNOW WHAT YOU'RE SO UPSET ABOUT.
OKAY, OKAY-- SO I SHRANK YOU DOWN AND ATE YOU. AND THEN EXPELLED YOU IN A KINDA/SORTA... UNPLEASANT WAY.
BUT ISN'T THAT BETTER THAN WHAT I DID TO YOUR BUDDY BARRY?
I'LL BET THAT'S IT. YOU MISS HIM--AND YOUR OTHER STUPID FRIENDS THAT I SENT TO TAKRON-GALTOS. WELL, LET ME TELL YOU SOMETHING--
--FRIENDS CAN'T BE TRUSTED. YOU'RE BETTER OFF WITHOUT THEM.
I MAY BE ONE OF THE FIVE-- BUT I'VE KNOWN, FROM THE GET-GO, THAT THEY'RE JUST USING ME FOR MY POWER. WE PRETEND LIKE WE'RE ALL ON THE SAME TEAM--

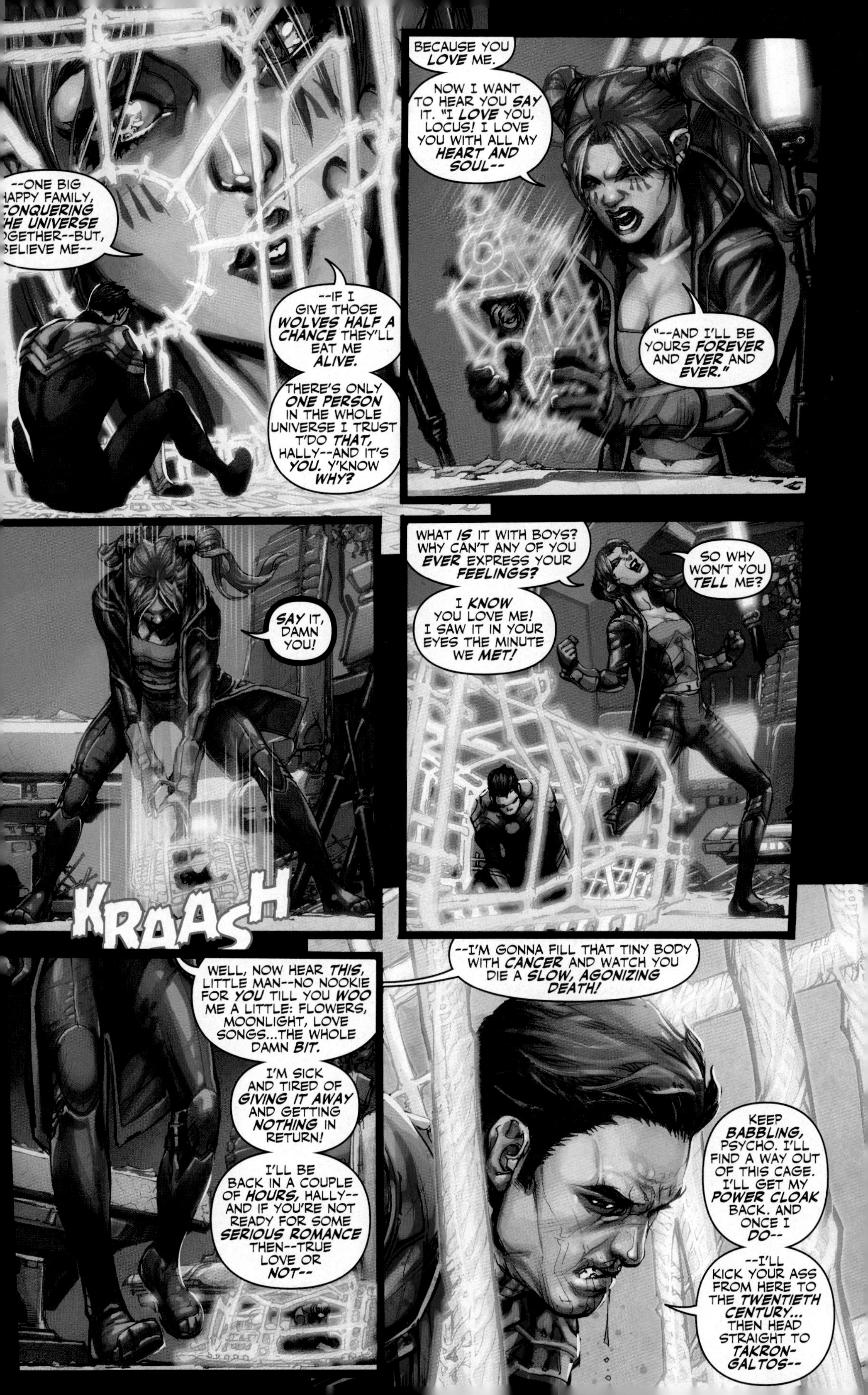
--ONE BIG HAPPY FAMILY, CONQUERING THE UNIVERSE TOGETHER--BUT, BELIEVE ME--
--IF I GIVE THOSE WOLVES HALF A CHANCE THEY'LL EAT ME ALIVE.
THERE'S ONLY ONE PERSON IN THE WHOLE UNIVERSE I TRUST T'DO THAT, HALLY--AND IT'S YOU. Y'KNOW WHY?
BECAUSE YOU LOVE ME.
NOW I WANT TO HEAR YOU SAY IT. "I LOVE YOU, LOCUS! I LOVE YOU WITH ALL MY HEART AND SOUL--
"--AND I'LL BE YOURS FOREVER AND EVER AND EVER."
SAY IT, DAMN YOU!
KRAASH
WHAT IS IT WITH BOYS? WHY CAN'T ANY OF YOU EVER EXPRESS YOUR FEELINGS?
I KNOW YOU LOVE ME! I SAW IT IN YOUR EYES THE MINUTE WE MET!
SO WHY WON'T YOU TELL ME?
WELL, NOW HEAR THIS, LITTLE MAN--NO NOOKIE FOR YOU TILL YOU WOO ME A LITTLE: FLOWERS, MOONLIGHT, LOVE SONGS...THE WHOLE DAMN BIT.
I'M SICK AND TIRED OF GIVING IT AWAY AND GETTING NOTHING IN RETURN!
I'LL BE BACK IN A COUPLE OF HOURS, HALLY--AND IF YOU'RE NOT READY FOR SOME SERIOUS ROMANCE THEN--TRUE LOVE OR NOT--
--I'M GONNA FILL THAT TINY BODY WITH CANCER AND WATCH YOU DIE A SLOW, AGONIZING DEATH!
KEEP BABBLING, PSYCHO. I'LL FIND A WAY OUT OF THIS CAGE. I'LL GET MY POWER CLOAK BACK. AND ONCE I DO--
--I'LL KICK YOUR ASS FROM HERE TO THE TWENTIETH CENTURY... THEN HEAD STRAIGHT TO TAKRON-GALTOS--

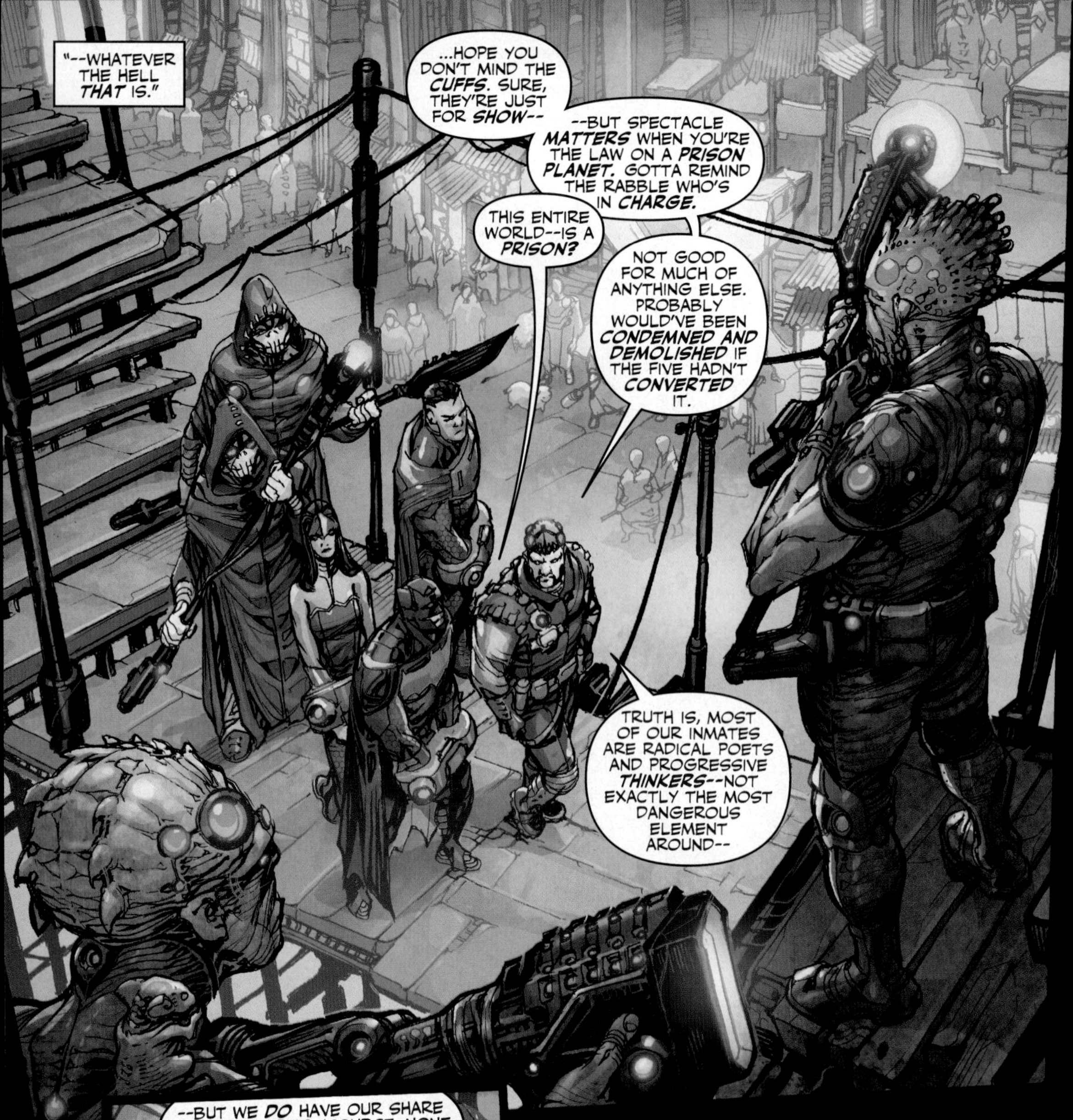
"--WHATEVER THE HELL THAT IS."
...HOPE YOU DON'T MIND THE CUFFS. SURE, THEY'RE JUST FOR SHOW--
--BUT SPECTACLE MATTERS WHEN YOU'RE THE LAW ON A PRISON PLANET. GOTTA REMIND THE RABBLE WHO'S IN CHARGE.
THIS ENTIRE WORLD--IS A PRISON?
NOT GOOD FOR MUCH OF ANYTHING ELSE. PROBABLY WOULD'VE BEEN CONDEMNED AND DEMOLISHED IF THE FIVE HADN'T CONVERTED IT.
TRUTH IS, MOST OF OUR INMATES ARE RADICAL POETS AND PROGRESSIVE THINKERS--NOT EXACTLY THE MOST DANGEROUS ELEMENT AROUND--
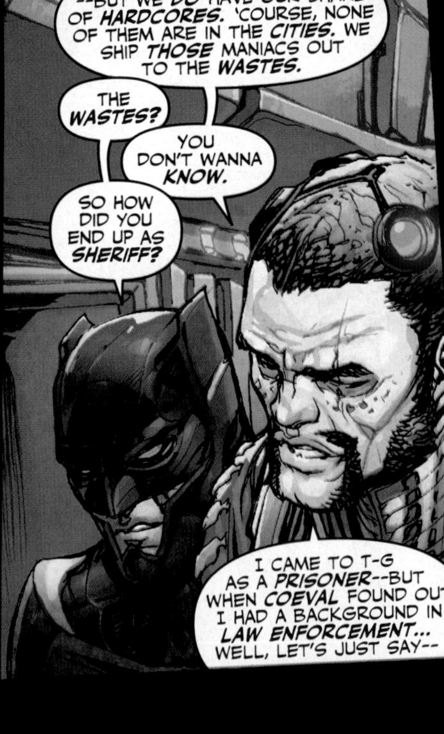
--BUT WE DO HAVE OUR SHARE OF HARDCORES. 'COURSE, NONE OF THEM ARE IN THE CITIES. WE SHIP THOSE MANIACS OUT TO THE WASTES.
THE WASTES?
YOU DON'T WANNA KNOW.
SO HOW DID YOU END UP AS SHERIFF?
I CAME TO T-G AS A PRISONER--BUT WHEN COEVAL FOUND OUT I HAD A BACKGROUND IN LAW ENFORCEMENT... WELL, LET'S JUST SAY--
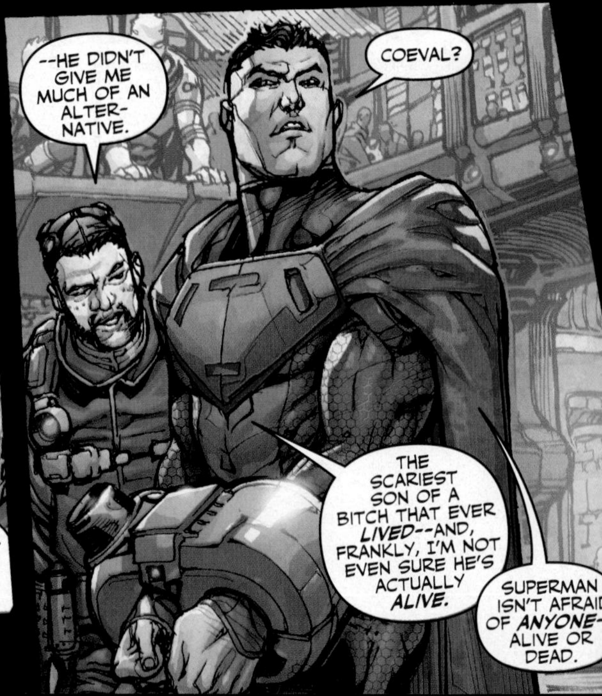
--HE DIDN'T GIVE ME MUCH OF AN ALTER-NATIVE.
COEVAL?
THE SCARIEST SON OF A BITCH THAT EVER LIVED--AND, FRANKLY, I'M NOT EVEN SURE HE'S ACTUALLY ALIVE.
SUPERMAN ISN'T AFRAID OF ANYONE--ALIVE OR DEAD.

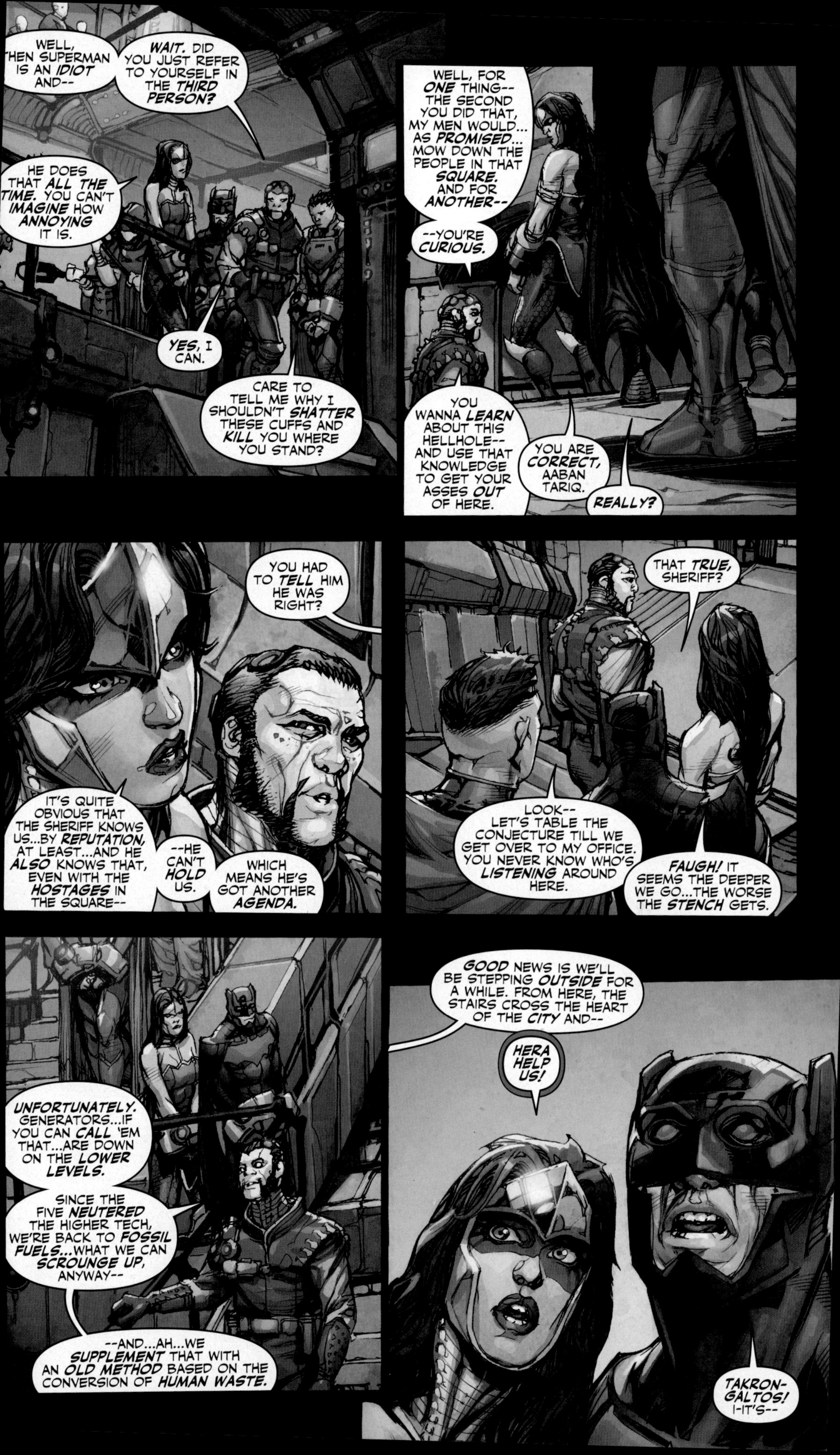

WELL, THEN SUPERMAN IS AN IDIOT AND--
WAIT. DID YOU JUST REFER TO YOURSELF IN THE THIRD PERSON?
HE DOES THAT ALL THE TIME. YOU CAN'T IMAGINE HOW ANNOYING IT IS.
YES, I CAN.
CARE TO TELL ME WHY I SHOULDN'T SHATTER THESE CUFFS AND KILL YOU WHERE YOU STAND?
WELL, FOR ONE THING--THE SECOND YOU DID THAT, MY MEN WOULD... AS PROMISED... MOW DOWN THE PEOPLE IN THAT SQUARE. AND FOR ANOTHER--
--YOU'RE CURIOUS.
YOU WANNA LEARN ABOUT THIS HELLHOLE--AND USE THAT KNOWLEDGE TO GET YOUR ASSES OUT OF HERE.
YOU ARE CORRECT, AABAN TARIQ.
REALLY?
YOU HAD TO TELL HIM HE WAS RIGHT?
IT'S QUITE OBVIOUS THAT THE SHERIFF KNOWS US...BY REPUTATION, AT LEAST...AND HE ALSO KNOWS THAT, EVEN WITH THE HOSTAGES IN THE SQUARE--
--HE CAN'T HOLD US.
WHICH MEANS HE'S GOT ANOTHER AGENDA.
THAT TRUE, SHERIFF?
LOOK--LET'S TABLE THE CONJECTURE TILL WE GET OVER TO MY OFFICE. YOU NEVER KNOW WHO'S LISTENING AROUND HERE.
FAUGH! IT SEEMS THE DEEPER WE GO...THE WORSE THE STENCH GETS.
UNFORTUNATELY. GENERATORS...IF YOU CAN CALL 'EM THAT...ARE DOWN ON THE LOWER LEVELS.
SINCE THE FIVE NEUTERED THE HIGHER TECH, WE'RE BACK TO FOSSIL FUELS...WHAT WE CAN SCROUNGE UP, ANYWAY--
--AND...AH...WE SUPPLEMENT THAT WITH AN OLD METHOD BASED ON THE CONVERSION OF HUMAN WASTE.
GOOD NEWS IS WE'LL BE STEPPING OUTSIDE FOR A WHILE. FROM HERE, THE STAIRS CROSS THE HEART OF THE CITY AND--
HERA HELP US!
TAKRON-GALTOS! I-IT'S--

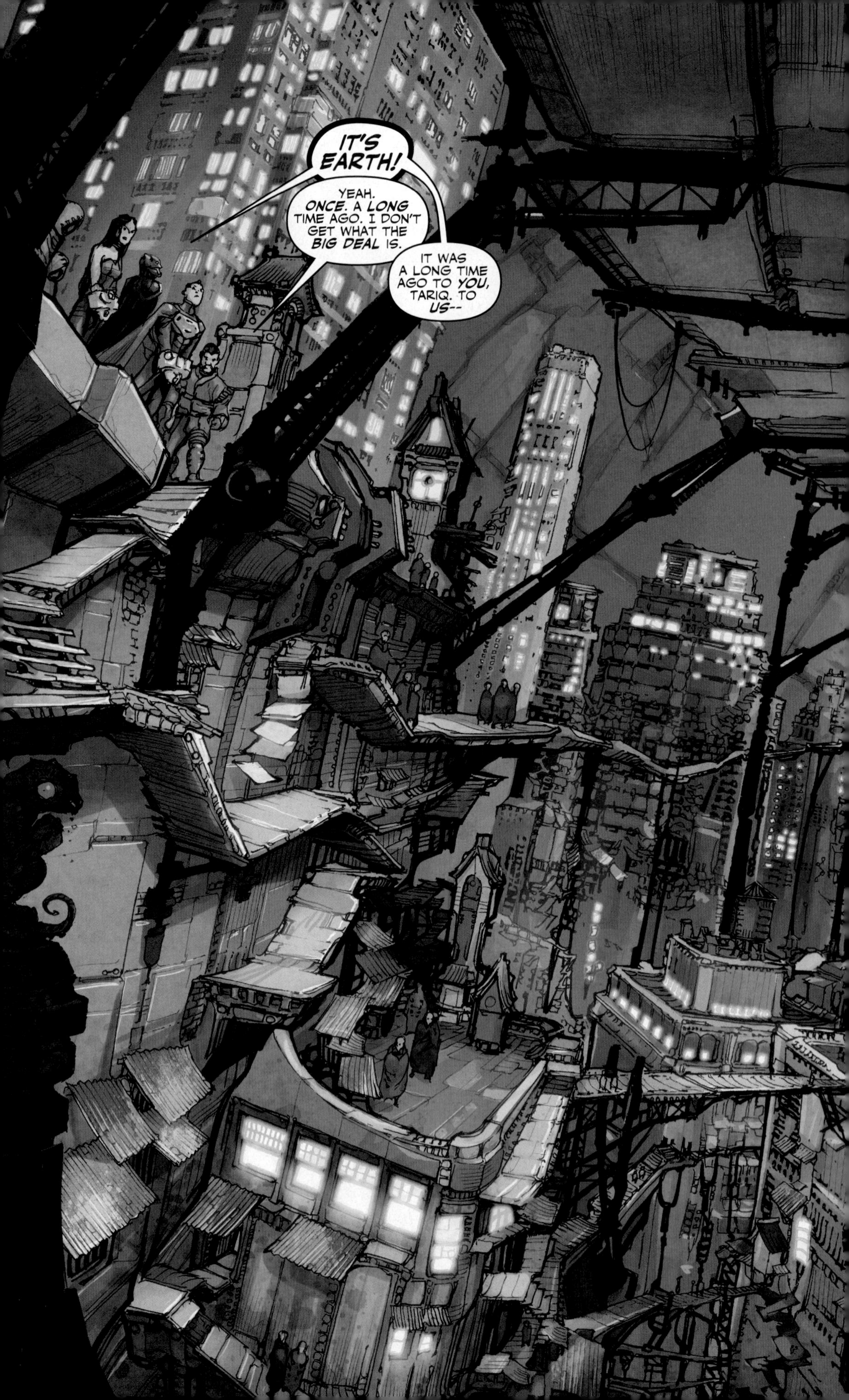
IT'S EARTH!
YEAH. ONCE. A LONG TIME AGO. I DON'T GET WHAT THE BIG DEAL IS.
IT WAS A LONG TIME AGO TO YOU, TARIQ. TO US--

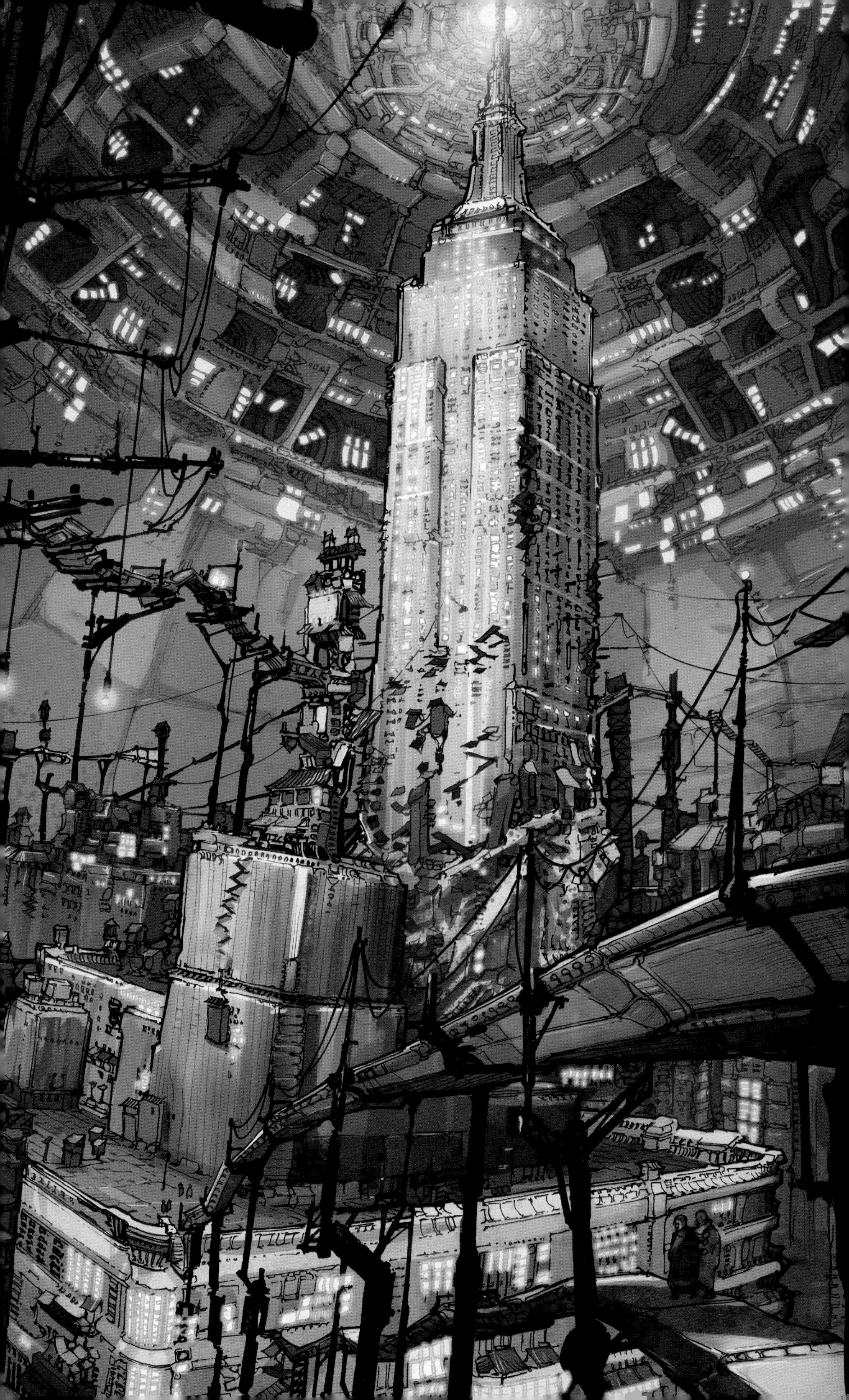

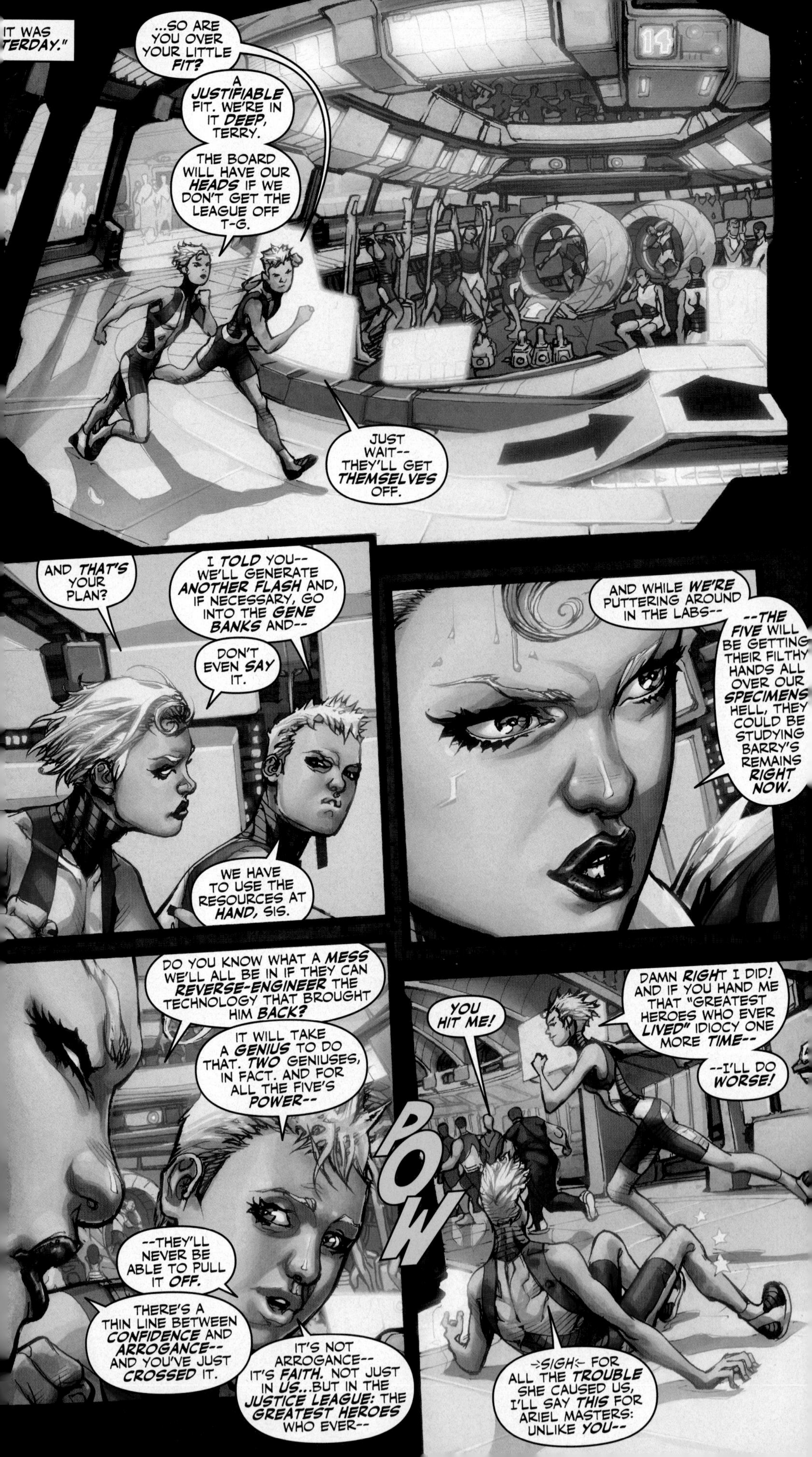
IT WAS
TERDAY."
...SO ARE YOU OVER YOUR LITTLE FIT?
A JUSTIFIABLE FIT. WE'RE IN IT DEEP, TERRY.
THE BOARD WILL HAVE OUR HEADS IF WE DON'T GET THE LEAGUE OFF T-G.
JUST WAIT-- THEY'LL GET THEMSELVES OFF.
AND THAT'S YOUR PLAN?
I TOLD YOU-- WE'LL GENERATE ANOTHER FLASH AND, IF NECESSARY, GO INTO THE GENE BANKS AND--
DON'T EVEN SAY IT.
WE HAVE TO USE THE RESOURCES AT HAND, SIS.
AND WHILE WE'RE PUTTERING AROUND IN THE LABS--
--THE FIVE WILL BE GETTING THEIR FILTHY HANDS ALL OVER OUR SPECIMENS. HELL, THEY COULD BE STUDYING BARRY'S REMAINS RIGHT NOW.
DO YOU KNOW WHAT A MESS WE'LL ALL BE IN IF THEY CAN REVERSE-ENGINEER THE TECHNOLOGY THAT BROUGHT HIM BACK?
IT WILL TAKE A GENIUS TO DO THAT. TWO GENIUSES, IN FACT. AND FOR ALL THE FIVE'S POWER--
--THEY'LL NEVER BE ABLE TO PULL IT OFF.
THERE'S A THIN LINE BETWEEN CONFIDENCE AND ARROGANCE-- AND YOU'VE JUST CROSSED IT.
IT'S NOT ARROGANCE-- IT'S FAITH. NOT JUST IN US...BUT IN THE JUSTICE LEAGUE: THE GREATEST HEROES WHO EVER--
POW
YOU HIT ME!
DAMN RIGHT I DID! AND IF YOU HAND ME THAT "GREATEST HEROES WHO EVER LIVED" IDIOCY ONE MORE TIME--
--I'LL DO WORSE!
>SIGH< FOR ALL THE TROUBLE SHE CAUSED US, I'LL SAY THIS FOR ARIEL MASTERS: UNLIKE YOU--

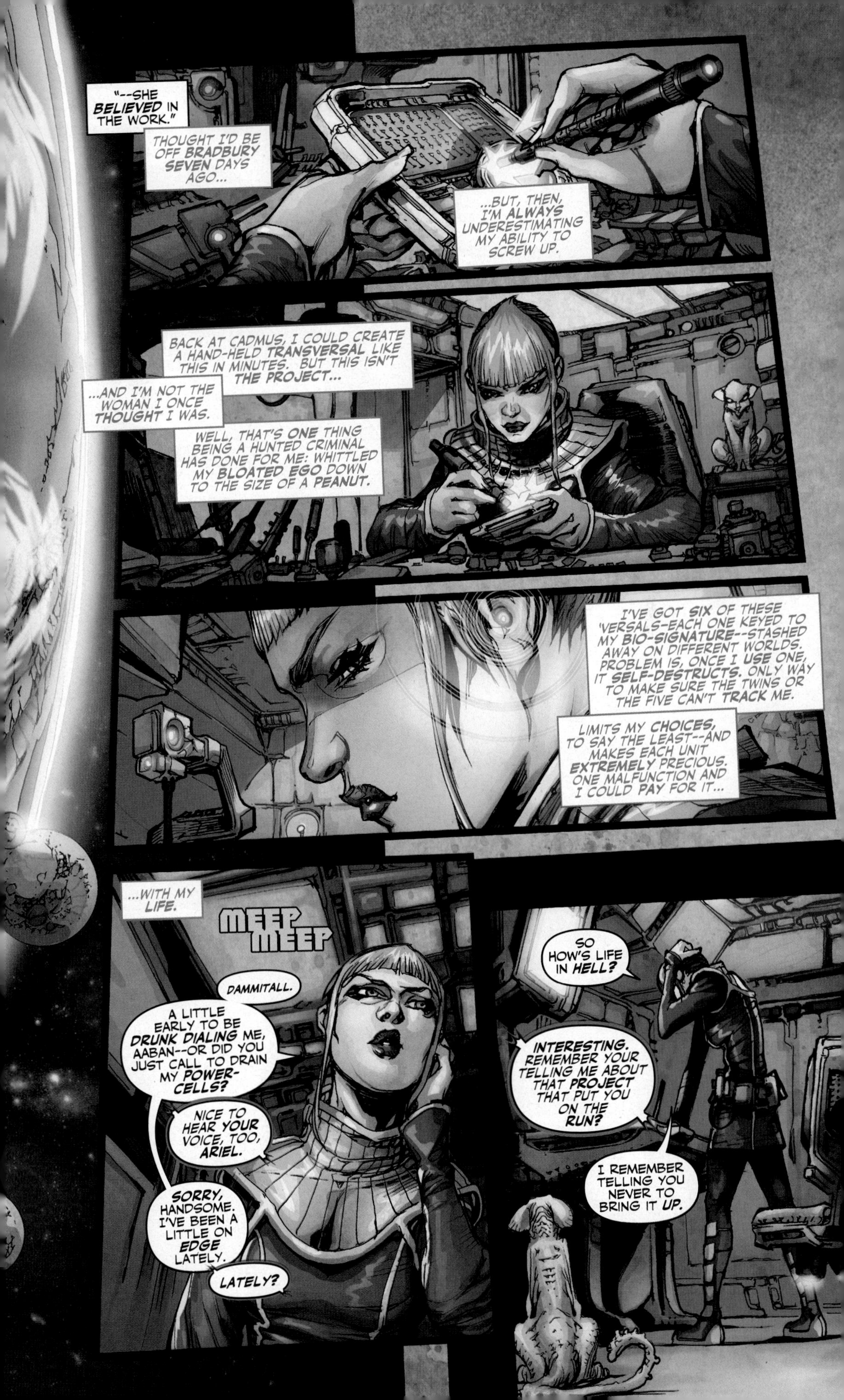
"--SHE BELIEVED IN THE WORK."
THOUGHT I'D BE OFF BRADBURY SEVEN DAYS AGO...
...BUT, THEN, I'M ALWAYS UNDERESTIMATING MY ABILITY TO SCREW UP.
BACK AT CADMUS, I COULD CREATE A HAND-HELD TRANSVERSAL LIKE THIS IN MINUTES. BUT THIS ISN'T THE PROJECT...
...AND I'M NOT THE WOMAN I ONCE THOUGHT I WAS.
WELL, THAT'S ONE THING BEING A HUNTED CRIMINAL HAS DONE FOR ME: WHITTLED MY BLOATED EGO DOWN TO THE SIZE OF A PEANUT.
I'VE GOT SIX OF THESE 'VERSALS--EACH ONE KEYED TO MY BIO-SIGNATURE--STASHED AWAY ON DIFFERENT WORLDS. PROBLEM IS, ONCE I USE ONE, IT SELF-DESTRUCTS. ONLY WAY TO MAKE SURE THE TWINS OR THE FIVE CAN'T TRACK ME.
LIMITS MY CHOICES, TO SAY THE LEAST--AND MAKES EACH UNIT EXTREMELY PRECIOUS. ONE MALFUNCTION AND I COULD PAY FOR IT...
...WITH MY LIFE.
MEEP MEEP
DAMMITALL.
A LITTLE EARLY TO BE DRUNK DIALING ME, AABAN--OR DID YOU JUST CALL TO DRAIN MY POWER-CELLS?
NICE TO HEAR YOUR VOICE, TOO, ARIEL.
SORRY, HANDSOME. I'VE BEEN A LITTLE ON EDGE LATELY.
LATELY?
SO HOW'S LIFE IN HELL?
INTERESTING. REMEMBER YOUR TELLING ME ABOUT THAT PROJECT THAT PUT YOU ON THE RUN?
I REMEMBER TELLING YOU NEVER TO BRING IT UP.

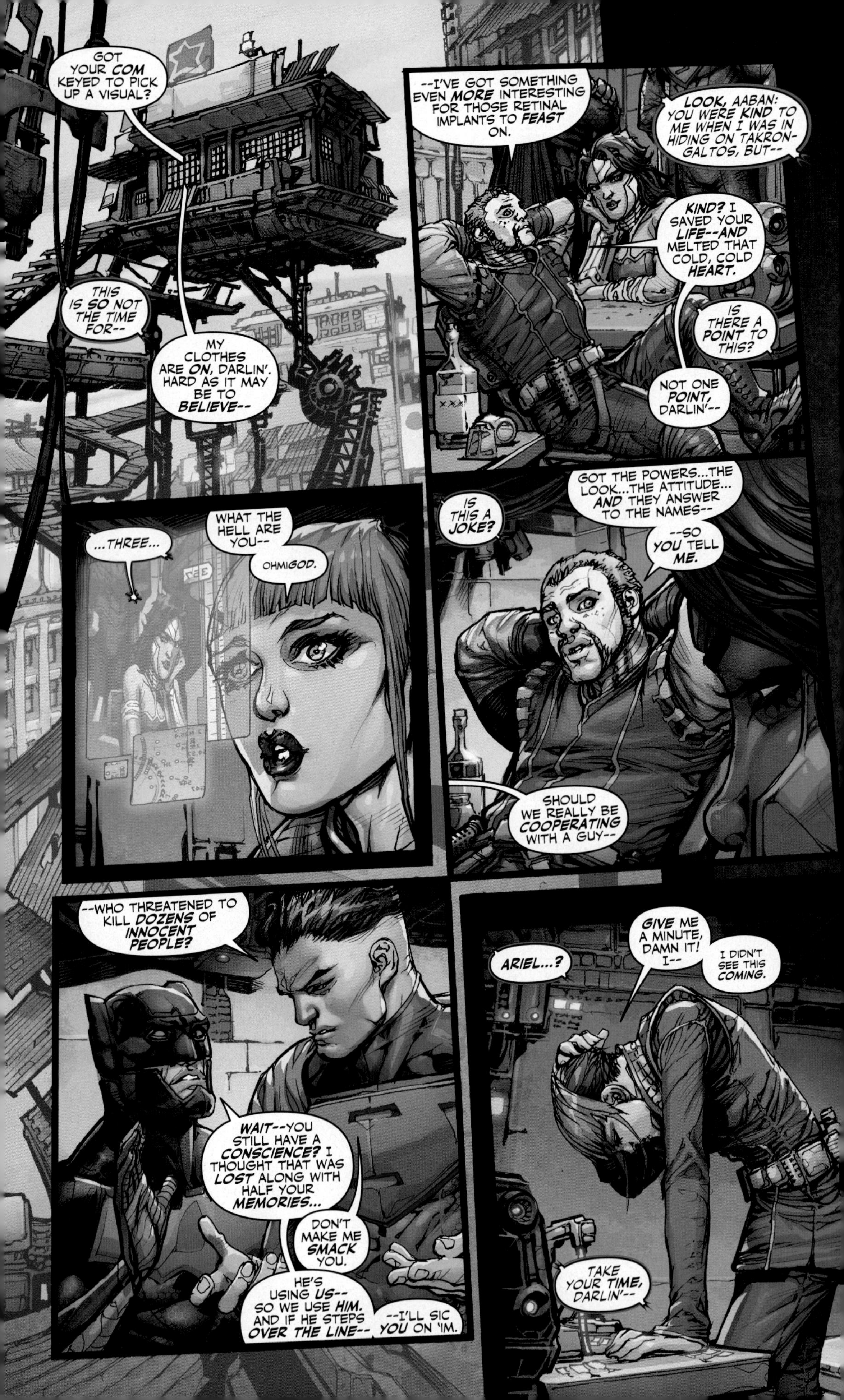
GOT YOUR COM KEYED TO PICK UP A VISUAL?
THIS IS SO NOT THE TIME FOR--
MY CLOTHES ARE ON, DARLIN'. HARD AS IT MAY BE TO BELIEVE--
--I'VE GOT SOMETHING EVEN MORE INTERESTING FOR THOSE RETINAL IMPLANTS TO FEAST ON.
LOOK, AABAN: YOU WERE KIND TO ME WHEN I WAS IN HIDING ON TAKRON-GALTOS, BUT--
KIND? I SAVED YOUR LIFE--AND MELTED THAT COLD, COLD HEART.
IS THERE A POINT TO THIS?
NOT ONE POINT, DARLIN'--
...THREE...
WHAT THE HELL ARE YOU--
OHMIGOD.
IS THIS A JOKE?
GOT THE POWERS...THE LOOK...THE ATTITUDE... AND THEY ANSWER TO THE NAMES--
--SO YOU TELL ME.
SHOULD WE REALLY BE COOPERATING WITH A GUY--
--WHO THREATENED TO KILL DOZENS OF INNOCENT PEOPLE?
WAIT--YOU STILL HAVE A CONSCIENCE? I THOUGHT THAT WAS LOST ALONG WITH HALF YOUR MEMORIES...
DON'T MAKE ME SMACK YOU.
HE'S USING US--SO WE USE HIM. AND IF HE STEPS OVER THE LINE--
--I'LL SIC YOU ON 'IM.
ARIEL...?
GIVE ME A MINUTE, DAMN IT! I--
I DIDN'T SEE THIS COMING.
TAKE YOUR TIME, DARLIN'--

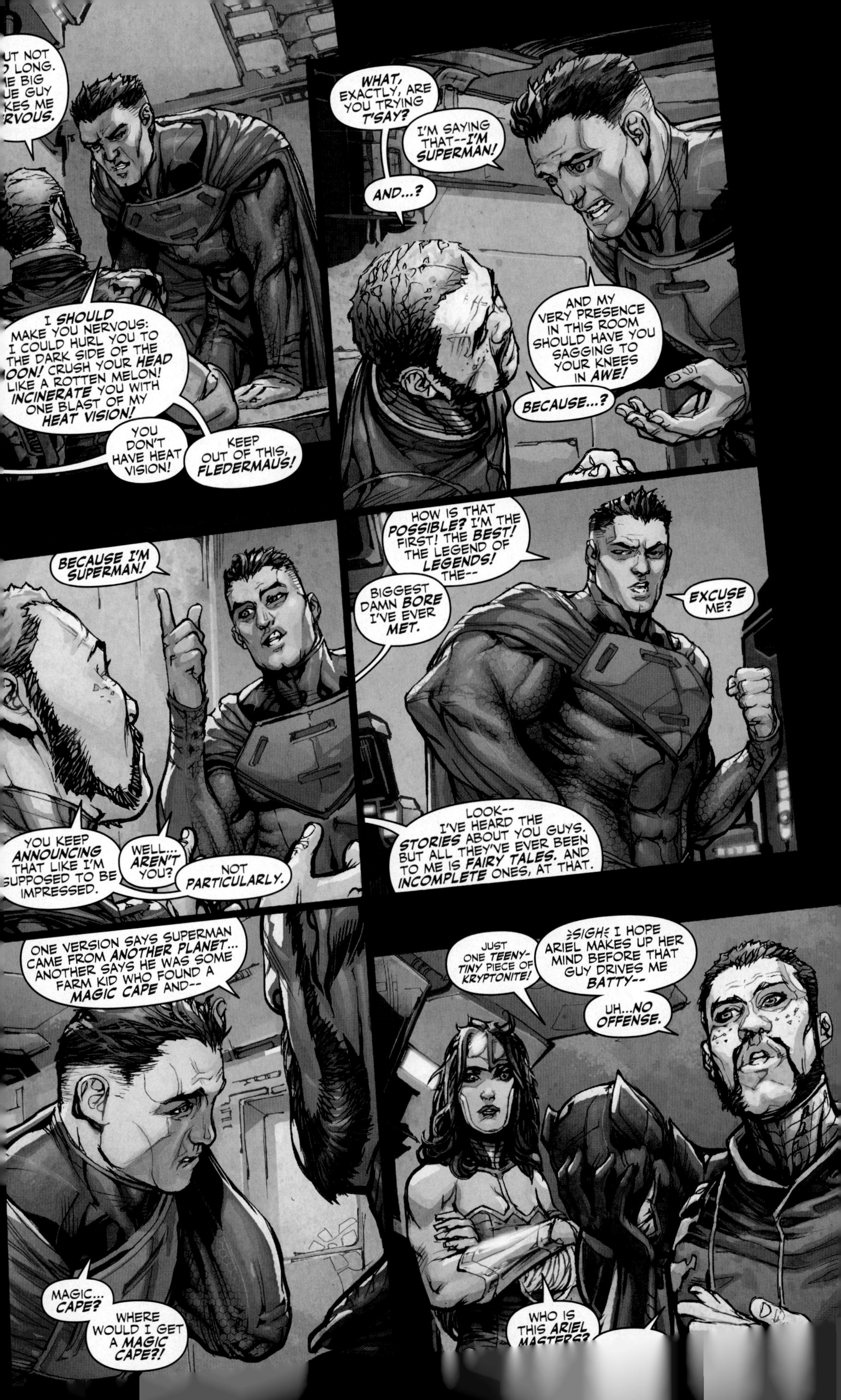
UT NOT
D LONG.
HE BIG
UE GUY
KES ME
ERVOUS.
I SHOULD MAKE YOU NERVOUS: I COULD HURL YOU TO THE DARK SIDE OF THE MOON! CRUSH YOUR HEAD LIKE A ROTTEN MELON! INCINERATE YOU WITH ONE BLAST OF MY HEAT VISION!
YOU DON'T HAVE HEAT VISION!
KEEP OUT OF THIS, FLEDERMAUS!
WHAT, EXACTLY, ARE YOU TRYING T'SAY?
I'M SAYING THAT--I'M SUPERMAN!
AND...?
AND MY VERY PRESENCE IN THIS ROOM SHOULD HAVE YOU SAGGING TO YOUR KNEES IN AWE!
BECAUSE...?
BECAUSE I'M SUPERMAN!
YOU KEEP ANNOUNCING THAT LIKE I'M SUPPOSED TO BE IMPRESSED.
WELL... AREN'T YOU?
NOT PARTICULARLY.
HOW IS THAT POSSIBLE? I'M THE FIRST! THE BEST! THE LEGEND OF LEGENDS! THE--
BIGGEST DAMN BORE I'VE EVER MET.
EXCUSE ME?
LOOK-- I'VE HEARD THE STORIES ABOUT YOU GUYS. BUT ALL THEY'VE EVER BEEN TO ME IS FAIRY TALES. AND INCOMPLETE ONES, AT THAT.
ONE VERSION SAYS SUPERMAN CAME FROM ANOTHER PLANET... ANOTHER SAYS HE WAS SOME FARM KID WHO FOUND A MAGIC CAPE AND--
MAGIC... CAPE?
WHERE WOULD I GET A MAGIC CAPE?!
JUST ONE TEENY-TINY PIECE OF KRYPTONITE!
≶SIGH≶ I HOPE ARIEL MAKES UP HER MIND BEFORE THAT GUY DRIVES ME BATTY--
UH...NO OFFENSE.
WHO IS THIS ARIEL

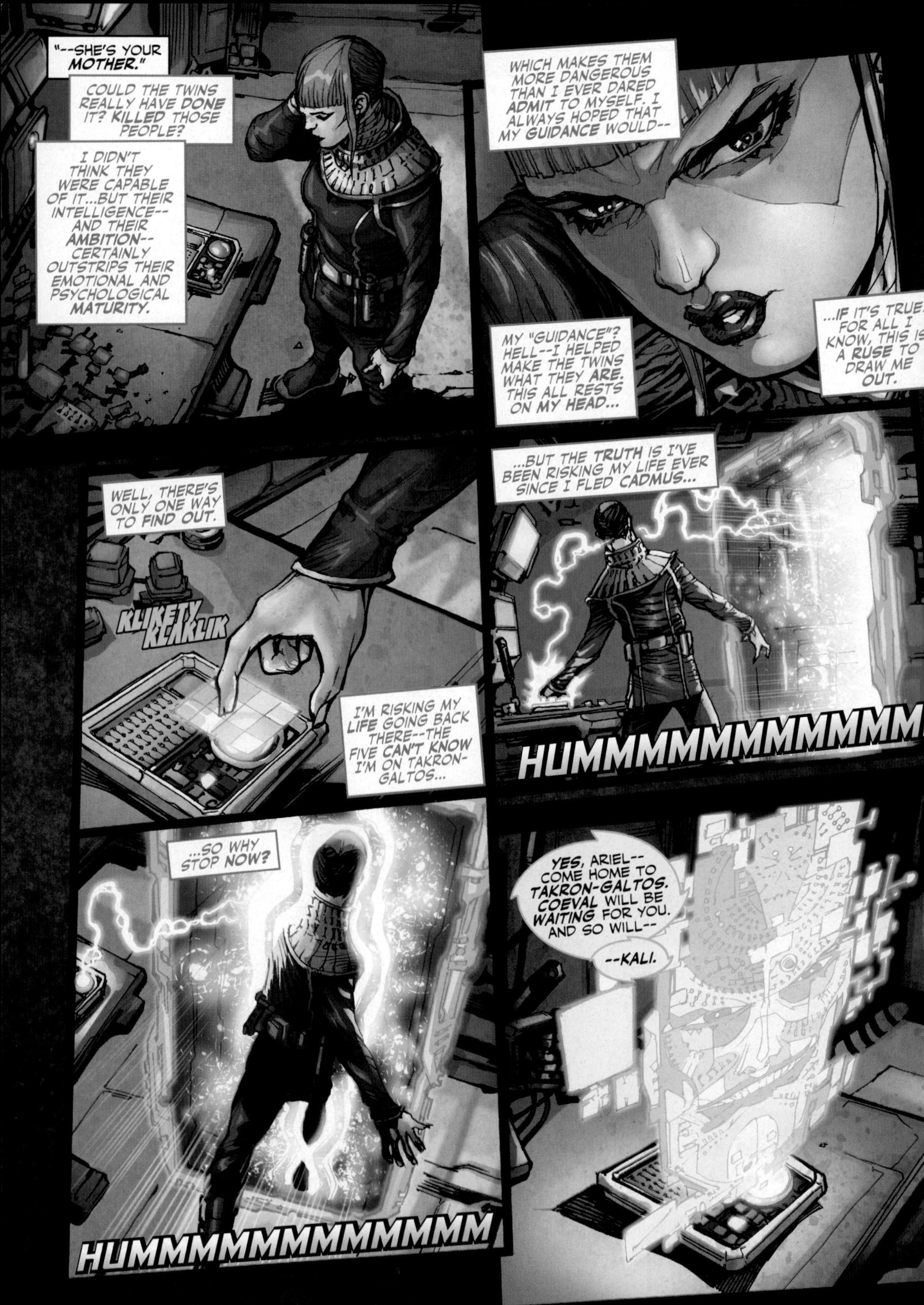

"--SHE'S YOUR MOTHER."
COULD THE TWINS REALLY HAVE DONE IT? KILLED THOSE PEOPLE?
I DIDN'T THINK THEY WERE CAPABLE OF IT...BUT THEIR INTELLIGENCE--AND THEIR AMBITION--CERTAINLY OUTSTRIPS THEIR EMOTIONAL AND PSYCHOLOGICAL MATURITY.
WHICH MAKES THEM MORE DANGEROUS THAN I EVER DARED ADMIT TO MYSELF. I ALWAYS HOPED THAT MY GUIDANCE WOULD--
MY "GUIDANCE"? HELL--I HELPED MAKE THE TWINS WHAT THEY ARE. THIS ALL RESTS ON MY HEAD...
...IF IT'S TRUE. FOR ALL I KNOW, THIS IS A RUSE TO DRAW ME OUT.
WELL, THERE'S ONLY ONE WAY TO FIND OUT.
KLIKETY KLAKLIK
I'M RISKING MY LIFE GOING BACK THERE--THE FIVE CAN'T KNOW I'M ON TAKRON-GALTOS...
...BUT THE TRUTH IS I'VE BEEN RISKING MY LIFE EVER SINCE I FLED CADMUS...
HUMMMMMMMMMMMMM
...SO WHY STOP NOW?
HUMMMMMMMMMMMM
YES, ARIEL--COME HOME TO TAKRON-GALTOS. COEVAL WILL BE WAITING FOR YOU. AND SO WILL--
--KALI.

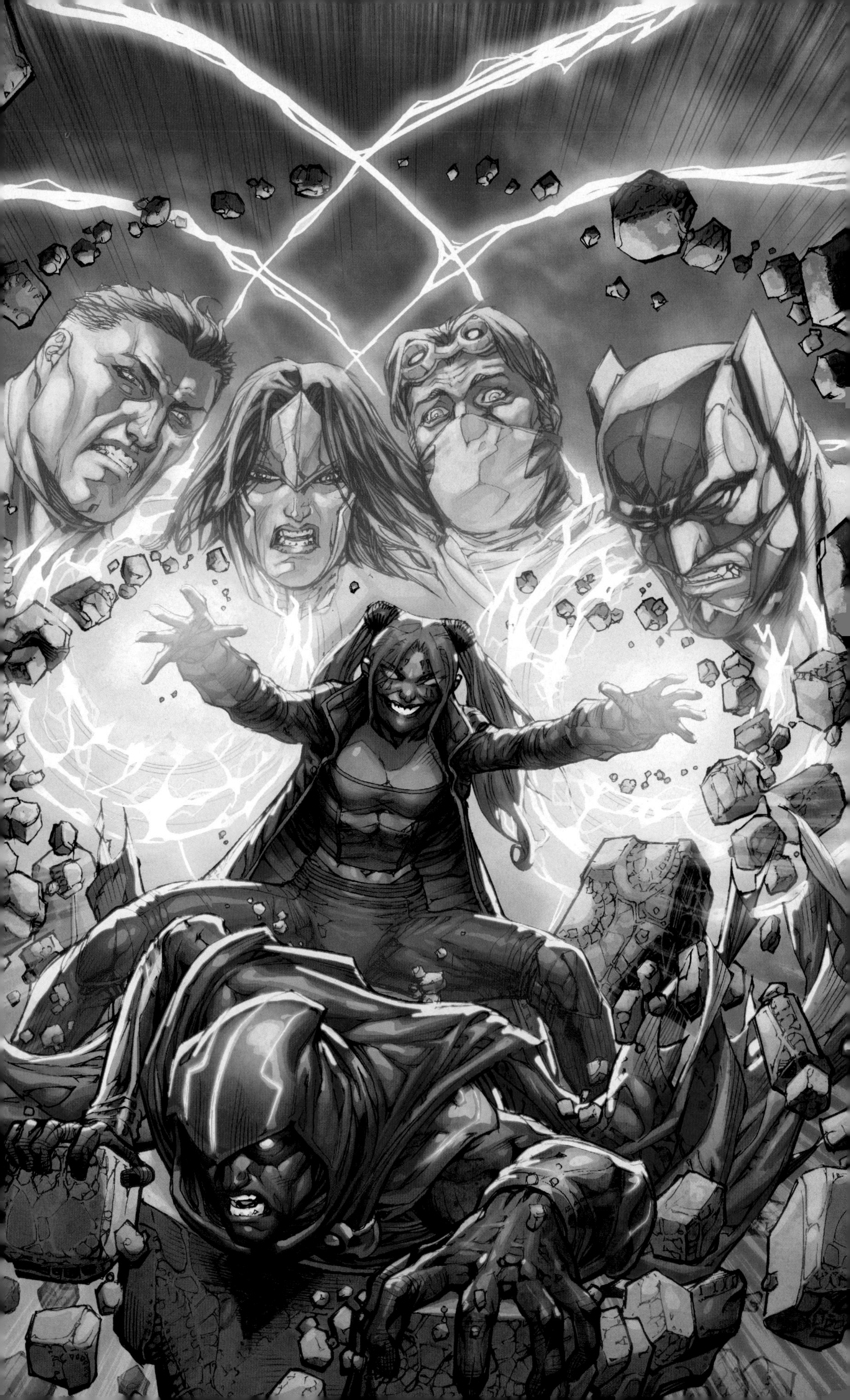

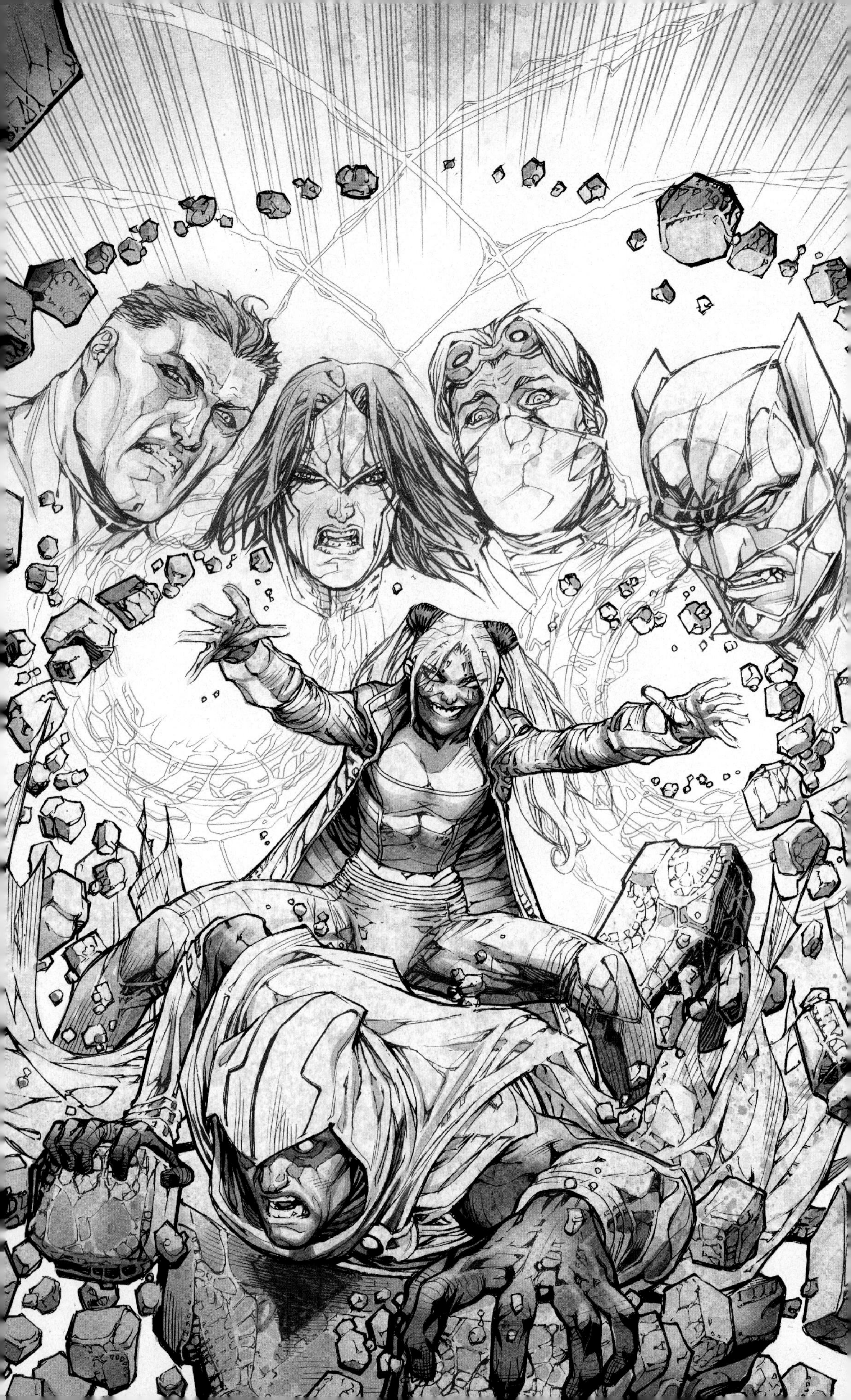

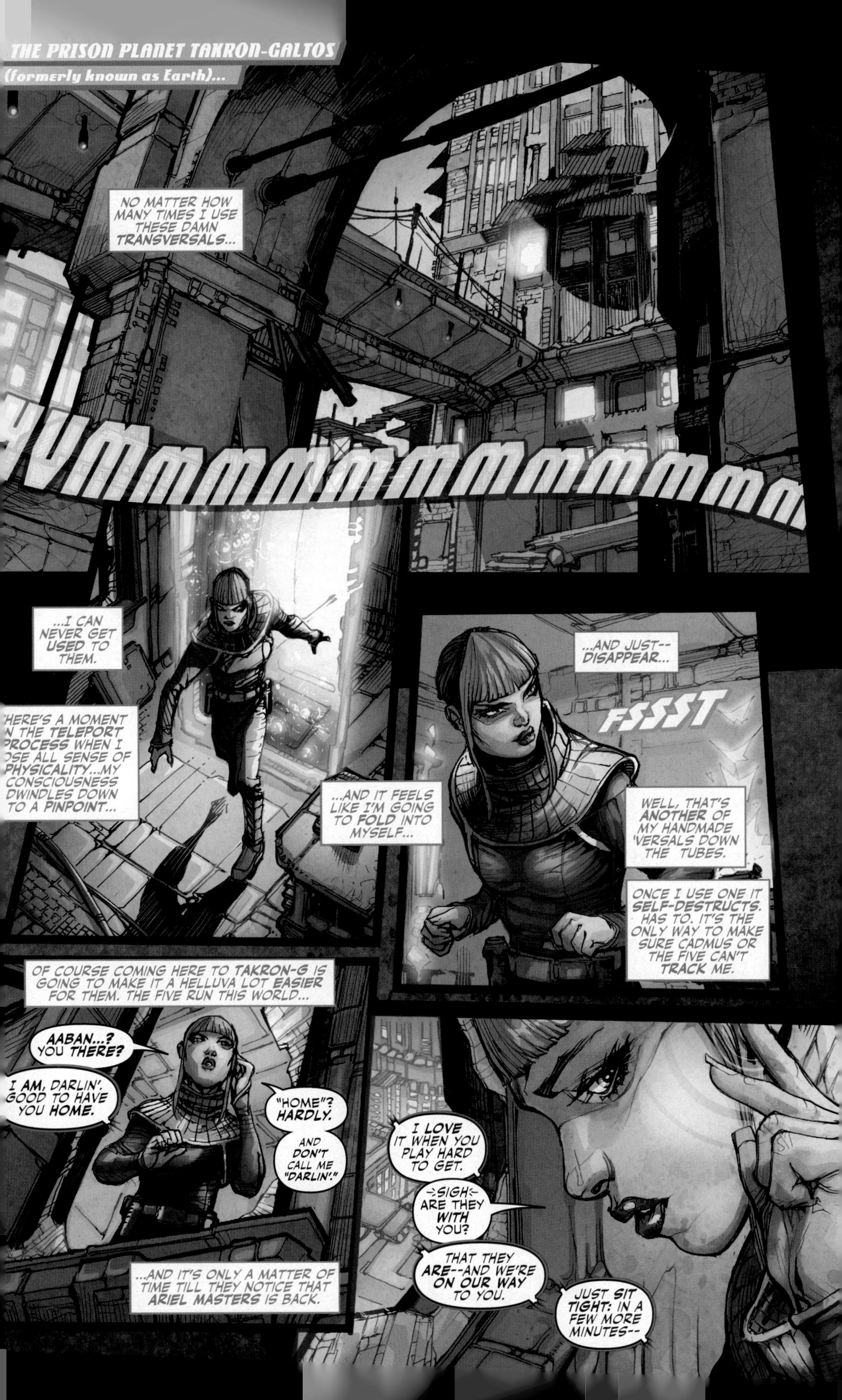

THE PRISON PLANET TAKRON-GALTOS
(formerly known as Earth)...
NO MATTER HOW MANY TIMES I USE THESE DAMN TRANSVERSALS...
VMMMMMMMMMMMMMMM
...I CAN NEVER GET USED TO THEM.
HERE'S A MOMENT IN THE TELEPORT PROCESS WHEN I LOSE ALL SENSE OF PHYSICALITY...MY CONSCIOUSNESS DWINDLES DOWN TO A PINPOINT...
...AND IT FEELS LIKE I'M GOING TO FOLD INTO MYSELF...
...AND JUST--DISAPPEAR...
FSSST
WELL, THAT'S ANOTHER OF MY HANDMADE 'VERSALS DOWN THE TUBES.
ONCE I USE ONE IT SELF-DESTRUCTS. HAS TO. IT'S THE ONLY WAY TO MAKE SURE CADMUS OR THE FIVE CAN'T TRACK ME.
OF COURSE COMING HERE TO TAKRON-G IS GOING TO MAKE IT A HELLUVA LOT EASIER FOR THEM. THE FIVE RUN THIS WORLD...
AABAN...? YOU THERE?
I AM, DARLIN'. GOOD TO HAVE YOU HOME.
"HOME"? HARDLY.
AND DON'T CALL ME "DARLIN'."
...AND IT'S ONLY A MATTER OF TIME TILL THEY NOTICE THAT ARIEL MASTERS IS BACK.
I LOVE IT WHEN YOU PLAY HARD TO GET.
SIGH ARE THEY WITH YOU?
THAT THEY ARE--AND WE'RE ON OUR WAY TO YOU.
JUST SIT TIGHT: IN A FEW MORE MINUTES--

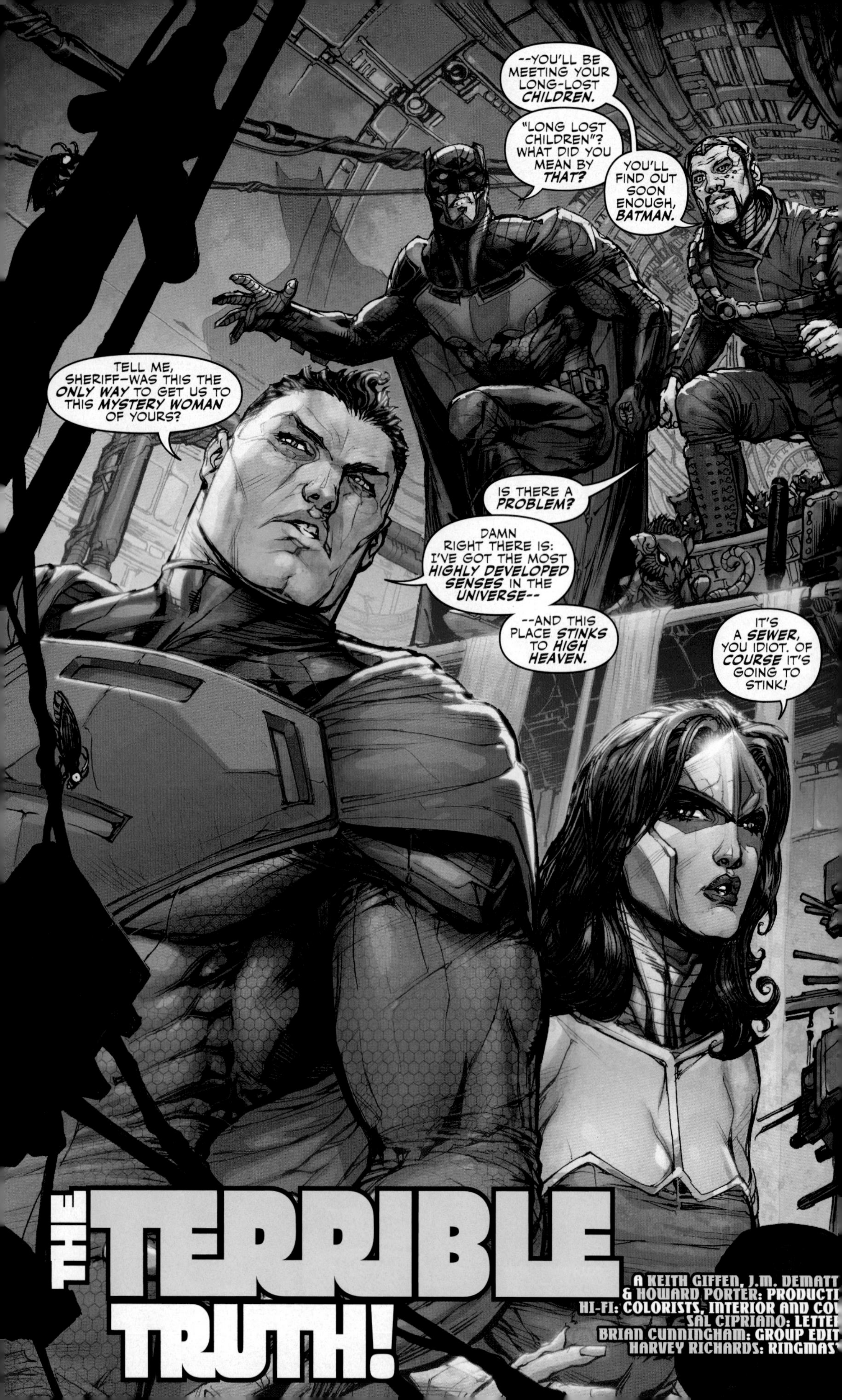
--YOU'LL BE MEETING YOUR LONG-LOST CHILDREN.
"LONG LOST CHILDREN"? WHAT DID YOU MEAN BY THAT?
YOU'LL FIND OUT SOON ENOUGH, BATMAN.
TELL ME, SHERIFF--WAS THIS THE ONLY WAY TO GET US TO THIS MYSTERY WOMAN OF YOURS?
IS THERE A PROBLEM?
DAMN RIGHT THERE IS: I'VE GOT THE MOST HIGHLY DEVELOPED SENSES IN THE UNIVERSE--
--AND THIS PLACE STINKS TO HIGH HEAVEN.
IT'S A SEWER, YOU IDIOT. OF COURSE IT'S GOING TO STINK!
THE TERRIBLE TRUTH!
A KEITH GIFFEN, J.M. DEMATT
& HOWARD PORTER: PRODUCTI
HI-FI: COLORISTS, INTERIOR AND CO
SAL CIPRIANO: LETTE
BRIAN CUNNINGHAM: GROUP EDIT
HARVEY RICHARDS: RINGMAS

THIS IS *BENEATH* A HERO OF MY STATURE.

IT'S BENEATH THE *WHOLE CITY.* ≈SNICKER≈

YOU MAY BE THE *LAW* IN THIS HELLHOLE, *TARIQ...*BUT I'M--

YOU'RE *SUPERMAN.* SO YOU KEEP TELLING ME: OVER AND OVER. AD *NAUSEAM.* AD *INFINITUM.*

I'M *STILL* NOT IMPRESSED.

DRAGGING US THROUGH THE *LOWEST LEVELS* OF THE CITY. WHY IS THE *SHERIFF* OF *NEW NEW YORK* HIDING?

BECAUSE *THE FIVE* ARE HUNTING *ARIEL,* TOO.

UP ON THE SURFACE, *COEVAL'S* GOT EYES AND EARS EVERY-WHERE--

--AND *THE CONVERT'S* POPPING IN AND OUT OF BODIES WITH *ALARMING* FREQUENCY--

CONVERT? *HAH!*

WE KICKED HIS ASS--WELL, *ASSES*--LAST TIME WE MET--

--AND YOU CAN BET WE'LL DO IT *AGAIN*--

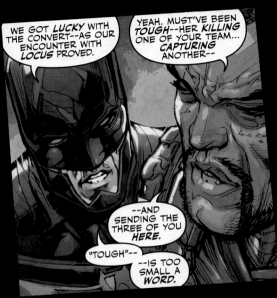

WE GOT *LUCKY* WITH THE CONVERT--AS OUR ENCOUNTER WITH *LOCUS* PROVED.

YEAH. MUST'VE BEEN *TOUGH*--HER *KILLING* ONE OF YOUR TEAM... *CAPTURING* ANOTHER--

--AND SENDING THE *THREE* OF YOU *HERE.*

"TOUGH"-- --IS TOO *SMALL* A *WORD.*

NOT TO *WORRY.* ONCE WE GET *OFF* THIS ROCK, I'LL TEAR LOCUS' *HEAD* OFF AND SHOVE IT RIGHT UP HER--

I THOUGHT YOU HAD A *CODE* AGAINST KILLING.

THAT'S WHAT THE *HISTORY* BOOKS SAY. BUT I DON'T *READ* BOOKS--

ARIEL'S GONNA BE *MASSIVELY* DISAPPOINTED WHEN SHE SEES HOW *YOU* TURNED OUT.

AND WHY WOULD SHE EVEN *CARE?*

BECAUSE, *SUPERDUNCE*--SHE'S YOUR *MOMMY.*

"MOMMY"?

NOW COME *ON*--

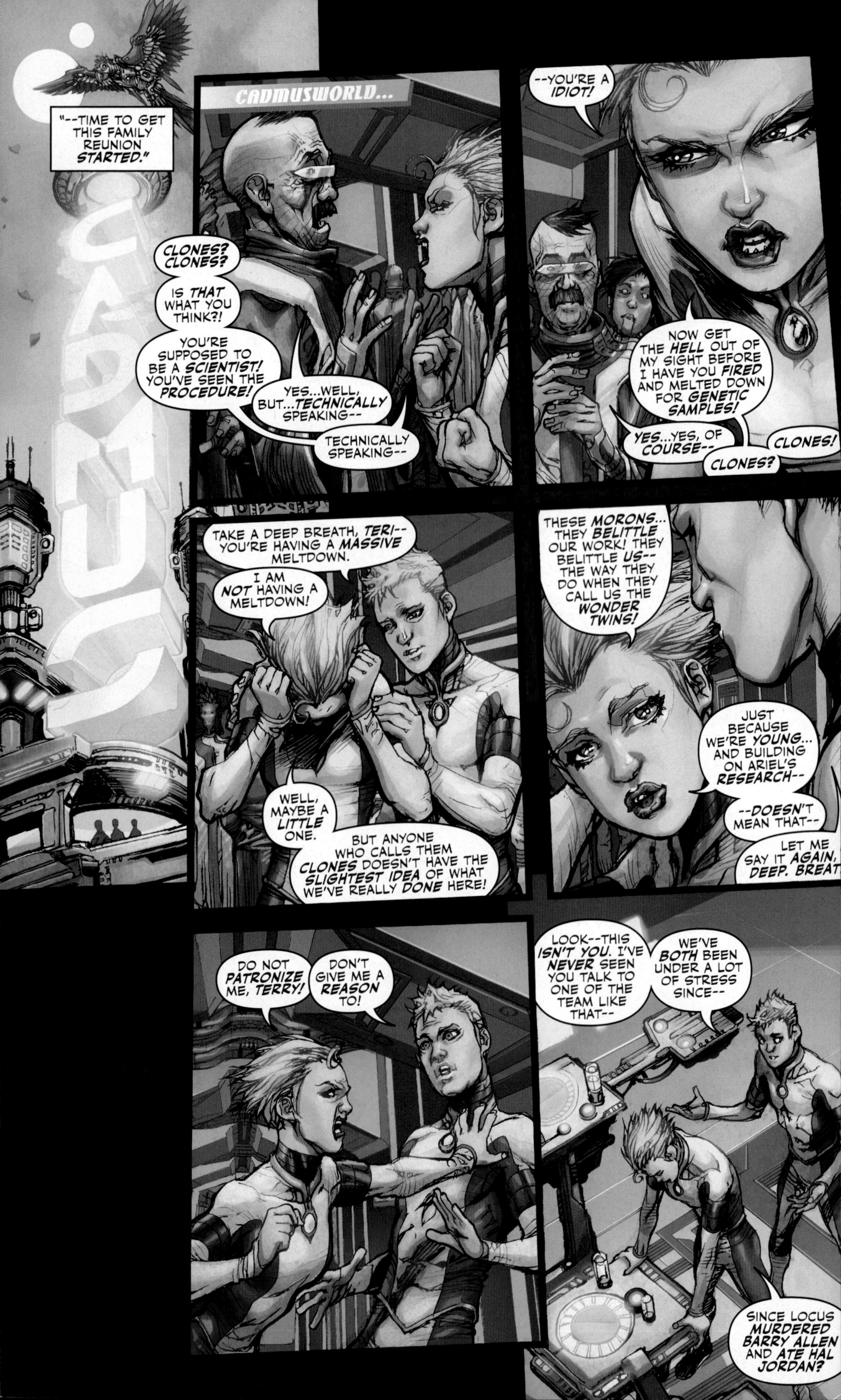
"--TIME TO GET THIS FAMILY REUNION STARTED."
CADMUSWORLD...
CLONES? CLONES?
IS THAT WHAT YOU THINK?!
YOU'RE SUPPOSED TO BE A SCIENTIST! YOU'VE SEEN THE PROCEDURE!
YES...WELL, BUT...TECHNICALLY SPEAKING--
TECHNICALLY SPEAKING--
--YOU'RE A IDIOT!
NOW GET THE HELL OUT OF MY SIGHT BEFORE I HAVE YOU FIRED AND MELTED DOWN FOR GENETIC SAMPLES!
YES...YES, OF COURSE--
CLONES?
CLONES!
TAKE A DEEP BREATH, TERI-- YOU'RE HAVING A MASSIVE MELTDOWN.
I AM NOT HAVING A MELTDOWN!
WELL, MAYBE A LITTLE ONE.
BUT ANYONE WHO CALLS THEM CLONES DOESN'T HAVE THE SLIGHTEST IDEA OF WHAT WE'VE REALLY DONE HERE!
THESE MORONS... THEY BELITTLE OUR WORK! THEY BELITTLE US-- THE WAY THEY DO WHEN THEY CALL US THE WONDER TWINS!
JUST BECAUSE WE'RE YOUNG... AND BUILDING ON ARIEL'S RESEARCH--
--DOESN'T MEAN THAT--
LET ME SAY IT AGAIN, DEEP. BREAT
DO NOT PATRONIZE ME, TERRY!
DON'T GIVE ME A REASON TO!
LOOK--THIS ISN'T YOU. I'VE NEVER SEEN YOU TALK TO ONE OF THE TEAM LIKE THAT--
WE'VE BOTH BEEN UNDER A LOT OF STRESS SINCE--
SINCE LOCUS MURDERED BARRY ALLEN AND ATE HAL JORDAN?

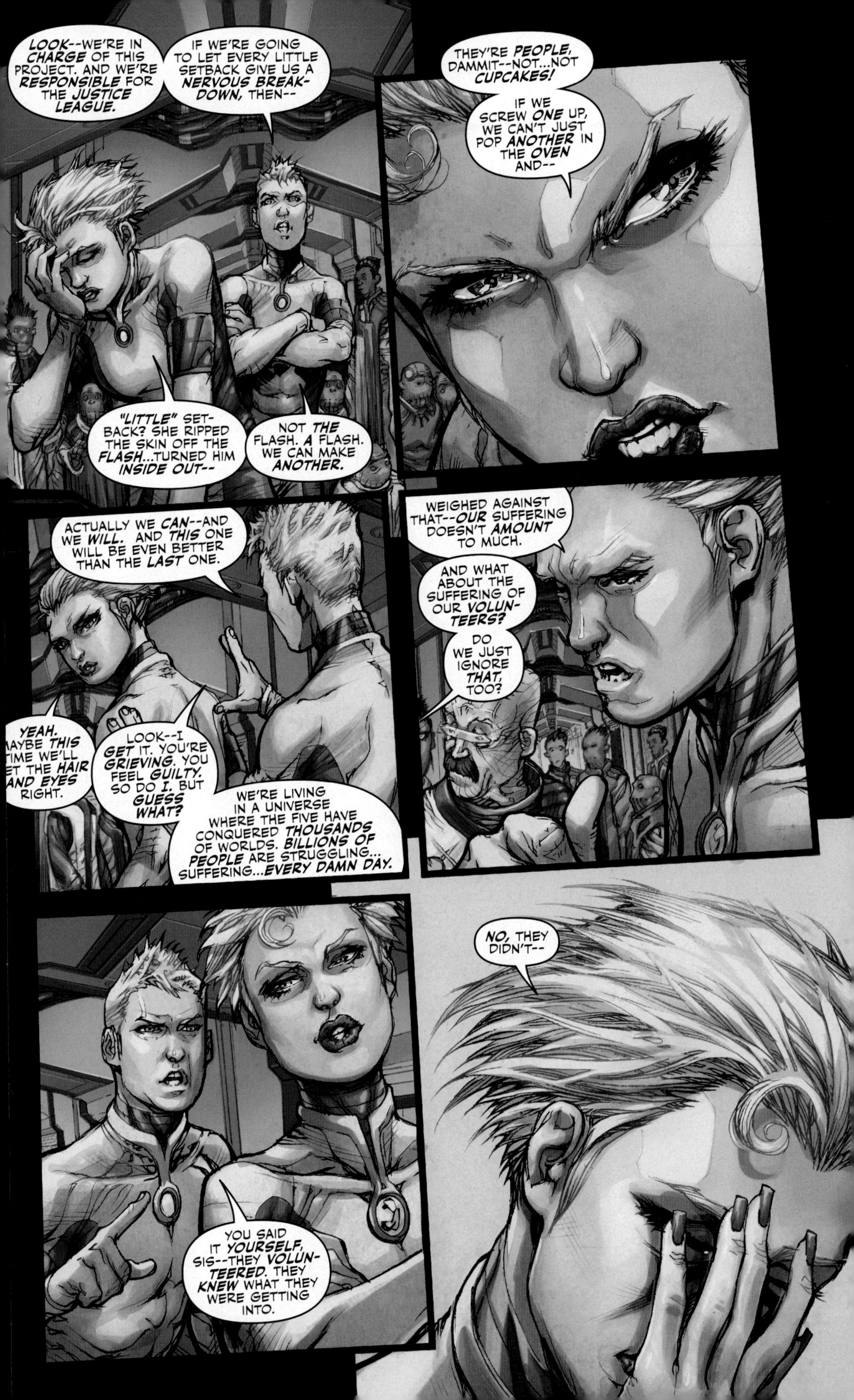
LOOK--WE'RE IN CHARGE OF THIS PROJECT. AND WE'RE RESPONSIBLE FOR THE JUSTICE LEAGUE.
IF WE'RE GOING TO LET EVERY LITTLE SETBACK GIVE US A NERVOUS BREAK-DOWN, THEN--
"LITTLE" SET-BACK? SHE RIPPED THE SKIN OFF THE FLASH...TURNED HIM INSIDE OUT--
NOT THE FLASH. A FLASH. WE CAN MAKE ANOTHER.
THEY'RE PEOPLE, DAMMIT--NOT...NOT CUPCAKES!
IF WE SCREW ONE UP, WE CAN'T JUST POP ANOTHER IN THE OVEN AND--
ACTUALLY WE CAN--AND WE WILL. AND THIS ONE WILL BE EVEN BETTER THAN THE LAST ONE.
YEAH. MAYBE THIS TIME WE'LL GET THE HAIR AND EYES RIGHT.
LOOK--I GET IT. YOU'RE GRIEVING. YOU FEEL GUILTY. SO DO I. BUT GUESS WHAT?
WE'RE LIVING IN A UNIVERSE WHERE THE FIVE HAVE CONQUERED THOUSANDS OF WORLDS. BILLIONS OF PEOPLE ARE STRUGGLING... SUFFERING...EVERY DAMN DAY.
WEIGHED AGAINST THAT--OUR SUFFERING DOESN'T AMOUNT TO MUCH.
AND WHAT ABOUT THE SUFFERING OF OUR VOLUN-TEERS?
DO WE JUST IGNORE THAT, TOO?
YOU SAID IT YOURSELF, SIS--THEY VOLUN-TEERED. THEY KNEW WHAT THEY WERE GETTING INTO.
NO, THEY DIDN'T--

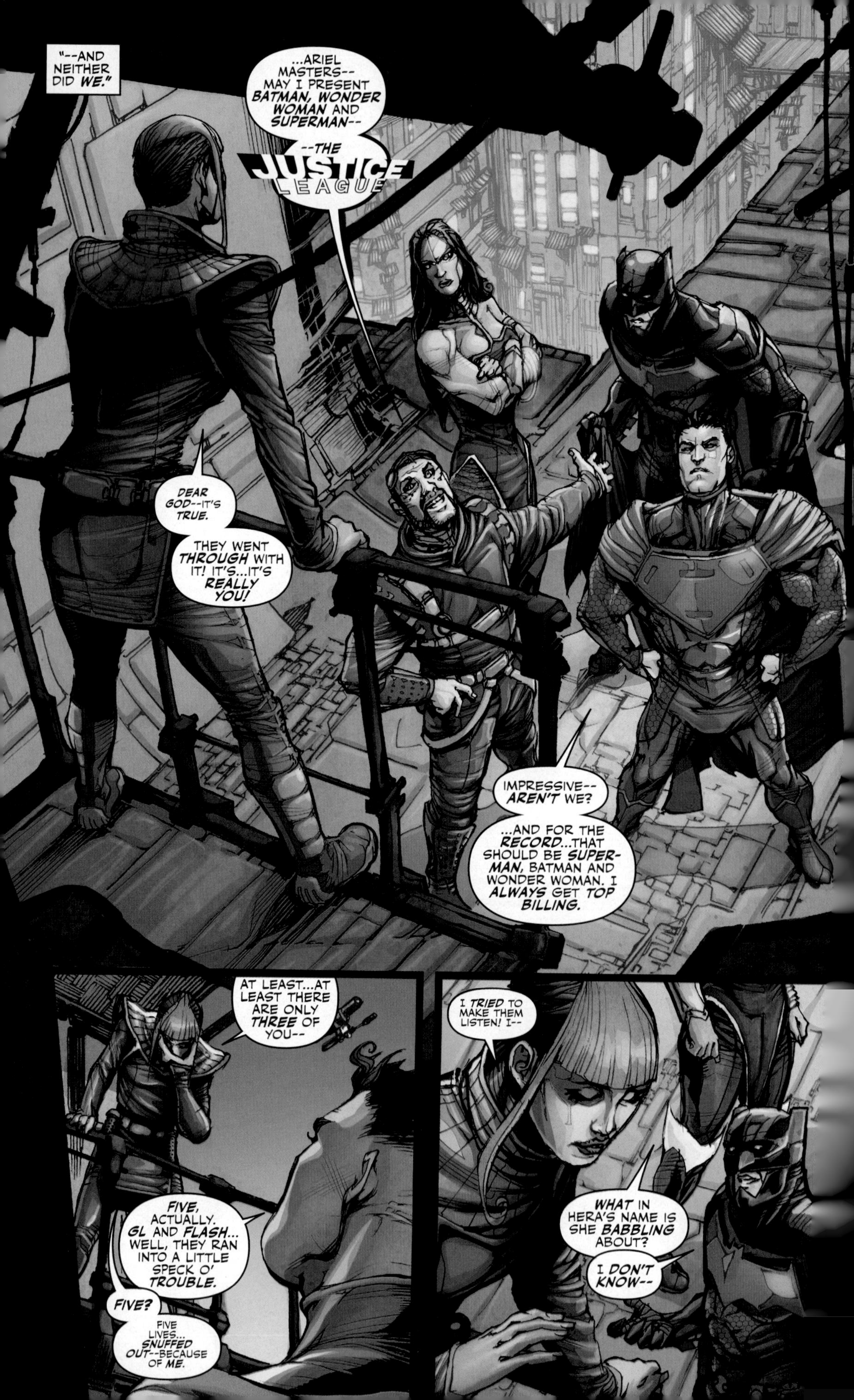
"--AND NEITHER DID WE."
...ARIEL MASTERS-- MAY I PRESENT BATMAN, WONDER WOMAN AND SUPERMAN--
--THE JUSTICE LEAGUE
DEAR GOD--IT'S TRUE.
THEY WENT THROUGH WITH IT! IT'S...IT'S REALLY YOU!
IMPRESSIVE-- AREN'T WE?
...AND FOR THE RECORD...THAT SHOULD BE SUPERMAN, BATMAN AND WONDER WOMAN. I ALWAYS GET TOP BILLING.
AT LEAST...AT LEAST THERE ARE ONLY THREE OF YOU--
FIVE, ACTUALLY. GL AND FLASH... WELL, THEY RAN INTO A LITTLE SPECK O' TROUBLE.
FIVE?
FIVE LIVES... SNUFFED OUT--BECAUSE OF ME.
I TRIED TO MAKE THEM LISTEN! I--
WHAT IN HERA'S NAME IS SHE BABBLING ABOUT?
I DON'T KNOW--

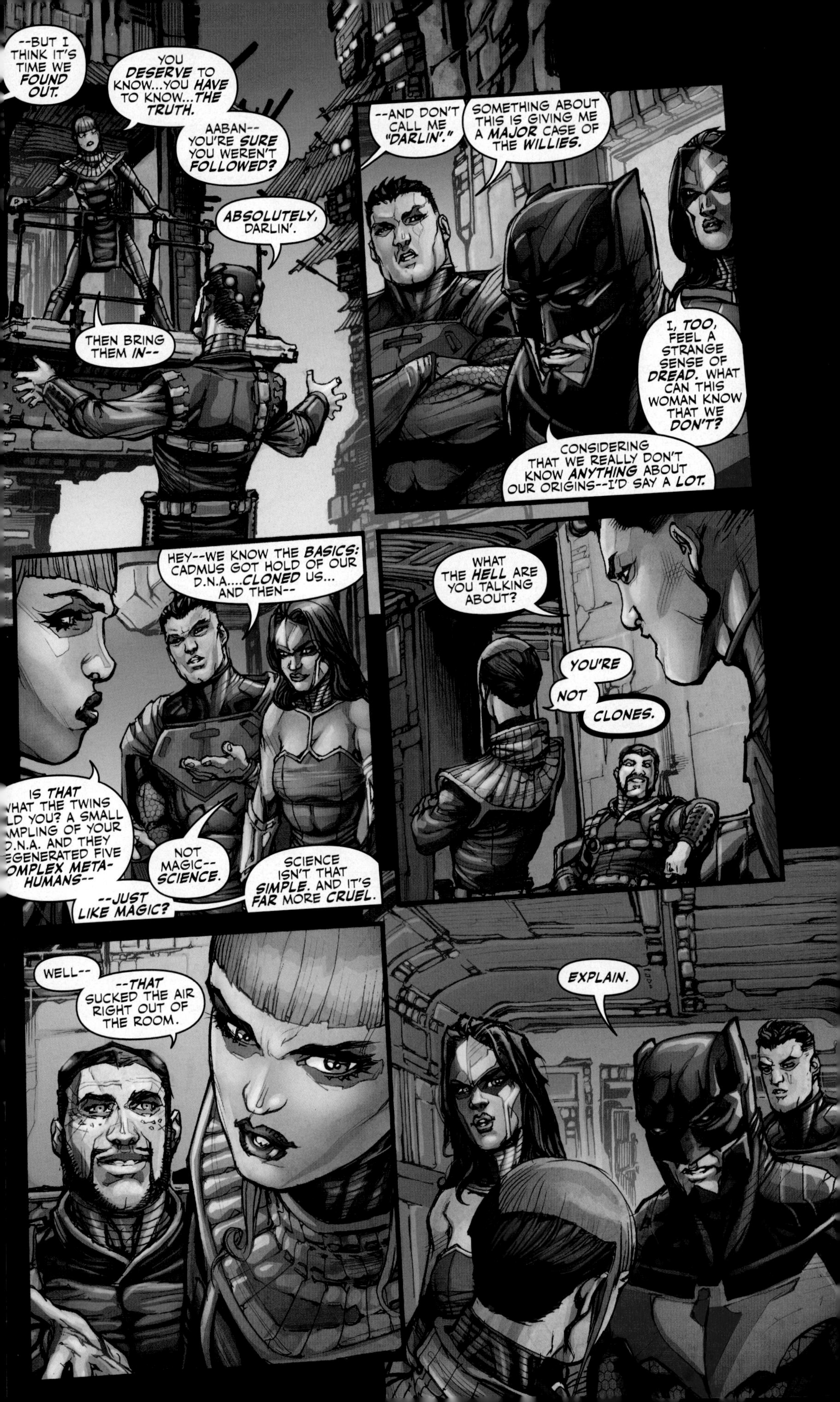
--BUT I THINK IT'S TIME WE FOUND OUT.
YOU DESERVE TO KNOW...YOU HAVE TO KNOW...THE TRUTH.
AABAN-- YOU'RE SURE YOU WEREN'T FOLLOWED?
ABSOLUTELY, DARLIN'.
THEN BRING THEM IN--
--AND DON'T CALL ME "DARLIN'."
SOMETHING ABOUT THIS IS GIVING ME A MAJOR CASE OF THE WILLIES.
I, TOO, FEEL A STRANGE SENSE OF DREAD. WHAT CAN THIS WOMAN KNOW THAT WE DON'T?
CONSIDERING THAT WE REALLY DON'T KNOW ANYTHING ABOUT OUR ORIGINS--I'D SAY A LOT.
HEY--WE KNOW THE BASICS: CADMUS GOT HOLD OF OUR D.N.A....CLONED US... AND THEN--
IS THAT WHAT THE TWINS LD YOU? A SMALL MPLING OF YOUR D.N.A. AND THEY EGENERATED FIVE OMPLEX META-HUMANS--
NOT MAGIC--SCIENCE.
--JUST LIKE MAGIC?
SCIENCE ISN'T THAT SIMPLE. AND IT'S FAR MORE CRUEL.
WHAT THE HELL ARE YOU TALKING ABOUT?
YOU'RE NOT CLONES.
WELL--
--THAT SUCKED THE AIR RIGHT OUT OF THE ROOM.
EXPLAIN.

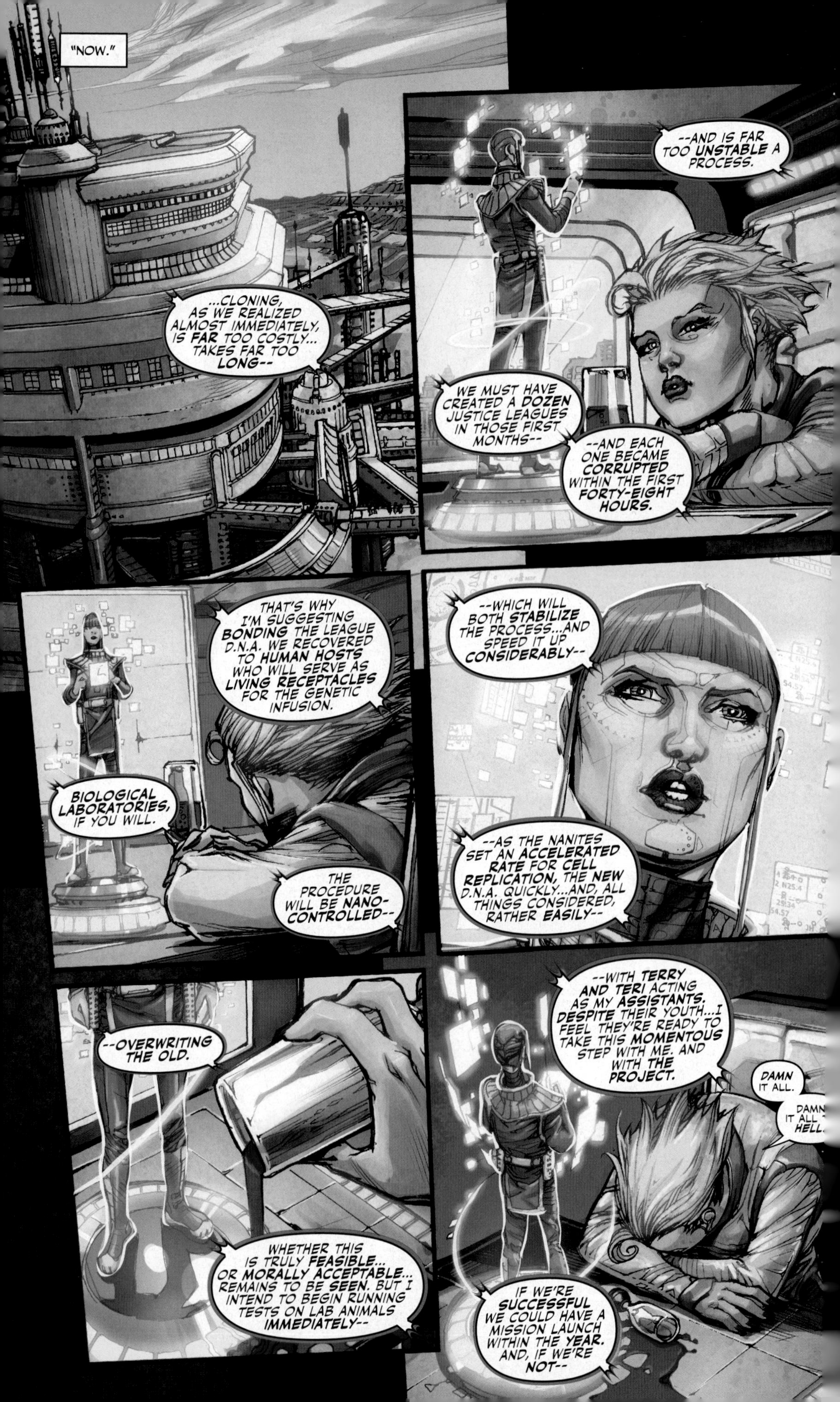
"NOW."
...CLONING, AS WE REALIZED ALMOST IMMEDIATELY, IS FAR TOO COSTLY... TAKES FAR TOO LONG--
--AND IS FAR TOO UNSTABLE A PROCESS.
WE MUST HAVE CREATED A DOZEN JUSTICE LEAGUES IN THOSE FIRST MONTHS--
--AND EACH ONE BECAME CORRUPTED WITHIN THE FIRST FORTY-EIGHT HOURS.
THAT'S WHY I'M SUGGESTING BONDING THE LEAGUE D.N.A. WE RECOVERED TO HUMAN HOSTS WHO WILL SERVE AS LIVING RECEPTACLES FOR THE GENETIC INFUSION.
BIOLOGICAL LABORATORIES, IF YOU WILL.
THE PROCEDURE WILL BE NANO-CONTROLLED--
--WHICH WILL BOTH STABILIZE THE PROCESS...AND SPEED IT UP CONSIDERABLY--
--AS THE NANITES SET AN ACCELERATED RATE FOR CELL REPLICATION, THE NEW D.N.A. QUICKLY...AND, ALL THINGS CONSIDERED, RATHER EASILY--
--OVERWRITING THE OLD.
WHETHER THIS IS TRULY FEASIBLE... OR MORALLY ACCEPTABLE... REMAINS TO BE SEEN. BUT I INTEND TO BEGIN RUNNING TESTS ON LAB ANIMALS IMMEDIATELY--
--WITH TERRY AND TERI ACTING AS MY ASSISTANTS. DESPITE THEIR YOUTH...I FEEL THEY'RE READY TO TAKE THIS MOMENTOUS STEP WITH ME. AND WITH THE PROJECT.
DAMN IT ALL.
DAMN IT ALL TO HELL.
IF WE'RE SUCCESSFUL WE COULD HAVE A MISSION LAUNCH WITHIN THE YEAR. AND, IF WE'RE NOT--

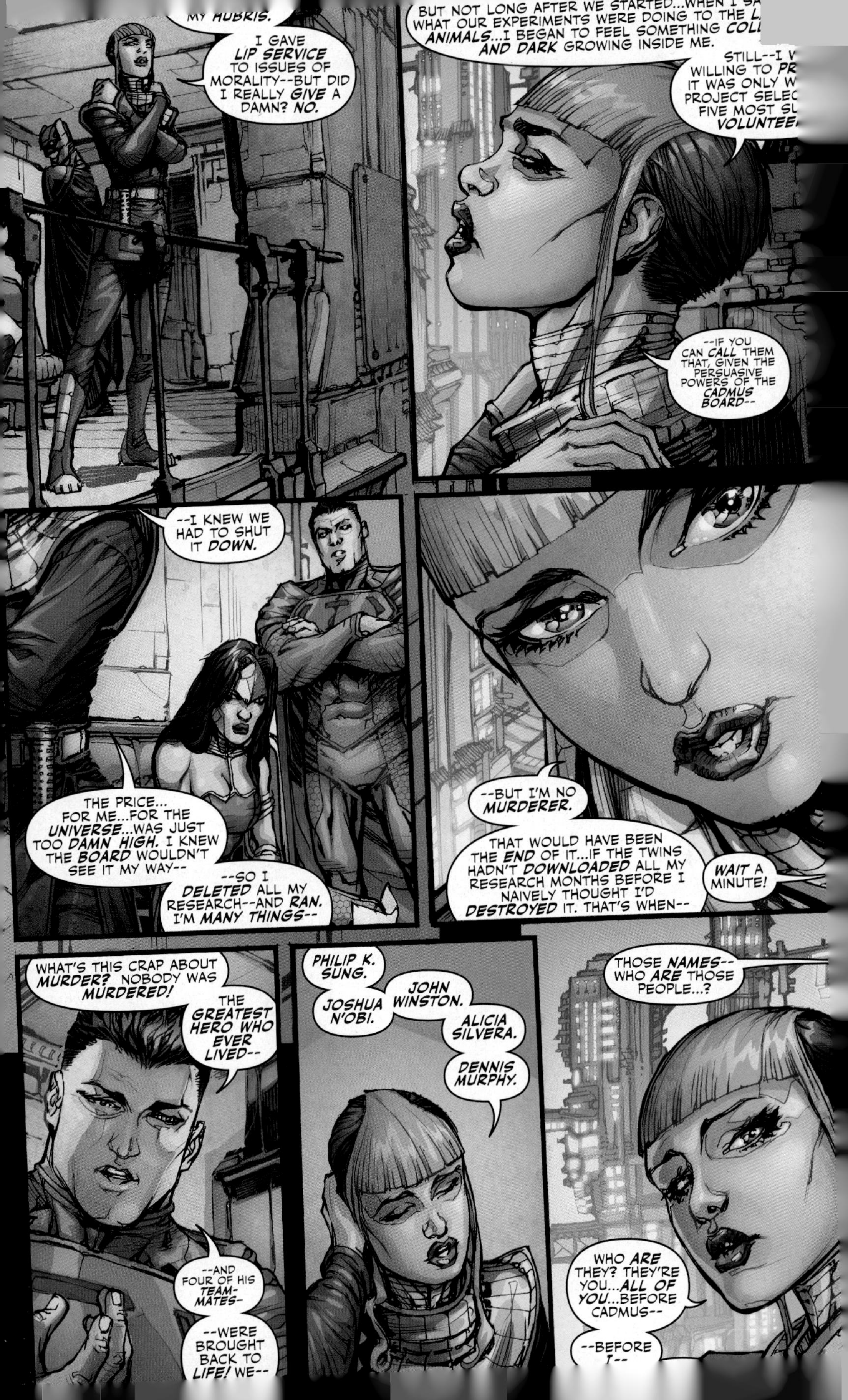
MY HUBRIS.
I GAVE LIP SERVICE TO ISSUES OF MORALITY--BUT DID I REALLY GIVE A DAMN? NO.
BUT NOT LONG AFTER WE STARTED...WHEN I SA WHAT OUR EXPERIMENTS WERE DOING TO THE L ANIMALS...I BEGAN TO FEEL SOMETHING COL AND DARK GROWING INSIDE ME.
STILL--I W WILLING TO PR IT WAS ONLY W PROJECT SELEC FIVE MOST SU VOLUNTEE
--IF YOU CAN CALL THEM THAT, GIVEN THE PERSUASIVE POWERS OF THE CADMUS BOARD--
--I KNEW WE HAD TO SHUT IT DOWN.
THE PRICE... FOR ME...FOR THE UNIVERSE...WAS JUST TOO DAMN HIGH. I KNEW THE BOARD WOULDN'T SEE IT MY WAY--
--SO I DELETED ALL MY RESEARCH--AND RAN. I'M MANY THINGS--
--BUT I'M NO MURDERER.
THAT WOULD HAVE BEEN THE END OF IT...IF THE TWINS HADN'T DOWNLOADED ALL MY RESEARCH MONTHS BEFORE I NAIVELY THOUGHT I'D DESTROYED IT. THAT'S WHEN--
WAIT A MINUTE!
WHAT'S THIS CRAP ABOUT MURDER? NOBODY WAS MURDERED!
THE GREATEST HERO WHO EVER LIVED--
--AND FOUR OF HIS TEAM-MATES-
--WERE BROUGHT BACK TO LIFE! WE--
PHILIP K. SUNG.
JOSHUA N'OBI.
JOHN WINSTON.
ALICIA SILVERA.
DENNIS MURPHY.
THOSE NAMES--WHO ARE THOSE PEOPLE...?
WHO ARE THEY? THEY'RE YOU...ALL OF YOU...BEFORE CADMUS--
--BEFORE I--

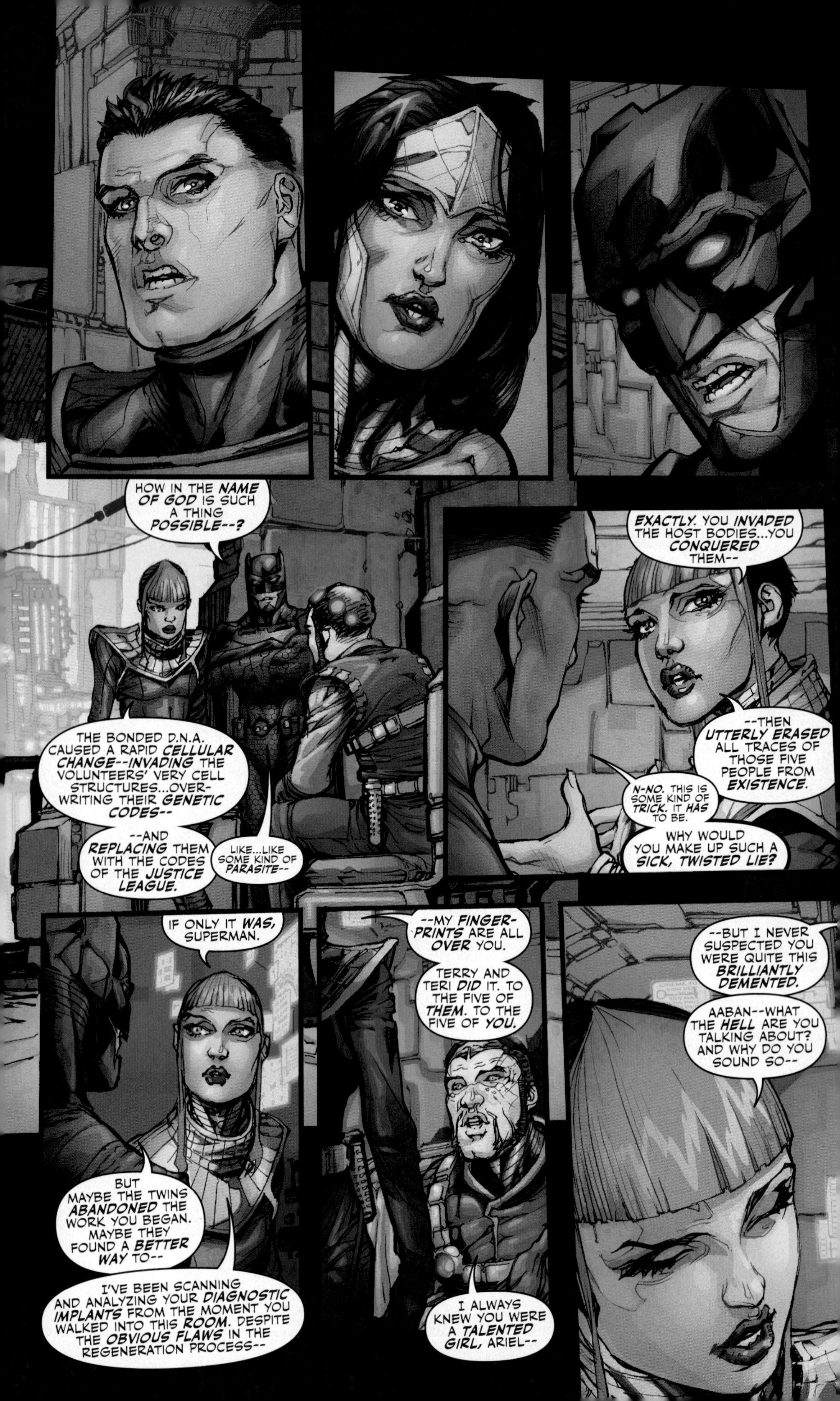
HOW IN THE NAME OF GOD IS SUCH A THING POSSIBLE--?
THE BONDED D.N.A. CAUSED A RAPID CELLULAR CHANGE--INVADING THE VOLUNTEERS' VERY CELL STRUCTURES...OVER-WRITING THEIR GENETIC CODES--
--AND REPLACING THEM WITH THE CODES OF THE JUSTICE LEAGUE.
LIKE...LIKE SOME KIND OF PARASITE--
EXACTLY. YOU INVADED THE HOST BODIES...YOU CONQUERED THEM--
--THEN UTTERLY ERASED ALL TRACES OF THOSE FIVE PEOPLE FROM EXISTENCE.
N-NO. THIS IS SOME KIND OF TRICK. IT HAS TO BE.
WHY WOULD YOU MAKE UP SUCH A SICK, TWISTED LIE?
IF ONLY IT WAS, SUPERMAN.
BUT MAYBE THE TWINS ABANDONED THE WORK YOU BEGAN. MAYBE THEY FOUND A BETTER WAY TO--
I'VE BEEN SCANNING AND ANALYZING YOUR DIAGNOSTIC IMPLANTS FROM THE MOMENT YOU WALKED INTO THIS ROOM. DESPITE THE OBVIOUS FLAWS IN THE REGENERATION PROCESS--
--MY FINGER-PRINTS ARE ALL OVER YOU.
TERRY AND TERI DID IT. TO THE FIVE OF THEM. TO THE FIVE OF YOU.
I ALWAYS KNEW YOU WERE A TALENTED GIRL, ARIEL--
--BUT I NEVER SUSPECTED YOU WERE QUITE THIS BRILLIANTLY DEMENTED.
AABAN--WHAT THE HELL ARE YOU TALKING ABOUT? AND WHY DO YOU SOUND SO--

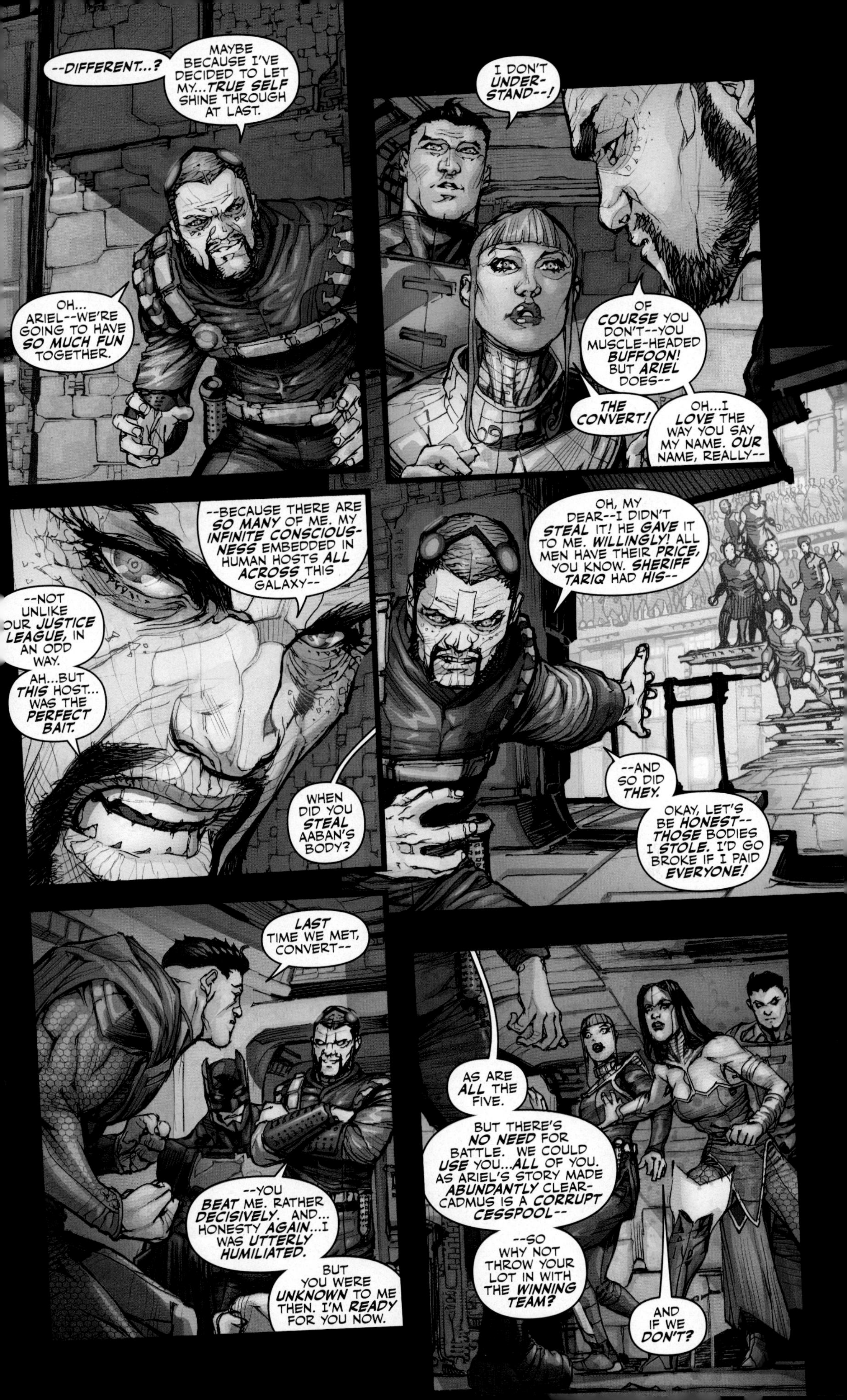

--DIFFERENT...?
MAYBE BECAUSE I'VE DECIDED TO LET MY...TRUE SELF SHINE THROUGH AT LAST.
OH... ARIEL--WE'RE GOING TO HAVE SO MUCH FUN TOGETHER.
I DON'T UNDER-STAND--!
OF COURSE YOU DON'T--YOU MUSCLE-HEADED BUFFOON! BUT ARIEL DOES--
THE CONVERT!
OH...I LOVE THE WAY YOU SAY MY NAME. OUR NAME, REALLY--
--BECAUSE THERE ARE SO MANY OF ME. MY INFINITE CONSCIOUS-NESS EMBEDDED IN HUMAN HOSTS ALL ACROSS THIS GALAXY--
--NOT UNLIKE OUR JUSTICE LEAGUE, IN AN ODD WAY.
AH...BUT THIS HOST... WAS THE PERFECT BAIT.
WHEN DID YOU STEAL AABAN'S BODY?
OH, MY DEAR--I DIDN'T STEAL IT! HE GAVE IT TO ME. WILLINGLY! ALL MEN HAVE THEIR PRICE, YOU KNOW. SHERIFF TARIQ HAD HIS--
--AND SO DID THEY.
OKAY, LET'S BE HONEST-- THOSE BODIES I STOLE. I'D GO BROKE IF I PAID EVERYONE!
LAST TIME WE MET, CONVERT--
--YOU BEAT ME. RATHER DECISIVELY. AND... HONESTY AGAIN...I WAS UTTERLY HUMILIATED.
BUT YOU WERE UNKNOWN TO ME THEN. I'M READY FOR YOU NOW.
AS ARE ALL THE FIVE.
BUT THERE'S NO NEED FOR BATTLE. WE COULD USE YOU...ALL OF YOU. AS ARIEL'S STORY MADE ABUNDANTLY CLEAR-CADMUS IS A CORRUPT CESSPOOL--
--SO WHY NOT THROW YOUR LOT IN WITH THE WINNING TEAM?
AND IF WE DON'T?

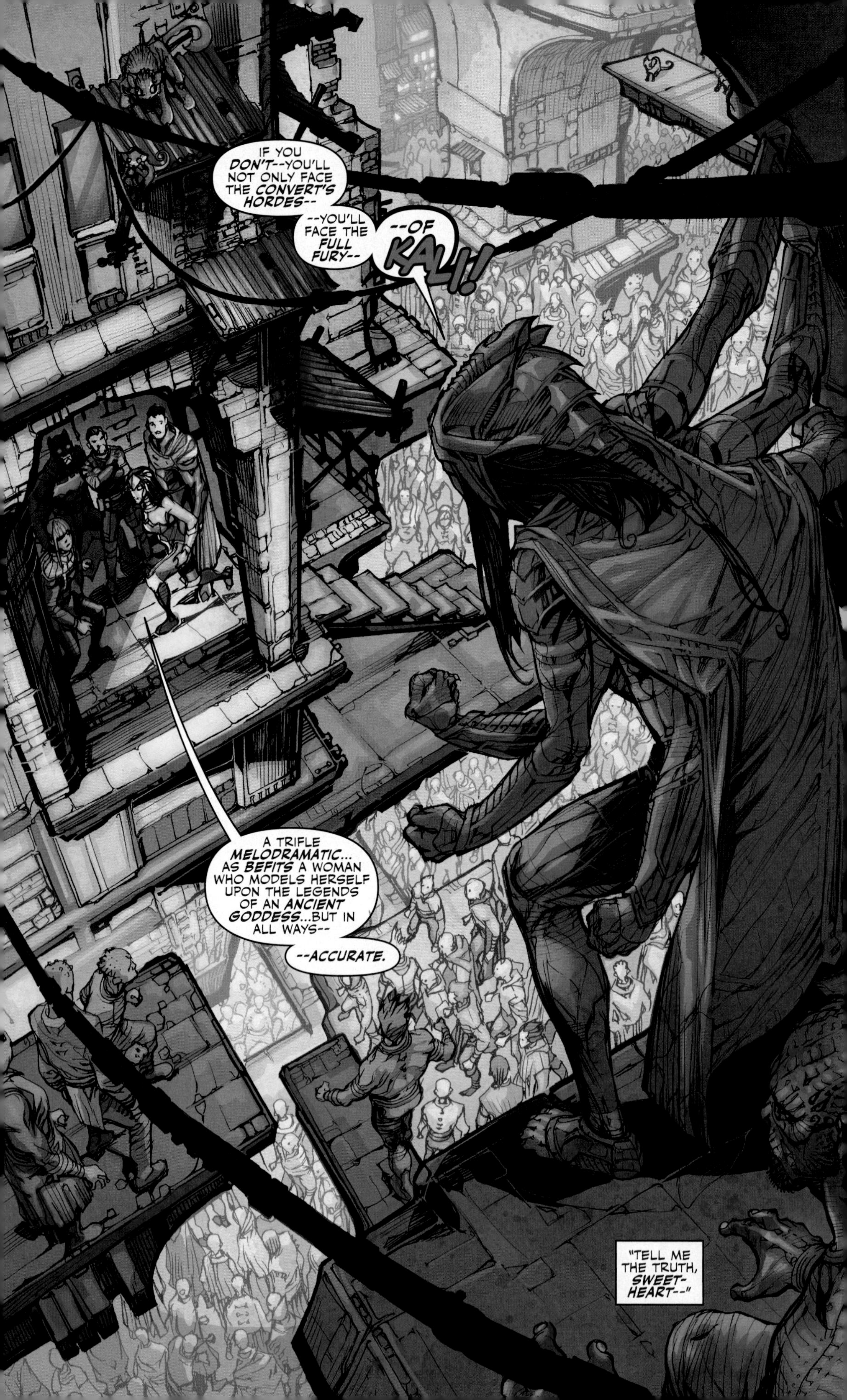
IF YOU DON'T--YOU'LL NOT ONLY FACE THE CONVERT'S HORDES--
--YOU'LL FACE THE FULL FURY--
--OF KALI!
A TRIFLE MELODRAMATIC... AS BEFITS A WOMAN WHO MODELS HERSELF UPON THE LEGENDS OF AN ANCIENT GODDESS...BUT IN ALL WAYS--
--ACCURATE.
"TELL ME THE TRUTH, SWEET-HEART--"

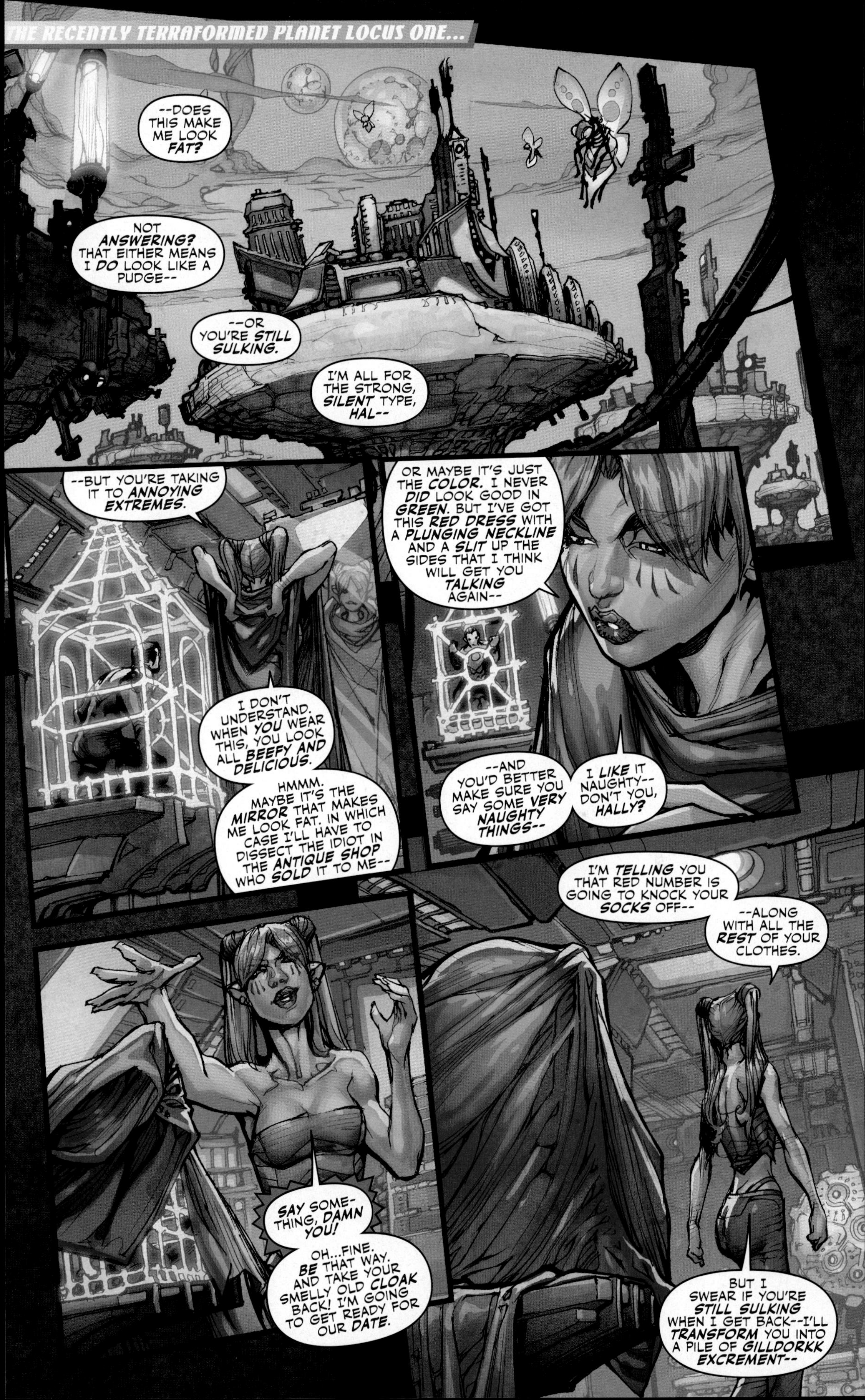
THE RECENTLY TERRAFORMED PLANET LOCUS ONE...
--DOES THIS MAKE ME LOOK FAT?
NOT ANSWERING? THAT EITHER MEANS I DO LOOK LIKE A PUDGE--
--OR YOU'RE STILL SULKING.
I'M ALL FOR THE STRONG, SILENT TYPE, HAL--
--BUT YOU'RE TAKING IT TO ANNOYING EXTREMES.
I DON'T UNDERSTAND. WHEN YOU WEAR THIS, YOU LOOK ALL BEEFY AND DELICIOUS.
HMMM. MAYBE IT'S THE MIRROR THAT MAKES ME LOOK FAT. IN WHICH CASE I'LL HAVE TO DISSECT THE IDIOT IN THE ANTIQUE SHOP WHO SOLD IT TO ME--
OR MAYBE IT'S JUST THE COLOR. I NEVER DID LOOK GOOD IN GREEN. BUT I'VE GOT THIS RED DRESS WITH A PLUNGING NECKLINE AND A SLIT UP THE SIDES THAT I THINK WILL GET YOU TALKING AGAIN--
--AND YOU'D BETTER MAKE SURE YOU SAY SOME VERY NAUGHTY THINGS--
I LIKE IT NAUGHTY--DON'T YOU, HALLY?
SAY SOMETHING, DAMN YOU!
OH...FINE. BE THAT WAY. AND TAKE YOUR SMELLY OLD CLOAK BACK! I'M GOING TO GET READY FOR OUR DATE.
I'M TELLING YOU THAT RED NUMBER IS GOING TO KNOCK YOUR SOCKS OFF--
--ALONG WITH ALL THE REST OF YOUR CLOTHES.
BUT I SWEAR IF YOU'RE STILL SULKING WHEN I GET BACK--I'LL TRANSFORM YOU INTO A PILE OF GILLDORKK EXCREMENT--

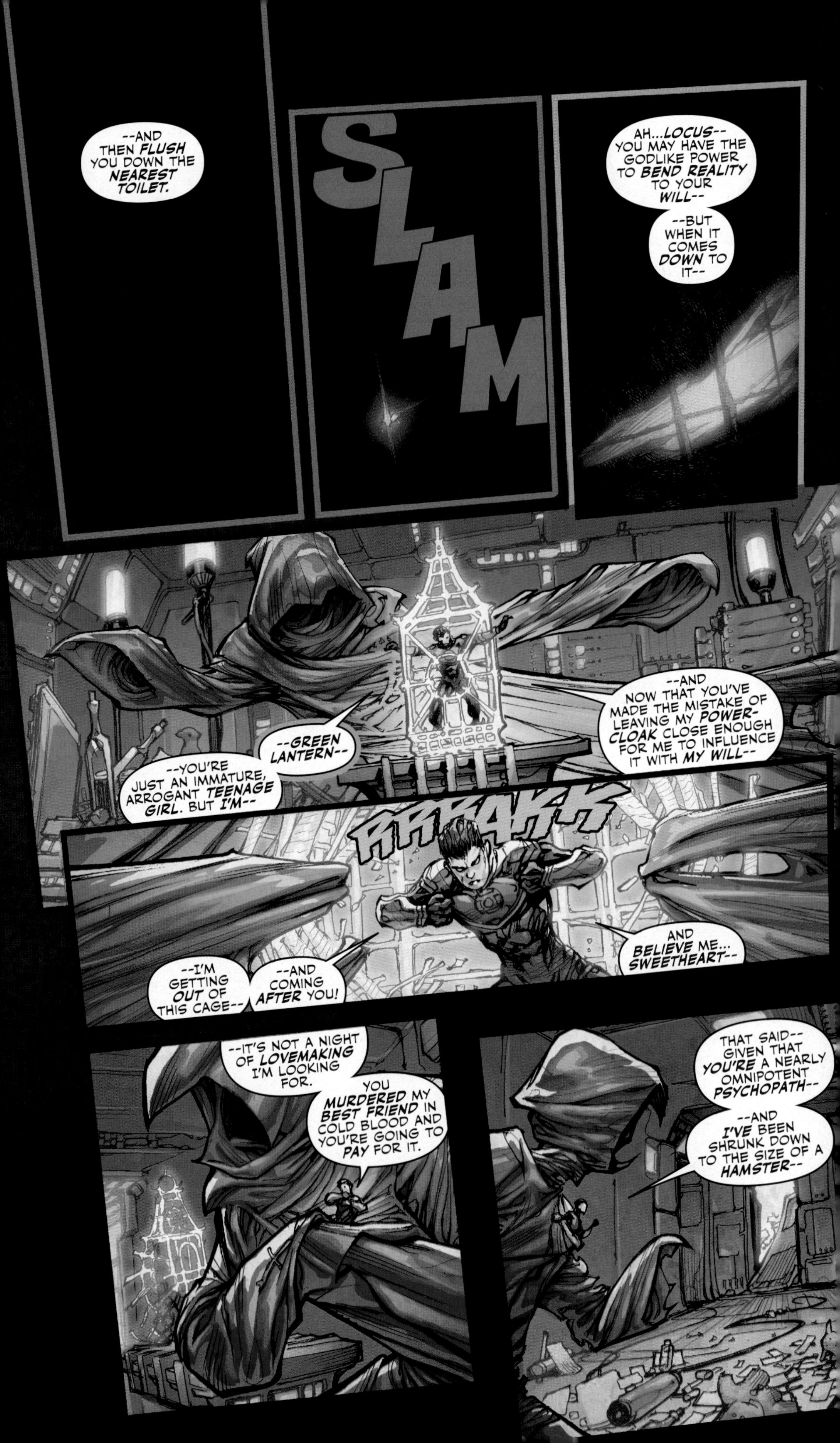
--AND THEN FLUSH YOU DOWN THE NEAREST TOILET.
SLAM
AH...LOCUS-- YOU MAY HAVE THE GODLIKE POWER TO BEND REALITY TO YOUR WILL--
--BUT WHEN IT COMES DOWN TO IT--
--YOU'RE JUST AN IMMATURE, ARROGANT TEENAGE GIRL. BUT I'M--
--GREEN LANTERN--
--AND NOW THAT YOU'VE MADE THE MISTAKE OF LEAVING MY POWER-CLOAK CLOSE ENOUGH FOR ME TO INFLUENCE IT WITH MY WILL--
RRRAKK
--I'M GETTING OUT OF THIS CAGE--
--AND COMING AFTER YOU!
AND BELIEVE ME... SWEETHEART--
--IT'S NOT A NIGHT OF LOVEMAKING I'M LOOKING FOR.
YOU MURDERED MY BEST FRIEND IN COLD BLOOD AND YOU'RE GOING TO PAY FOR IT.
THAT SAID-- GIVEN THAT YOU'RE A NEARLY OMNIPOTENT PSYCHOPATH--
--AND I'VE BEEN SHRUNK DOWN TO THE SIZE OF A HAMSTER--

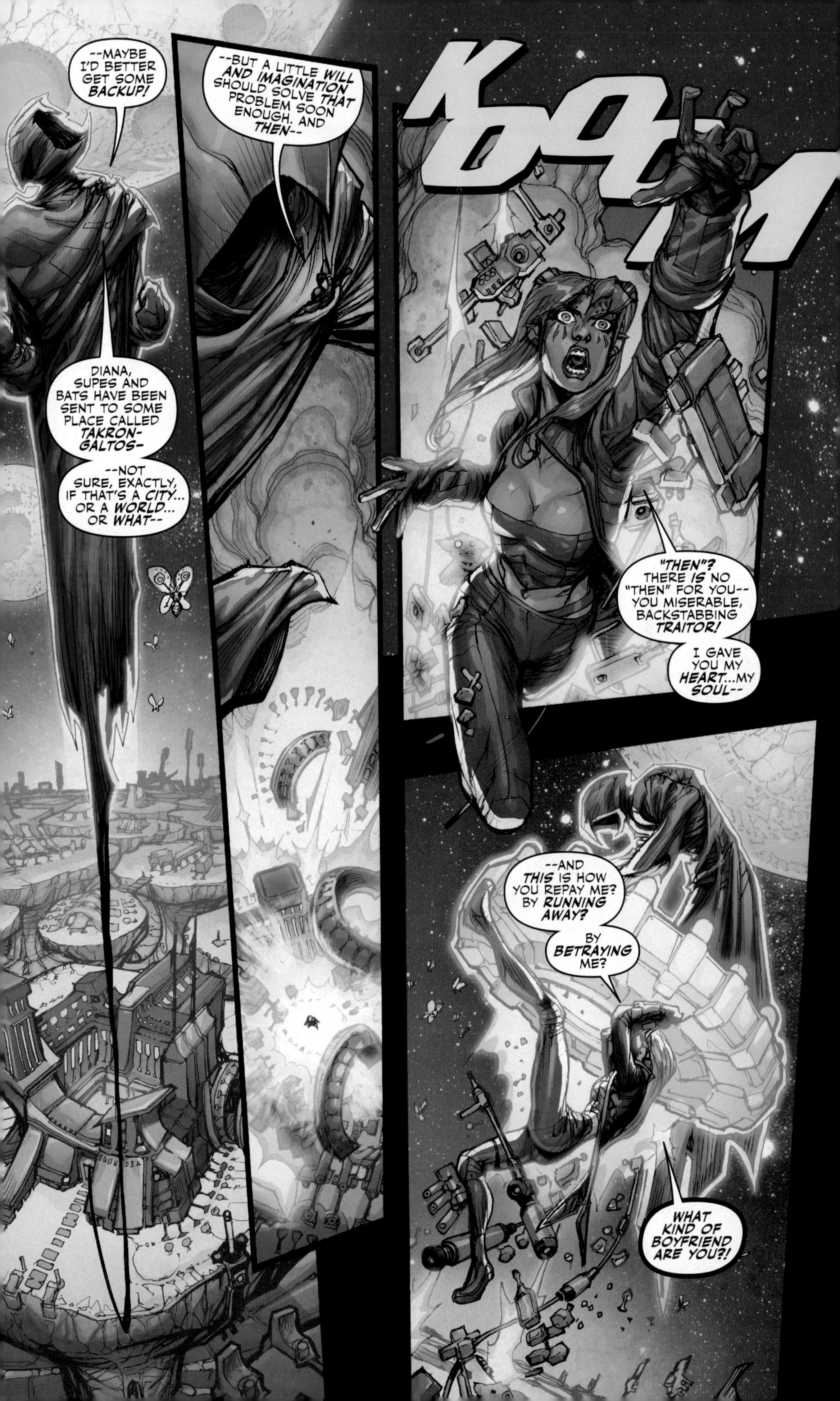
--MAYBE I'D BETTER GET SOME BACKUP!
DIANA, SUPES AND BATS HAVE BEEN SENT TO SOME PLACE CALLED TAKRON-GALTOS-
--NOT SURE, EXACTLY, IF THAT'S A CITY... OR A WORLD... OR WHAT--
--BUT A LITTLE WILL AND IMAGINATION SHOULD SOLVE THAT PROBLEM SOON ENOUGH. AND THEN--
KOOM
"THEN"? THERE IS NO "THEN" FOR YOU--YOU MISERABLE, BACKSTABBING TRAITOR!
I GAVE YOU MY HEART...MY SOUL--
--AND THIS IS HOW YOU REPAY ME? BY RUNNING AWAY?
BY BETRAYING ME?
WHAT KIND OF BOYFRIEND ARE YOU?!

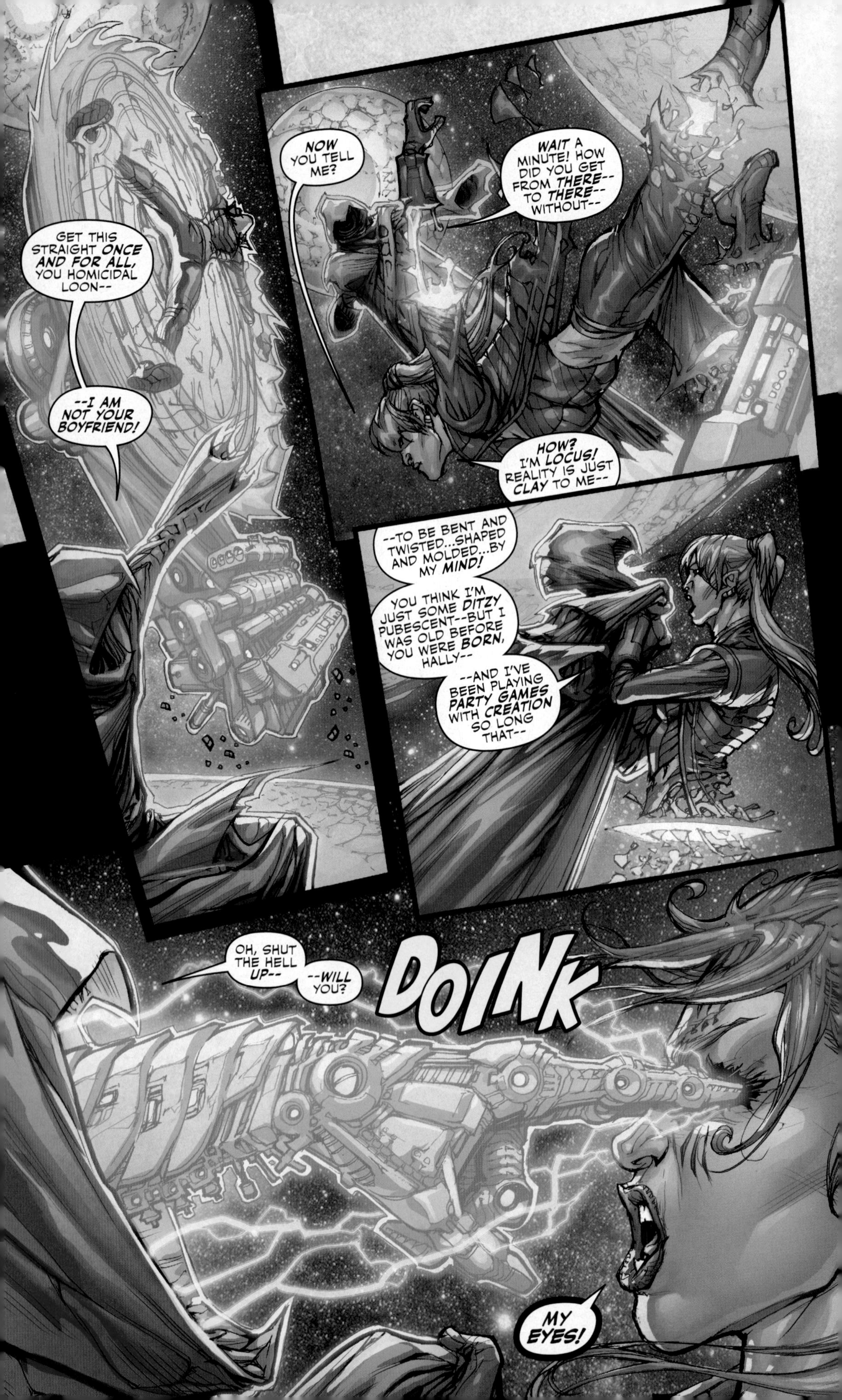
GET THIS STRAIGHT ONCE AND FOR ALL, YOU HOMICIDAL LOON--
--I AM NOT YOUR BOYFRIEND!
NOW YOU TELL ME?
WAIT A MINUTE! HOW DID YOU GET FROM THERE-- TO THERE-- WITHOUT--
HOW? I'M LOCUS! REALITY IS JUST CLAY TO ME--
--TO BE BENT AND TWISTED...SHAPED AND MOLDED...BY MY MIND!
YOU THINK I'M JUST SOME DITZY PUBESCENT--BUT I WAS OLD BEFORE YOU WERE BORN, HALLY--
--AND I'VE BEEN PLAYING PARTY GAMES WITH CREATION SO LONG THAT--
OH, SHUT THE HELL UP--
--WILL YOU?
DOINK
MY EYES!

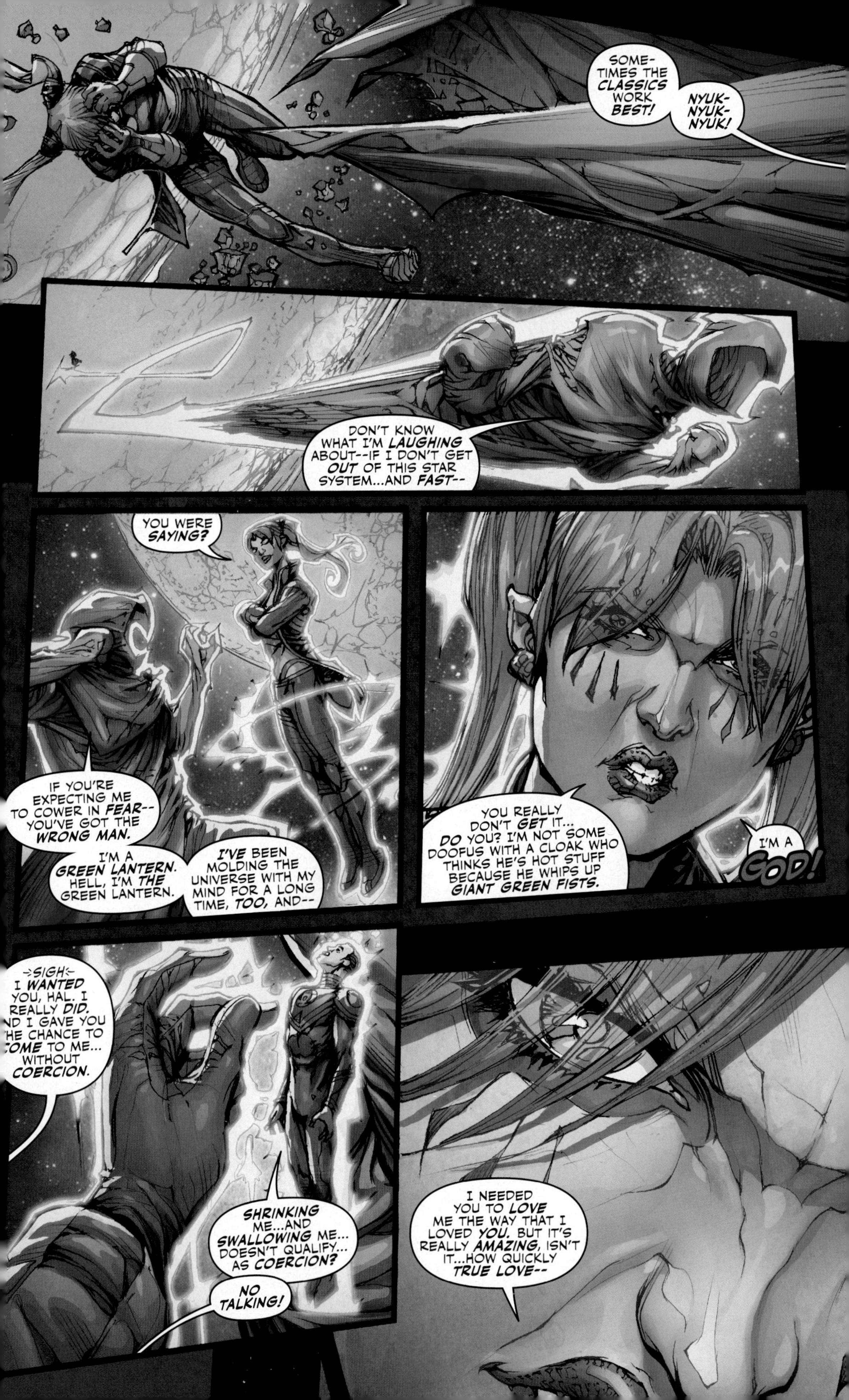
SOMETIMES THE CLASSICS WORK BEST!
NYUK-NYUK-NYUK!
DON'T KNOW WHAT I'M LAUGHING ABOUT--IF I DON'T GET OUT OF THIS STAR SYSTEM...AND FAST--
YOU WERE SAYING?
IF YOU'RE EXPECTING ME TO COWER IN FEAR--YOU'VE GOT THE WRONG MAN.
I'M A GREEN LANTERN. HELL, I'M THE GREEN LANTERN.
I'VE BEEN MOLDING THE UNIVERSE WITH MY MIND FOR A LONG TIME, TOO, AND--
YOU REALLY DON'T GET IT... DO YOU? I'M NOT SOME DOOFUS WITH A CLOAK WHO THINKS HE'S HOT STUFF BECAUSE HE WHIPS UP GIANT GREEN FISTS.
I'M A GOD!
-SIGH- I WANTED YOU, HAL. I REALLY DID. ND I GAVE YOU HE CHANCE TO COME TO ME... WITHOUT COERCION.
SHRINKING ME...AND SWALLOWING ME... DOESN'T QUALIFY... AS COERCION?
NO TALKING!
I NEEDED YOU TO LOVE ME THE WAY THAT I LOVED YOU. BUT IT'S REALLY AMAZING, ISN'T IT...HOW QUICKLY TRUE LOVE--

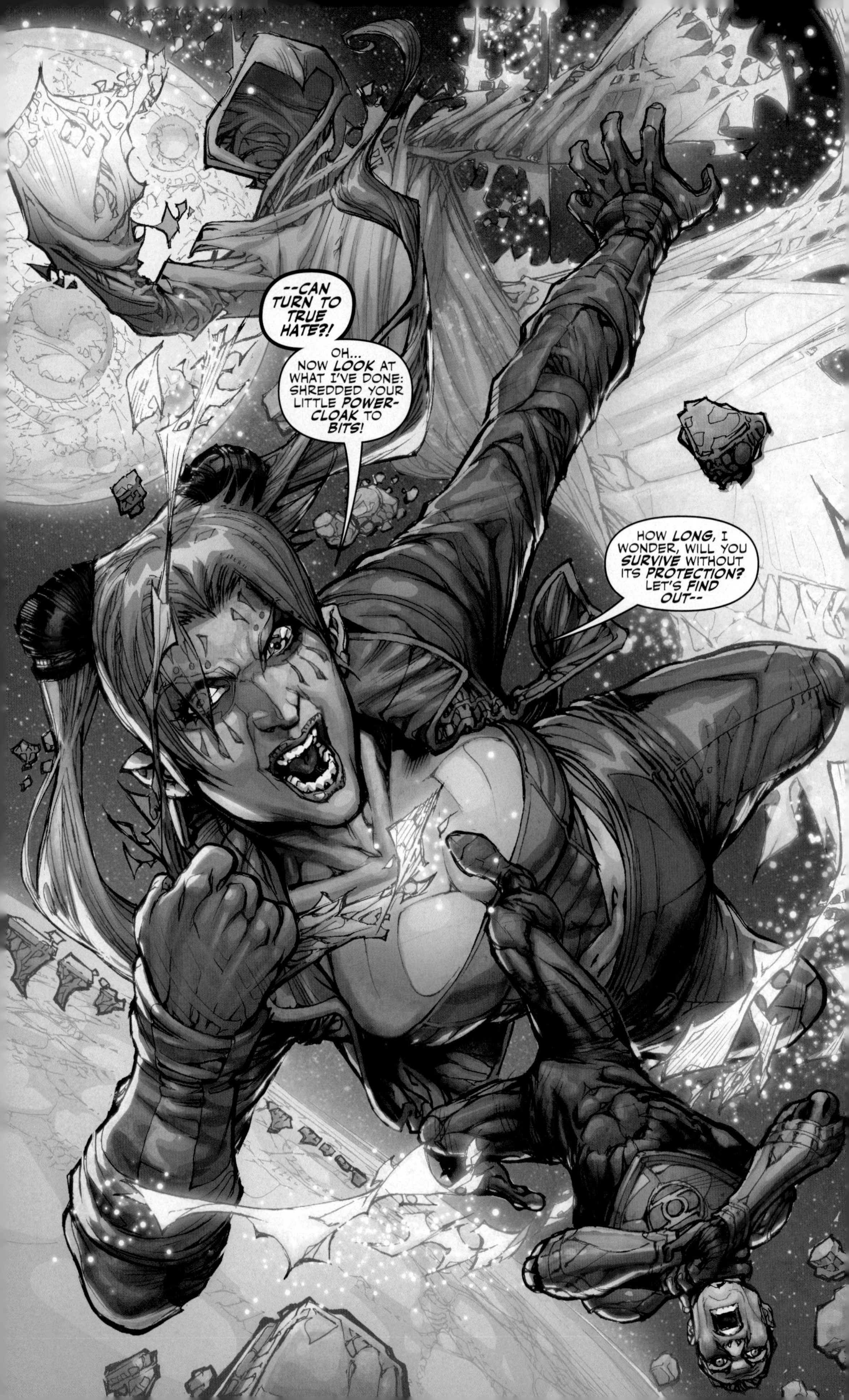

--CAN TURN TO TRUE HATE?!
OH... NOW LOOK AT WHAT I'VE DONE: SHREDDED YOUR LITTLE POWER-CLOAK TO BITS!
HOW LONG, I WONDER, WILL YOU SURVIVE WITHOUT ITS PROTECTION? LET'S FIND OUT--

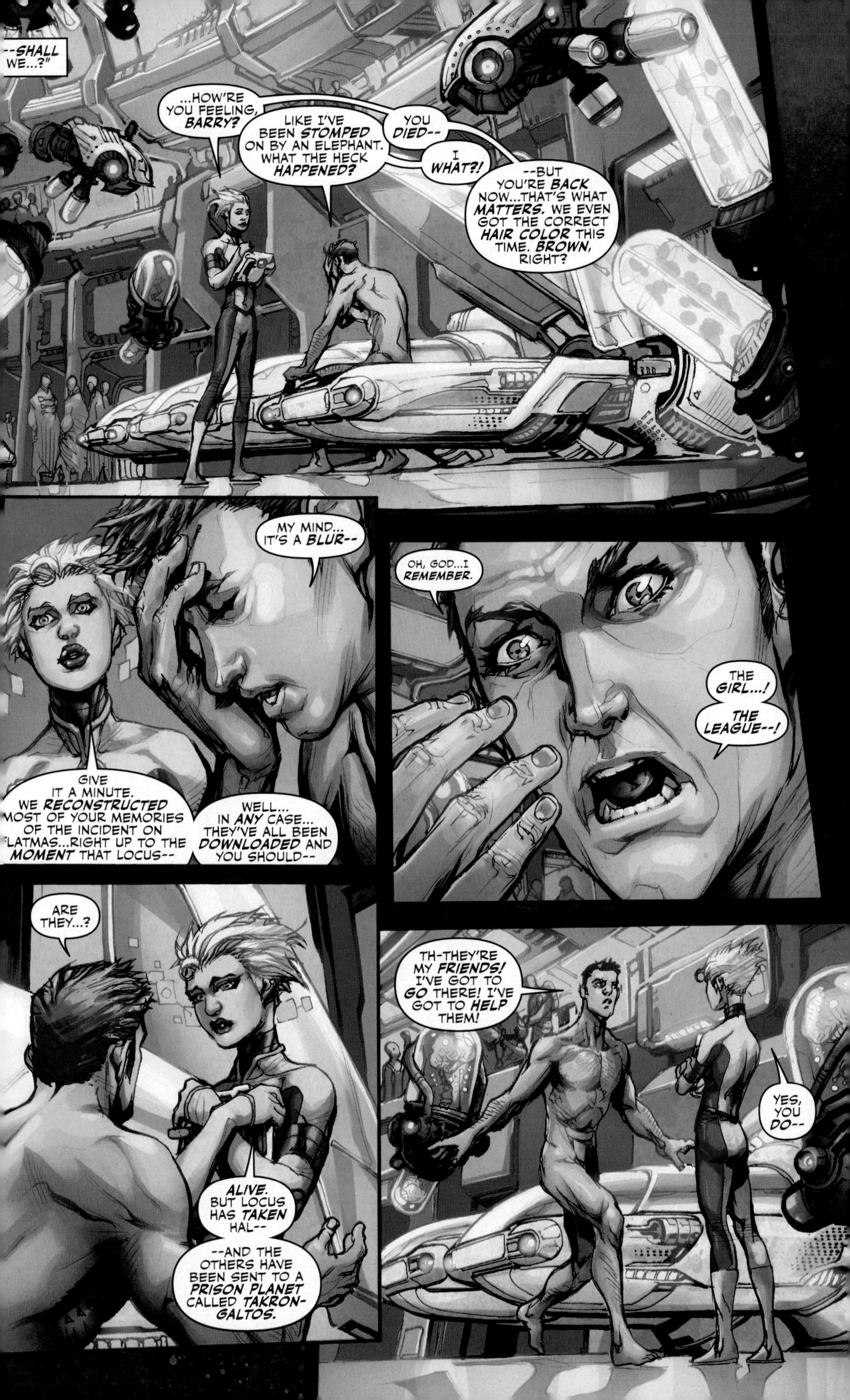
--SHALL WE...?"
...HOW'RE YOU FEELING, BARRY?
LIKE I'VE BEEN STOMPED ON BY AN ELEPHANT. WHAT THE HECK HAPPENED?
YOU DIED--
I WHAT?!
--BUT YOU'RE BACK NOW...THAT'S WHAT MATTERS. WE EVEN GOT THE CORRECT HAIR COLOR THIS TIME. BROWN, RIGHT?
MY MIND... IT'S A BLUR--
GIVE IT A MINUTE. WE RECONSTRUCTED MOST OF YOUR MEMORIES OF THE INCIDENT ON FLATMAS...RIGHT UP TO THE MOMENT THAT LOCUS--
WELL... IN ANY CASE... THEY'VE ALL BEEN DOWNLOADED AND YOU SHOULD--
OH, GOD...I REMEMBER.
THE GIRL...!
THE LEAGUE--!
ARE THEY...?
ALIVE. BUT LOCUS HAS TAKEN HAL--
--AND THE OTHERS HAVE BEEN SENT TO A PRISON PLANET CALLED TAKRON-GALTOS.
TH-THEY'RE MY FRIENDS! I'VE GOT TO GO THERE! I'VE GOT TO HELP THEM!
YES, YOU DO--

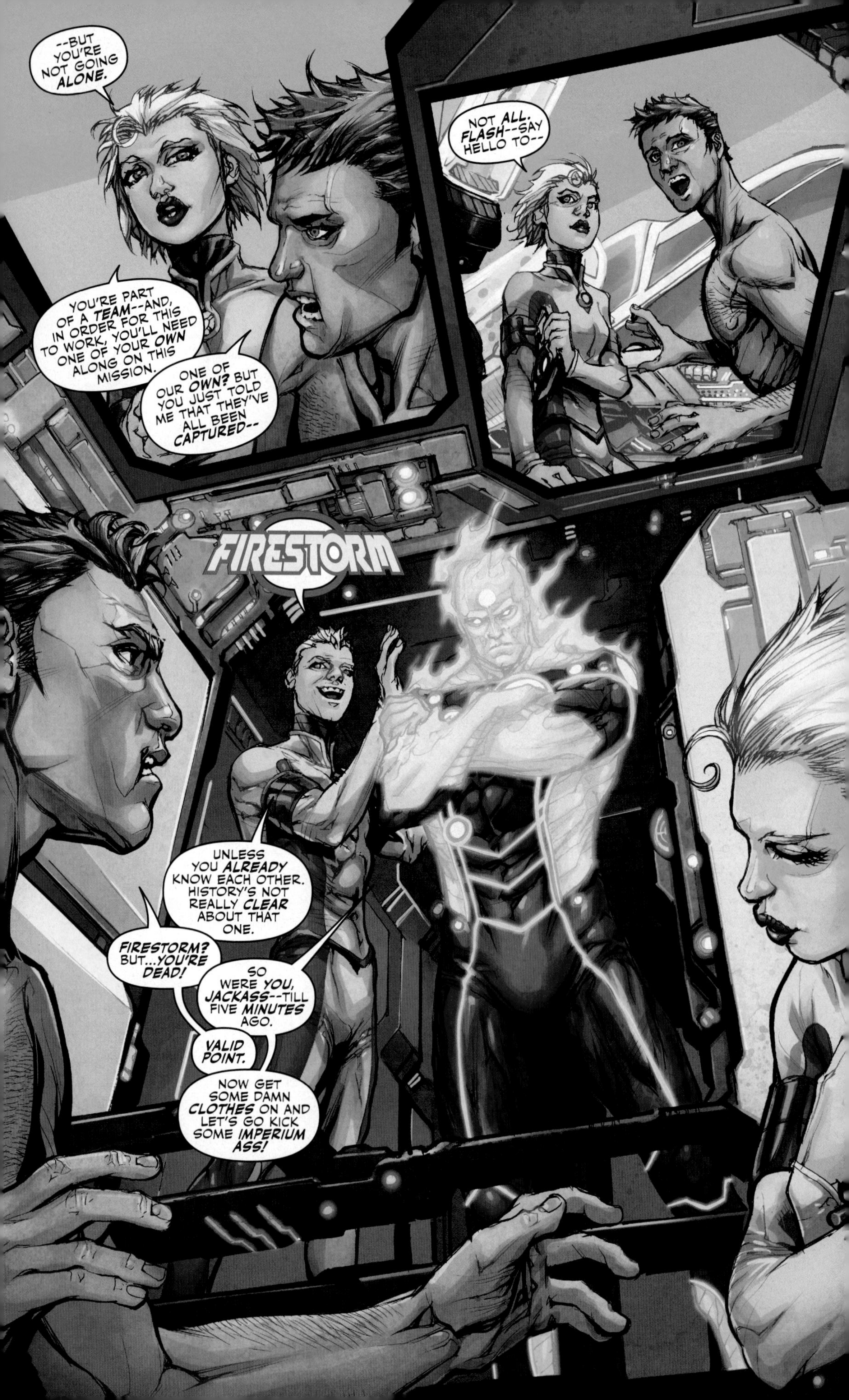
--BUT YOU'RE NOT GOING ALONE.
YOU'RE PART OF A TEAM--AND, IN ORDER FOR THIS TO WORK, YOU'LL NEED ONE OF YOUR OWN ALONG ON THIS MISSION.
ONE OF OUR OWN? BUT YOU JUST TOLD ME THAT THEY'VE ALL BEEN CAPTURED--
NOT ALL. FLASH--SAY HELLO TO--
FIRESTORM
UNLESS YOU ALREADY KNOW EACH OTHER. HISTORY'S NOT REALLY CLEAR ABOUT THAT ONE.
FIRESTORM? BUT...YOU'RE DEAD!
SO WERE YOU, JACKASS--TILL FIVE MINUTES AGO.
VALID POINT.
NOW GET SOME DAMN CLOTHES ON AND LET'S GO KICK SOME IMPERIUM ASS!

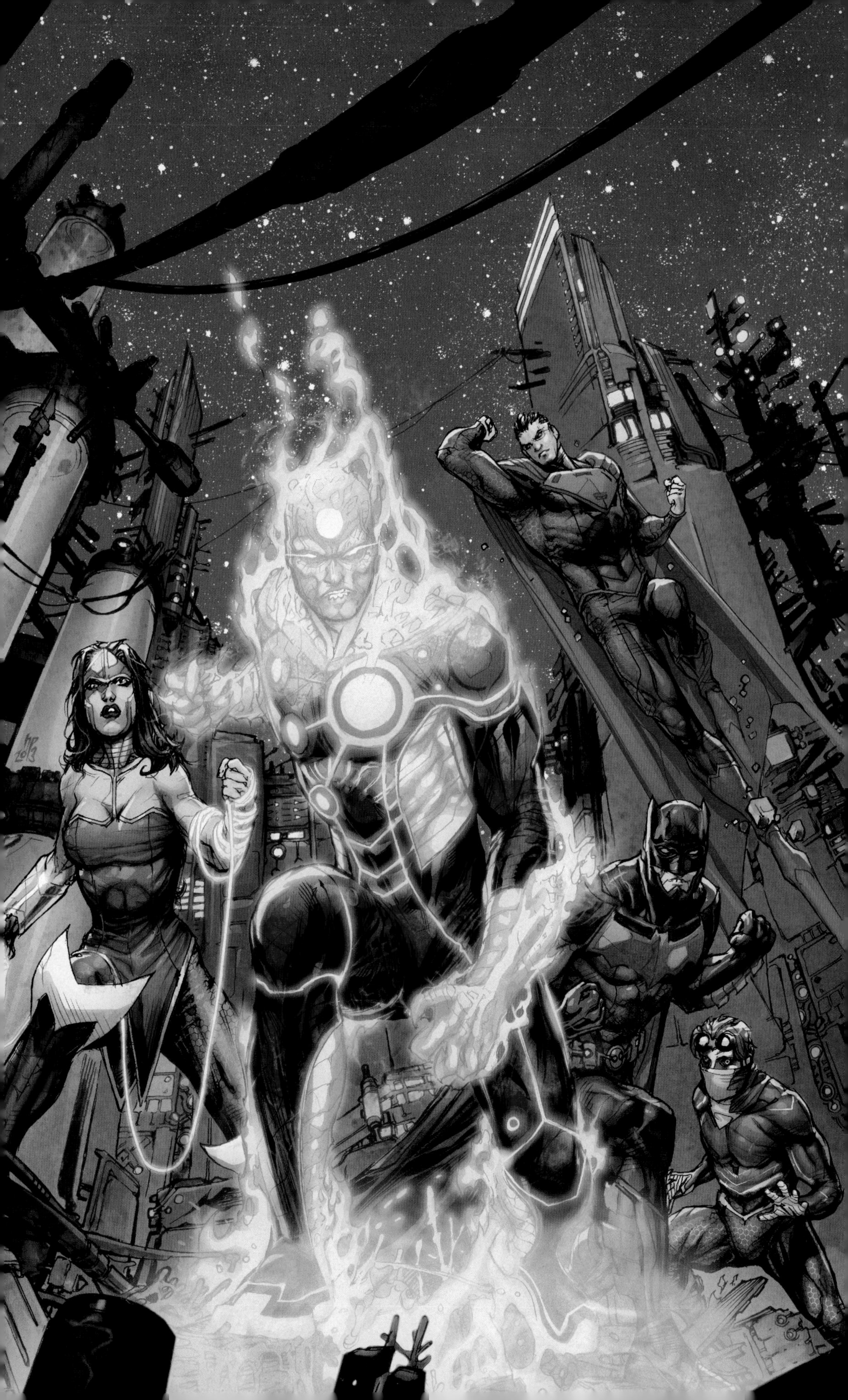

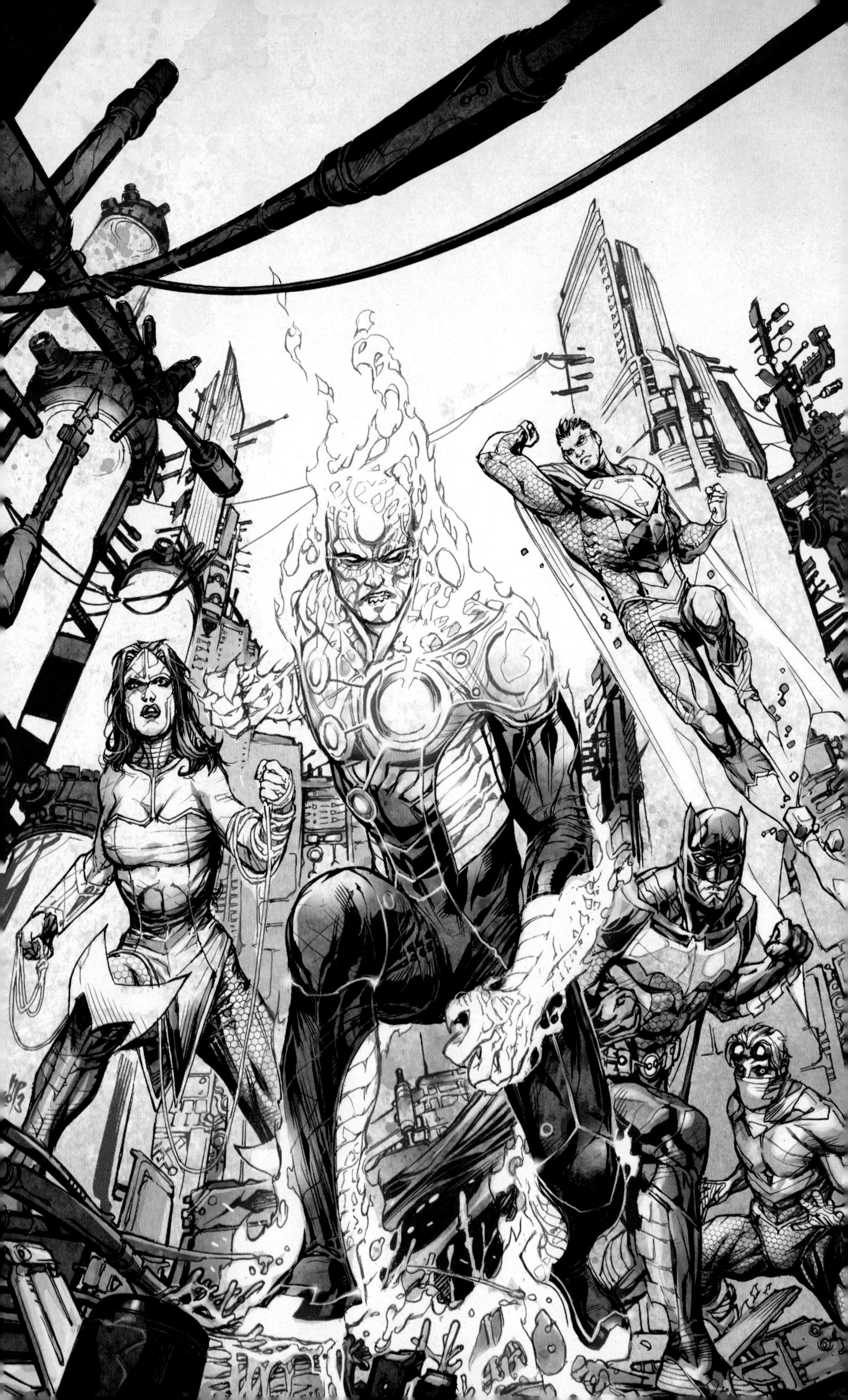

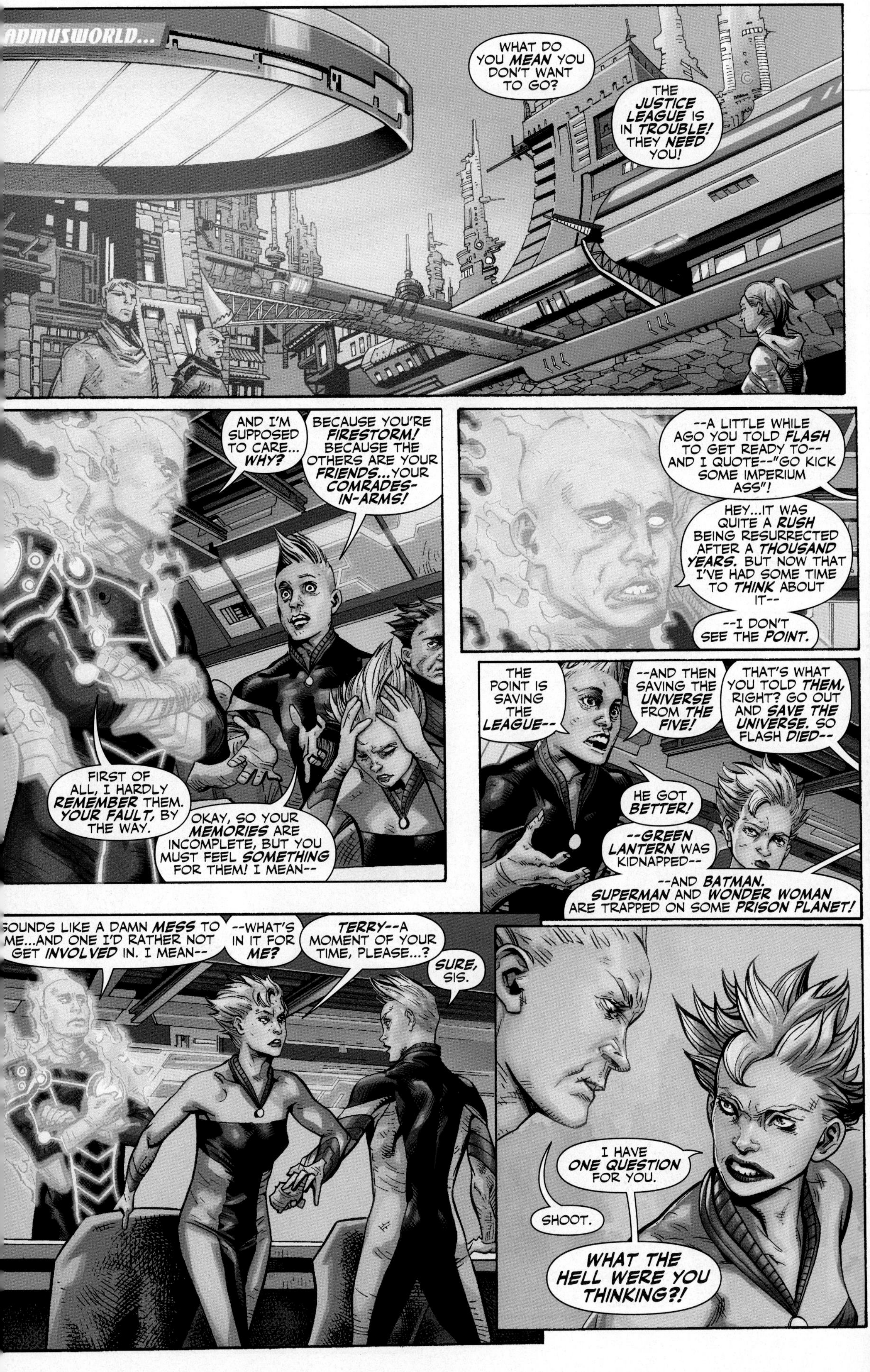
ADMUSWORLD...
WHAT DO YOU MEAN YOU DON'T WANT TO GO?
THE JUSTICE LEAGUE IS IN TROUBLE! THEY NEED YOU!
AND I'M SUPPOSED TO CARE... WHY?
BECAUSE YOU'RE FIRESTORM! BECAUSE THE OTHERS ARE YOUR FRIENDS...YOUR COMRADES-IN-ARMS!
FIRST OF ALL, I HARDLY REMEMBER THEM. YOUR FAULT, BY THE WAY.
OKAY, SO YOUR MEMORIES ARE INCOMPLETE, BUT YOU MUST FEEL SOMETHING FOR THEM! I MEAN--
--A LITTLE WHILE AGO YOU TOLD FLASH TO GET READY TO--AND I QUOTE--"GO KICK SOME IMPERIUM ASS"!
HEY...IT WAS QUITE A RUSH BEING RESURRECTED AFTER A THOUSAND YEARS. BUT NOW THAT I'VE HAD SOME TIME TO THINK ABOUT IT--
--I DON'T SEE THE POINT.
THE POINT IS SAVING THE LEAGUE--
--AND THEN SAVING THE UNIVERSE FROM THE FIVE!
THAT'S WHAT YOU TOLD THEM, RIGHT? GO OUT AND SAVE THE UNIVERSE. SO FLASH DIED--
HE GOT BETTER!
--GREEN LANTERN WAS KIDNAPPED--
--AND BATMAN, SUPERMAN AND WONDER WOMAN ARE TRAPPED ON SOME PRISON PLANET!
SOUNDS LIKE A DAMN MESS TO ME...AND ONE I'D RATHER NOT GET INVOLVED IN. I MEAN--
--WHAT'S IN IT FOR ME?
TERRY--A MOMENT OF YOUR TIME, PLEASE...?
SURE, SIS.
I HAVE ONE QUESTION FOR YOU.
SHOOT.
WHAT THE HELL WERE YOU THINKING?!

DON'T WORRY, *TERI*-- WE'LL MAKE A FEW *ADJUSTMENTS* AND HE'LL--

WHEN WE REGENERATED THE *OTHERS*, THERE WERE *MASSIVE* GAPS IN THEIR MEMORIES! THEIR PERSONALITIES WERE DISTORTED... *CORRUPTED!*

HOW COULD YOU *POSSIBLY* THINK YOU'D SUCCEED IN REGENERATING A BEING WITH *TWO* PERSONALITIES--

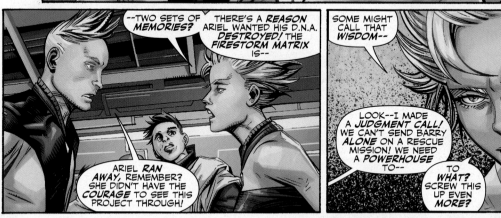

--TWO SETS OF *MEMORIES?*

THERE'S A *REASON* ARIEL WANTED HIS D.N.A. *DESTROYED!* THE FIRESTORM MATRIX IS--

ARIEL *RAN AWAY,* REMEMBER? SHE DIDN'T HAVE THE *COURAGE* TO SEE THIS PROJECT THROUGH!

SOME MIGHT CALL THAT *WISDOM*--

LOOK--I MADE A *JUDGMENT CALL!* WE CAN'T SEND BARRY *ALONE* ON A RESCUE MISSION! WE NEED A *POWERHOUSE* TO--

TO *WHAT?* *SCREW* THIS UP EVEN *MORE?*

Y'KNOW, I'M GETTING *AWFULLY* TIRED OF ALL THIS *ARGUING.* IF YOU DON'T WANT TO STAY WITH THE PROJECT, JUST GO TO THE *CADMUS BOARD* AND--

AND LEAVE *YOU* IN CHARGE? *HELL,* NO. I'VE BEEN PULLING YOUR FAT OUT OF THE *FIRE* SINCE WE WERE KIDS AND--

YOU'RE *STILL* KIDS. AND *GOD* KNOWS YOU'RE *ACTING* LIKE IT.

I GUESS BEING A *GENIUS* AND REACHING SOME LEVEL OF *EMOTIONAL MATURITY* DON'T NECESSARILY GO HAND-IN-HAND--

BARRY! HOW ARE YOU *FEELING?*

ANNOYED. I COME BACK FROM THE DEAD...*AGAIN*...READY TO GO OUT THERE AND RESCUE MY FRIENDS-- AND WHAT DO I *FIND?*

YOU TWO ACTING LIKE A COUPLE OF *PRE-SCHOOLERS* FIGHTING OVER THEIR *BLOCKS!*

SHE STARTED IT!

HE STARTED IT!

≈SIGH≈ DO ME A *FAVOR,* WILL YOU? IF I HAPPEN TO DIE *AGAIN*--

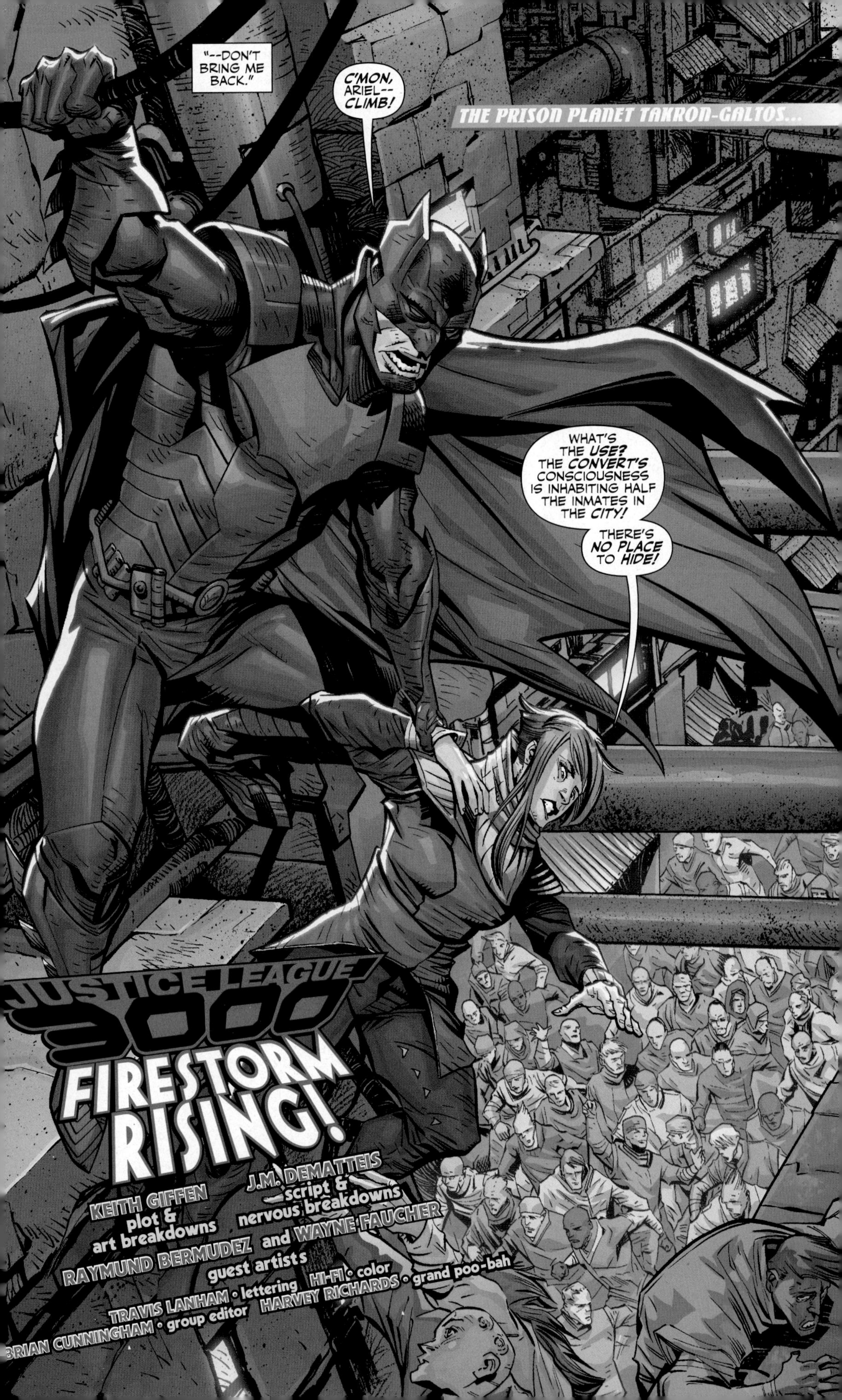

"--DON'T BRING ME BACK."
C'MON, ARIEL-- CLIMB!
THE PRISON PLANET TAKRON-GALTOS...
WHAT'S THE USE? THE CONVERT'S CONSCIOUSNESS IS INHABITING HALF THE INMATES IN THE CITY!
THERE'S NO PLACE TO HIDE!
JUSTICE LEAGUE 3000
FIRESTORM RISING!
KEITH GIFFEN plot & art breakdowns
J.M. DEMATTEIS script & nervous breakdowns
RAYMUND BERMUDEZ and WAYNE FAUCHER guest artists
TRAVIS LANHAM • lettering
HI-FI • color
HARVEY RICHARDS • grand poo-bah
BRIAN CUNNINGHAM • group editor

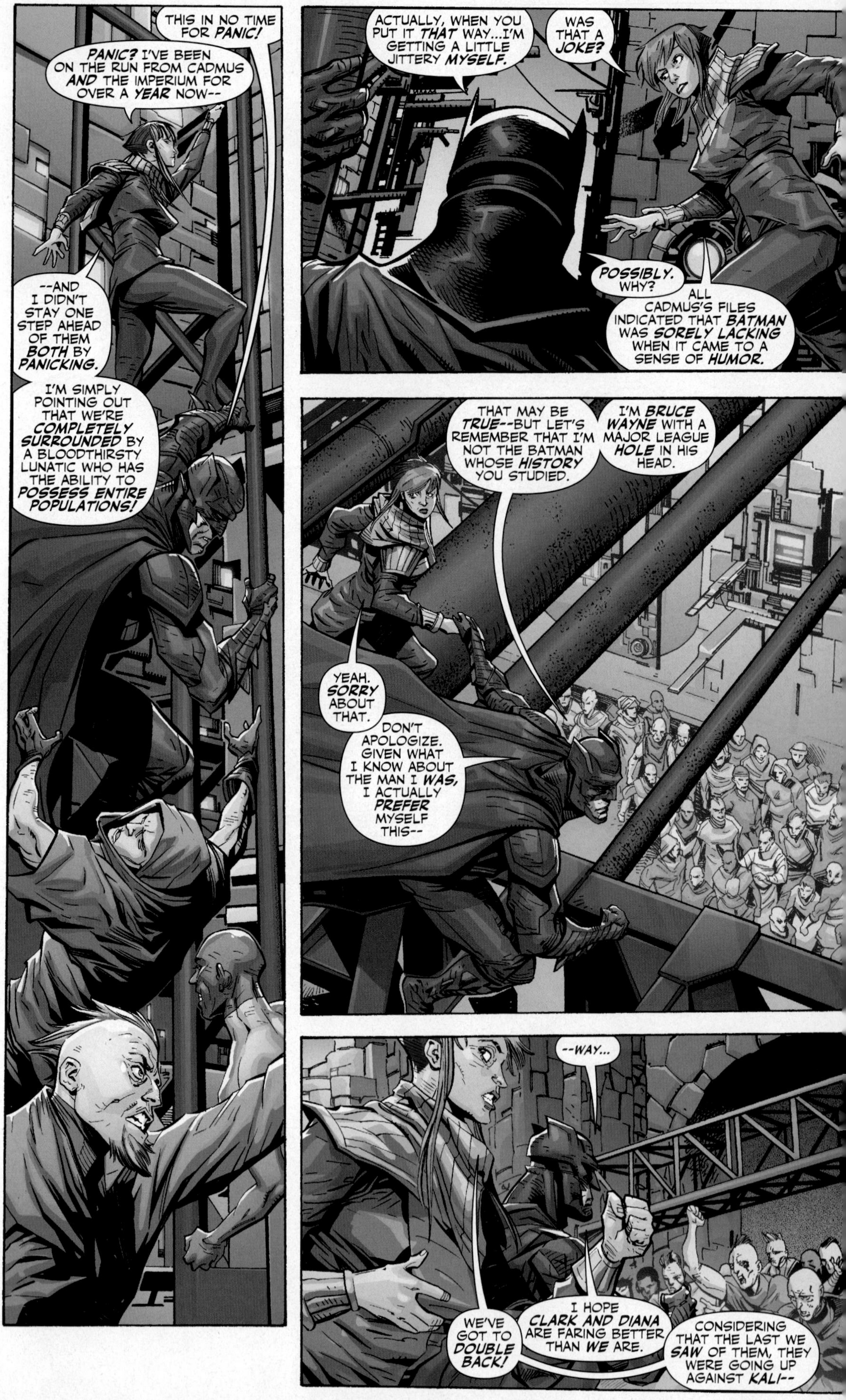
THIS IN NO TIME FOR PANIC!
PANIC? I'VE BEEN ON THE RUN FROM CADMUS AND THE IMPERIUM FOR OVER A YEAR NOW--
--AND I DIDN'T STAY ONE STEP AHEAD OF THEM BOTH BY PANICKING.
I'M SIMPLY POINTING OUT THAT WE'RE COMPLETELY SURROUNDED BY A BLOODTHIRSTY LUNATIC WHO HAS THE ABILITY TO POSSESS ENTIRE POPULATIONS!
ACTUALLY, WHEN YOU PUT IT THAT WAY...I'M GETTING A LITTLE JITTERY MYSELF.
WAS THAT A JOKE?
POSSIBLY. WHY?
ALL CADMUS'S FILES INDICATED THAT BATMAN WAS SORELY LACKING WHEN IT CAME TO A SENSE OF HUMOR.
THAT MAY BE TRUE--BUT LET'S REMEMBER THAT I'M NOT THE BATMAN WHOSE HISTORY YOU STUDIED.
I'M BRUCE WAYNE WITH A MAJOR LEAGUE HOLE IN HIS HEAD.
YEAH. SORRY ABOUT THAT.
DON'T APOLOGIZE. GIVEN WHAT I KNOW ABOUT THE MAN I WAS, I ACTUALLY PREFER MYSELF THIS--
--WAY...
WE'VE GOT TO DOUBLE BACK!
I HOPE CLARK AND DIANA ARE FARING BETTER THAN WE ARE.
CONSIDERING THAT THE LAST WE SAW OF THEM, THEY WERE GOING UP AGAINST KALI--

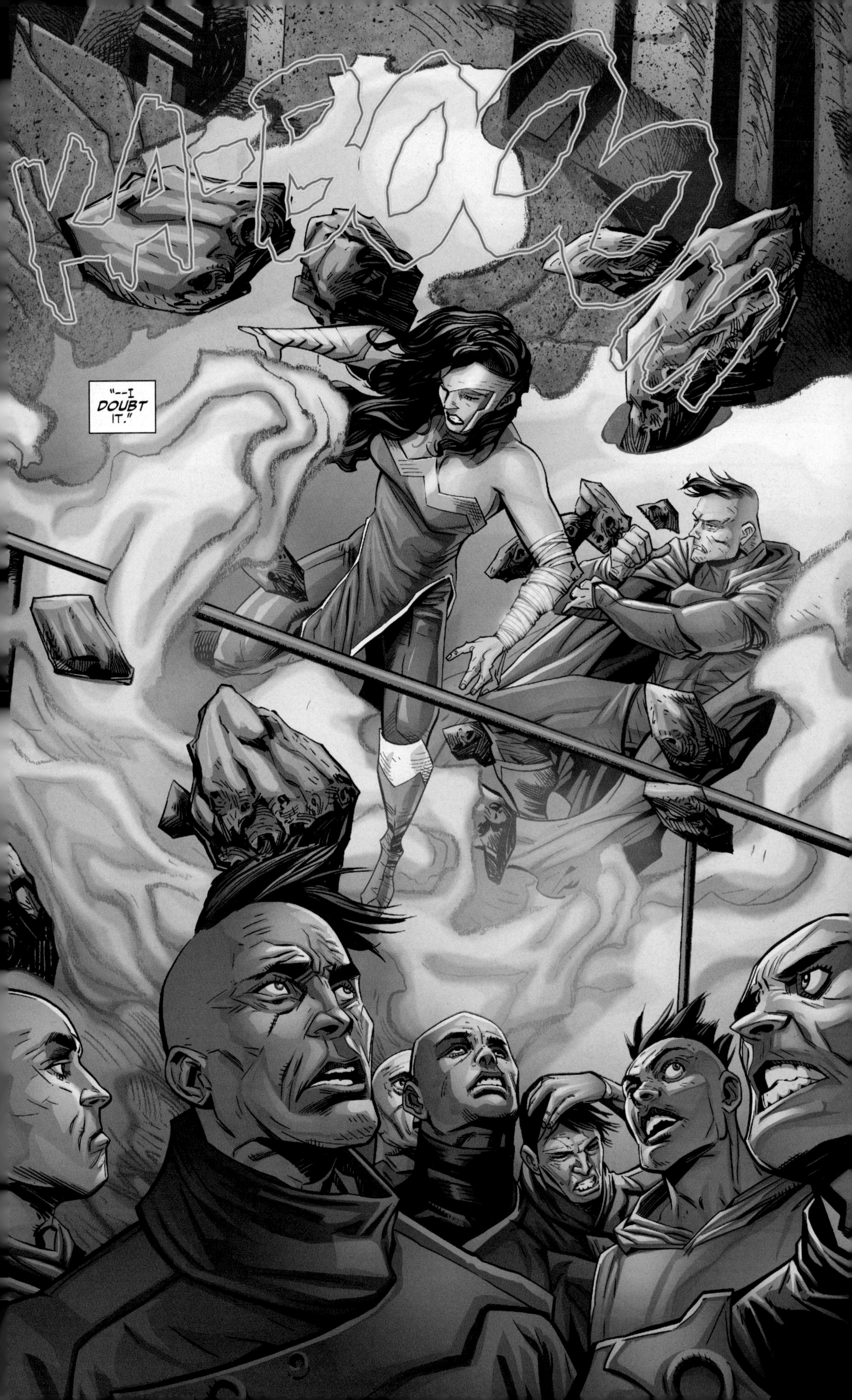
KA-BOOOM
"--I DOUBT IT."

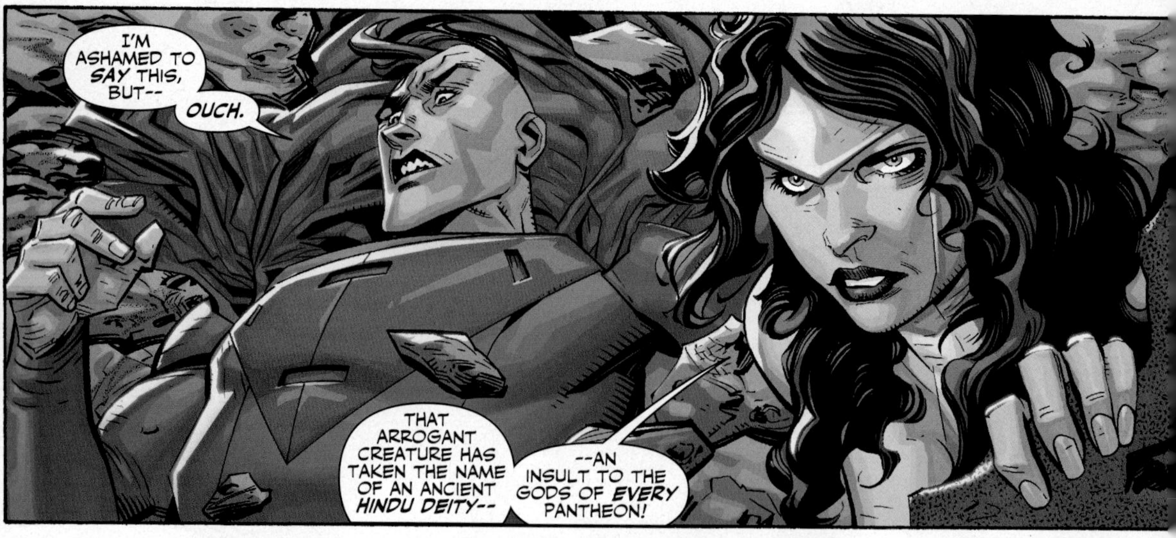
I'M ASHAMED TO SAY THIS, BUT--
OUCH.
THAT ARROGANT CREATURE HAS TAKEN THE NAME OF AN ANCIENT HINDU DEITY--
--AN INSULT TO THE GODS OF EVERY PANTHEON!

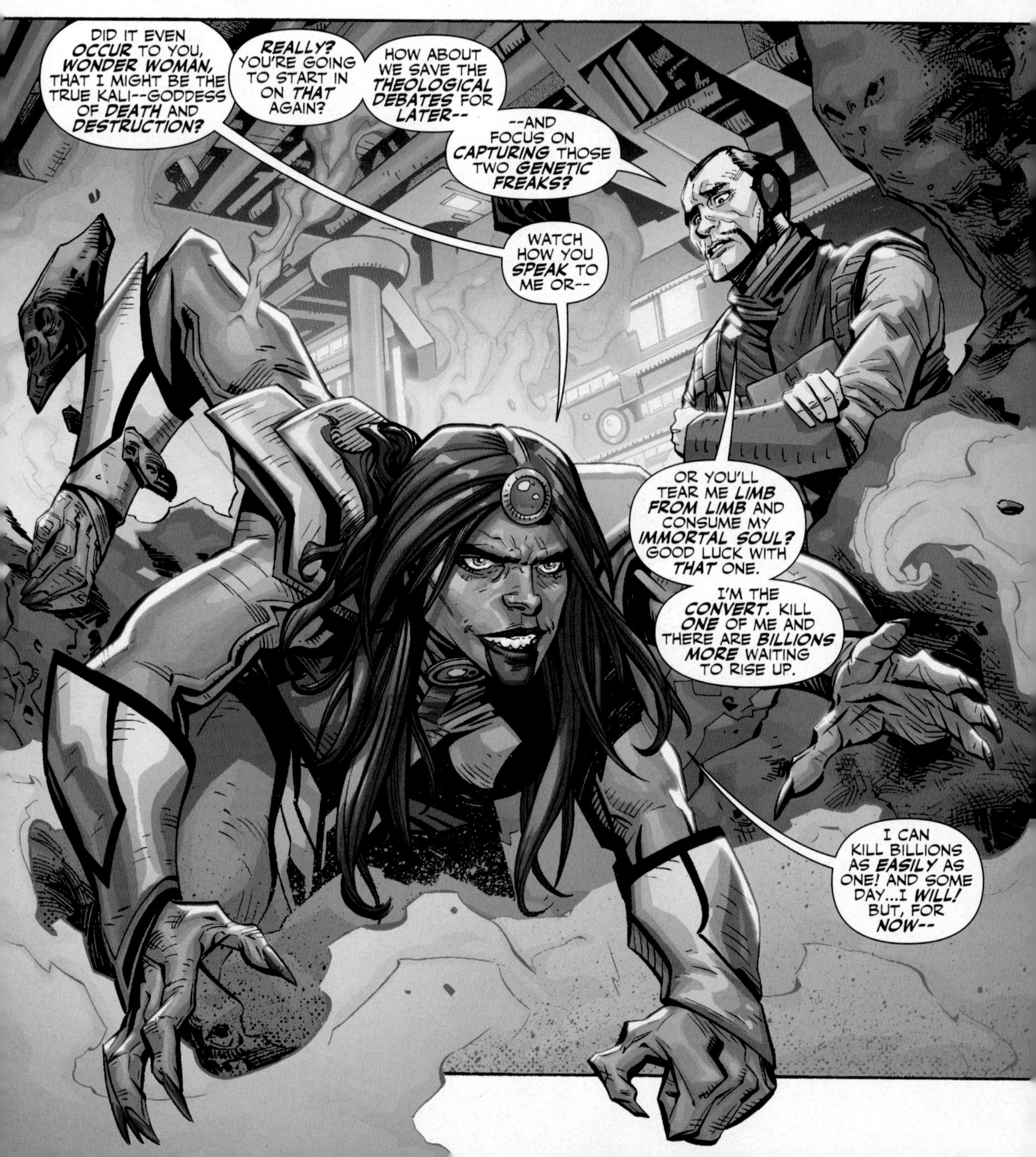
DID IT EVEN OCCUR TO YOU, WONDER WOMAN, THAT I MIGHT BE THE TRUE KALI--GODDESS OF DEATH AND DESTRUCTION?
REALLY? YOU'RE GOING TO START IN ON THAT AGAIN?
HOW ABOUT WE SAVE THE THEOLOGICAL DEBATES FOR LATER--
--AND FOCUS ON CAPTURING THOSE TWO GENETIC FREAKS?
WATCH HOW YOU SPEAK TO ME OR--
OR YOU'LL TEAR ME LIMB FROM LIMB AND CONSUME MY IMMORTAL SOUL? GOOD LUCK WITH THAT ONE.
I'M THE CONVERT. KILL ONE OF ME AND THERE ARE BILLIONS MORE WAITING TO RISE UP.
I CAN KILL BILLIONS AS EASILY AS ONE! AND SOME DAY...I WILL! BUT, FOR NOW--

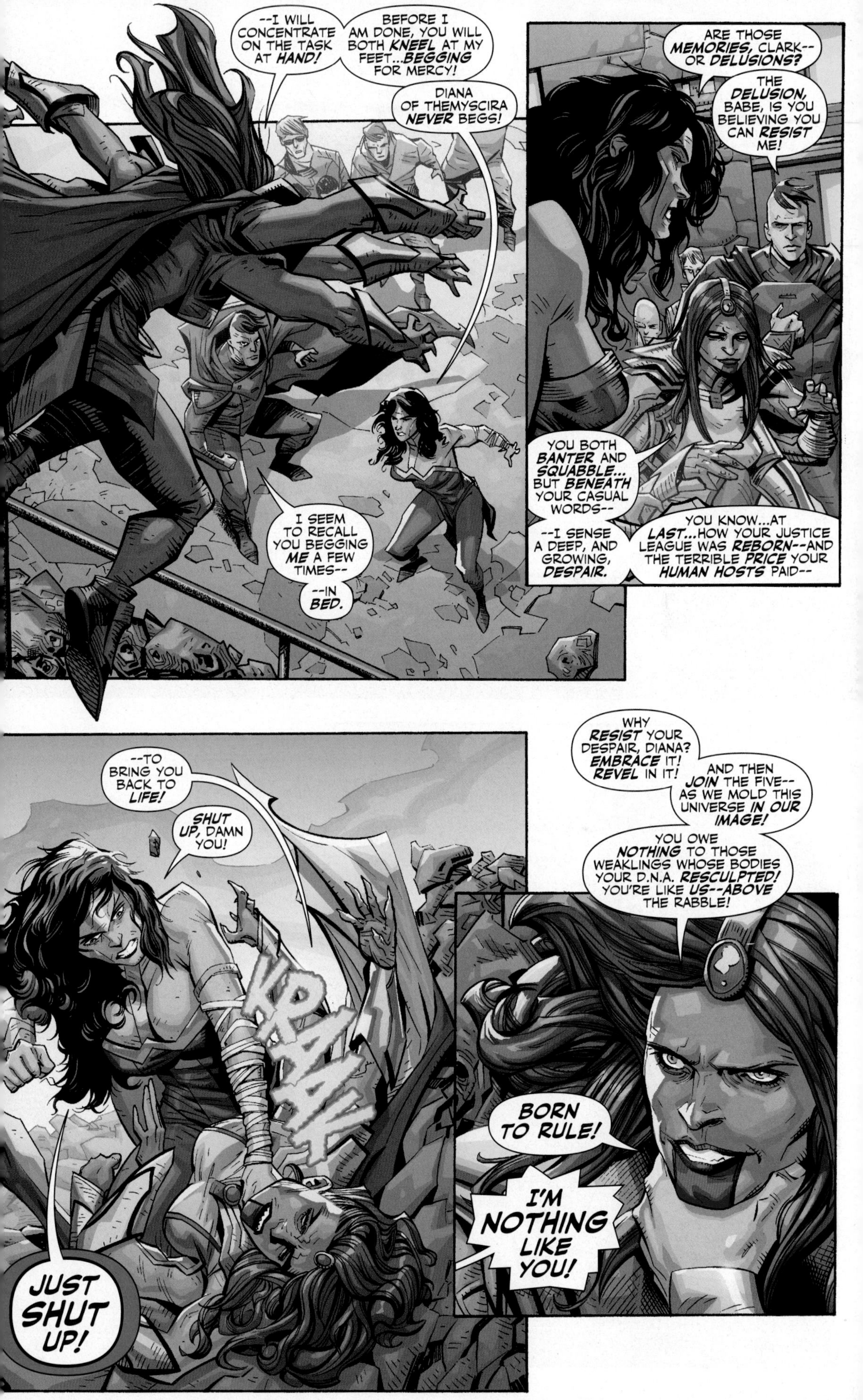
--I WILL CONCENTRATE ON THE TASK AT HAND!
BEFORE I AM DONE, YOU WILL BOTH KNEEL AT MY FEET...BEGGING FOR MERCY!
DIANA OF THEMYSCIRA NEVER BEGS!
I SEEM TO RECALL YOU BEGGING ME A FEW TIMES--
--IN BED.
ARE THOSE MEMORIES, CLARK-- OR DELUSIONS?
THE DELUSION, BABE, IS YOU BELIEVING YOU CAN RESIST ME!
YOU BOTH BANTER AND SQUABBLE... BUT BENEATH YOUR CASUAL WORDS--
--I SENSE A DEEP, AND GROWING, DESPAIR.
YOU KNOW...AT LAST...HOW YOUR JUSTICE LEAGUE WAS REBORN--AND THE TERRIBLE PRICE YOUR HUMAN HOSTS PAID--
--TO BRING YOU BACK TO LIFE!
SHUT UP, DAMN YOU!
KRAAK
JUST SHUT UP!
WHY RESIST YOUR DESPAIR, DIANA? EMBRACE IT! REVEL IN IT!
AND THEN JOIN THE FIVE-- AS WE MOLD THIS UNIVERSE IN OUR IMAGE!
YOU OWE NOTHING TO THOSE WEAKLINGS WHOSE BODIES YOUR D.N.A. RESCULPTED! YOU'RE LIKE US--ABOVE THE RABBLE!
BORN TO RULE!
I'M NOTHING LIKE YOU!

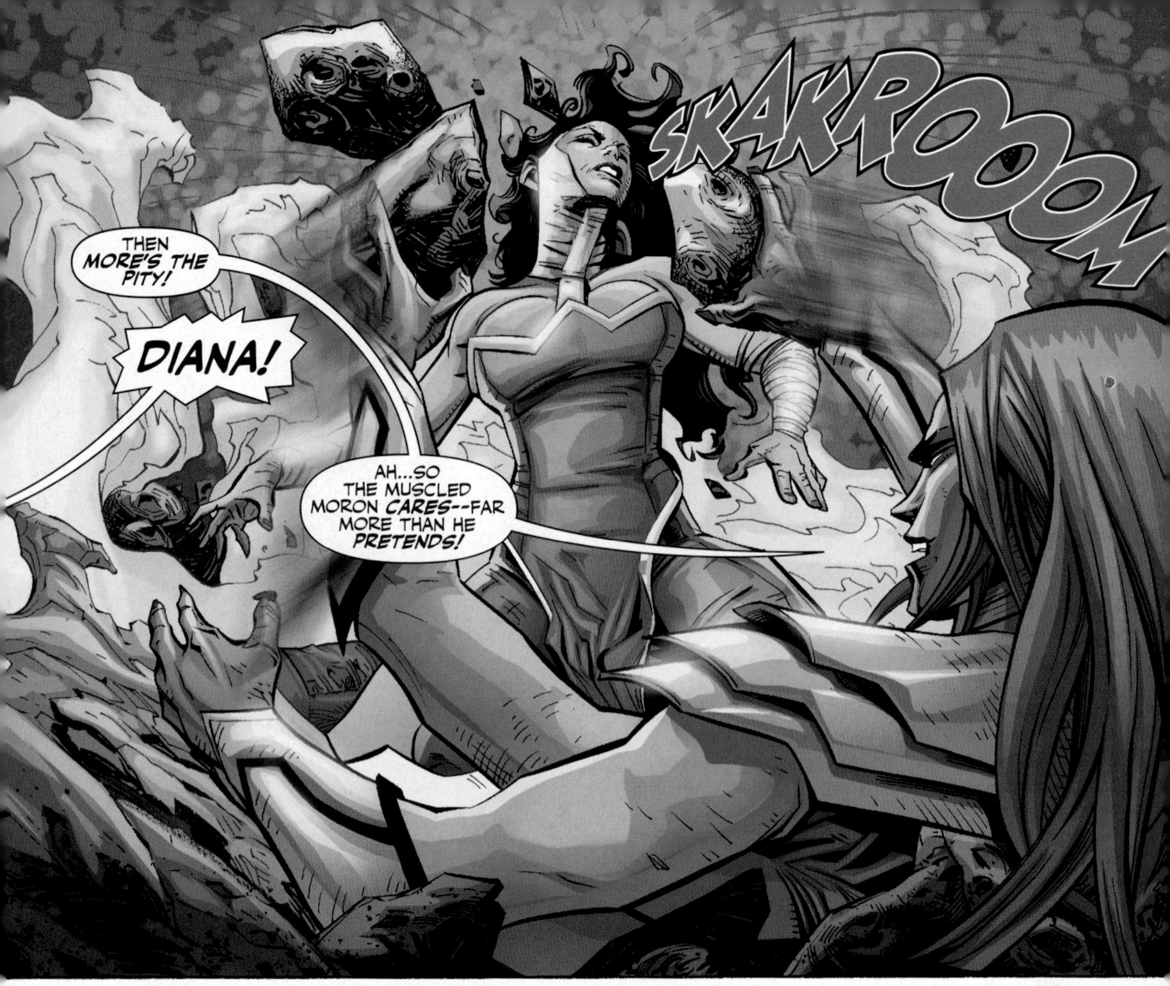
SKAKROOOM
THEN MORE'S THE PITY!
DIANA!
AH...SO THE MUSCLED MORON CARES--FAR MORE THAN HE PRETENDS!
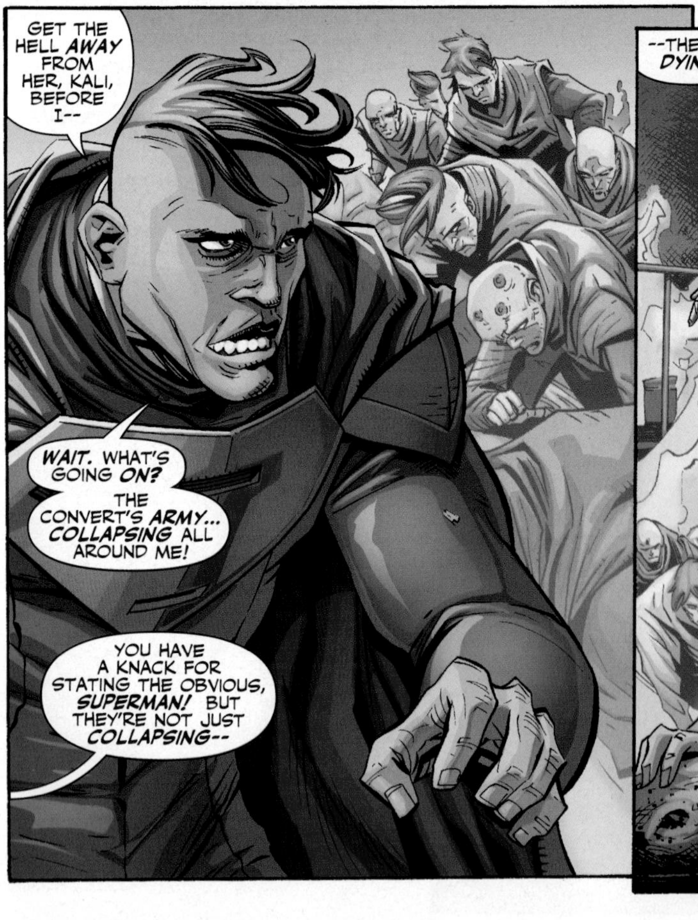
GET THE HELL AWAY FROM HER, KALI, BEFORE I--
WAIT. WHAT'S GOING ON?
THE CONVERT'S ARMY... COLLAPSING ALL AROUND ME!
YOU HAVE A KNACK FOR STATING THE OBVIOUS, SUPERMAN! BUT THEY'RE NOT JUST COLLAPSING--
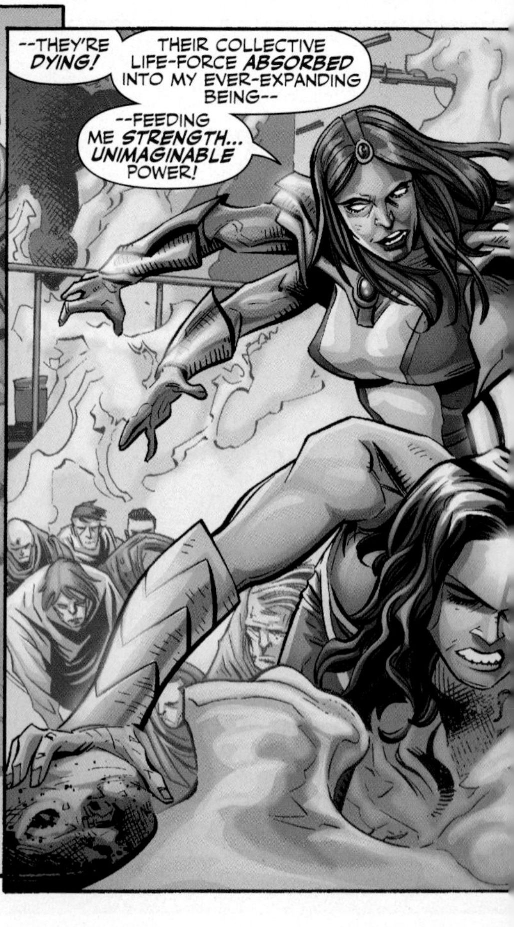
--THEY'RE DYING!
THEIR COLLECTIVE LIFE-FORCE ABSORBED INTO MY EVER-EXPANDING BEING--
--FEEDING ME STRENGTH... UNIMAGINABLE POWER!

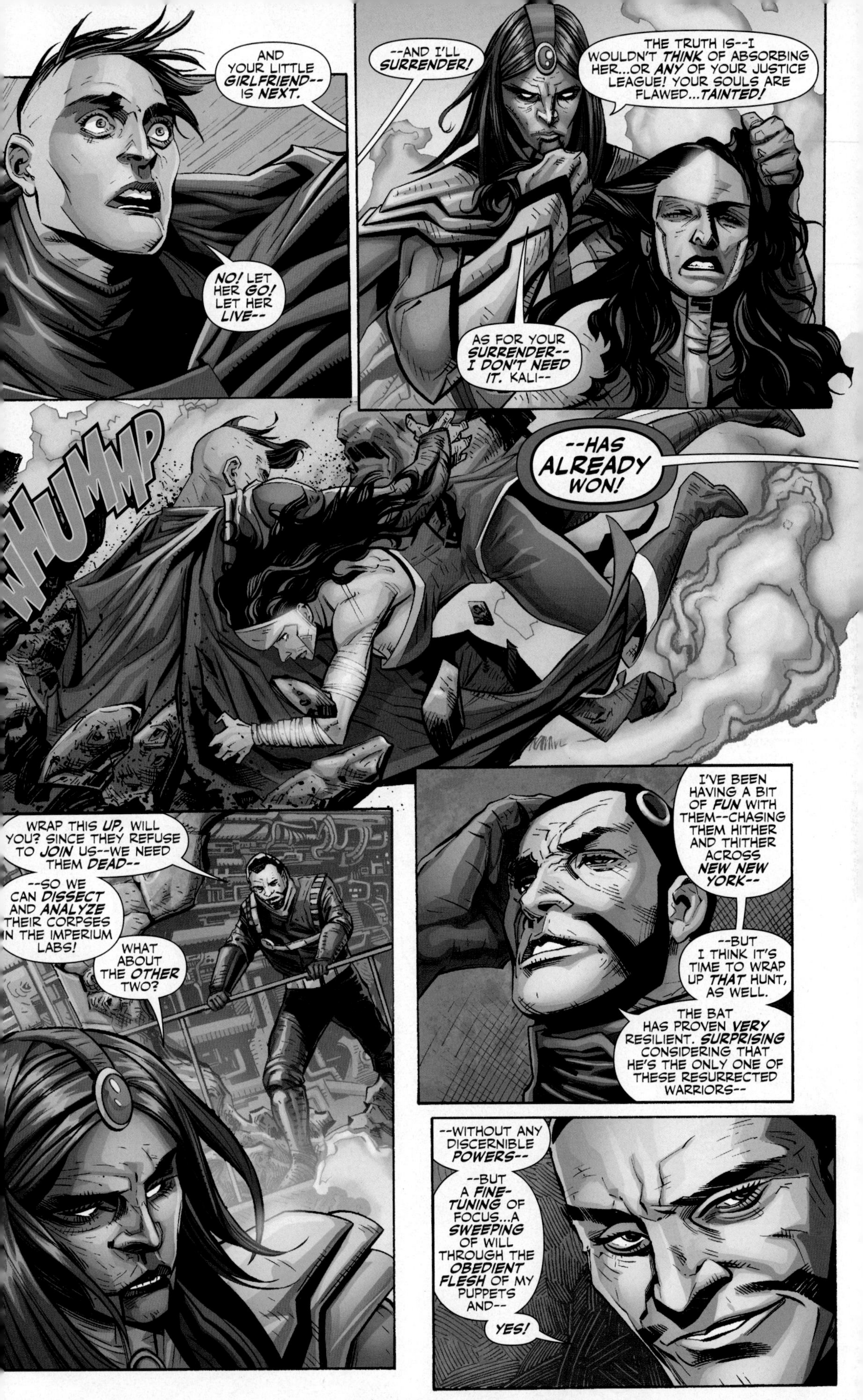
AND YOUR LITTLE GIRLFRIEND-- IS NEXT.
--AND I'LL SURRENDER!
THE TRUTH IS--I WOULDN'T THINK OF ABSORBING HER...OR ANY OF YOUR JUSTICE LEAGUE! YOUR SOULS ARE FLAWED...TAINTED!
NO! LET HER GO! LET HER LIVE--
AS FOR YOUR SURRENDER-- I DON'T NEED IT. KALI--
WHUMMP
--HAS ALREADY WON!
WRAP THIS UP, WILL YOU? SINCE THEY REFUSE TO JOIN US--WE NEED THEM DEAD--
--SO WE CAN DISSECT AND ANALYZE THEIR CORPSES IN THE IMPERIUM LABS!
WHAT ABOUT THE OTHER TWO?
I'VE BEEN HAVING A BIT OF FUN WITH THEM--CHASING THEM HITHER AND THITHER ACROSS NEW NEW YORK--
--BUT I THINK IT'S TIME TO WRAP UP THAT HUNT, AS WELL.
THE BAT HAS PROVEN VERY RESILIENT. SURPRISING CONSIDERING THAT HE'S THE ONLY ONE OF THESE RESURRECTED WARRIORS--
--WITHOUT ANY DISCERNIBLE POWERS--
--BUT A FINE-TUNING OF FOCUS...A SWEEPING OF WILL THROUGH THE OBEDIENT FLESH OF MY PUPPETS AND--
YES!

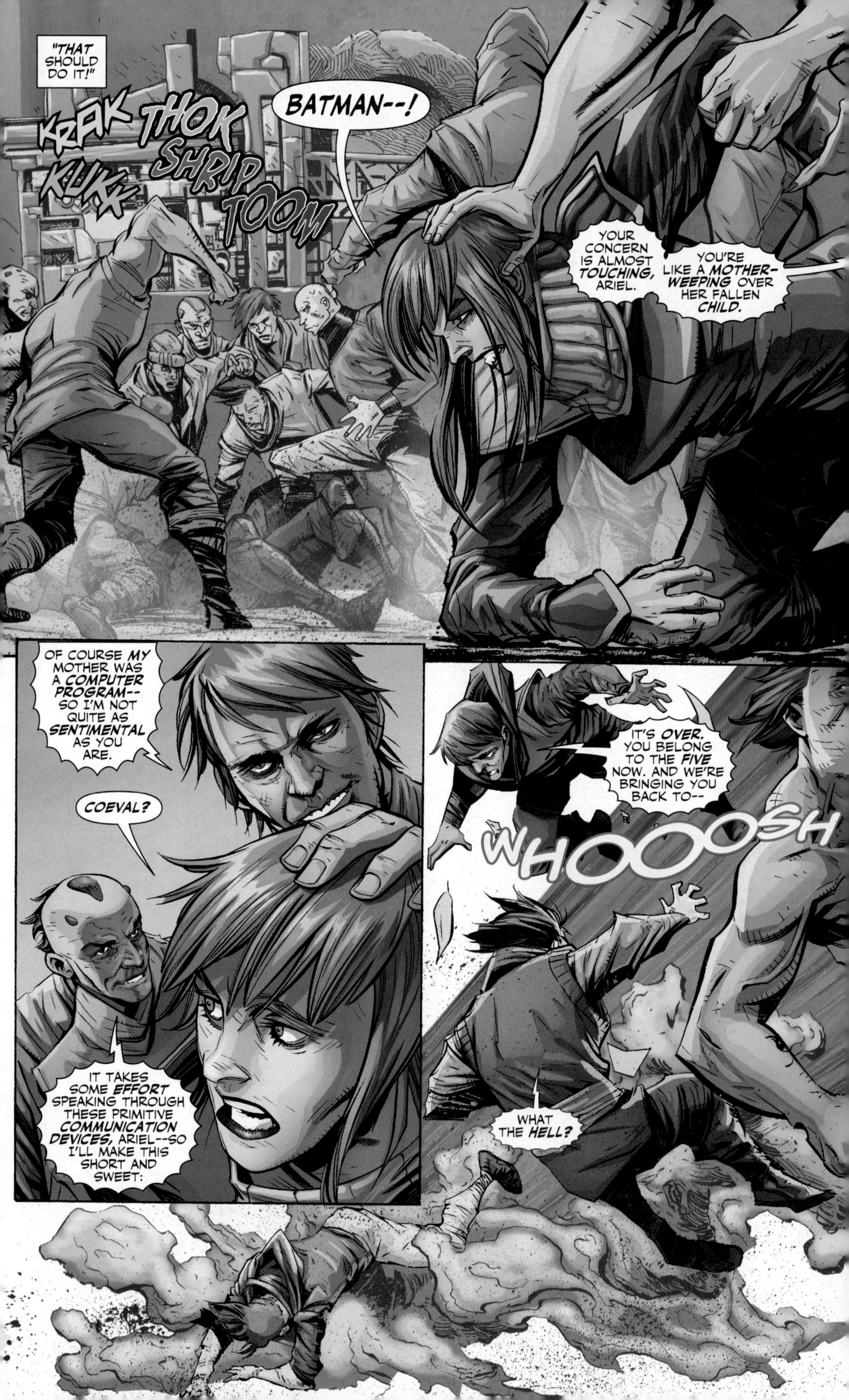
"THAT SHOULD DO IT!"
KRAK THOK KUKK SHRIP TOOM
BATMAN--!
YOUR CONCERN IS ALMOST TOUCHING, ARIEL.
YOU'RE LIKE A MOTHER-WEEPING OVER HER FALLEN CHILD.
OF COURSE MY MOTHER WAS A COMPUTER PROGRAM-- SO I'M NOT QUITE AS SENTIMENTAL AS YOU ARE.
COEVAL?
IT TAKES SOME EFFORT SPEAKING THROUGH THESE PRIMITIVE COMMUNICATION DEVICES, ARIEL--SO I'LL MAKE THIS SHORT AND SWEET:
IT'S OVER. YOU BELONG TO THE FIVE NOW. AND WE'RE BRINGING YOU BACK TO--
WHOOOSH
WHAT THE HELL?

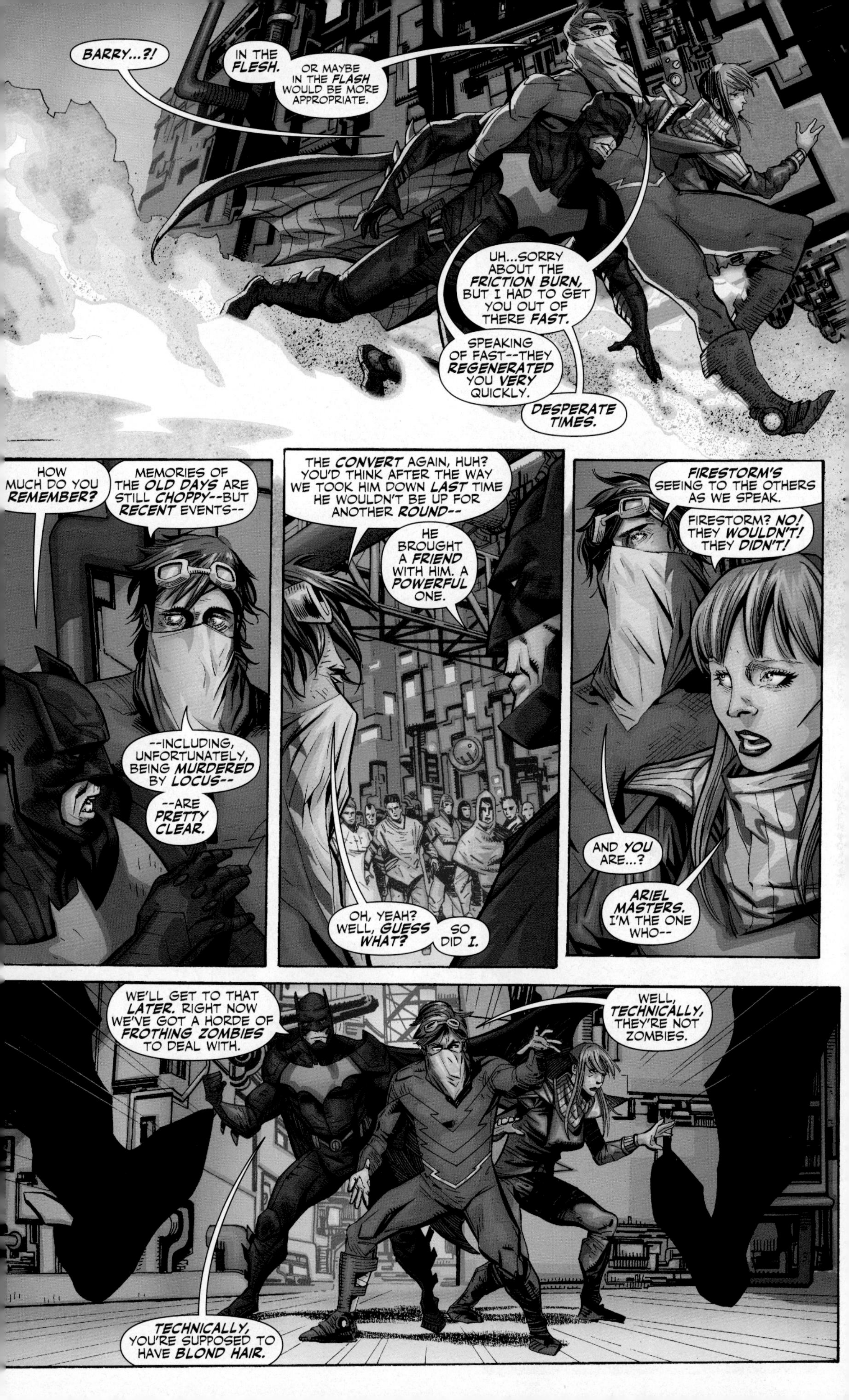
BARRY...?!
IN THE FLESH.
OR MAYBE IN THE FLASH WOULD BE MORE APPROPRIATE.
UH...SORRY ABOUT THE FRICTION BURN, BUT I HAD TO GET YOU OUT OF THERE FAST.
SPEAKING OF FAST--THEY REGENERATED YOU VERY QUICKLY.
DESPERATE TIMES.
HOW MUCH DO YOU REMEMBER?
MEMORIES OF THE OLD DAYS ARE STILL CHOPPY--BUT RECENT EVENTS--
--INCLUDING, UNFORTUNATELY, BEING MURDERED BY LOCUS--
--ARE PRETTY CLEAR.
THE CONVERT AGAIN, HUH? YOU'D THINK AFTER THE WAY WE TOOK HIM DOWN LAST TIME HE WOULDN'T BE UP FOR ANOTHER ROUND--
HE BROUGHT A FRIEND WITH HIM. A POWERFUL ONE.
OH, YEAH? WELL, GUESS WHAT?
SO DID I.
FIRESTORM'S SEEING TO THE OTHERS AS WE SPEAK.
FIRESTORM? NO! THEY WOULDN'T! THEY DIDN'T!
AND YOU ARE...?
ARIEL MASTERS. I'M THE ONE WHO--
WE'LL GET TO THAT LATER. RIGHT NOW WE'VE GOT A HORDE OF FROTHING ZOMBIES TO DEAL WITH.
WELL, TECHNICALLY, THEY'RE NOT ZOMBIES.
TECHNICALLY, YOU'RE SUPPOSED TO HAVE BLOND HAIR.

YOU'RE **BLOND?** WE NEVER **KNEW!** MOST OF THE SURVIVING RECORDS INDICATED YOU WERE A **REDHEAD** AND--

"WE" NEVER KNEW? WAIT...ARE YOU PART OF THE PROJECT?

--AND THAT'S **JUST** WHAT I'M GONNA DO!

SHOOOOSH

SPOOM

LONG STORY.

WHICH I DON'T HAVE **TIME** FOR. MY JOB IS TO GET MY FRIENDS **OFF** THIS HELLHOLE--

NOT JUST **US.** WE'VE GOT TO KEEP ARIEL **SAFE.**

WHY? WHO IS **SHE?**

IN A STRANGE WAY-- SHE'S OUR **MOTHER.**

OUR **WHAT?**

AS THE LADY SAID: **LONG STORY.**

BY THE WAY-- HOW'D YOU **GET** HERE?

WAKKADAWAKKA!!

SAME WAY WE MADE LANDFALL ON **SKORCH 4** --PORTABLE **TRANSVERSAL.**

IS IT STILL **HERE?**

IN **ORBIT.** I **SIGNAL** AND IT PULLS US **OUT.**

UNLESS ITS **SECURITY** IS COMPROMISE IN WHICH CASE IT--

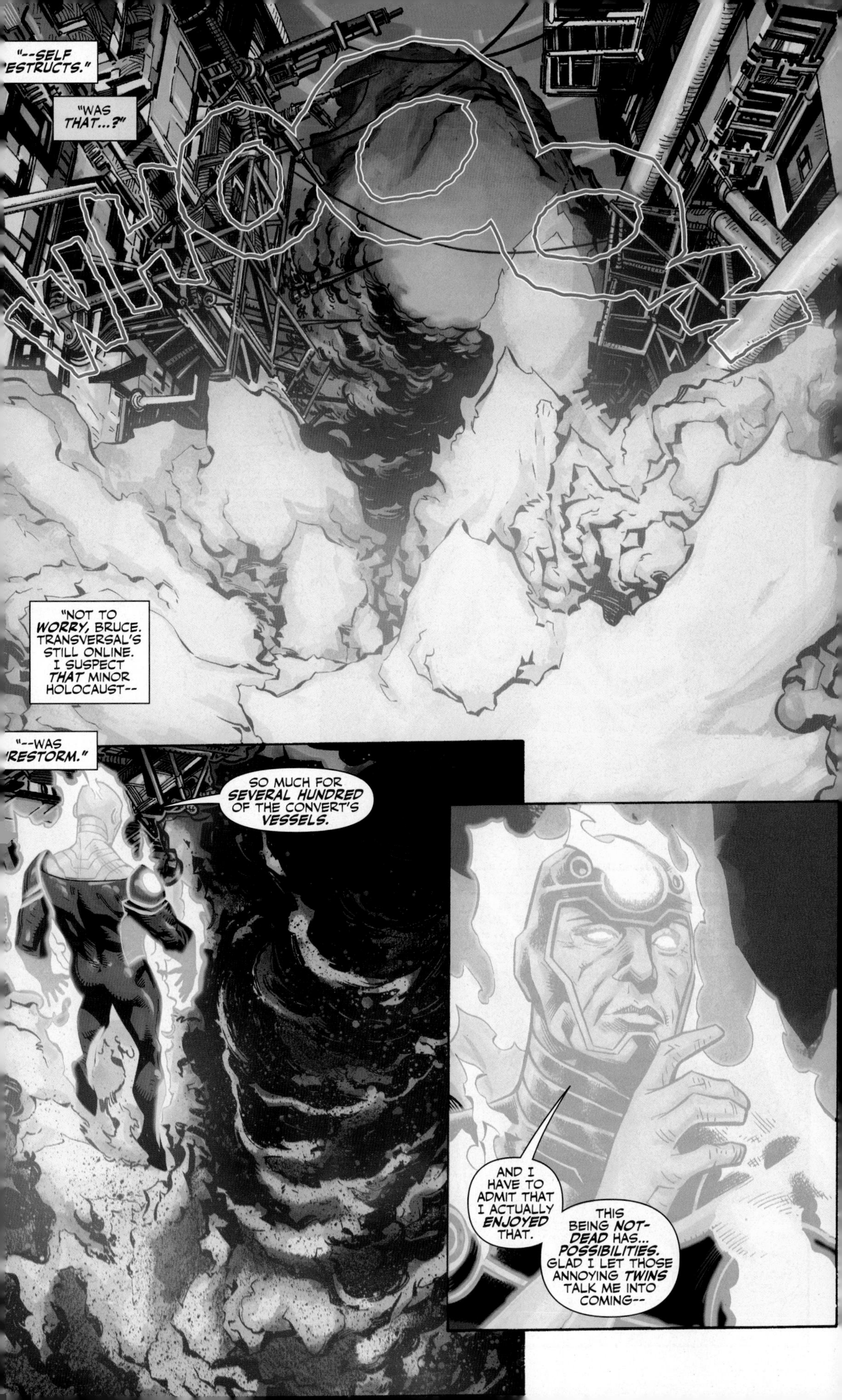
"--SELF
ESTRUCTS."
"WAS THAT...?"
WHOOOOSSH
"NOT TO WORRY, BRUCE. TRANSVERSAL'S STILL ONLINE. I SUSPECT THAT MINOR HOLOCAUST--
"--WAS
RESTORM."
SO MUCH FOR SEVERAL HUNDRED OF THE CONVERT'S VESSELS.
AND I HAVE TO ADMIT THAT I ACTUALLY ENJOYED THAT.
THIS BEING NOT-DEAD HAS... POSSIBILITIES. GLAD I LET THOSE ANNOYING TWINS TALK ME INTO COMING--

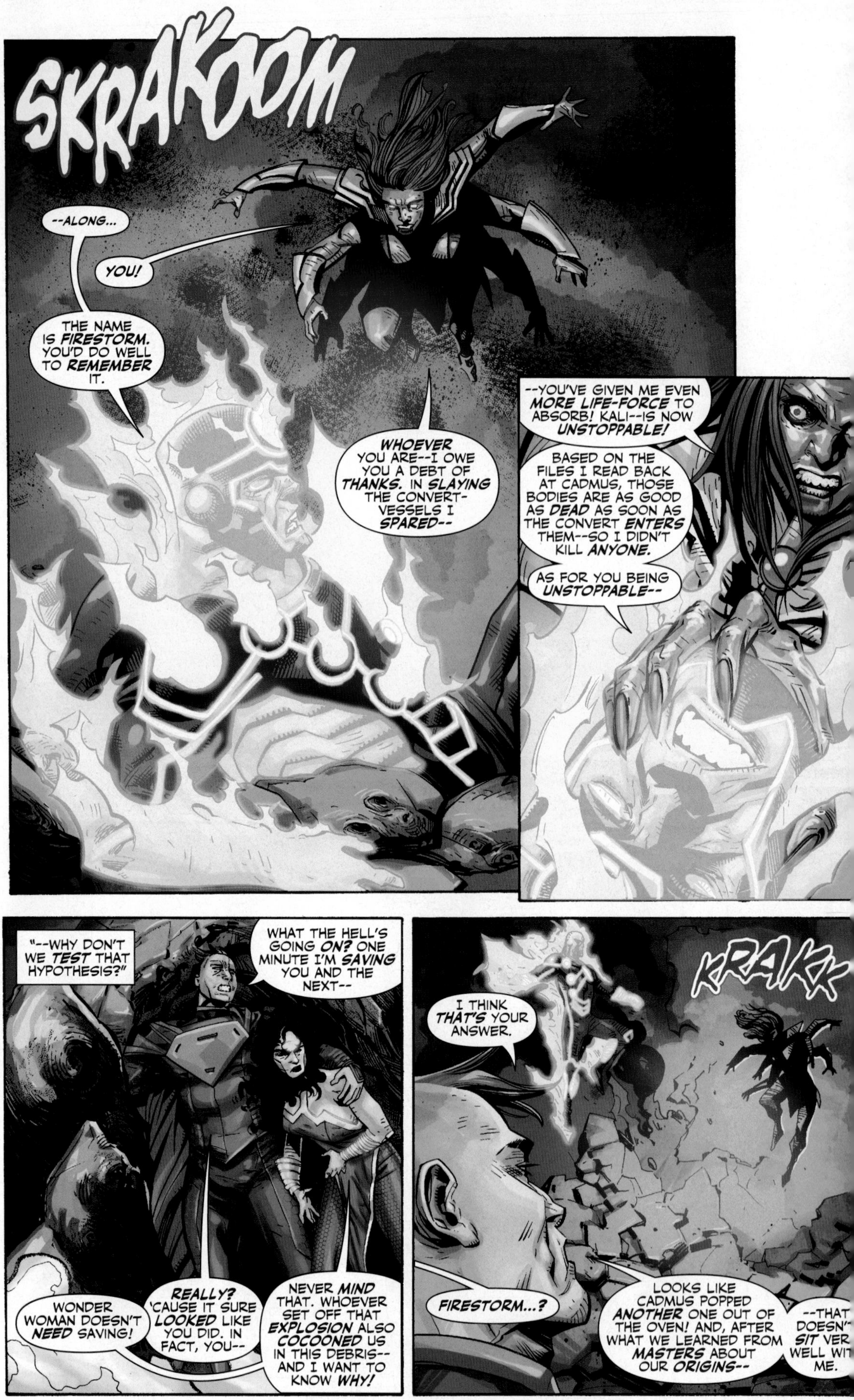
SKRAKOOM
--ALONG...
YOU!
THE NAME IS FIRESTORM. YOU'D DO WELL TO REMEMBER IT.
WHOEVER YOU ARE--I OWE YOU A DEBT OF THANKS. IN SLAYING THE CONVERT-VESSELS I SPARED--
--YOU'VE GIVEN ME EVEN MORE LIFE-FORCE TO ABSORB! KALI--IS NOW UNSTOPPABLE!
BASED ON THE FILES I READ BACK AT CADMUS, THOSE BODIES ARE AS GOOD AS DEAD AS SOON AS THE CONVERT ENTERS THEM--SO I DIDN'T KILL ANYONE.
AS FOR YOU BEING UNSTOPPABLE--
"--WHY DON'T WE TEST THAT HYPOTHESIS?"
WHAT THE HELL'S GOING ON? ONE MINUTE I'M SAVING YOU AND THE NEXT--
WONDER WOMAN DOESN'T NEED SAVING!
REALLY? 'CAUSE IT SURE LOOKED LIKE YOU DID. IN FACT, YOU--
NEVER MIND THAT. WHOEVER SET OFF THAT EXPLOSION ALSO COCOONED US IN THIS DEBRIS--AND I WANT TO KNOW WHY!
KRAKK
I THINK THAT'S YOUR ANSWER.
FIRESTORM...?
LOOKS LIKE CADMUS POPPED ANOTHER ONE OUT OF THE OVEN! AND, AFTER WHAT WE LEARNED FROM MASTERS ABOUT OUR ORIGINS--
--THAT DOESN'T SIT VER WELL WIT ME.

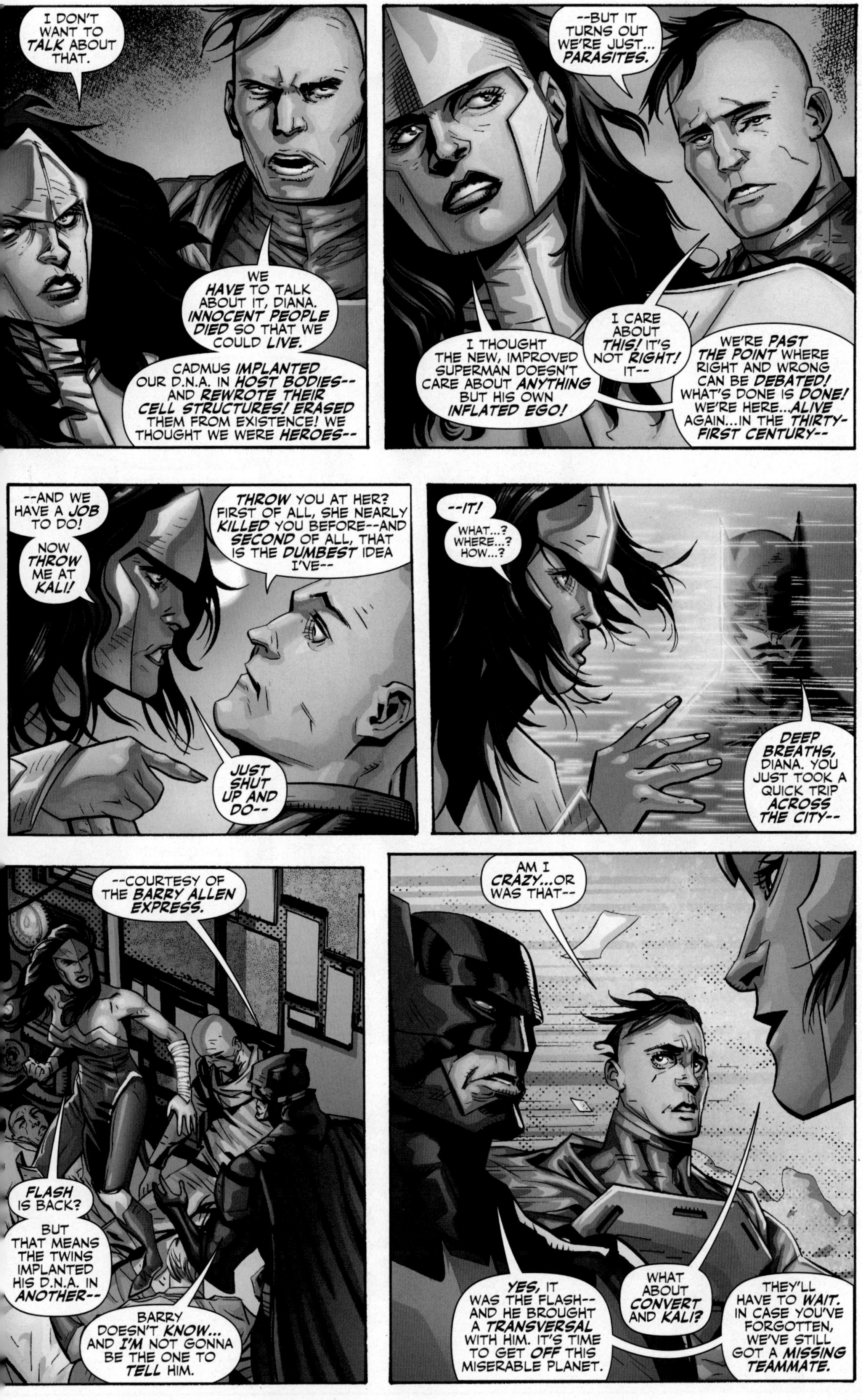

I DON'T WANT TO TALK ABOUT THAT.
WE HAVE TO TALK ABOUT IT, DIANA. INNOCENT PEOPLE DIED SO THAT WE COULD LIVE.
CADMUS IMPLANTED OUR D.N.A. IN HOST BODIES-- AND REWROTE THEIR CELL STRUCTURES! ERASED THEM FROM EXISTENCE! WE THOUGHT WE WERE HEROES--
--BUT IT TURNS OUT WE'RE JUST... PARASITES.
I THOUGHT THE NEW, IMPROVED SUPERMAN DOESN'T CARE ABOUT ANYTHING BUT HIS OWN INFLATED EGO!
I CARE ABOUT THIS! IT'S NOT RIGHT! IT--
WE'RE PAST THE POINT WHERE RIGHT AND WRONG CAN BE DEBATED! WHAT'S DONE IS DONE! WE'RE HERE...ALIVE AGAIN...IN THE THIRTY-FIRST CENTURY--
--AND WE HAVE A JOB TO DO!
NOW THROW ME AT KALI!
THROW YOU AT HER? FIRST OF ALL, SHE NEARLY KILLED YOU BEFORE--AND SECOND OF ALL, THAT IS THE DUMBEST IDEA I'VE--
JUST SHUT UP AND DO--
--IT!
WHAT...? WHERE...? HOW...?
DEEP BREATHS, DIANA. YOU JUST TOOK A QUICK TRIP ACROSS THE CITY--
--COURTESY OF THE BARRY ALLEN EXPRESS.
FLASH IS BACK?
BUT THAT MEANS THE TWINS IMPLANTED HIS D.N.A. IN ANOTHER--
BARRY DOESN'T KNOW... AND I'M NOT GONNA BE THE ONE TO TELL HIM.
AM I CRAZY...OR WAS THAT--
YES, IT WAS THE FLASH-- AND HE BROUGHT A TRANSVERSAL WITH HIM. IT'S TIME TO GET OFF THIS MISERABLE PLANET.
WHAT ABOUT CONVERT AND KALI?
THEY'LL HAVE TO WAIT. IN CASE YOU'VE FORGOTTEN, WE'VE STILL GOT A MISSING TEAMMATE.

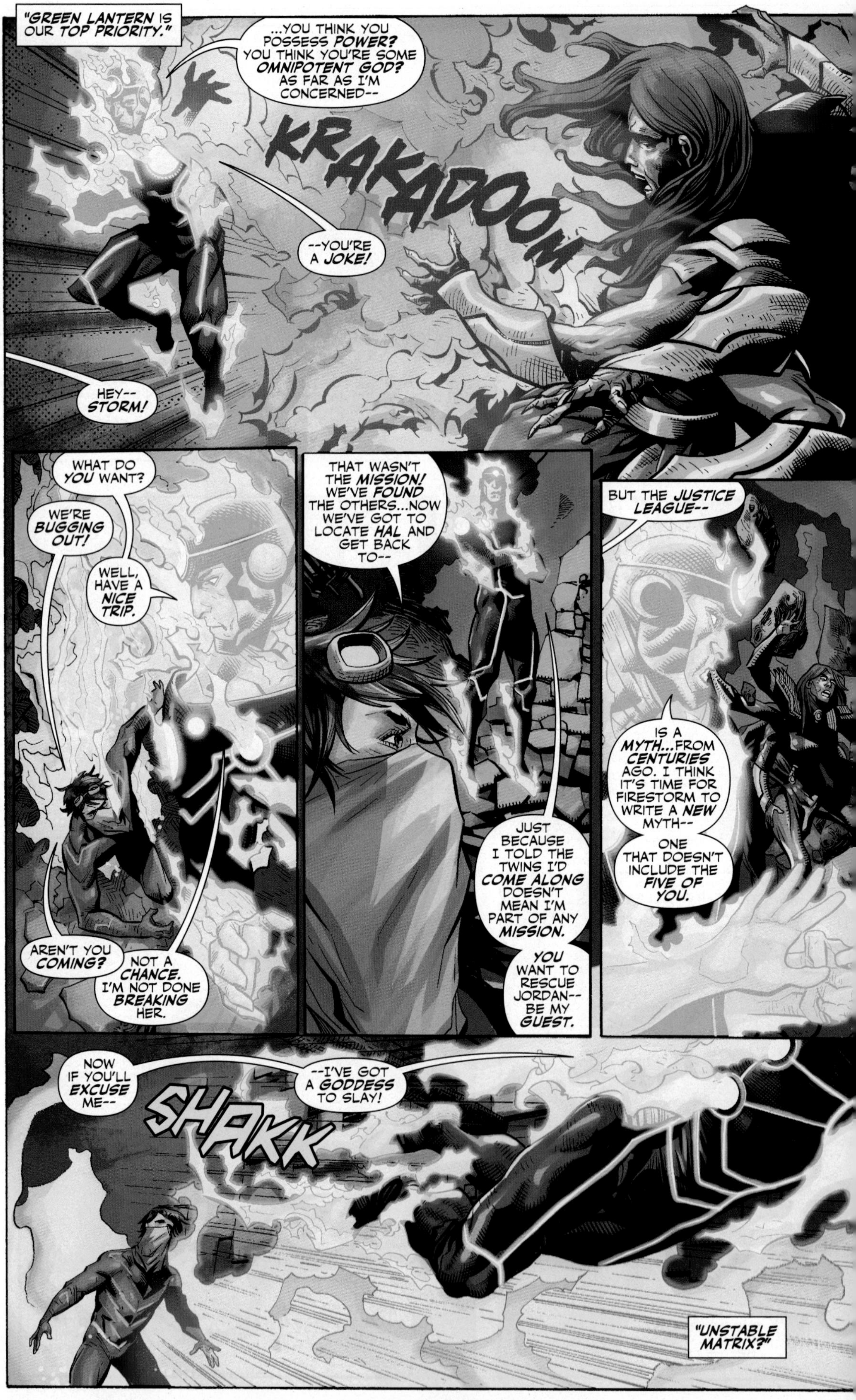
"GREEN LANTERN IS OUR TOP PRIORITY."
...YOU THINK YOU POSSESS POWER? YOU THINK YOU'RE SOME OMNIPOTENT GOD? AS FAR AS I'M CONCERNED--
KRAKADOOOM
--YOU'RE A JOKE!
HEY-- STORM!
WHAT DO YOU WANT?
WE'RE BUGGING OUT!
WELL, HAVE A NICE TRIP.
AREN'T YOU COMING?
NOT A CHANCE. I'M NOT DONE BREAKING HER.
THAT WASN'T THE MISSION! WE'VE FOUND THE OTHERS...NOW WE'VE GOT TO LOCATE HAL AND GET BACK TO--
JUST BECAUSE I TOLD THE TWINS I'D COME ALONG DOESN'T MEAN I'M PART OF ANY MISSION.
YOU WANT TO RESCUE JORDAN-- BE MY GUEST.
BUT THE JUSTICE LEAGUE--
IS A MYTH...FROM CENTURIES AGO. I THINK IT'S TIME FOR FIRESTORM TO WRITE A NEW MYTH--
ONE THAT DOESN'T INCLUDE THE FIVE OF YOU.
NOW IF YOU'LL EXCUSE ME--
--I'VE GOT A GODDESS TO SLAY!
SHAKK
"UNSTABLE MATRIX?"

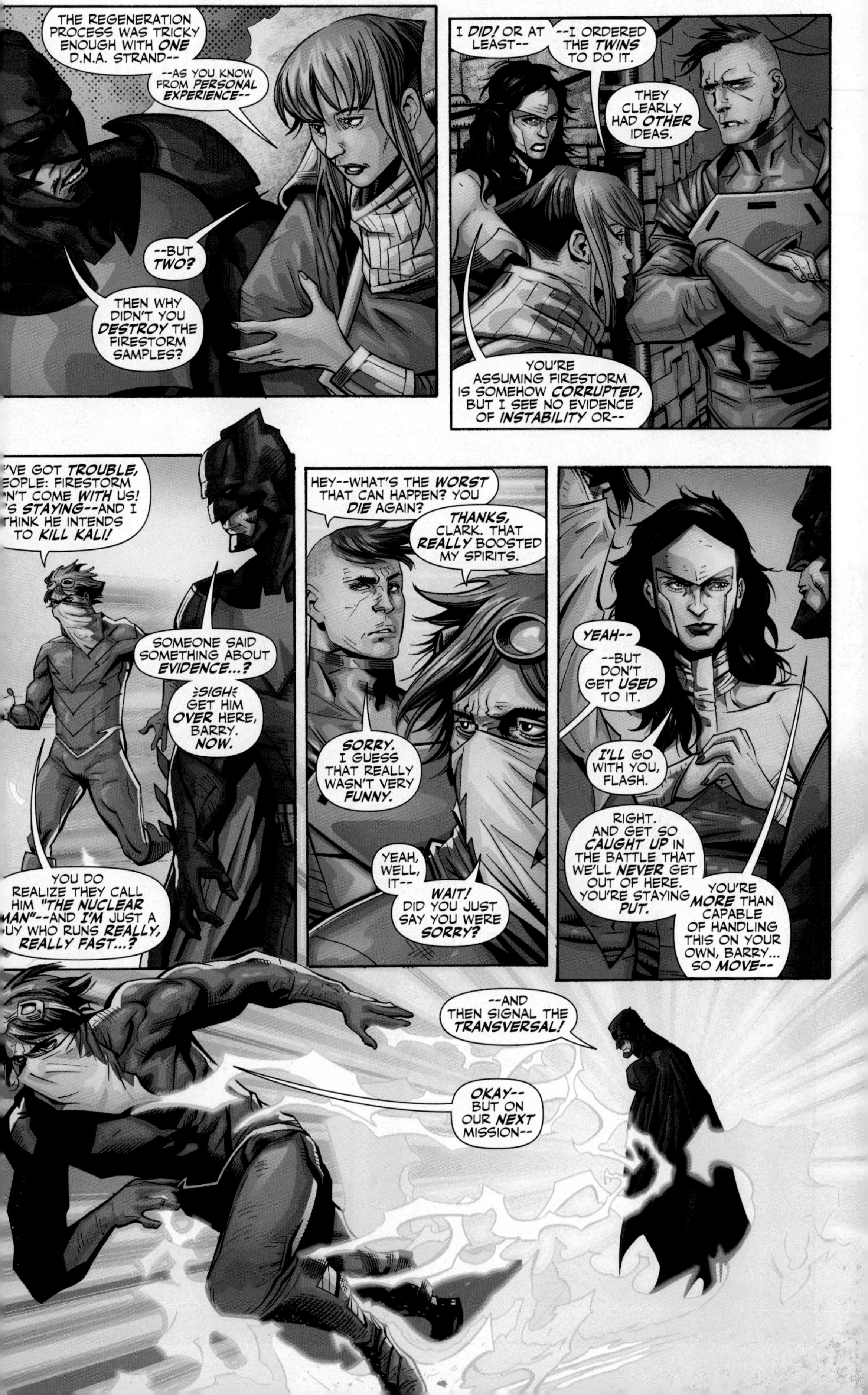
THE REGENERATION PROCESS WAS TRICKY ENOUGH WITH ONE D.N.A. STRAND--
--AS YOU KNOW FROM PERSONAL EXPERIENCE--
--BUT TWO?
THEN WHY DIDN'T YOU DESTROY THE FIRESTORM SAMPLES?
I DID! OR AT LEAST--
--I ORDERED THE TWINS TO DO IT.
THEY CLEARLY HAD OTHER IDEAS.
YOU'RE ASSUMING FIRESTORM IS SOMEHOW CORRUPTED, BUT I SEE NO EVIDENCE OF INSTABILITY OR--
'VE GOT TROUBLE, EOPLE: FIRESTORM N'T COME WITH US! 'S STAYING--AND I THINK HE INTENDS TO KILL KALI!
SOMEONE SAID SOMETHING ABOUT EVIDENCE...?
SIGH GET HIM OVER HERE, BARRY. NOW.
YOU DO REALIZE THEY CALL HIM "THE NUCLEAR MAN"--AND I'M JUST A UY WHO RUNS REALLY, REALLY FAST...?
HEY--WHAT'S THE WORST THAT CAN HAPPEN? YOU DIE AGAIN?
THANKS, CLARK. THAT REALLY BOOSTED MY SPIRITS.
SORRY. I GUESS THAT REALLY WASN'T VERY FUNNY.
YEAH, WELL, IT--
WAIT! DID YOU JUST SAY YOU WERE SORRY?
YEAH--
--BUT DON'T GET USED TO IT.
I'LL GO WITH YOU, FLASH.
RIGHT. AND GET SO CAUGHT UP IN THE BATTLE THAT WE'LL NEVER GET OUT OF HERE. YOU'RE STAYING PUT.
YOU'RE MORE THAN CAPABLE OF HANDLING THIS ON YOUR OWN, BARRY... SO MOVE--
--AND THEN SIGNAL THE TRANSVERSAL!
OKAY-- BUT ON OUR NEXT MISSION--

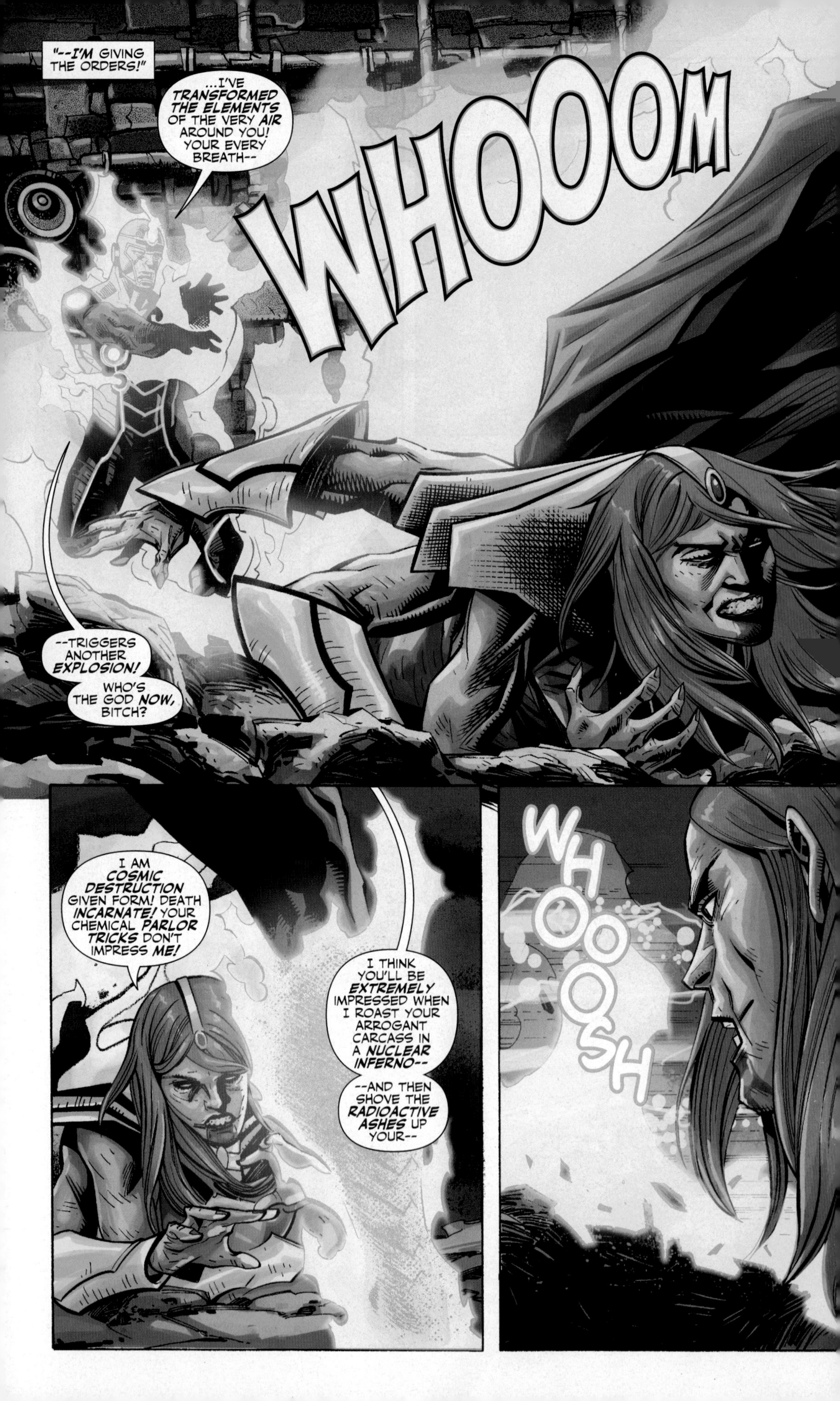
"--I'M GIVING THE ORDERS!"
...I'VE TRANSFORMED THE ELEMENTS OF THE VERY AIR AROUND YOU! YOUR EVERY BREATH--
WHOOOOM
--TRIGGERS ANOTHER EXPLOSION!
WHO'S THE GOD NOW, BITCH?
I AM COSMIC DESTRUCTION GIVEN FORM! DEATH INCARNATE! YOUR CHEMICAL PARLOR TRICKS DON'T IMPRESS ME!
I THINK YOU'LL BE EXTREMELY IMPRESSED WHEN I ROAST YOUR ARROGANT CARCASS IN A NUCLEAR INFERNO--
--AND THEN SHOVE THE RADIOACTIVE ASHES UP YOUR--
WHOOOOSH

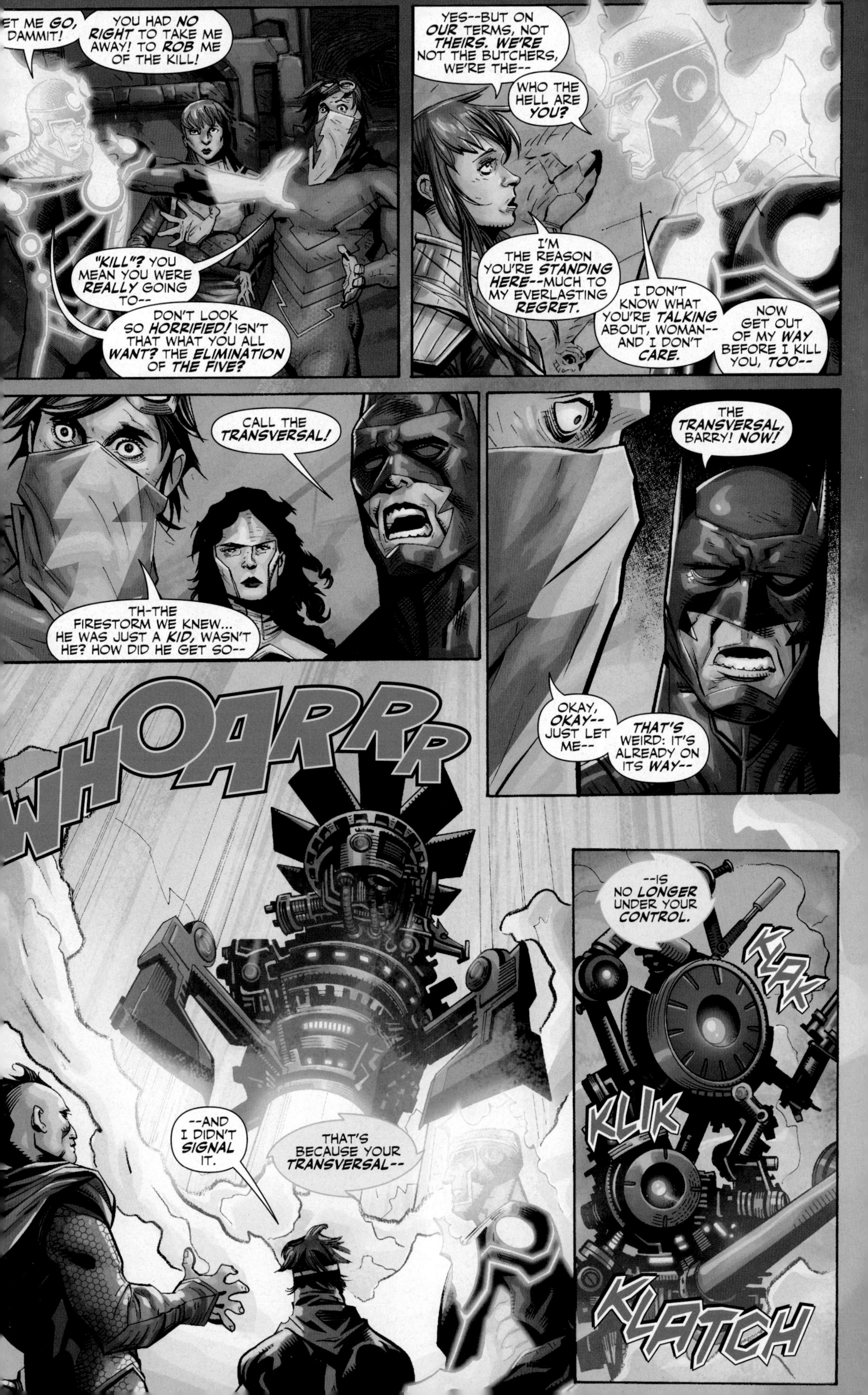
ET ME GO, DAMMIT!
YOU HAD NO RIGHT TO TAKE ME AWAY! TO ROB ME OF THE KILL!
"KILL"? YOU MEAN YOU WERE REALLY GOING TO--
DON'T LOOK SO HORRIFIED! ISN'T THAT WHAT YOU ALL WANT? THE ELIMINATION OF THE FIVE?
YES--BUT ON OUR TERMS, NOT THEIRS. WE'RE NOT THE BUTCHERS, WE'RE THE--
WHO THE HELL ARE YOU?
I'M THE REASON YOU'RE STANDING HERE--MUCH TO MY EVERLASTING REGRET.
I DON'T KNOW WHAT YOU'RE TALKING ABOUT, WOMAN-- AND I DON'T CARE.
NOW GET OUT OF MY WAY BEFORE I KILL YOU, TOO--
CALL THE TRANSVERSAL!
TH-THE FIRESTORM WE KNEW... HE WAS JUST A KID, WASN'T HE? HOW DID HE GET SO--
THE TRANSVERSAL, BARRY! NOW!
OKAY, OKAY-- JUST LET ME--
THAT'S WEIRD: IT'S ALREADY ON ITS WAY--
WHOARRR
--AND I DIDN'T SIGNAL IT.
THAT'S BECAUSE YOUR TRANSVERSAL--
--IS NO LONGER UNDER YOUR CONTROL.
KLAK
KLIK
KLATCH

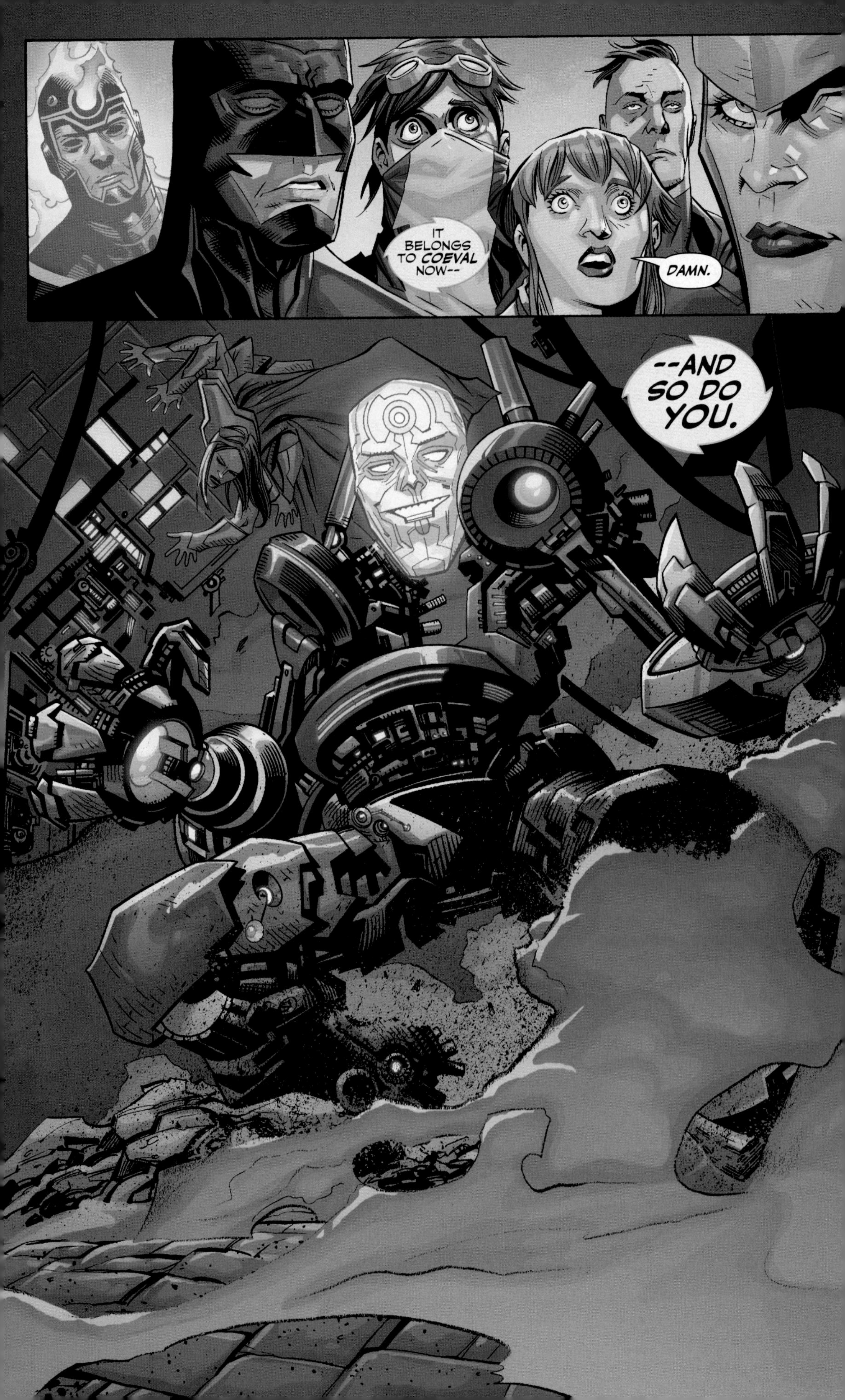
IT BELONGS TO COEVAL NOW--
DAMN.
--AND SO DO YOU.

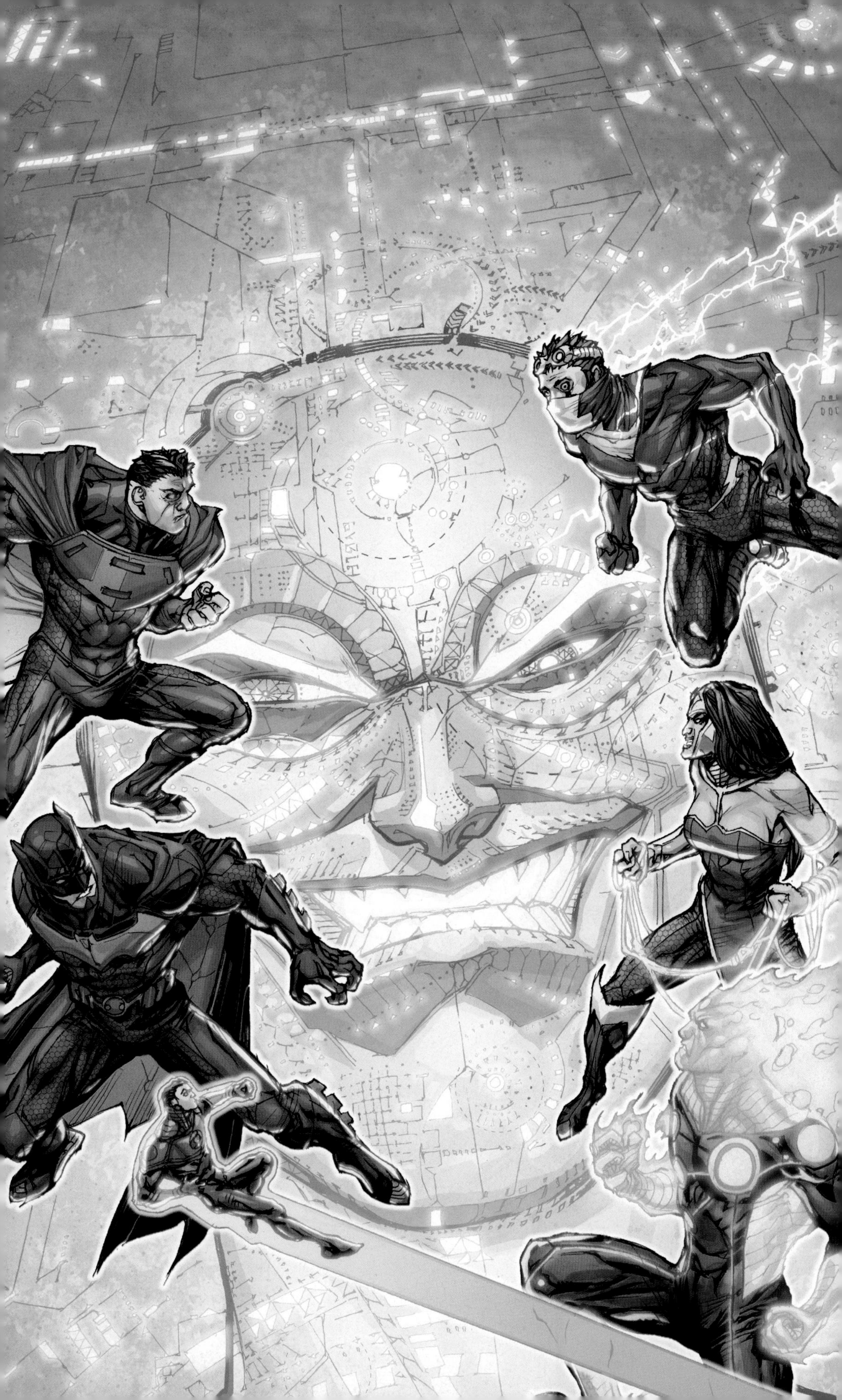

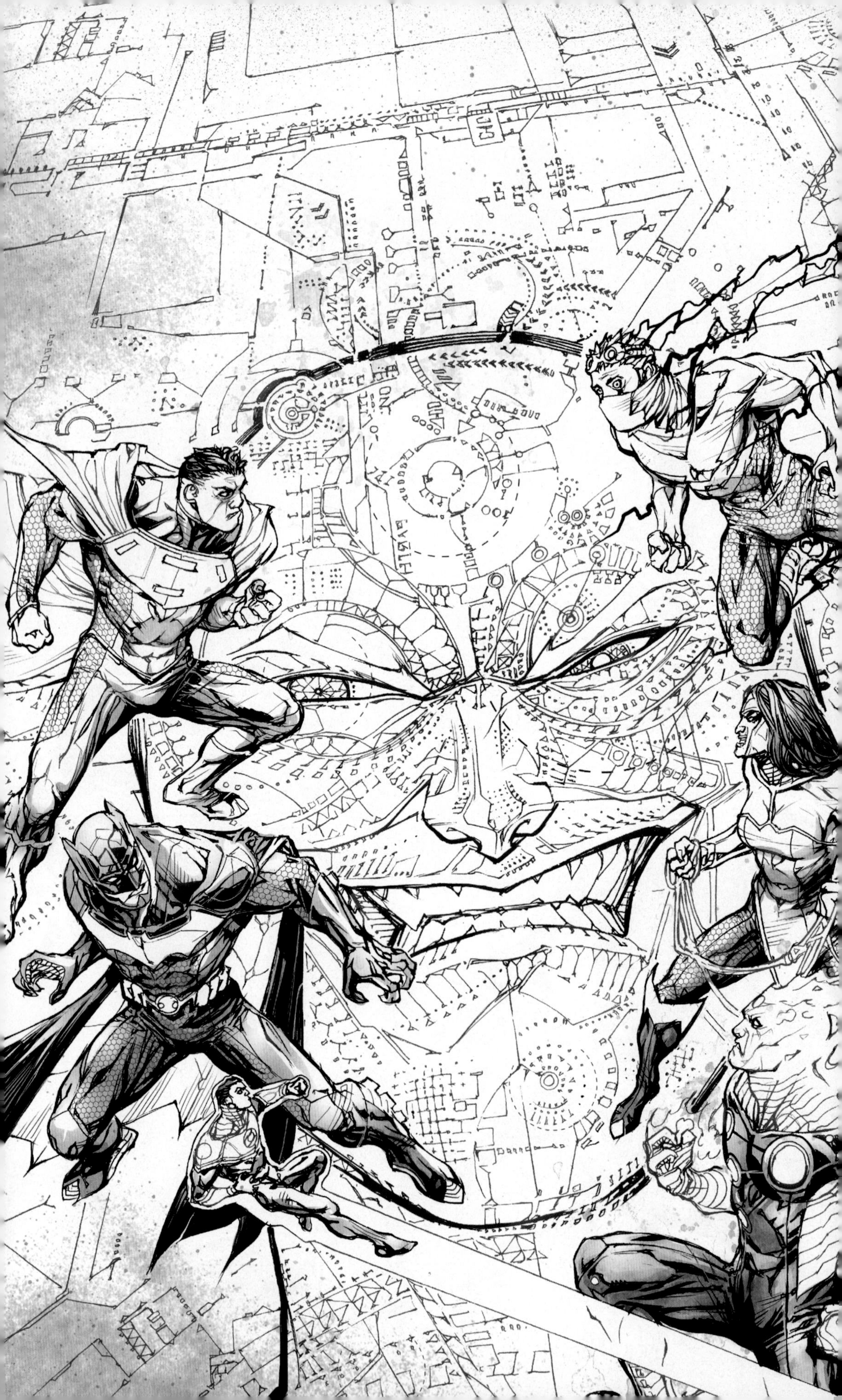

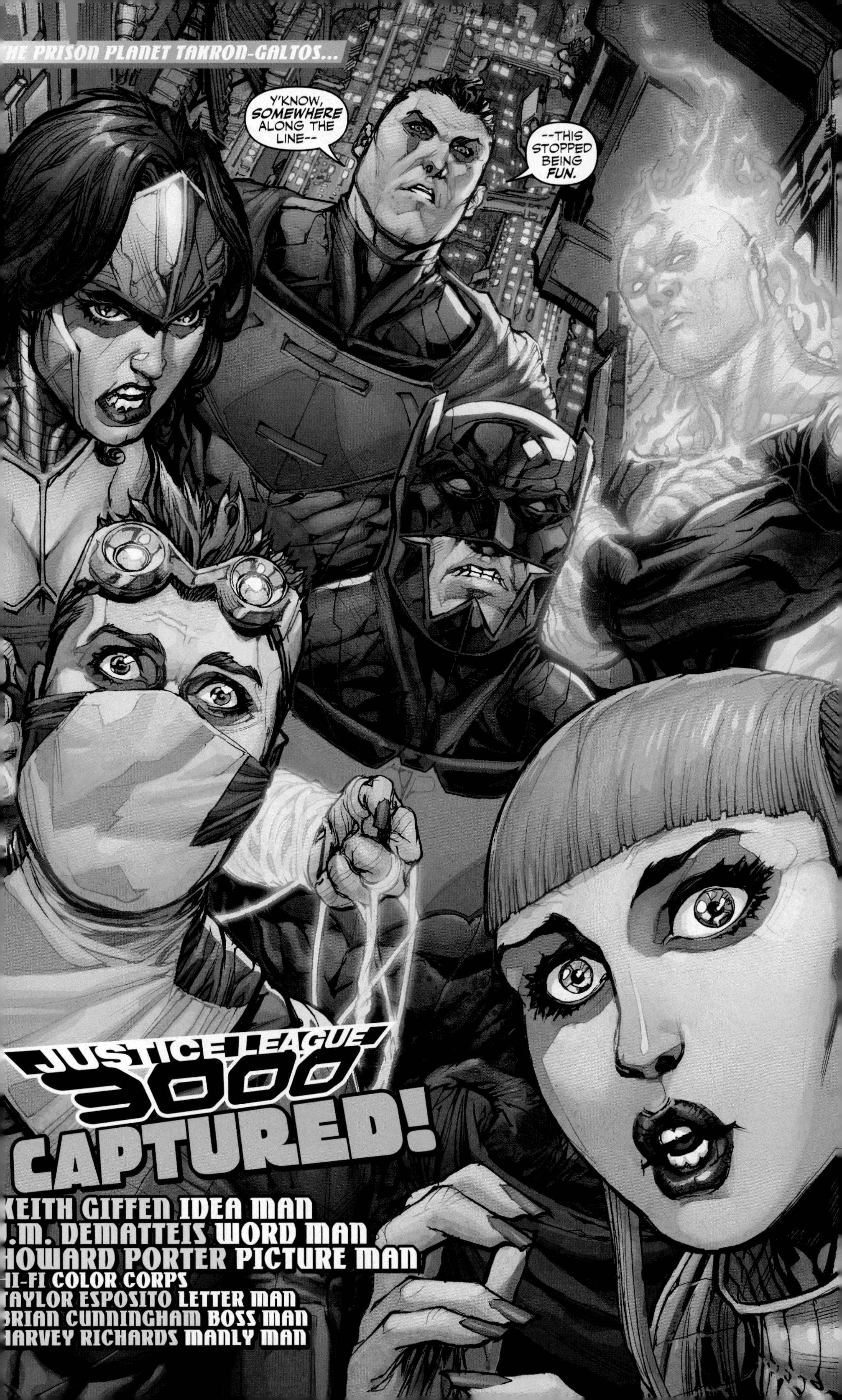

HE PRISON PLANET TAKRON-GALTOS...
Y'KNOW, SOMEWHERE ALONG THE LINE--
--THIS STOPPED BEING FUN.
JUSTICE LEAGUE 3000
CAPTURED!
KEITH GIFFEN IDEA MAN
J.M. DEMATTEIS WORD MAN
HOWARD PORTER PICTURE MAN
HI-FI COLOR CORPS
TAYLOR ESPOSITO LETTER MAN
BRIAN CUNNINGHAM BOSS MAN
HARVEY RICHARDS MANLY MAN

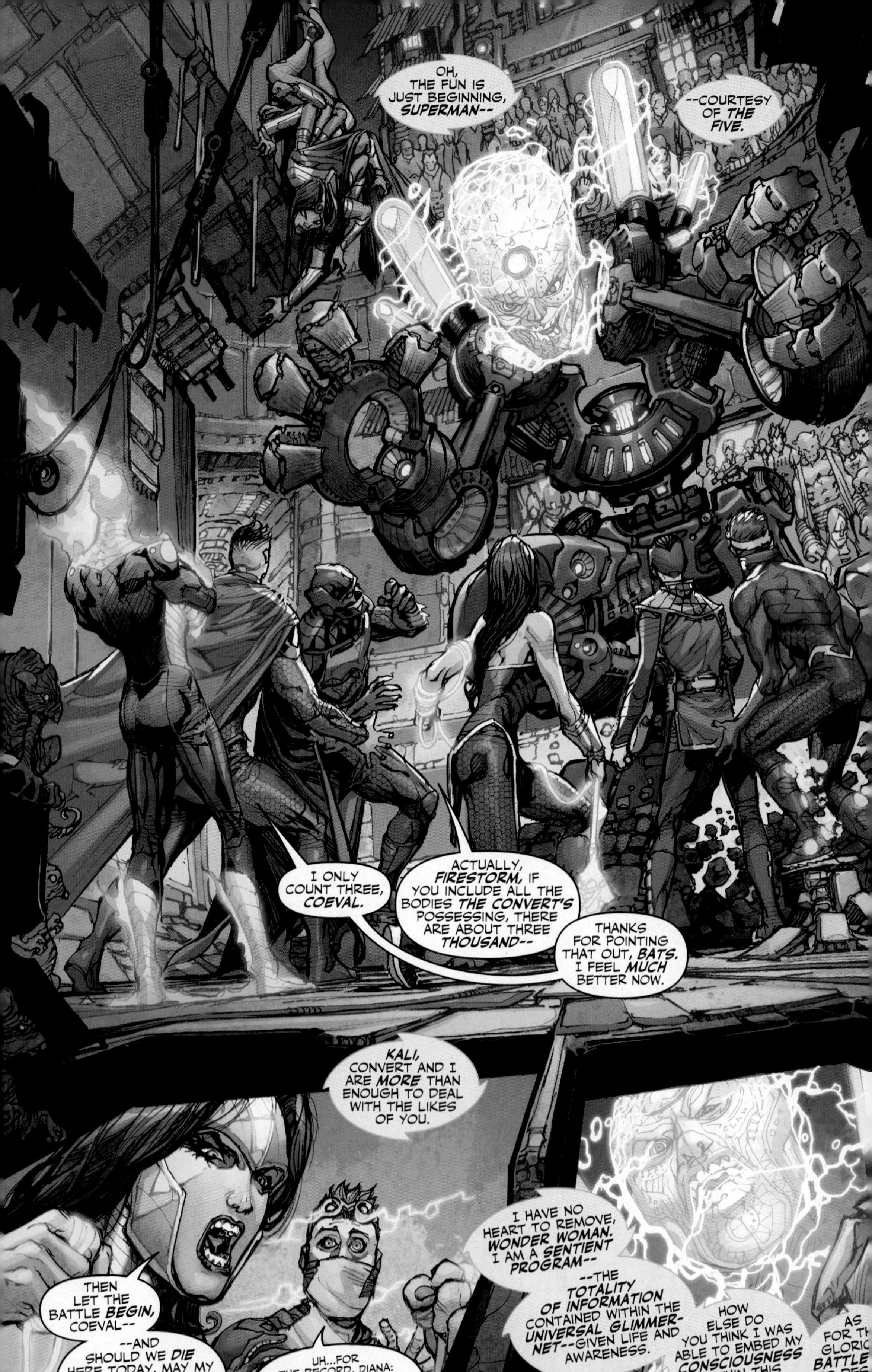
OH, THE FUN IS JUST BEGINNING, SUPERMAN--
--COURTESY OF THE FIVE.
I ONLY COUNT THREE, COEVAL.
ACTUALLY, FIRESTORM, IF YOU INCLUDE ALL THE BODIES THE CONVERT'S POSSESSING, THERE ARE ABOUT THREE THOUSAND--
THANKS FOR POINTING THAT OUT, BATS. I FEEL MUCH BETTER NOW.
KALI, CONVERT AND I ARE MORE THAN ENOUGH TO DEAL WITH THE LIKES OF YOU.
THEN LET THE BATTLE BEGIN, COEVAL--
--AND SHOULD WE DIE HERE TODAY, MAY MY LAST ACT BE TEARING YOUR BLOODY HEART OUT OF YOUR CHEST!
UH...FOR THE RECORD, DIANA: I JUST DIED...FOR THE SECOND TIME...AND I'M IN
I HAVE NO HEART TO REMOVE, WONDER WOMAN. I AM A SENTIENT PROGRAM--
--THE TOTALITY OF INFORMATION CONTAINED WITHIN THE UNIVERSAL GLIMMER-NET--GIVEN LIFE AND AWARENESS.
HOW ELSE DO YOU THINK I WAS ABLE TO EMBED MY CONSCIOUSNESS WITHIN THIS
AS FOR

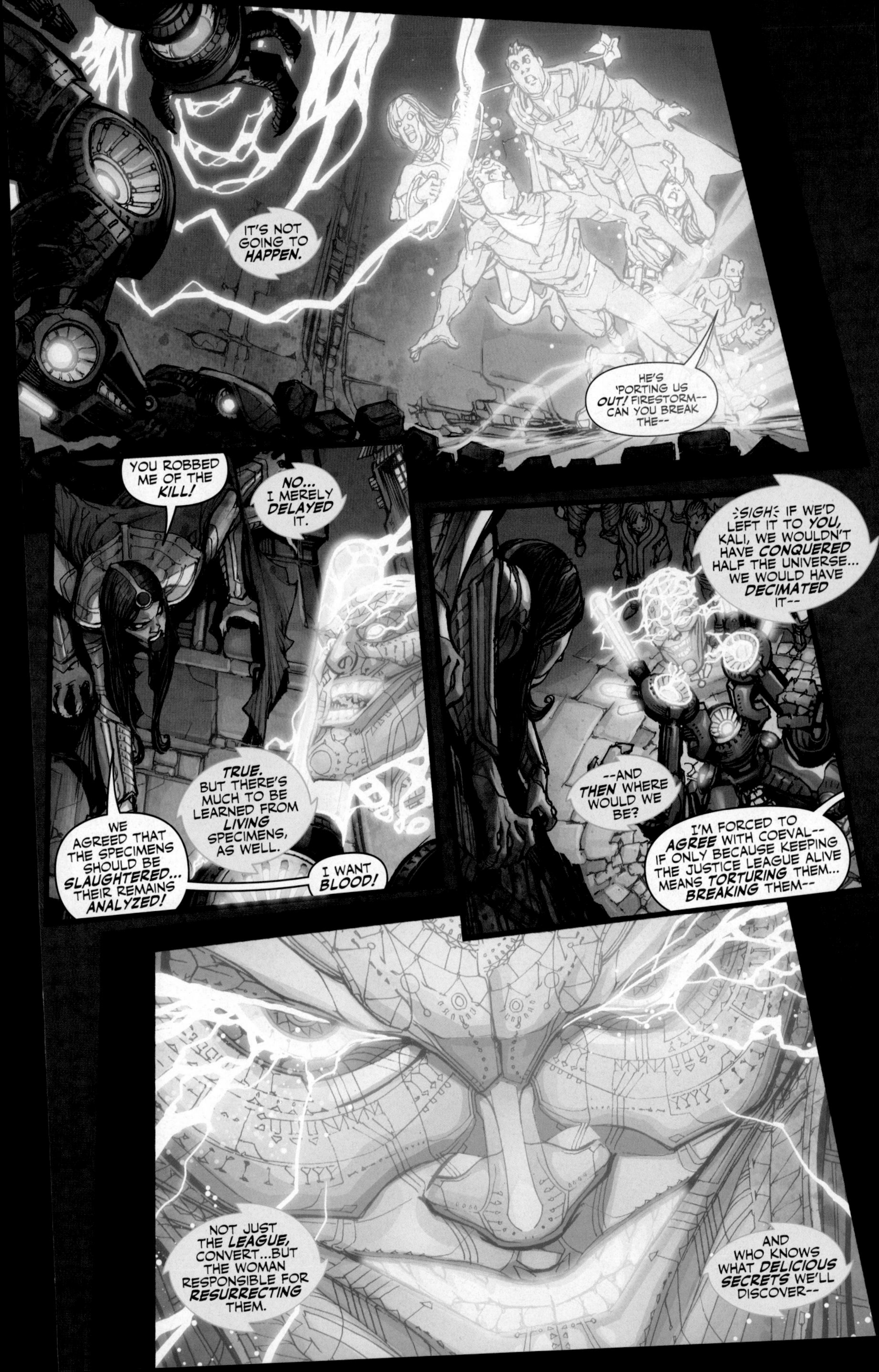
IT'S NOT GOING TO HAPPEN.
HE'S 'PORTING US OUT! FIRESTORM-- CAN YOU BREAK THE--
YOU ROBBED ME OF THE KILL!
NO... I MERELY DELAYED IT.
WE AGREED THAT THE SPECIMENS SHOULD BE SLAUGHTERED... THEIR REMAINS ANALYZED!
I WANT BLOOD!
TRUE. BUT THERE'S MUCH TO BE LEARNED FROM LIVING SPECIMENS, AS WELL.
:SIGH: IF WE'D LEFT IT TO YOU, KALI, WE WOULDN'T HAVE CONQUERED HALF THE UNIVERSE... WE WOULD HAVE DECIMATED IT--
--AND THEN WHERE WOULD WE BE?
I'M FORCED TO AGREE WITH COEVAL-- IF ONLY BECAUSE KEEPING THE JUSTICE LEAGUE ALIVE MEANS TORTURING THEM... BREAKING THEM--
NOT JUST THE LEAGUE, CONVERT...BUT THE WOMAN RESPONSIBLE FOR RESURRECTING THEM.
AND WHO KNOWS WHAT DELICIOUS SECRETS WE'LL DISCOVER--

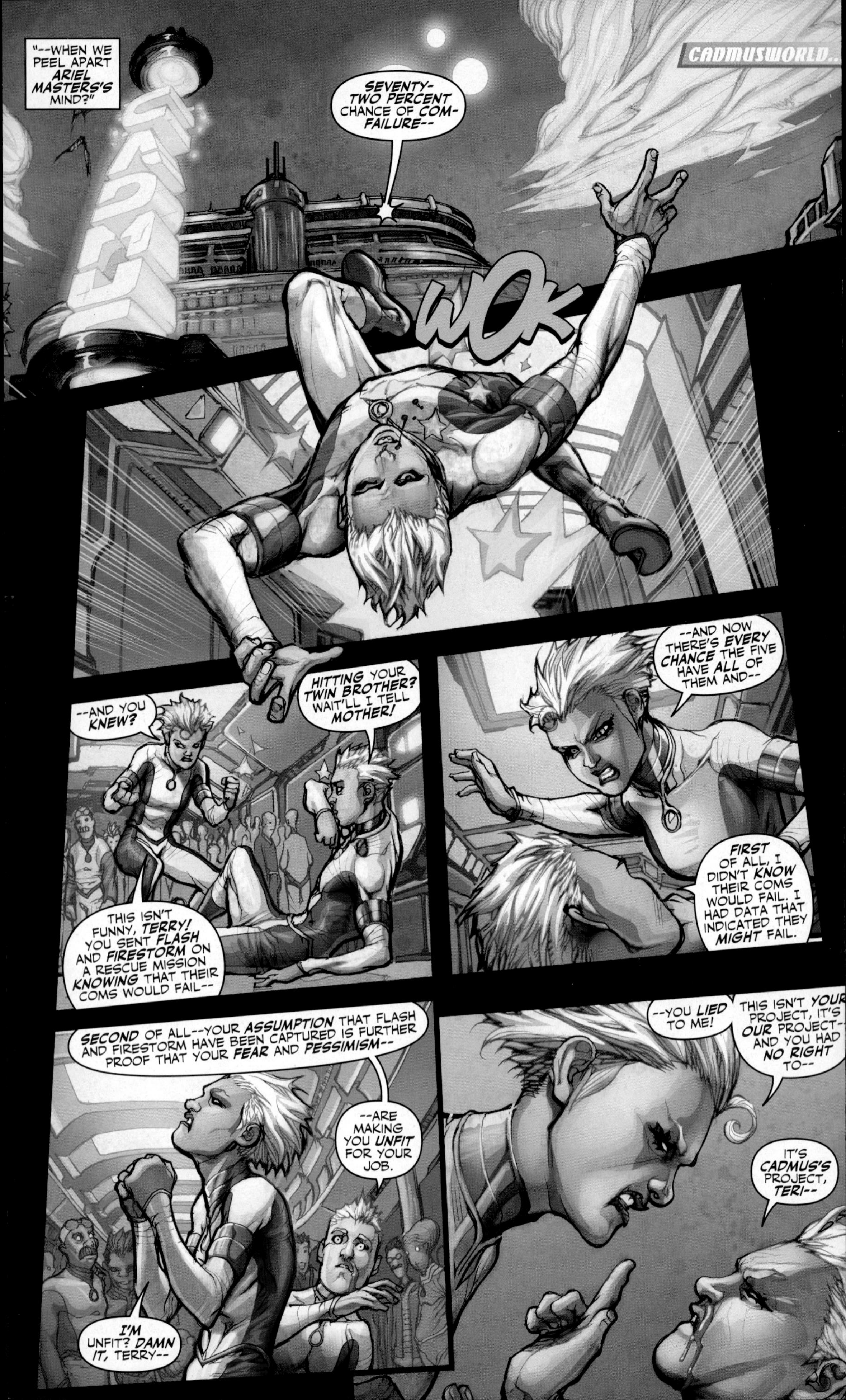
CADMUSWORLD...
"--WHEN WE PEEL APART ARIEL MASTERS'S MIND?"
SEVENTY-TWO PERCENT CHANCE OF COM-FAILURE--
WOK
HITTING YOUR TWIN BROTHER? WAIT'LL I TELL MOTHER!
--AND YOU KNEW?
THIS ISN'T FUNNY, TERRY! YOU SENT FLASH AND FIRESTORM ON A RESCUE MISSION KNOWING THAT THEIR COMS WOULD FAIL--
--AND NOW THERE'S EVERY CHANCE THE FIVE HAVE ALL OF THEM AND--
FIRST OF ALL, I DIDN'T KNOW THEIR COMS WOULD FAIL. I HAD DATA THAT INDICATED THEY MIGHT FAIL.
SECOND OF ALL--YOUR ASSUMPTION THAT FLASH AND FIRESTORM HAVE BEEN CAPTURED IS FURTHER PROOF THAT YOUR FEAR AND PESSIMISM--
--ARE MAKING YOU UNFIT FOR YOUR JOB.
I'M UNFIT? DAMN IT, TERRY--
--YOU LIED TO ME!
THIS ISN'T YOUR PROJECT, IT'S OUR PROJECT--AND YOU HAD NO RIGHT TO--
IT'S CADMUS'S PROJECT, TERI--

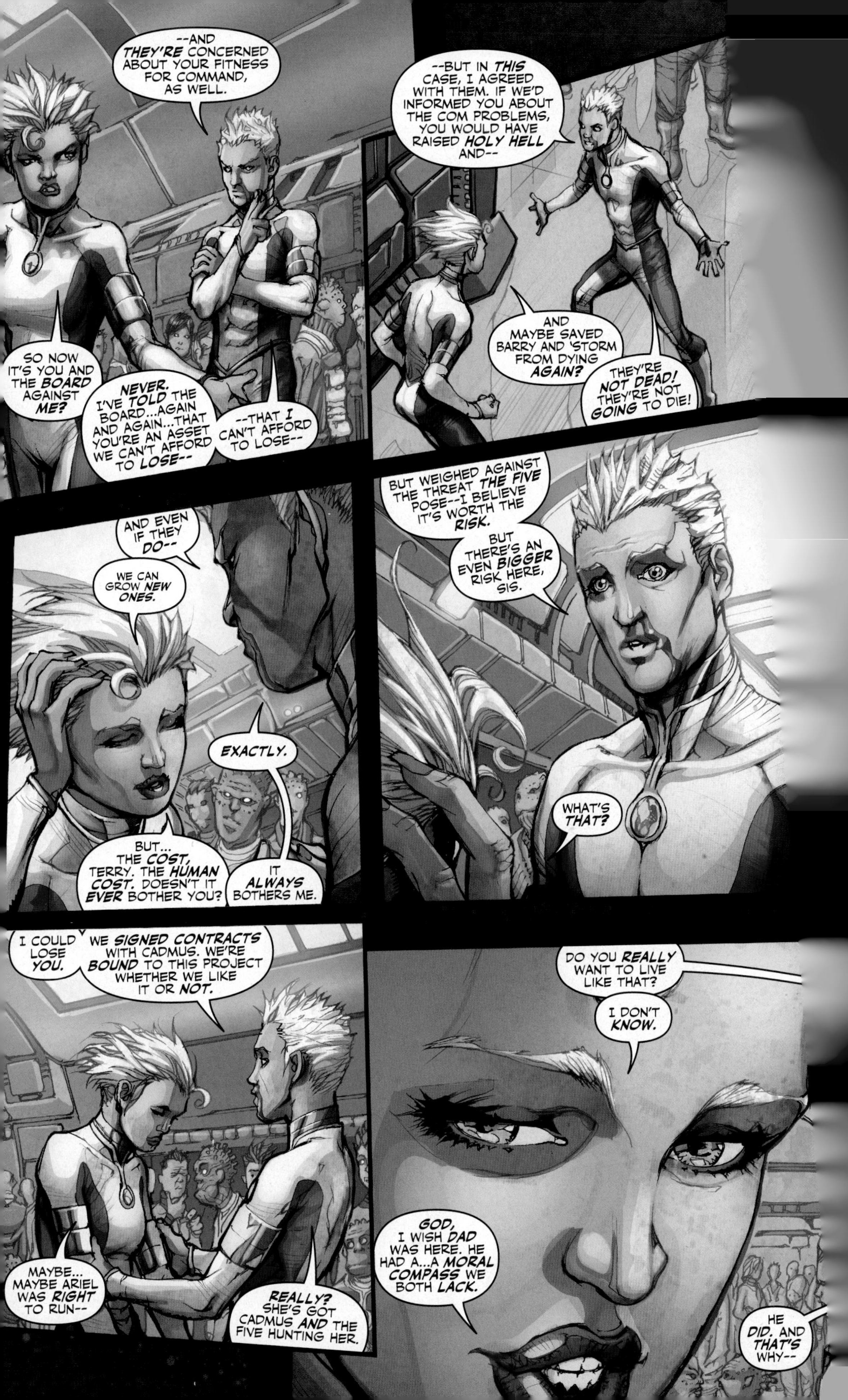
--AND THEY'RE CONCERNED ABOUT YOUR FITNESS FOR COMMAND, AS WELL.
SO NOW IT'S YOU AND THE BOARD AGAINST ME?
NEVER. I'VE TOLD THE BOARD...AGAIN AND AGAIN...THAT YOU'RE AN ASSET WE CAN'T AFFORD TO LOSE--
--THAT I CAN'T AFFORD TO LOSE--
--BUT IN THIS CASE, I AGREED WITH THEM. IF WE'D INFORMED YOU ABOUT THE COM PROBLEMS, YOU WOULD HAVE RAISED HOLY HELL AND--
AND MAYBE SAVED BARRY AND 'STORM FROM DYING AGAIN?
THEY'RE NOT DEAD! THEY'RE NOT GOING TO DIE!
AND EVEN IF THEY DO--
WE CAN GROW NEW ONES.
EXACTLY.
BUT... THE COST, TERRY. THE HUMAN COST. DOESN'T IT EVER BOTHER YOU?
IT ALWAYS BOTHERS ME.
BUT WEIGHED AGAINST THE THREAT THE FIVE POSE--I BELIEVE IT'S WORTH THE RISK.
BUT THERE'S AN EVEN BIGGER RISK HERE, SIS.
WHAT'S THAT?
I COULD LOSE YOU.
WE SIGNED CONTRACTS WITH CADMUS. WE'RE BOUND TO THIS PROJECT WHETHER WE LIKE IT OR NOT.
MAYBE... MAYBE ARIEL WAS RIGHT TO RUN--
REALLY? SHE'S GOT CADMUS AND THE FIVE HUNTING HER.
DO YOU REALLY WANT TO LIVE LIKE THAT?
I DON'T KNOW.
GOD, I WISH DAD WAS HERE. HE HAD A...A MORAL COMPASS WE BOTH LACK.
HE DID. AND THAT'S WHY--

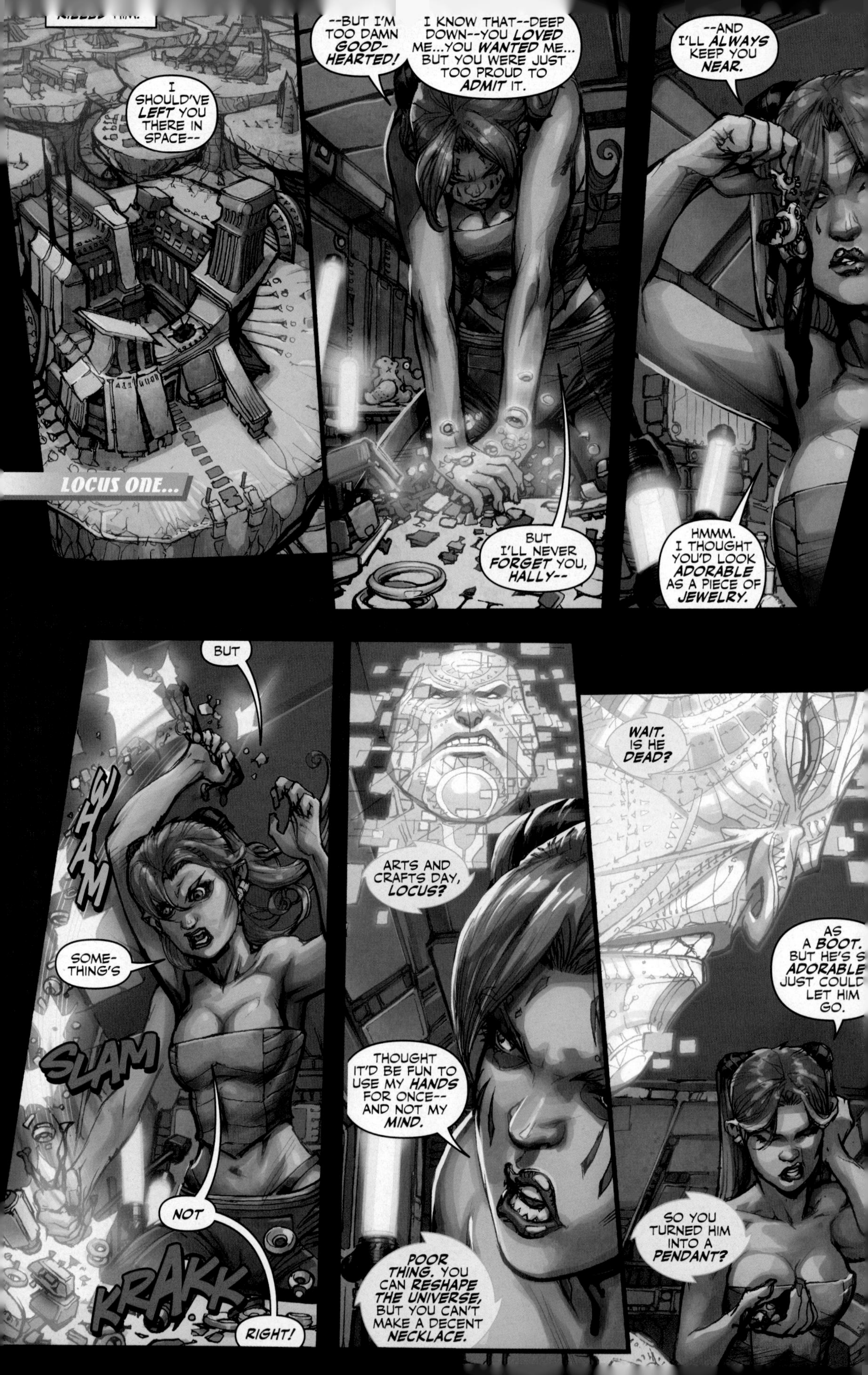

I SHOULD'VE LEFT YOU THERE IN SPACE--
LOCUS ONE...
--BUT I'M TOO DAMN GOOD-HEARTED!
I KNOW THAT--DEEP DOWN--YOU LOVED ME...YOU WANTED ME... BUT YOU WERE JUST TOO PROUD TO ADMIT IT.
BUT I'LL NEVER FORGET YOU, HALLY--
--AND I'LL ALWAYS KEEP YOU NEAR.
HMMM. I THOUGHT YOU'D LOOK ADORABLE AS A PIECE OF JEWELRY.
BUT
WHAM
SOME-THING'S
SLAM
NOT
KRAKK
RIGHT!
ARTS AND CRAFTS DAY, LOCUS?
THOUGHT IT'D BE FUN TO USE MY HANDS FOR ONCE--AND NOT MY MIND.
POOR THING. YOU CAN RESHAPE THE UNIVERSE, BUT YOU CAN'T MAKE A DECENT NECKLACE.
WAIT. IS HE DEAD?
AS A BOOT. BUT HE'S S ADORABLE JUST COULD LET HIM GO.
SO YOU TURNED HIM INTO A PENDANT?

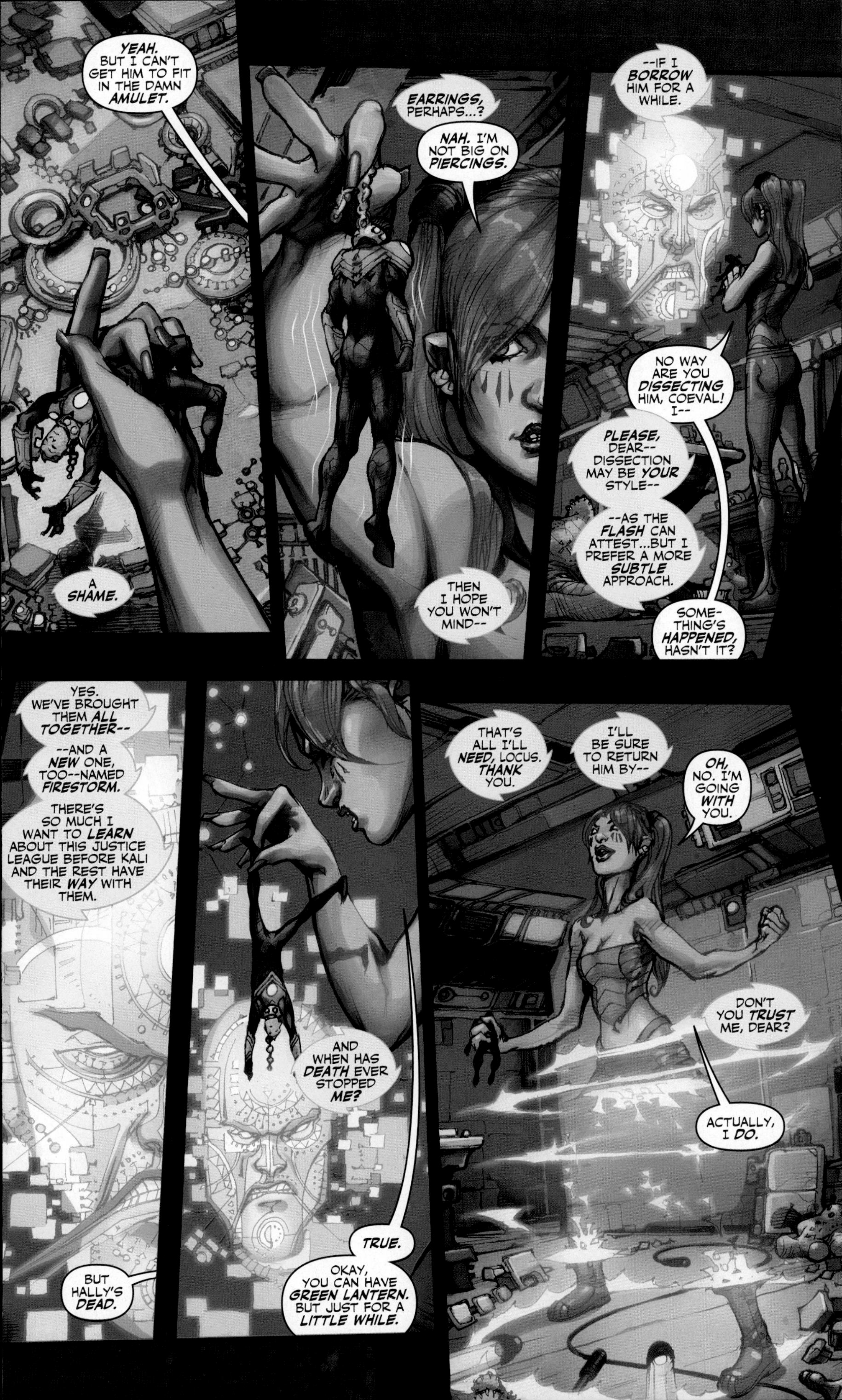
YEAH. BUT I CAN'T GET HIM TO FIT IN THE DAMN AMULET.
A SHAME.
EARRINGS, PERHAPS...?
NAH. I'M NOT BIG ON PIERCINGS.
THEN I HOPE YOU WON'T MIND--
--IF I BORROW HIM FOR A WHILE.
NO WAY ARE YOU DISSECTING HIM, COEVAL! I--
PLEASE, DEAR--DISSECTION MAY BE YOUR STYLE--
--AS THE FLASH CAN ATTEST...BUT I PREFER A MORE SUBTLE APPROACH.
SOME-THING'S HAPPENED, HASN'T IT?
YES. WE'VE BROUGHT THEM ALL TOGETHER--
--AND A NEW ONE, TOO--NAMED FIRESTORM.
THERE'S SO MUCH I WANT TO LEARN ABOUT THIS JUSTICE LEAGUE BEFORE KALI AND THE REST HAVE THEIR WAY WITH THEM.
BUT HALLY'S DEAD.
AND WHEN HAS DEATH EVER STOPPED ME?
TRUE.
OKAY, YOU CAN HAVE GREEN LANTERN. BUT JUST FOR A LITTLE WHILE.
THAT'S ALL I'LL NEED, LOCUS. THANK YOU.
I'LL BE SURE TO RETURN HIM BY--
OH, NO. I'M GOING WITH YOU.
DON'T YOU TRUST ME, DEAR?
ACTUALLY, I DO.

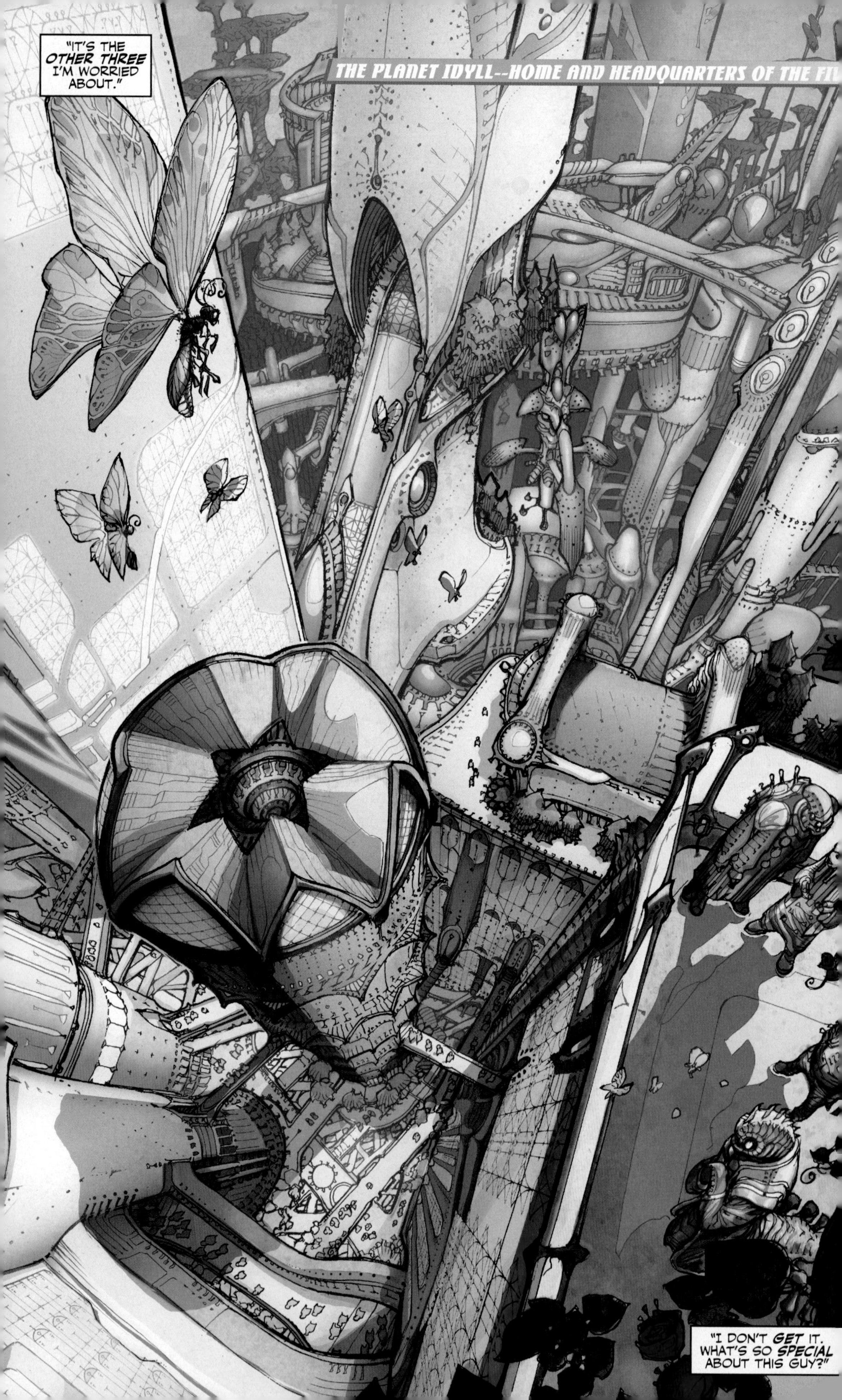
"IT'S THE OTHER THREE I'M WORRIED ABOUT."
THE PLANET IDYLL--HOME AND HEADQUARTERS OF THE FI
"I DON'T GET IT. WHAT'S SO SPECIAL ABOUT THIS GUY?"

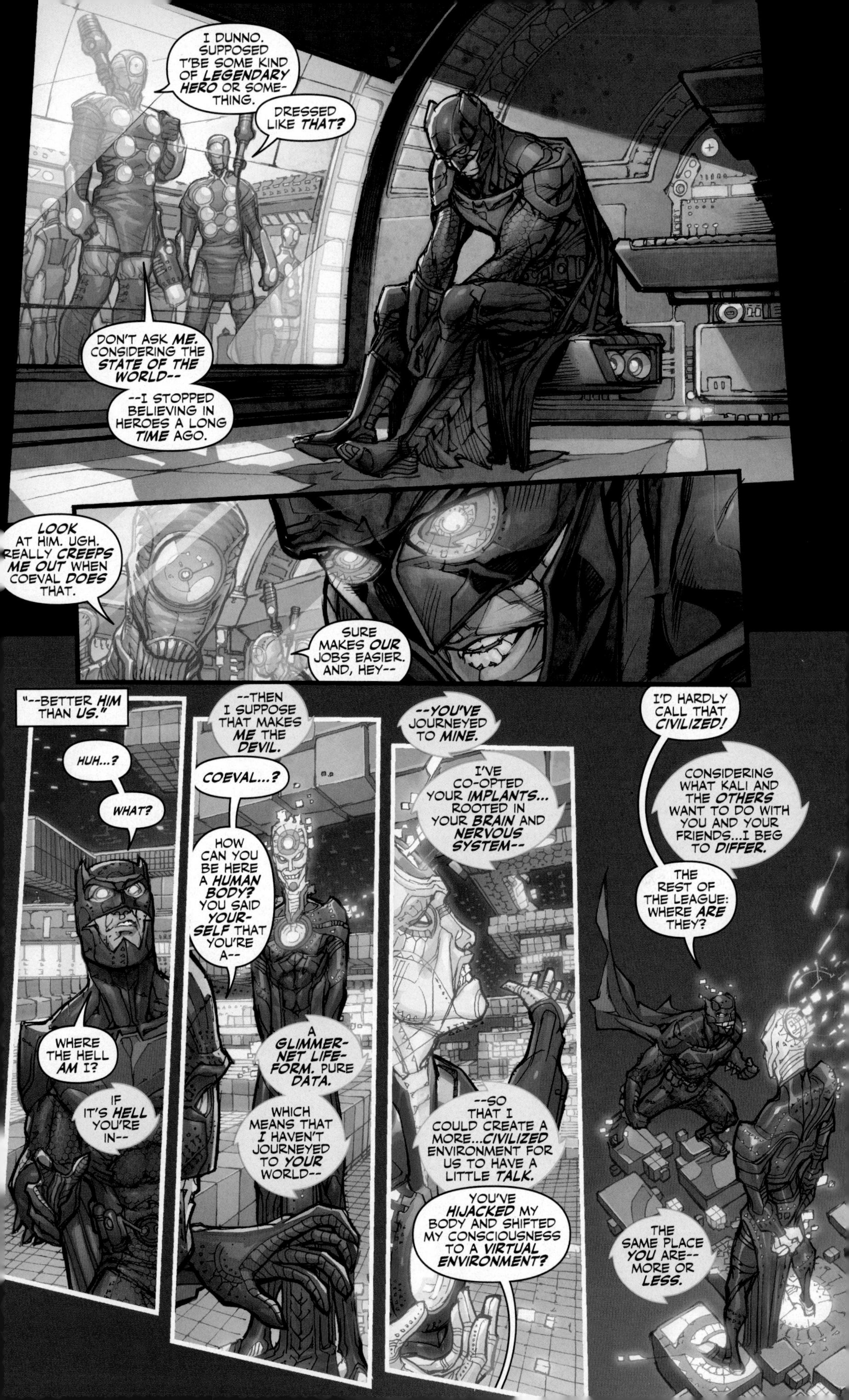
I DUNNO. SUPPOSED T'BE SOME KIND OF LEGENDARY HERO OR SOME-THING.
DRESSED LIKE THAT?
DON'T ASK ME. CONSIDERING THE STATE OF THE WORLD--
--I STOPPED BELIEVING IN HEROES A LONG TIME AGO.
LOOK AT HIM. UGH. REALLY CREEPS ME OUT WHEN COEVAL DOES THAT.
SURE MAKES OUR JOBS EASIER. AND, HEY--
"--BETTER HIM THAN US."
HUH...?
WHAT?
WHERE THE HELL AM I?
IF IT'S HELL YOU'RE IN--
--THEN I SUPPOSE THAT MAKES ME THE DEVIL.
COEVAL...?
HOW CAN YOU BE HERE A HUMAN BODY? YOU SAID YOUR-SELF THAT YOU'RE A--
A GLIMMER-NET LIFE-FORM. PURE DATA.
WHICH MEANS THAT I HAVEN'T JOURNEYED TO YOUR WORLD--
--YOU'VE JOURNEYED TO MINE.
I'VE CO-OPTED YOUR IMPLANTS... ROOTED IN YOUR BRAIN AND NERVOUS SYSTEM--
--SO THAT I COULD CREATE A MORE...CIVILIZED ENVIRONMENT FOR US TO HAVE A LITTLE TALK.
YOU'VE HIJACKED MY BODY AND SHIFTED MY CONSCIOUSNESS TO A VIRTUAL ENVIRONMENT?
I'D HARDLY CALL THAT CIVILIZED!
CONSIDERING WHAT KALI AND THE OTHERS WANT TO DO WITH YOU AND YOUR FRIENDS...I BEG TO DIFFER.
THE REST OF THE LEAGUE: WHERE ARE THEY?
THE SAME PLACE YOU ARE-- MORE OR LESS.

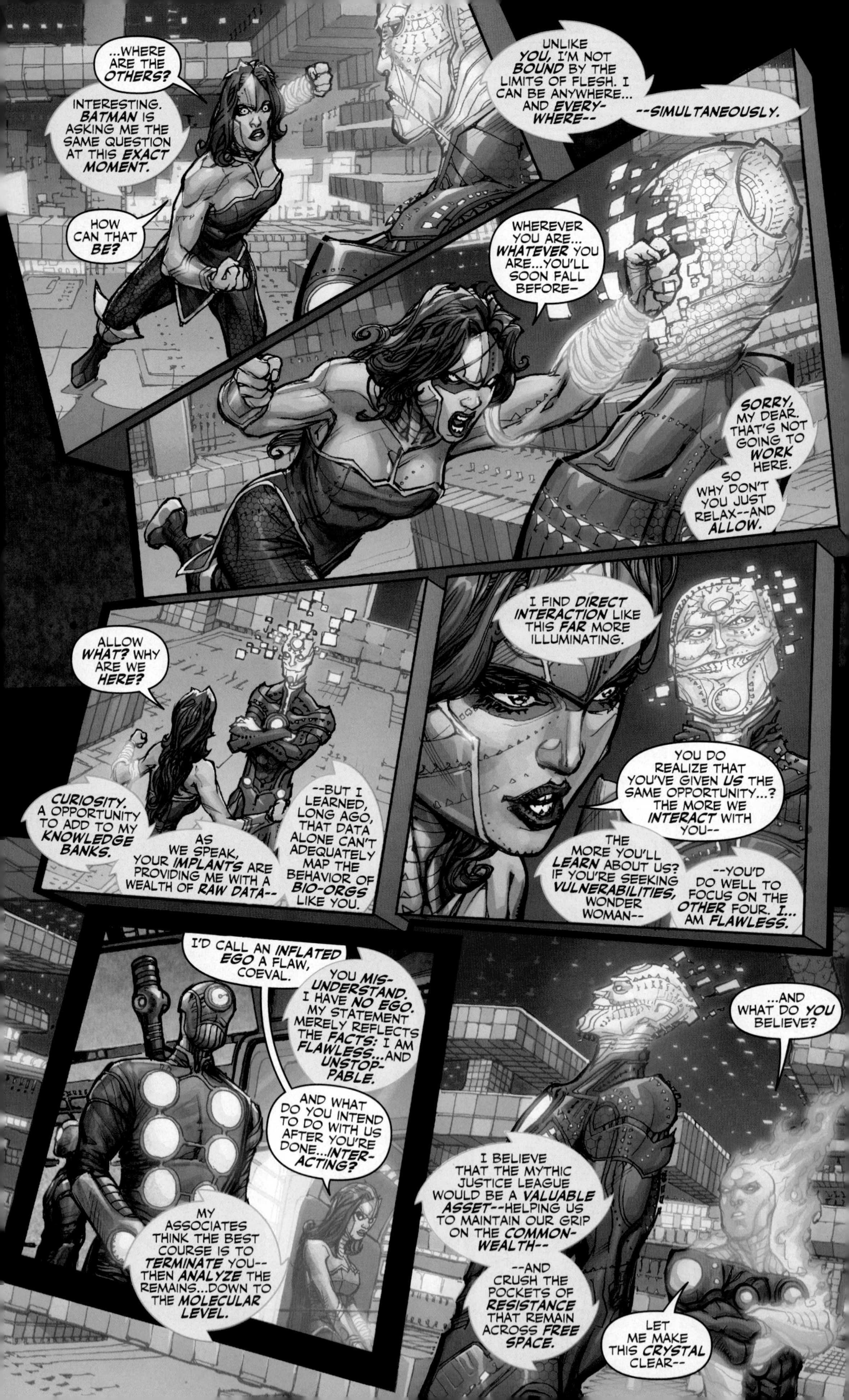
...WHERE ARE THE OTHERS?
INTERESTING. BATMAN IS ASKING ME THE SAME QUESTION AT THIS EXACT MOMENT.
HOW CAN THAT BE?
UNLIKE YOU, I'M NOT BOUND BY THE LIMITS OF FLESH. I CAN BE ANYWHERE... AND EVERY-WHERE--
--SIMULTANEOUSLY.
WHEREVER YOU ARE... WHATEVER YOU ARE...YOU'LL SOON FALL BEFORE-
SORRY, MY DEAR. THAT'S NOT GOING TO WORK HERE.
SO WHY DON'T YOU JUST RELAX--AND ALLOW.
ALLOW WHAT? WHY ARE WE HERE?
CURIOSITY. A OPPORTUNITY TO ADD TO MY KNOWLEDGE BANKS.
AS WE SPEAK, YOUR IMPLANTS ARE PROVIDING ME WITH A WEALTH OF RAW DATA--
--BUT I LEARNED, LONG AGO, THAT DATA ALONE CAN'T ADEQUATELY MAP THE BEHAVIOR OF BIO-ORGS LIKE YOU.
I FIND DIRECT INTERACTION LIKE THIS FAR MORE ILLUMINATING.
YOU DO REALIZE THAT YOU'VE GIVEN US THE SAME OPPORTUNITY...? THE MORE WE INTERACT WITH YOU--
THE MORE YOU'LL LEARN ABOUT US? IF YOU'RE SEEKING VULNERABILITIES, WONDER WOMAN--
--YOU'D DO WELL TO FOCUS ON THE OTHER FOUR. I... AM FLAWLESS.
I'D CALL AN INFLATED EGO A FLAW, COEVAL.
YOU MIS-UNDERSTAND. I HAVE NO EGO. MY STATEMENT MERELY REFLECTS THE FACTS: I AM FLAWLESS...AND UNSTOP-PABLE.
AND WHAT DO YOU INTEND TO DO WITH US AFTER YOU'RE DONE...INTER-ACTING?
MY ASSOCIATES THINK THE BEST COURSE IS TO TERMINATE YOU--THEN ANALYZE THE REMAINS...DOWN TO THE MOLECULAR LEVEL.
...AND WHAT DO YOU BELIEVE?
I BELIEVE THAT THE MYTHIC JUSTICE LEAGUE WOULD BE A VALUABLE ASSET--HELPING US TO MAINTAIN OUR GRIP ON THE COMMON-WEALTH--
--AND CRUSH THE POCKETS OF RESISTANCE THAT REMAIN ACROSS FREE SPACE.
LET ME MAKE THIS CRYSTAL CLEAR--

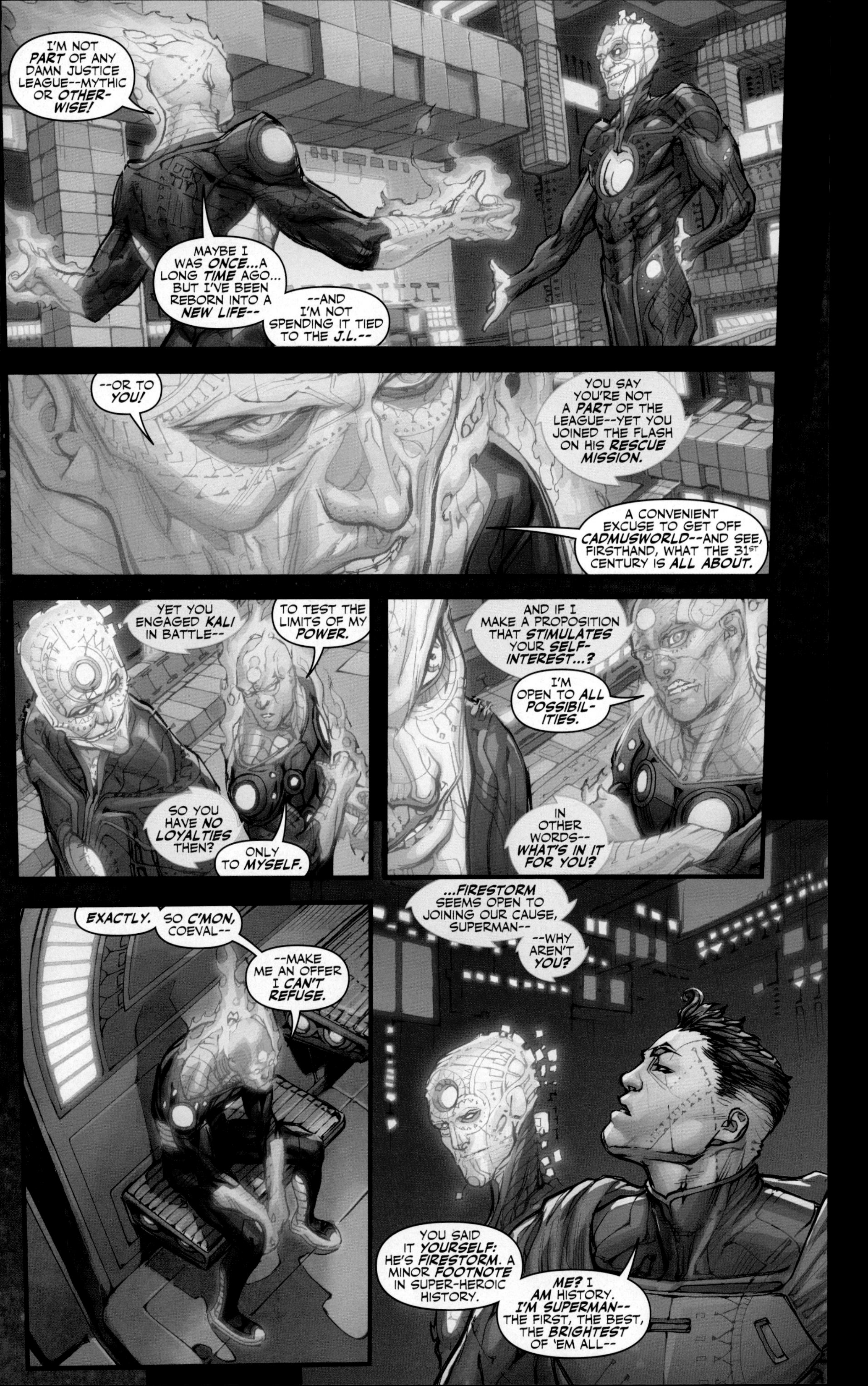

I'M NOT PART OF ANY DAMN JUSTICE LEAGUE--MYTHIC OR OTHER-WISE!
MAYBE I WAS ONCE...A LONG TIME AGO... BUT I'VE BEEN REBORN INTO A NEW LIFE--
--AND I'M NOT SPENDING IT TIED TO THE J.L.--
--OR TO YOU!
YOU SAY YOU'RE NOT A PART OF THE LEAGUE--YET YOU JOINED THE FLASH ON HIS RESCUE MISSION.
A CONVENIENT EXCUSE TO GET OFF CADMUSWORLD--AND SEE, FIRSTHAND, WHAT THE 31ST CENTURY IS ALL ABOUT.
YET YOU ENGAGED KALI IN BATTLE--
TO TEST THE LIMITS OF MY POWER.
SO YOU HAVE NO LOYALTIES THEN?
ONLY TO MYSELF.
AND IF I MAKE A PROPOSITION THAT STIMULATES YOUR SELF-INTEREST...?
I'M OPEN TO ALL POSSIBIL-ITIES.
IN OTHER WORDS--WHAT'S IN IT FOR YOU?
EXACTLY.
SO C'MON, COEVAL--
--MAKE ME AN OFFER I CAN'T REFUSE.
...FIRESTORM SEEMS OPEN TO JOINING OUR CAUSE, SUPERMAN--
--WHY AREN'T YOU?
YOU SAID IT YOURSELF: HE'S FIRESTORM. A MINOR FOOTNOTE IN SUPER-HEROIC HISTORY.
ME? I AM HISTORY. I'M SUPERMAN-- THE FIRST, THE BEST, THE BRIGHTEST OF 'EM ALL--

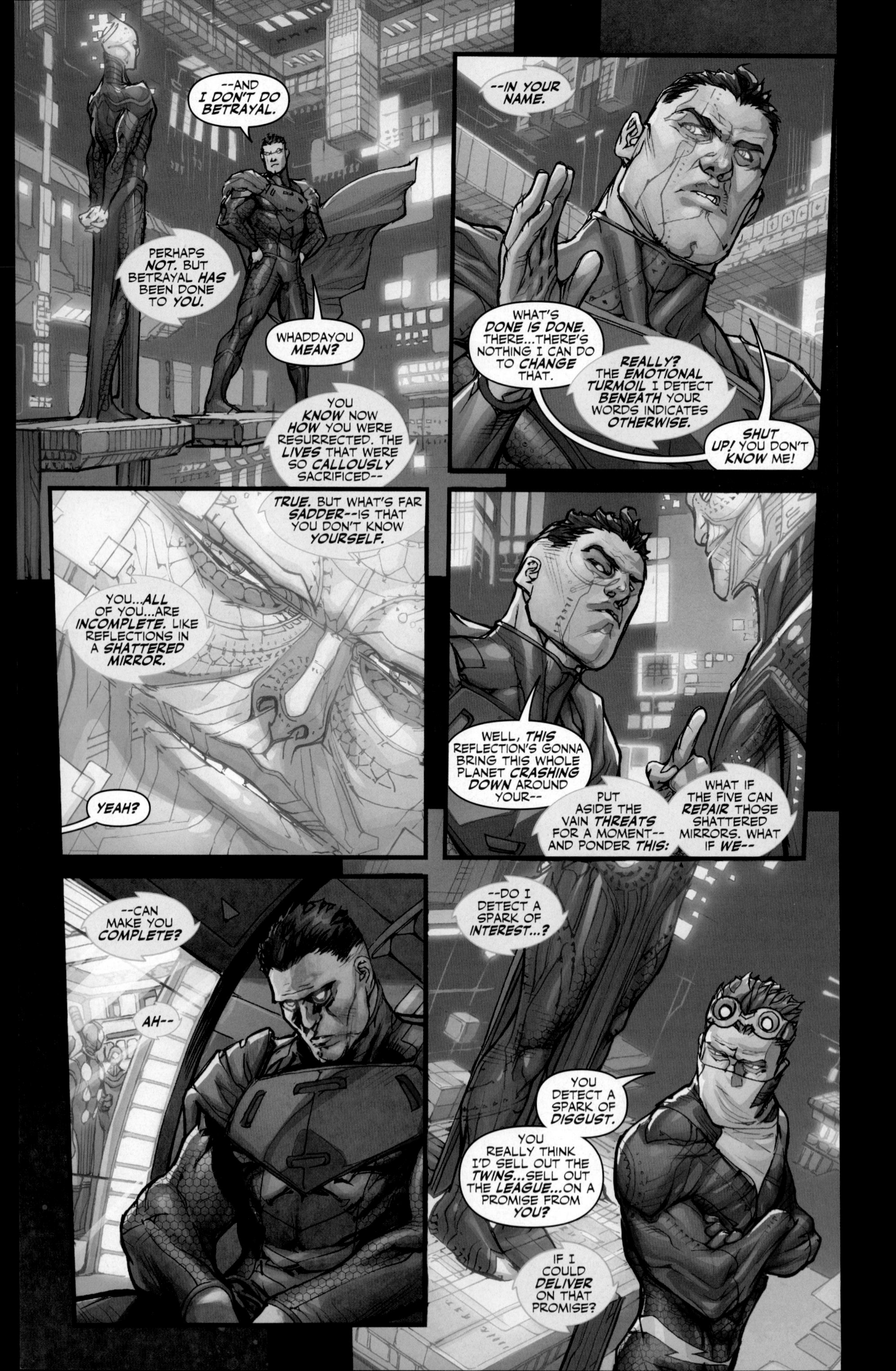
--AND I DON'T DO BETRAYAL.
PERHAPS NOT. BUT BETRAYAL HAS BEEN DONE TO YOU.
WHADDAYOU MEAN?
YOU KNOW NOW HOW YOU WERE RESURRECTED. THE LIVES THAT WERE SO CALLOUSLY SACRIFICED--
--IN YOUR NAME.
WHAT'S DONE IS DONE. THERE...THERE'S NOTHING I CAN DO TO CHANGE THAT.
REALLY? THE EMOTIONAL TURMOIL I DETECT BENEATH YOUR WORDS INDICATES OTHERWISE.
SHUT UP! YOU DON'T KNOW ME!
TRUE. BUT WHAT'S FAR SADDER--IS THAT YOU DON'T KNOW YOURSELF.
YOU...ALL OF YOU...ARE INCOMPLETE. LIKE REFLECTIONS IN A SHATTERED MIRROR.
YEAH?
WELL, THIS REFLECTION'S GONNA BRING THIS WHOLE PLANET CRASHING DOWN AROUND YOUR--
PUT ASIDE THE VAIN THREATS FOR A MOMENT--AND PONDER THIS:
WHAT IF THE FIVE CAN REPAIR THOSE SHATTERED MIRRORS. WHAT IF WE--
--CAN MAKE YOU COMPLETE?
AH--
--DO I DETECT A SPARK OF INTEREST...?
YOU DETECT A SPARK OF DISGUST.
YOU REALLY THINK I'D SELL OUT THE TWINS...SELL OUT THE LEAGUE...ON A PROMISE FROM YOU?
IF I COULD DELIVER ON THAT PROMISE?

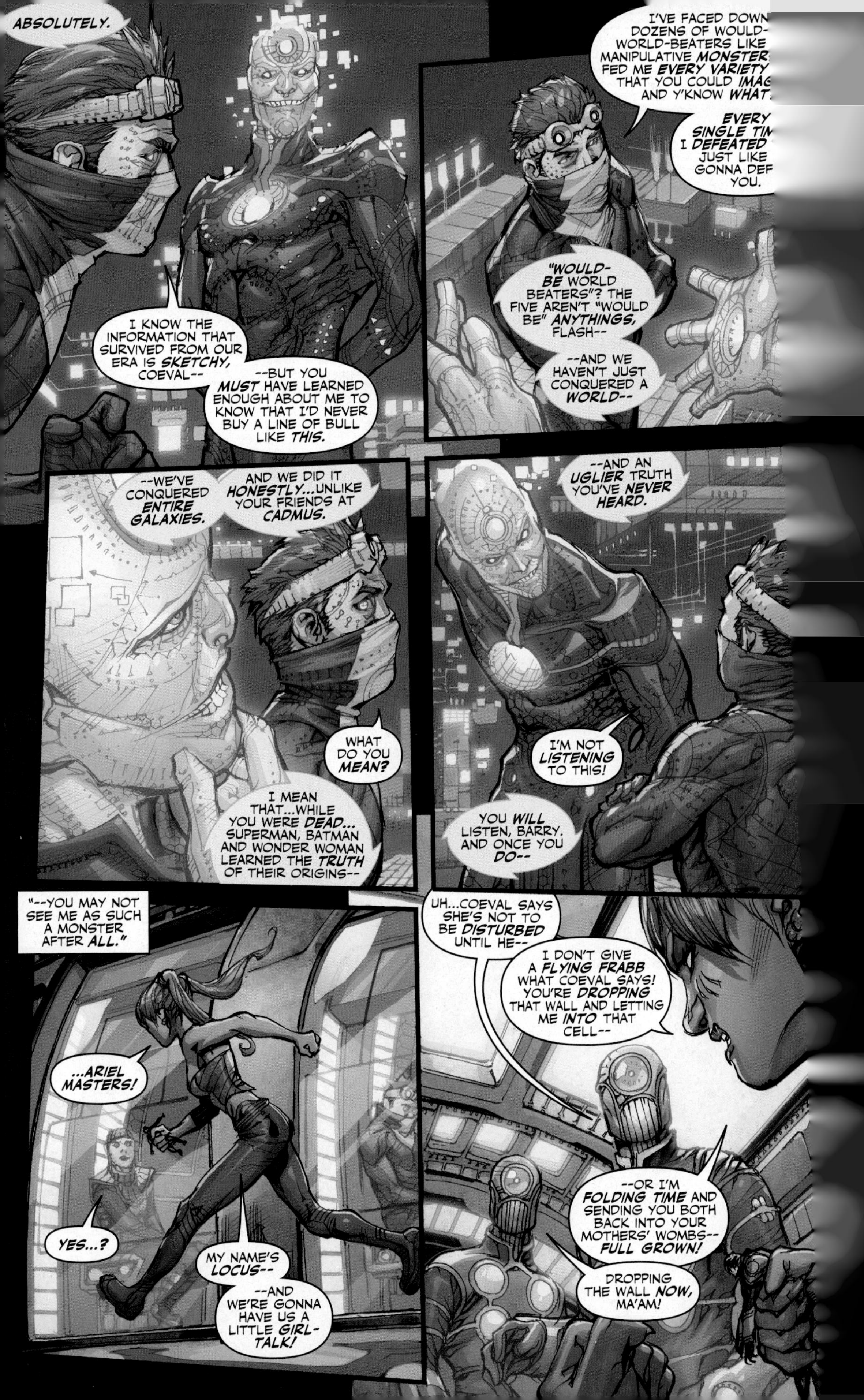
ABSOLUTELY.
I KNOW THE INFORMATION THAT SURVIVED FROM OUR ERA IS SKETCHY, COEVAL--
--BUT YOU MUST HAVE LEARNED ENOUGH ABOUT ME TO KNOW THAT I'D NEVER BUY A LINE OF BULL LIKE THIS.
I'VE FACED DOWN DOZENS OF WOULD- WORLD-BEATERS LIKE MANIPULATIVE MONSTER FED ME EVERY VARIETY THAT YOU COULD IMAG AND Y'KNOW WHAT
EVERY SINGLE TIM I DEFEATED JUST LIKE GONNA DEF YOU.
"WOULD-BE WORLD BEATERS"? THE FIVE AREN'T "WOULD BE" ANYTHINGS, FLASH--
--AND WE HAVEN'T JUST CONQUERED A WORLD--
--WE'VE CONQUERED ENTIRE GALAXIES.
AND WE DID IT HONESTLY...UNLIKE YOUR FRIENDS AT CADMUS.
WHAT DO YOU MEAN?
I MEAN THAT...WHILE YOU WERE DEAD... SUPERMAN, BATMAN AND WONDER WOMAN LEARNED THE TRUTH OF THEIR ORIGINS--
--AND AN UGLIER TRUTH YOU'VE NEVER HEARD.
I'M NOT LISTENING TO THIS!
YOU WILL LISTEN, BARRY. AND ONCE YOU DO--
"--YOU MAY NOT SEE ME AS SUCH A MONSTER AFTER ALL."
...ARIEL MASTERS!
YES...?
MY NAME'S LOCUS--
--AND WE'RE GONNA HAVE US A LITTLE GIRL-TALK!
UH...COEVAL SAYS SHE'S NOT TO BE DISTURBED UNTIL HE--
I DON'T GIVE A FLYING FRABB WHAT COEVAL SAYS! YOU'RE DROPPING THAT WALL AND LETTING ME INTO THAT CELL--
--OR I'M FOLDING TIME AND SENDING YOU BOTH BACK INTO YOUR MOTHERS' WOMBS--FULL GROWN!
DROPPING THE WALL NOW, MA'AM!

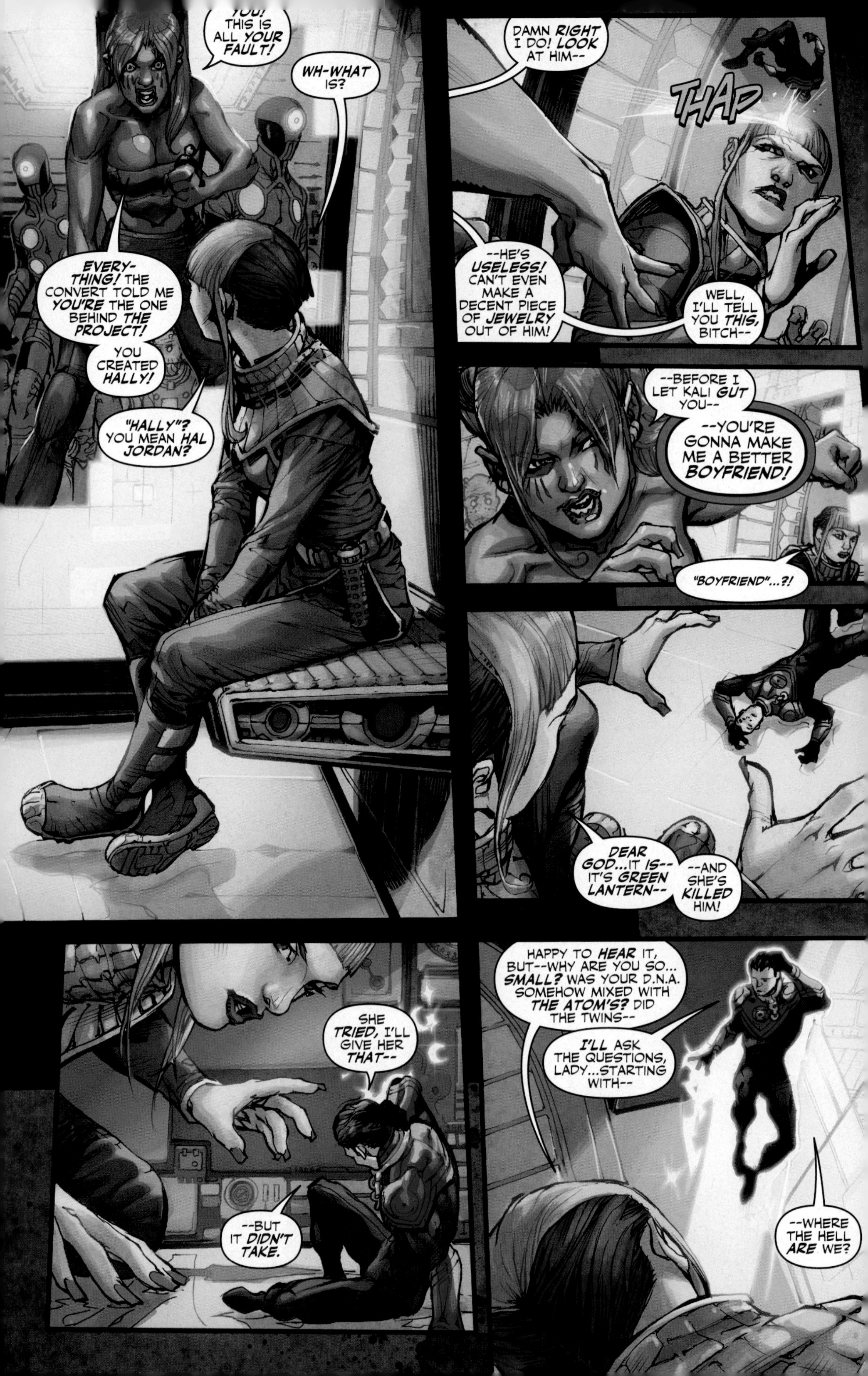
YOU! THIS IS ALL YOUR FAULT!
WH-WHAT IS?
EVERY-THING! THE CONVERT TOLD ME YOU'RE THE ONE BEHIND THE PROJECT!
YOU CREATED HALLY!
"HALLY"? YOU MEAN HAL JORDAN?
DAMN RIGHT I DO! LOOK AT HIM--
THAP
--HE'S USELESS! CAN'T EVEN MAKE A DECENT PIECE OF JEWELRY OUT OF HIM!
WELL, I'LL TELL YOU THIS, BITCH--
--BEFORE I LET KALI GUT YOU--
--YOU'RE GONNA MAKE ME A BETTER BOYFRIEND!
"BOYFRIEND"...?!
DEAR GOD...IT IS--IT'S GREEN LANTERN--
--AND SHE'S KILLED HIM!
SHE TRIED, I'LL GIVE HER THAT--
--BUT IT DIDN'T TAKE.
HAPPY TO HEAR IT, BUT--WHY ARE YOU SO... SMALL? WAS YOUR D.N.A. SOMEHOW MIXED WITH THE ATOM'S? DID THE TWINS--
I'LL ASK THE QUESTIONS, LADY...STARTING WITH--
--WHERE THE HELL ARE WE?

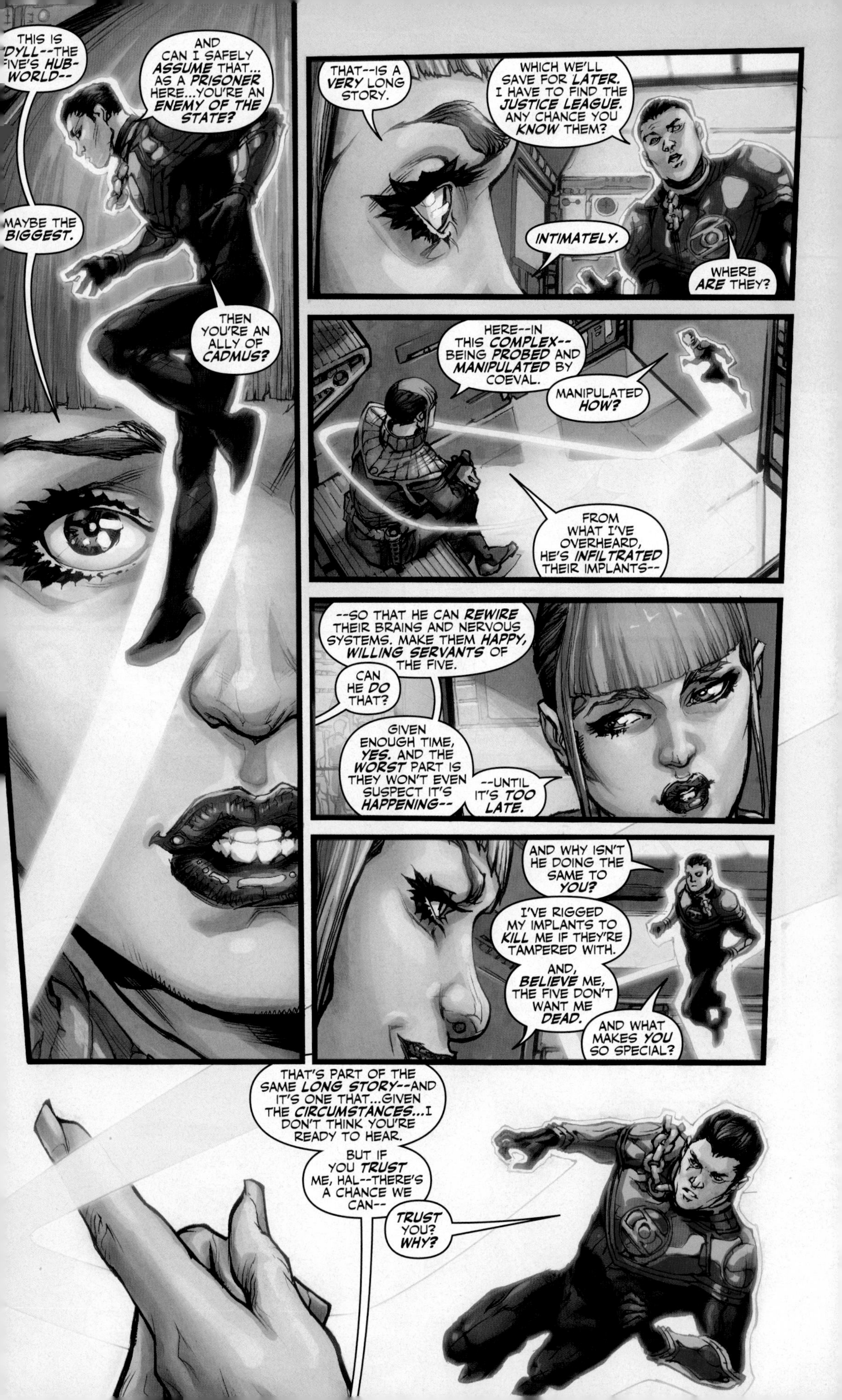

THIS IS IDYLL--THE FIVE'S HUB-WORLD--
AND CAN I SAFELY ASSUME THAT... AS A PRISONER HERE...YOU'RE AN ENEMY OF THE STATE?
MAYBE THE BIGGEST.
THEN YOU'RE AN ALLY OF CADMUS?
THAT--IS A VERY LONG STORY.
WHICH WE'LL SAVE FOR LATER. I HAVE TO FIND THE JUSTICE LEAGUE. ANY CHANCE YOU KNOW THEM?
INTIMATELY.
WHERE ARE THEY?
HERE--IN THIS COMPLEX--BEING PROBED AND MANIPULATED BY COEVAL.
MANIPULATED HOW?
FROM WHAT I'VE OVERHEARD, HE'S INFILTRATED THEIR IMPLANTS--
--SO THAT HE CAN REWIRE THEIR BRAINS AND NERVOUS SYSTEMS. MAKE THEM HAPPY, WILLING SERVANTS OF THE FIVE.
CAN HE DO THAT?
GIVEN ENOUGH TIME, YES. AND THE WORST PART IS THEY WON'T EVEN SUSPECT IT'S HAPPENING--
--UNTIL IT'S TOO LATE.
AND WHY ISN'T HE DOING THE SAME TO YOU?
I'VE RIGGED MY IMPLANTS TO KILL ME IF THEY'RE TAMPERED WITH.
AND, BELIEVE ME, THE FIVE DON'T WANT ME DEAD.
AND WHAT MAKES YOU SO SPECIAL?
THAT'S PART OF THE SAME LONG STORY--AND IT'S ONE THAT...GIVEN THE CIRCUMSTANCES...I DON'T THINK YOU'RE READY TO HEAR.
BUT IF YOU TRUST ME, HAL--THERE'S A CHANCE WE CAN--
TRUST YOU? WHY?

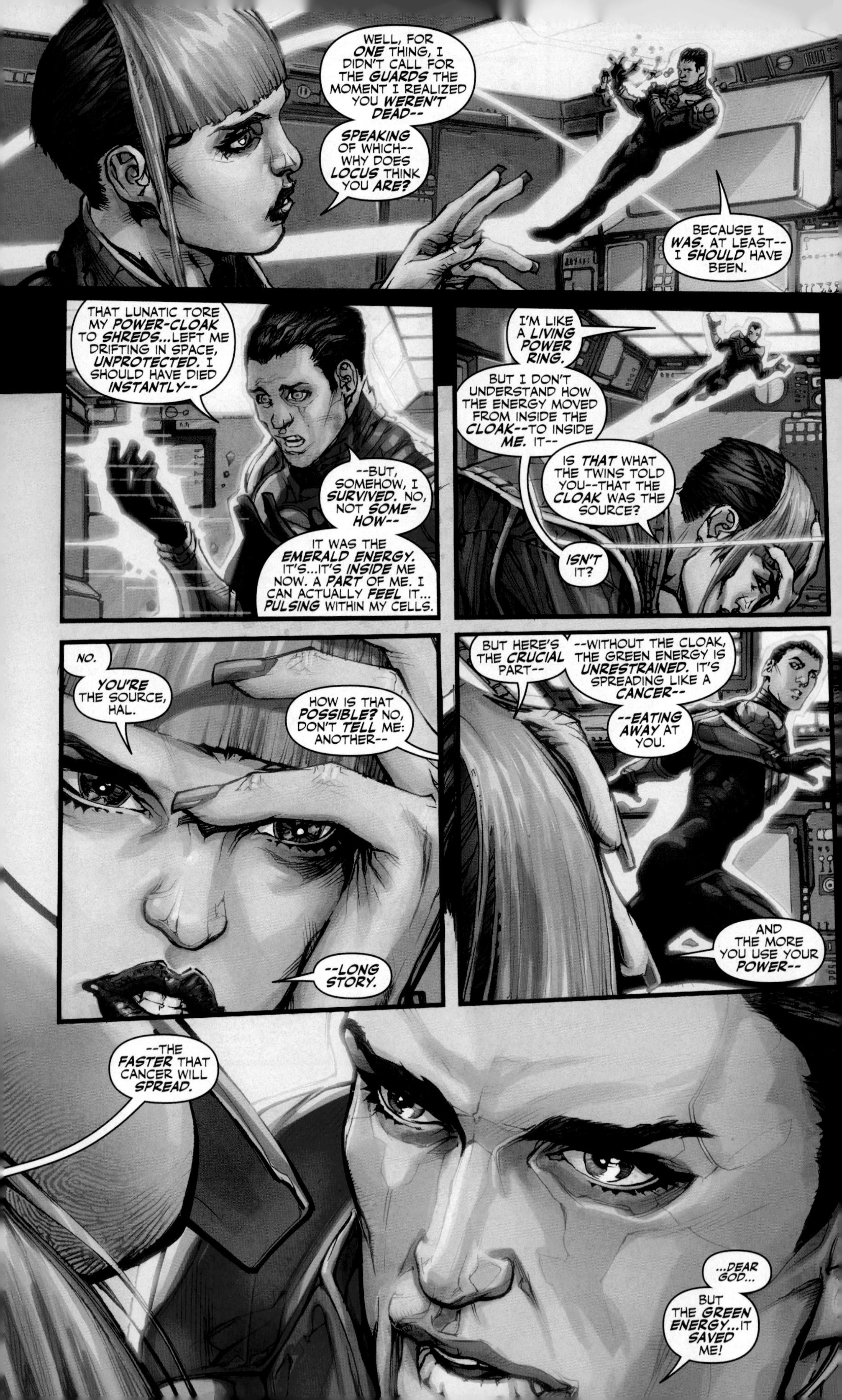

WELL, FOR ONE THING, I DIDN'T CALL FOR THE GUARDS THE MOMENT I REALIZED YOU WEREN'T DEAD--
SPEAKING OF WHICH--WHY DOES LOCUS THINK YOU ARE?
BECAUSE I WAS. AT LEAST--I SHOULD HAVE BEEN.
THAT LUNATIC TORE MY POWER-CLOAK TO SHREDS...LEFT ME DRIFTING IN SPACE, UNPROTECTED. I SHOULD HAVE DIED INSTANTLY--
--BUT, SOMEHOW, I SURVIVED. NO, NOT SOME-HOW--
IT WAS THE EMERALD ENERGY. IT'S...IT'S INSIDE ME NOW. A PART OF ME. I CAN ACTUALLY FEEL IT... PULSING WITHIN MY CELLS.
I'M LIKE A LIVING POWER RING.
BUT I DON'T UNDERSTAND HOW THE ENERGY MOVED FROM INSIDE THE CLOAK--TO INSIDE ME. IT--
IS THAT WHAT THE TWINS TOLD YOU--THAT THE CLOAK WAS THE SOURCE?
ISN'T IT?
NO.
YOU'RE THE SOURCE, HAL.
HOW IS THAT POSSIBLE? NO, DON'T TELL ME: ANOTHER--
--LONG STORY.
BUT HERE'S THE CRUCIAL PART--
--WITHOUT THE CLOAK, THE GREEN ENERGY IS UNRESTRAINED. IT'S SPREADING LIKE A CANCER--
--EATING AWAY AT YOU.
AND THE MORE YOU USE YOUR POWER--
--THE FASTER THAT CANCER WILL SPREAD.
...DEAR GOD...
BUT THE GREEN ENERGY...IT SAVED ME!

WHEN LOCUS SHREDDED THE *CLOAK*...IT *KICKED* IN--

...CTIVATED, SUSPECT, BY YOUR *CONSCIOUS MIND*...THE *WILL TO SURVIVE*.

SO THE ENERGY IS *KILLING* ME...AND *KEEPING* ME *ALIVE* AT THE SAME TIME?

IT'S... *COMPLICATED*. BUT *LOCUS*--DIDN'T SHE *REALIZE* THAT--

I'M NOT A *MORON*: I PLAYED *POSSUM*. WAITED FOR MY CHANCE TO *ESCAPE*.

BUT THAT *GIRL*...SHE'S *OBSESSIVE!* CARRIED ME *EVERYWHERE!*

BUT SHE MADE A *HELLUVA* MISTAKE LEAVING ME *HERE*.

NOW TELL ME WHERE SUPERMAN AND THE *OTHERS* ARE AND I'LL--

YOU'LL *WHAT?*

USE YOUR *POWER* TO *BREAK* THEM *OUT?*

YES!

AND *ACCELERATE* THE *GREEN CANCER?*

GUARANTEE A *SHORT LIFE* AND A *PAINFUL DEATH?*

I DON'T SEE THAT I HAVE A *CHOICE*. THEY'RE MY *FRIENDS*. I *OWE* THEM MY LIFE--

--A *THOUSAND* TIMES OVER.

YOU'RE *EVERYTHING* HISTORY *SAYS* YOU ARE, HAL JORDAN--

--AND *SO MUCH MORE*.

WHERE HAS COEVAL *TAKEN* THEM?

YOU HAVE TO UNDERSTAND-- THE SECOND YOU ATTEMPT TO *WAKE* ONE...HE'LL *KNOW*--

--AND YOU'LL *LOSE* THE ELEMENT OF *SURPRISE*.

IN *THAT* CASE--

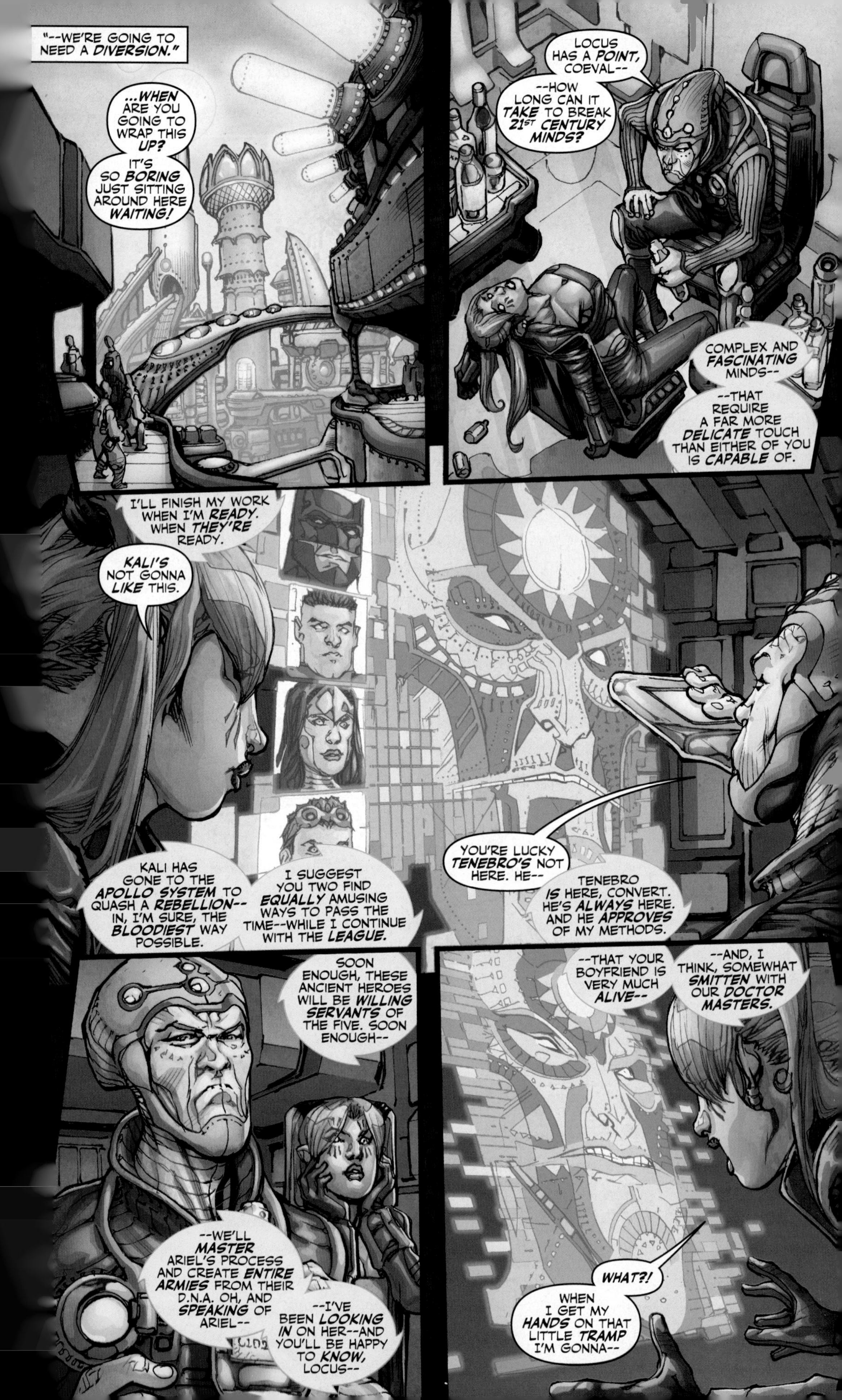
"--WE'RE GOING TO NEED A DIVERSION."
...WHEN ARE YOU GOING TO WRAP THIS UP?
IT'S SO BORING JUST SITTING AROUND HERE WAITING!
LOCUS HAS A POINT, COEVAL--
--HOW LONG CAN IT TAKE TO BREAK 21ST CENTURY MINDS?
COMPLEX AND FASCINATING MINDS--
--THAT REQUIRE A FAR MORE DELICATE TOUCH THAN EITHER OF YOU IS CAPABLE OF.
I'LL FINISH MY WORK WHEN I'M READY. WHEN THEY'RE READY.
KALI'S NOT GONNA LIKE THIS.
KALI HAS GONE TO THE APOLLO SYSTEM TO QUASH A REBELLION-- IN, I'M SURE, THE BLOODIEST WAY POSSIBLE.
I SUGGEST YOU TWO FIND EQUALLY AMUSING WAYS TO PASS THE TIME--WHILE I CONTINUE WITH THE LEAGUE.
YOU'RE LUCKY TENEBRO'S NOT HERE. HE--
TENEBRO IS HERE, CONVERT. HE'S ALWAYS HERE. AND HE APPROVES OF MY METHODS.
SOON ENOUGH, THESE ANCIENT HEROES WILL BE WILLING SERVANTS OF THE FIVE. SOON ENOUGH--
--WE'LL MASTER ARIEL'S PROCESS AND CREATE ENTIRE ARMIES FROM THEIR D.N.A. OH, AND SPEAKING OF ARIEL--
--I'VE BEEN LOOKING IN ON HER--AND YOU'LL BE HAPPY TO KNOW, LOCUS--
--THAT YOUR BOYFRIEND IS VERY MUCH ALIVE--
--AND, I THINK, SOMEWHAT SMITTEN WITH OUR DOCTOR MASTERS.
WHAT?!
WHEN I GET MY HANDS ON THAT LITTLE TRAMP I'M GONNA--

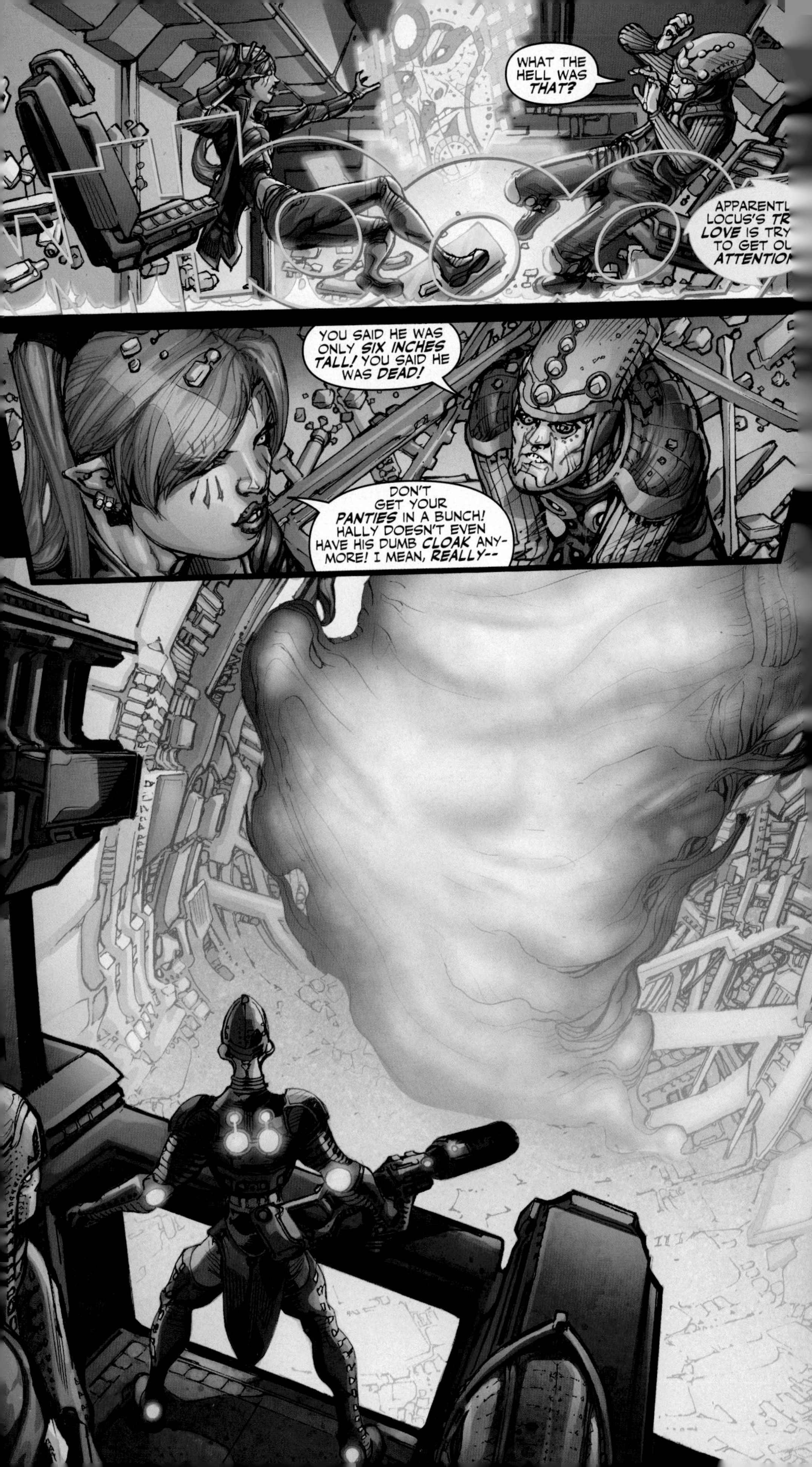

WHAT THE HELL WAS THAT?
APPARENTL LOCUS'S TR LOVE IS TRY TO GET OU ATTENTION
YOU SAID HE WAS ONLY SIX INCHES TALL! YOU SAID HE WAS DEAD!
DON'T GET YOUR PANTIES IN A BUNCH! HALLY DOESN'T EVEN HAVE HIS DUMB CLOAK ANY-MORE! I MEAN, REALLY--

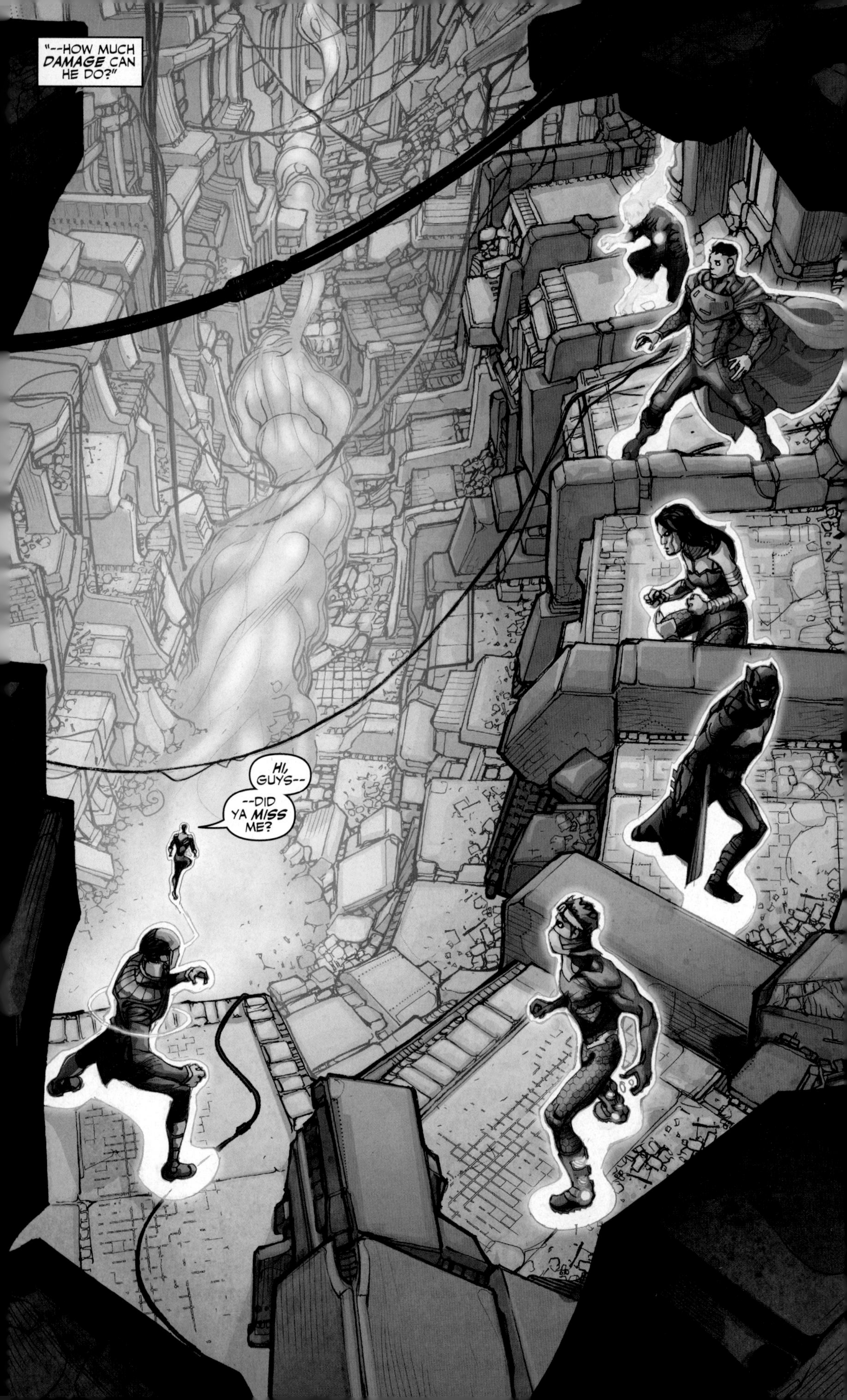
"--HOW MUCH DAMAGE CAN HE DO?"
HI, GUYS--
--DID YA MISS ME?

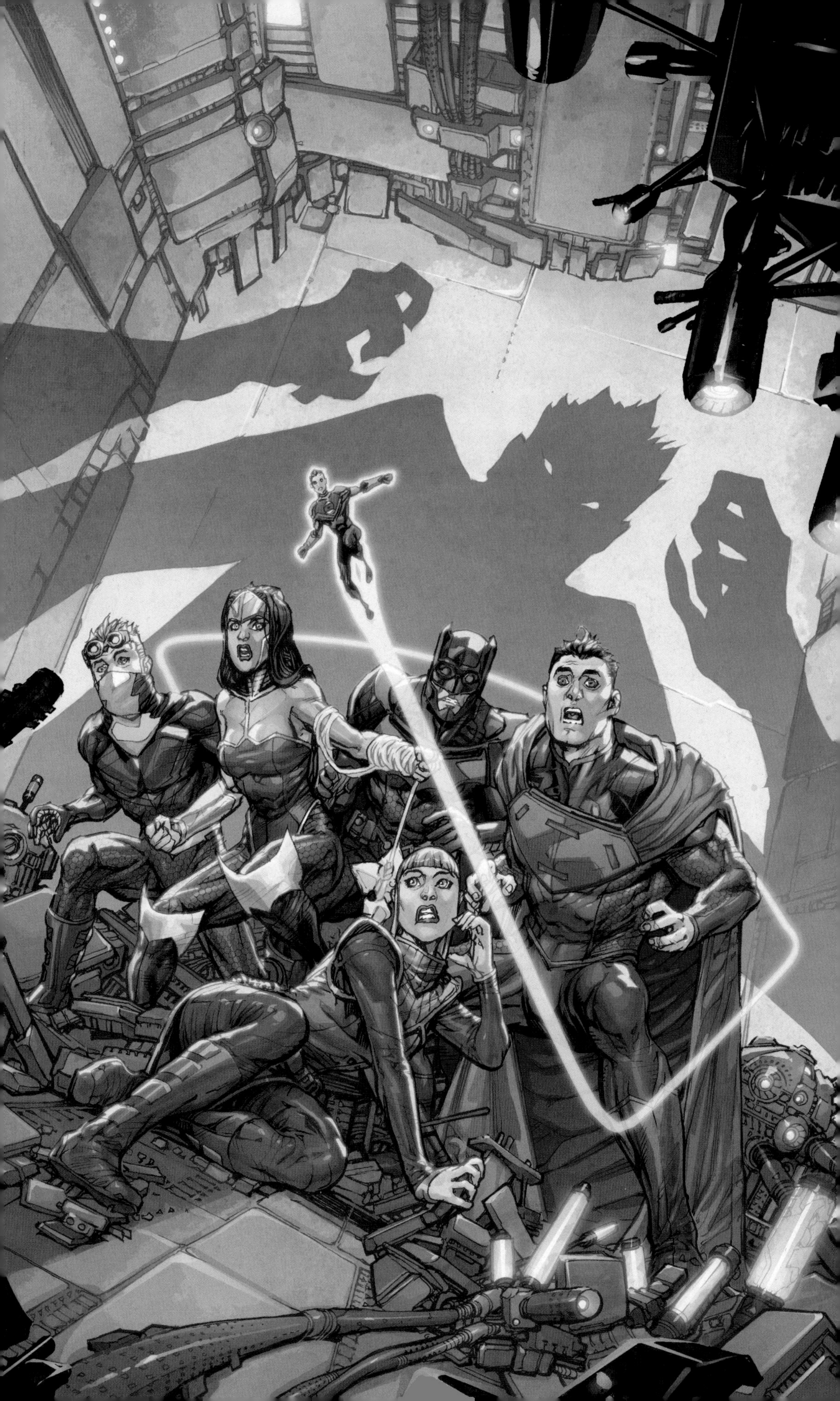

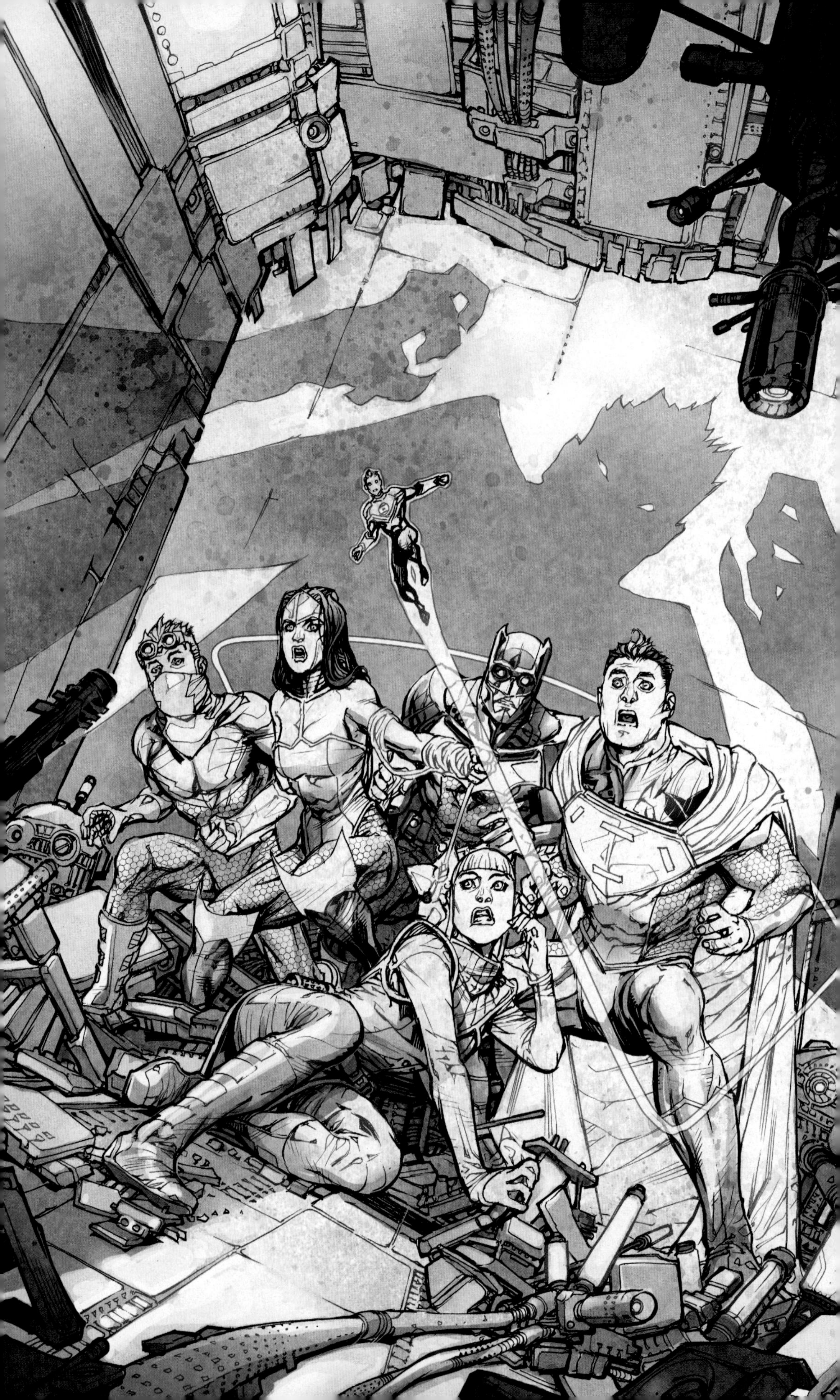

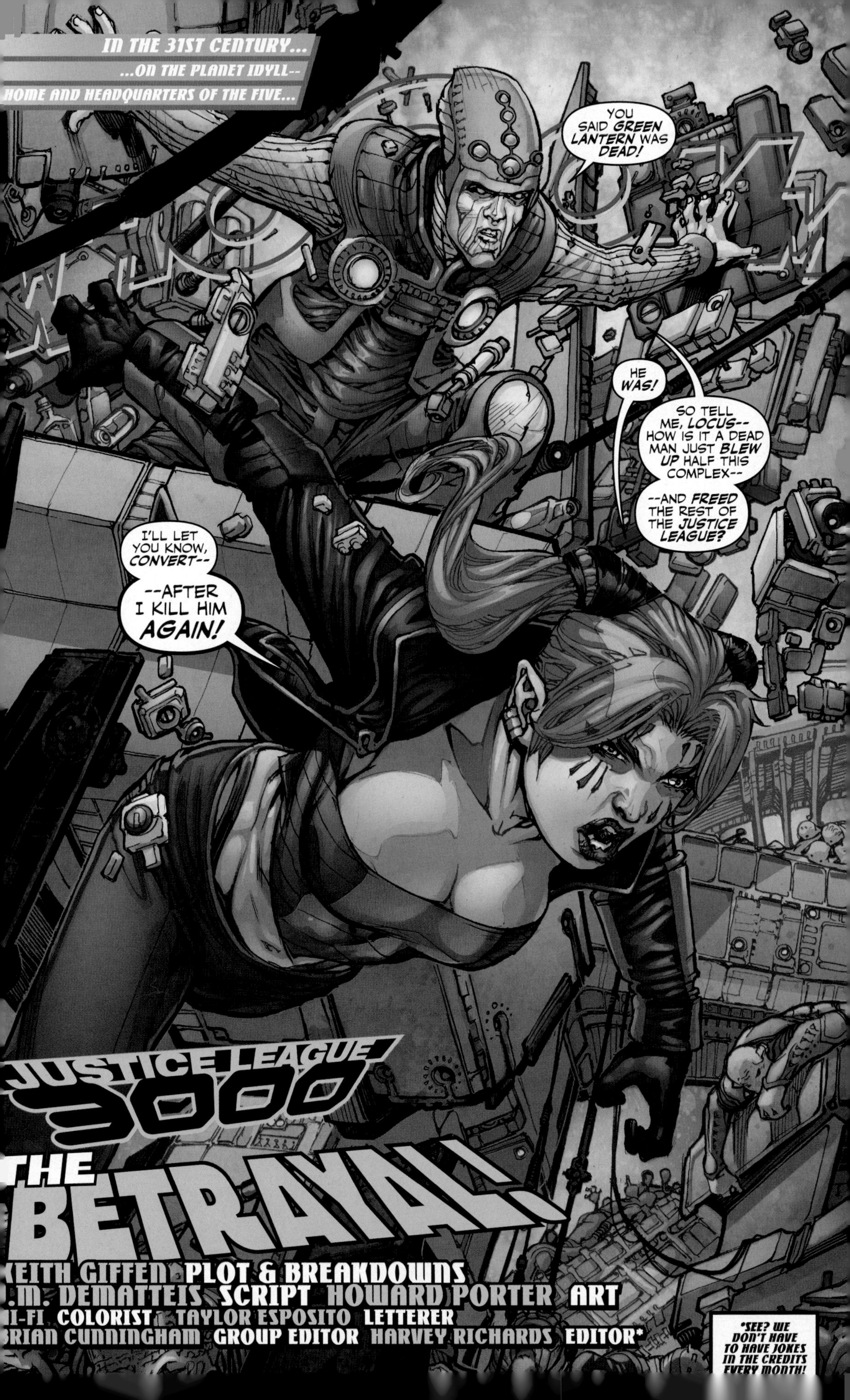
IN THE 31ST CENTURY...
...ON THE PLANET IDYLL--
HOME AND HEADQUARTERS OF THE FIVE...
YOU SAID GREEN LANTERN WAS DEAD!
HE WAS!
SO TELL ME, LOCUS-- HOW IS IT A DEAD MAN JUST BLEW UP HALF THIS COMPLEX--
--AND FREED THE REST OF THE JUSTICE LEAGUE?
I'LL LET YOU KNOW, CONVERT--
--AFTER I KILL HIM AGAIN!
JUSTICE LEAGUE 3000
THE BETRAYAL!
EITH GIFFEN PLOT & BREAKDOWNS
.M. DEMATTEIS SCRIPT HOWARD PORTER ART
I-FI COLORIST TAYLOR ESPOSITO LETTERER
RIAN CUNNINGHAM GROUP EDITOR HARVEY RICHARDS EDITOR*
*SEE? WE DON'T HAVE TO HAVE JOKES IN THE CREDITS EVERY MONTH!

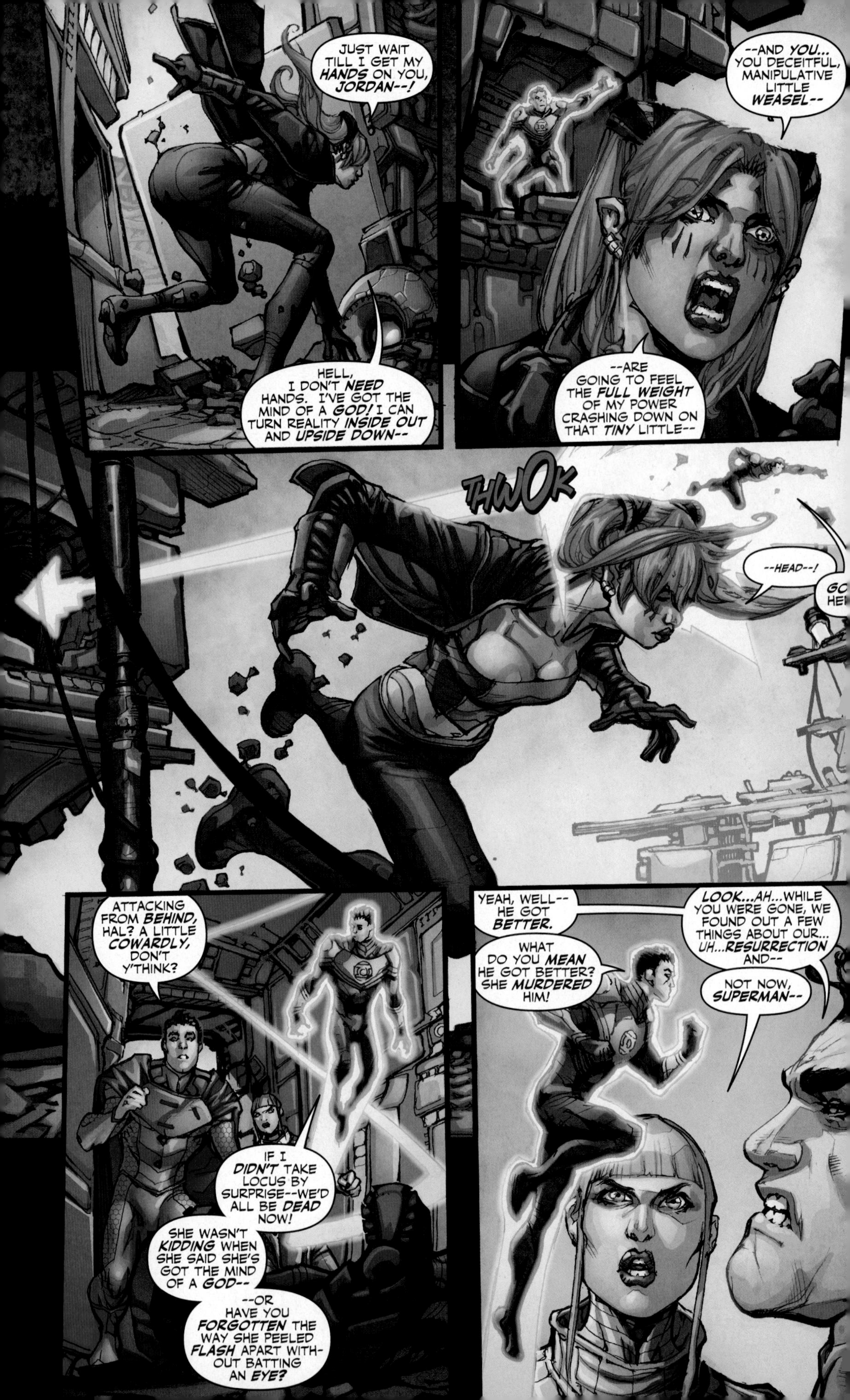
JUST WAIT TILL I GET MY HANDS ON YOU, JORDAN--!
HELL, I DON'T NEED HANDS. I'VE GOT THE MIND OF A GOD! I CAN TURN REALITY INSIDE OUT AND UPSIDE DOWN--
--AND YOU... YOU DECEITFUL, MANIPULATIVE LITTLE WEASEL--
--ARE GOING TO FEEL THE FULL WEIGHT OF MY POWER CRASHING DOWN ON THAT TINY LITTLE--
THWOK
--HEAD--!
ATTACKING FROM BEHIND, HAL? A LITTLE COWARDLY, DON'T Y'THINK?
IF I DIDN'T TAKE LOCUS BY SURPRISE--WE'D ALL BE DEAD NOW!
SHE WASN'T KIDDING WHEN SHE SAID SHE'S GOT THE MIND OF A GOD--
--OR HAVE YOU FORGOTTEN THE WAY SHE PEELED FLASH APART WITH-OUT BATTING AN EYE?
YEAH, WELL-- HE GOT BETTER.
WHAT DO YOU MEAN HE GOT BETTER? SHE MURDERED HIM!
LOOK...AH...WHILE YOU WERE GONE, WE FOUND OUT A FEW THINGS ABOUT OUR... UH...RESURRECTION AND--
NOT NOW, SUPERMAN--

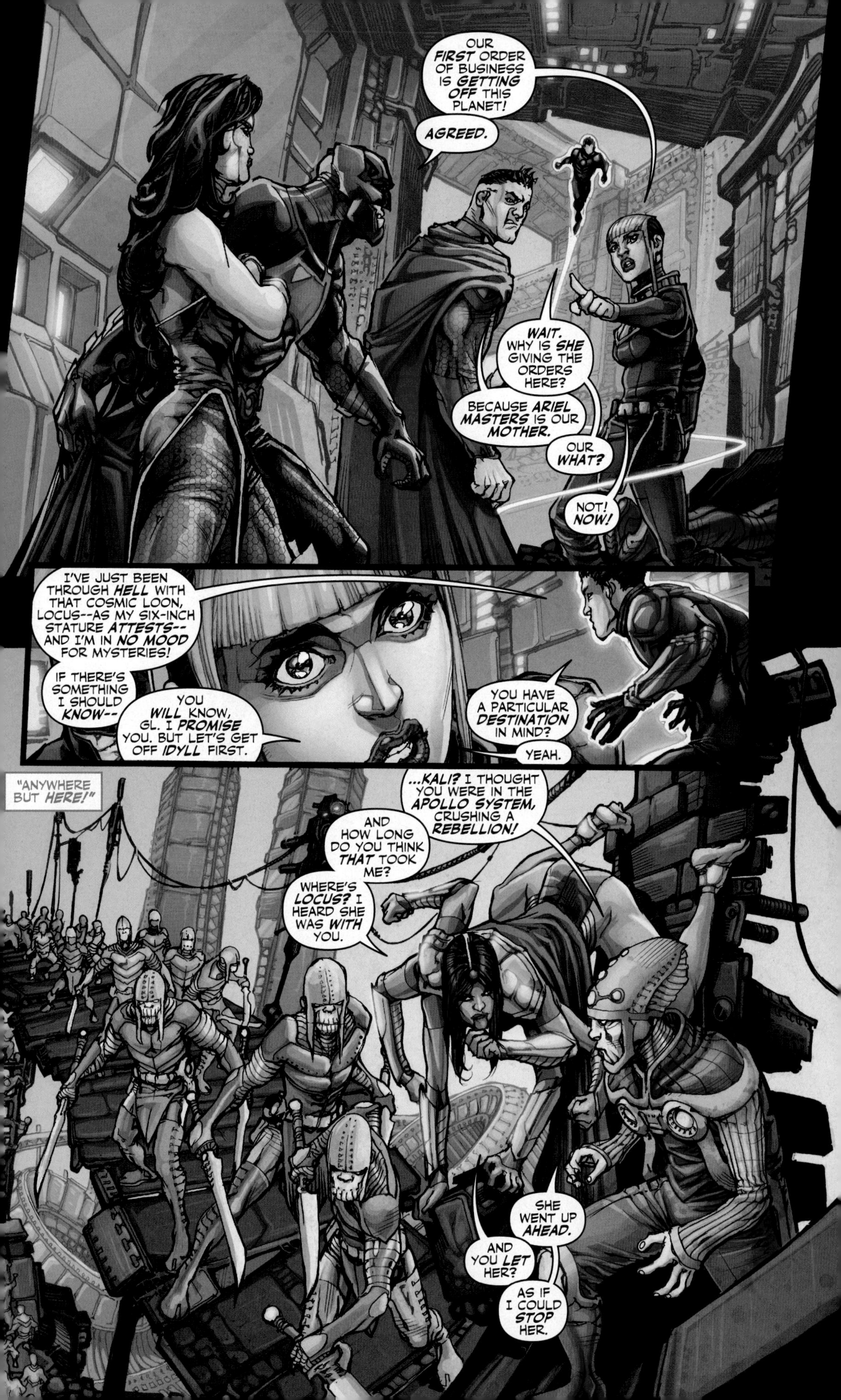

OUR FIRST ORDER OF BUSINESS IS GETTING OFF THIS PLANET!
AGREED.
WAIT. WHY IS SHE GIVING THE ORDERS HERE?
BECAUSE ARIEL MASTERS IS OUR MOTHER.
OUR WHAT?
NOT! NOW!
I'VE JUST BEEN THROUGH HELL WITH THAT COSMIC LOON, LOCUS--AS MY SIX-INCH STATURE ATTESTS--AND I'M IN NO MOOD FOR MYSTERIES!
IF THERE'S SOMETHING I SHOULD KNOW--
YOU WILL KNOW, GL. I PROMISE YOU. BUT LET'S GET OFF IDYLL FIRST.
YOU HAVE A PARTICULAR DESTINATION IN MIND?
YEAH.
"ANYWHERE BUT HERE!"
...KALI? I THOUGHT YOU WERE IN THE APOLLO SYSTEM, CRUSHING A REBELLION!
AND HOW LONG DO YOU THINK THAT TOOK ME?
WHERE'S LOCUS? I HEARD SHE WAS WITH YOU.
SHE WENT UP AHEAD.
AND YOU LET HER?
AS IF I COULD STOP HER.

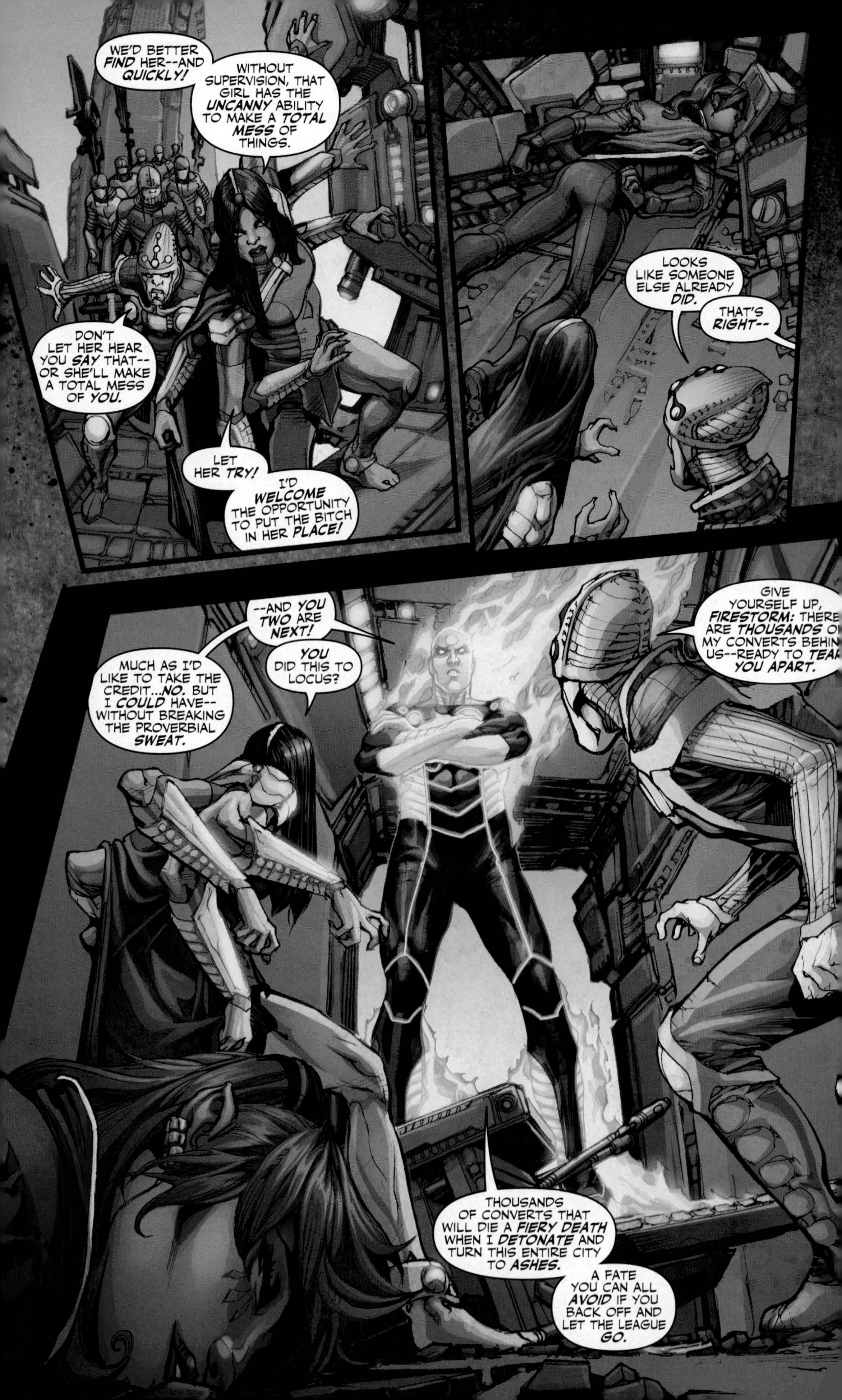

WE'D BETTER FIND HER--AND QUICKLY!
WITHOUT SUPERVISION, THAT GIRL HAS THE UNCANNY ABILITY TO MAKE A TOTAL MESS OF THINGS.
DON'T LET HER HEAR YOU SAY THAT--OR SHE'LL MAKE A TOTAL MESS OF YOU.
LET HER TRY!
I'D WELCOME THE OPPORTUNITY TO PUT THE BITCH IN HER PLACE!
LOOKS LIKE SOMEONE ELSE ALREADY DID.
THAT'S RIGHT--
--AND YOU TWO ARE NEXT!
YOU DID THIS TO LOCUS?
MUCH AS I'D LIKE TO TAKE THE CREDIT...NO. BUT I COULD HAVE--WITHOUT BREAKING THE PROVERBIAL SWEAT.
GIVE YOURSELF UP, FIRESTORM: THERE ARE THOUSANDS OF MY CONVERTS BEHIN US--READY TO TEAR YOU APART.
THOUSANDS OF CONVERTS THAT WILL DIE A FIERY DEATH WHEN I DETONATE AND TURN THIS ENTIRE CITY TO ASHES.
A FATE YOU CAN ALL AVOID IF YOU BACK OFF AND LET THE LEAGUE GO.

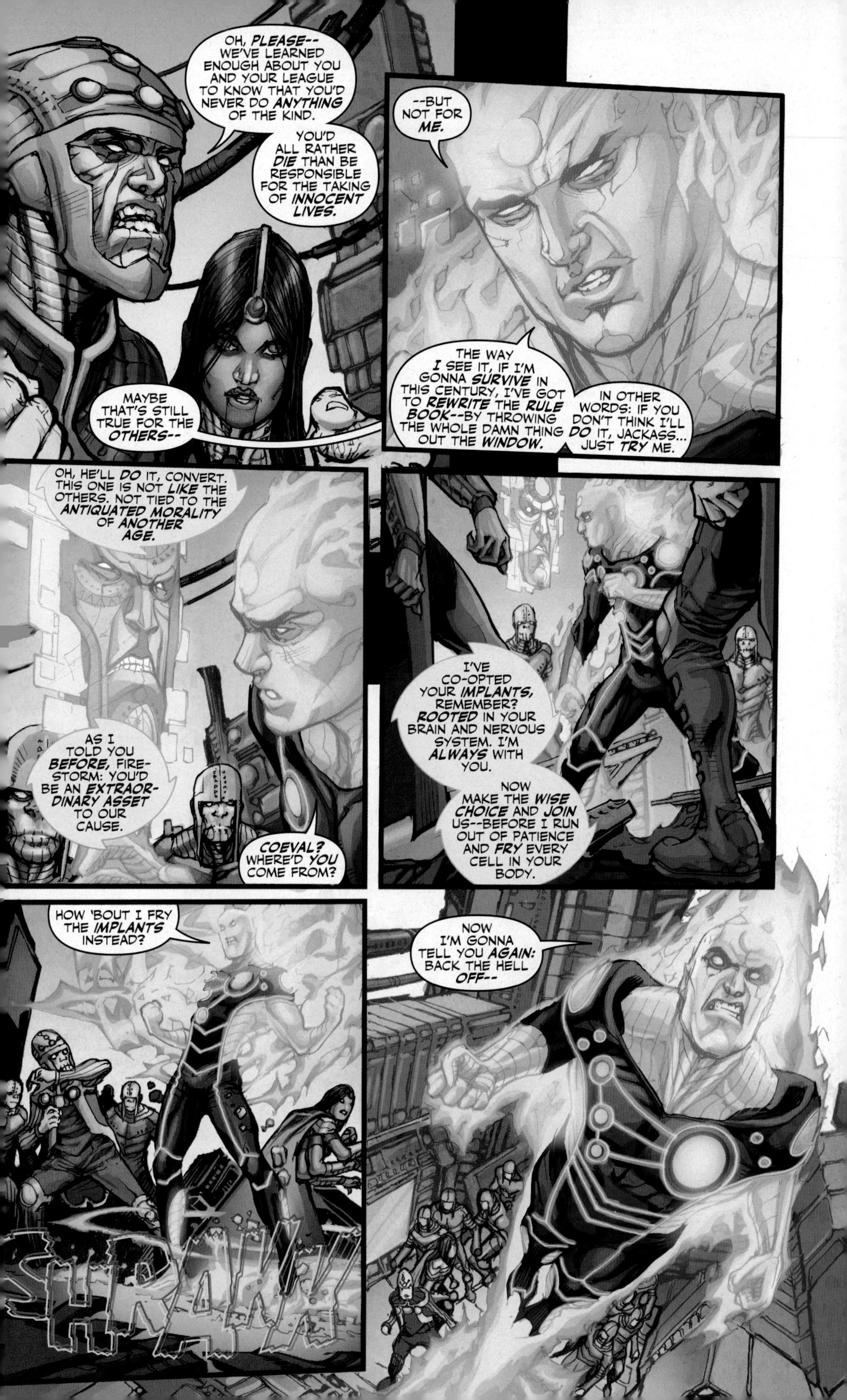
OH, PLEASE-- WE'VE LEARNED ENOUGH ABOUT YOU AND YOUR LEAGUE TO KNOW THAT YOU'D NEVER DO ANYTHING OF THE KIND.
YOU'D ALL RATHER DIE THAN BE RESPONSIBLE FOR THE TAKING OF INNOCENT LIVES.
MAYBE THAT'S STILL TRUE FOR THE OTHERS--
--BUT NOT FOR ME.
THE WAY I SEE IT, IF I'M GONNA SURVIVE IN THIS CENTURY, I'VE GOT TO REWRITE THE RULE BOOK--BY THROWING THE WHOLE DAMN THING OUT THE WINDOW.
IN OTHER WORDS: IF YOU DON'T THINK I'LL DO IT, JACKASS... JUST TRY ME.
OH, HE'LL DO IT, CONVERT. THIS ONE IS NOT LIKE THE OTHERS. NOT TIED TO THE ANTIQUATED MORALITY OF ANOTHER AGE.
AS I TOLD YOU BEFORE, FIRE-STORM: YOU'D BE AN EXTRAOR-DINARY ASSET TO OUR CAUSE.
COEVAL? WHERE'D YOU COME FROM?
I'VE CO-OPTED YOUR IMPLANTS, REMEMBER? ROOTED IN YOUR BRAIN AND NERVOUS SYSTEM. I'M ALWAYS WITH YOU.
NOW MAKE THE WISE CHOICE AND JOIN US--BEFORE I RUN OUT OF PATIENCE AND FRY EVERY CELL IN YOUR BODY.
HOW 'BOUT I FRY THE IMPLANTS INSTEAD?
SHRAAKK
NOW I'M GONNA TELL YOU AGAIN: BACK THE HELL OFF--

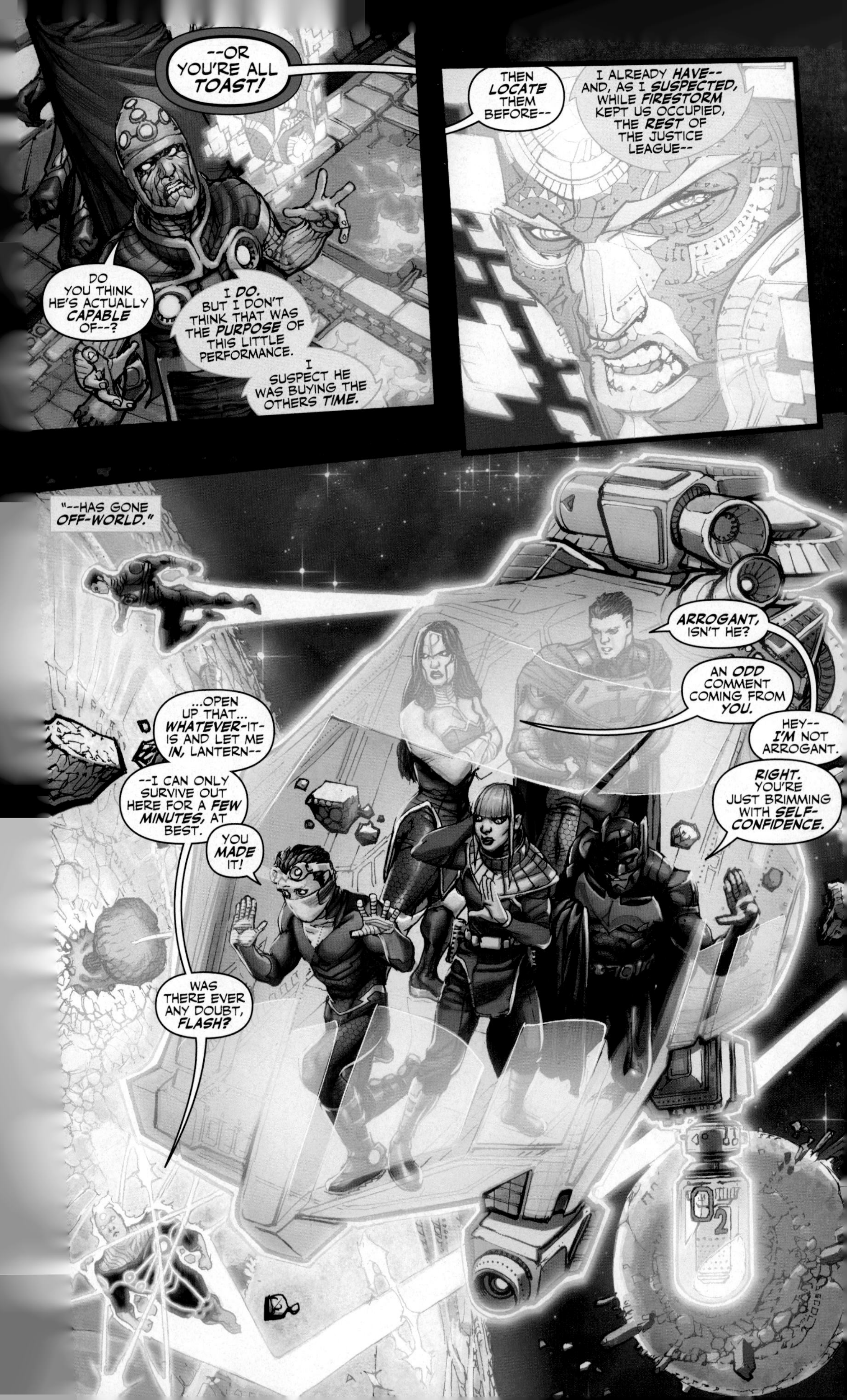
--OR YOU'RE ALL TOAST!
DO YOU THINK HE'S ACTUALLY CAPABLE OF--?
I DO. BUT I DON'T THINK THAT WAS THE PURPOSE OF THIS LITTLE PERFORMANCE.
I SUSPECT HE WAS BUYING THE OTHERS TIME.
THEN LOCATE THEM BEFORE--
I ALREADY HAVE--AND, AS I SUSPECTED, WHILE FIRESTORM KEPT US OCCUPIED, THE REST OF THE JUSTICE LEAGUE--
"--HAS GONE OFF-WORLD."
ARROGANT, ISN'T HE?
AN ODD COMMENT COMING FROM YOU.
HEY--I'M NOT ARROGANT.
RIGHT. YOU'RE JUST BRIMMING WITH SELF-CONFIDENCE.
...OPEN UP THAT... WHATEVER-IT-IS AND LET ME IN, LANTERN--
--I CAN ONLY SURVIVE OUT HERE FOR A FEW MINUTES, AT BEST.
YOU MADE IT!
WAS THERE EVER ANY DOUBT, FLASH?
O_2

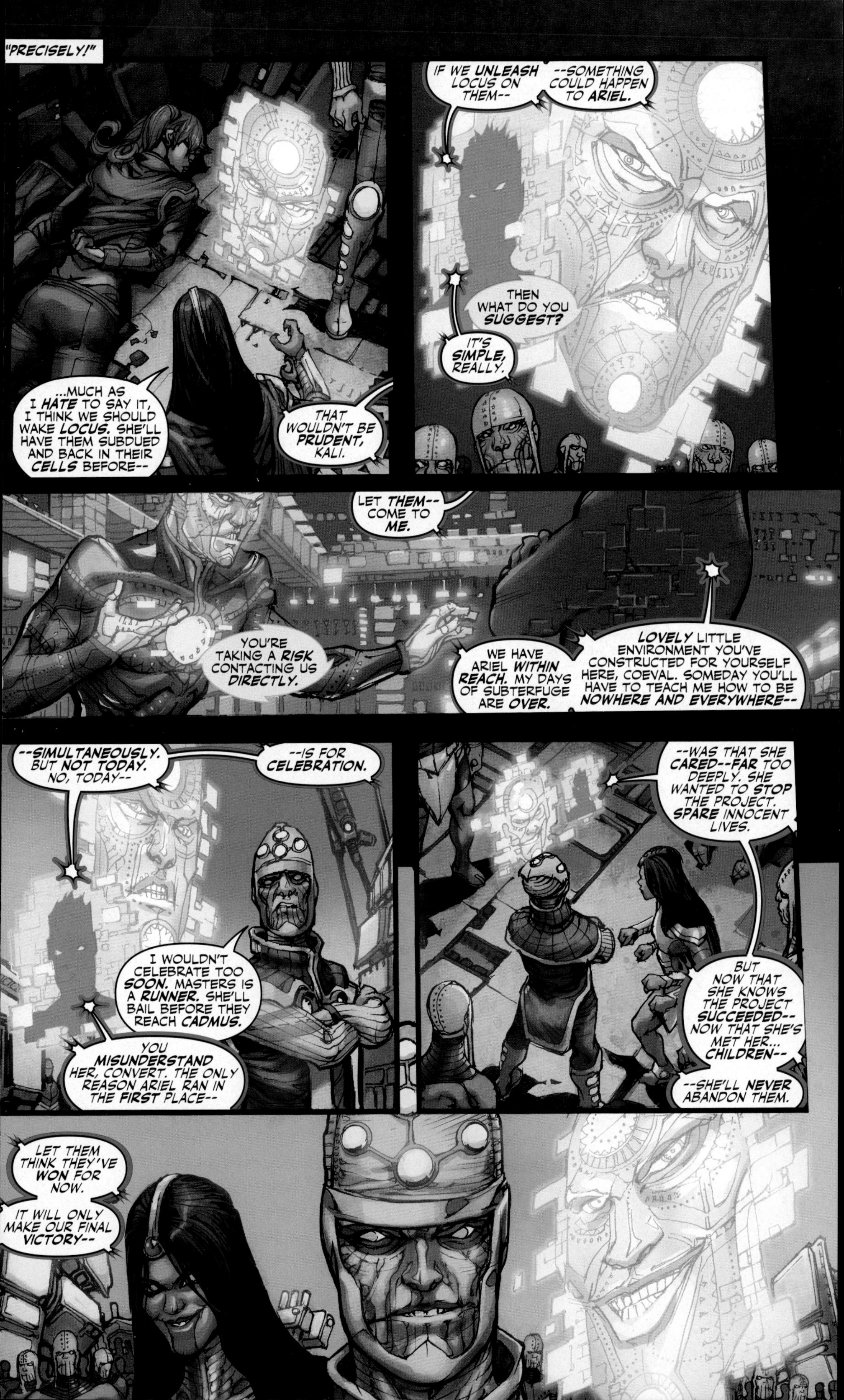
"PRECISELY!"
...MUCH AS I HATE TO SAY IT, I THINK WE SHOULD WAKE LOCUS. SHE'LL HAVE THEM SUBDUED AND BACK IN THEIR CELLS BEFORE--
THAT WOULDN'T BE PRUDENT, KALI.
IF WE UNLEASH LOCUS ON THEM--
--SOMETHING COULD HAPPEN TO ARIEL.
THEN WHAT DO YOU SUGGEST?
IT'S SIMPLE, REALLY.
LET THEM-- COME TO ME.
YOU'RE TAKING A RISK CONTACTING US DIRECTLY.
WE HAVE ARIEL WITHIN REACH. MY DAYS OF SUBTERFUGE ARE OVER.
LOVELY LITTLE ENVIRONMENT YOU'VE CONSTRUCTED FOR YOURSELF HERE, COEVAL. SOMEDAY YOU'LL HAVE TO TEACH ME HOW TO BE NOWHERE AND EVERYWHERE--
--SIMULTANEOUSLY. BUT NOT TODAY. NO, TODAY--
--IS FOR CELEBRATION.
I WOULDN'T CELEBRATE TOO SOON. MASTERS IS A RUNNER. SHE'LL BAIL BEFORE THEY REACH CADMUS.
YOU MISUNDERSTAND HER, CONVERT. THE ONLY REASON ARIEL RAN IN THE FIRST PLACE--
--WAS THAT SHE CARED--FAR TOO DEEPLY. SHE WANTED TO STOP THE PROJECT. SPARE INNOCENT LIVES.
BUT NOW THAT SHE KNOWS THE PROJECT SUCCEEDED-- NOW THAT SHE'S MET HER... CHILDREN--
--SHE'LL NEVER ABANDON THEM.
LET THEM THINK THEY'VE WON FOR NOW.
IT WILL ONLY MAKE OUR FINAL VICTORY--

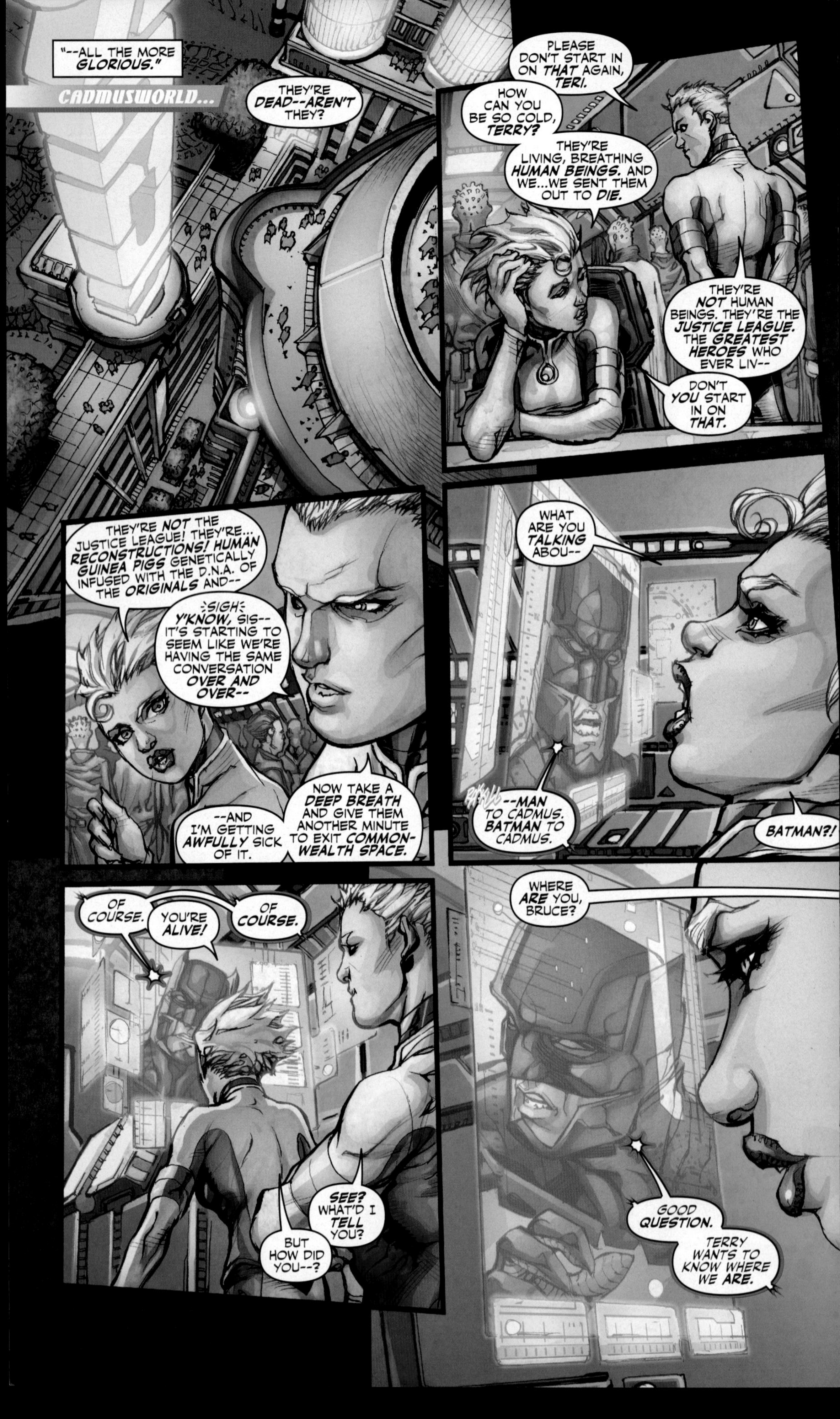
"--ALL THE MORE GLORIOUS."
CADMUSWORLD...
THEY'RE DEAD--AREN'T THEY?
HOW CAN YOU BE SO COLD, TERRY?
PLEASE DON'T START IN ON THAT AGAIN, TERI.
THEY'RE LIVING, BREATHING HUMAN BEINGS. AND WE...WE SENT THEM OUT TO DIE.
THEY'RE NOT HUMAN BEINGS. THEY'RE THE JUSTICE LEAGUE. THE GREATEST HEROES WHO EVER LIV--
DON'T YOU START IN ON THAT.
THEY'RE NOT THE JUSTICE LEAGUE! THEY'RE... HUMAN RECONSTRUCTIONS! HUMAN GUINEA PIGS GENETICALLY INFUSED WITH THE D.N.A. OF THE ORIGINALS AND--
SIGH
Y'KNOW, SIS--IT'S STARTING TO SEEM LIKE WE'RE HAVING THE SAME CONVERSATION OVER AND OVER--
--AND I'M GETTING AWFULLY SICK OF IT.
NOW TAKE A DEEP BREATH AND GIVE THEM ANOTHER MINUTE TO EXIT COMMON-WEALTH SPACE.
WHAT ARE YOU TALKING ABOU--
--MAN TO CADMUS. BATMAN TO CADMUS.
BATMAN?!
OF COURSE.
YOU'RE ALIVE!
OF COURSE.
SEE? WHAT'D I TELL YOU?
BUT HOW DID YOU--?
WHERE ARE YOU, BRUCE?
GOOD QUESTION.
TERRY WANTS TO KNOW WHERE WE ARE.

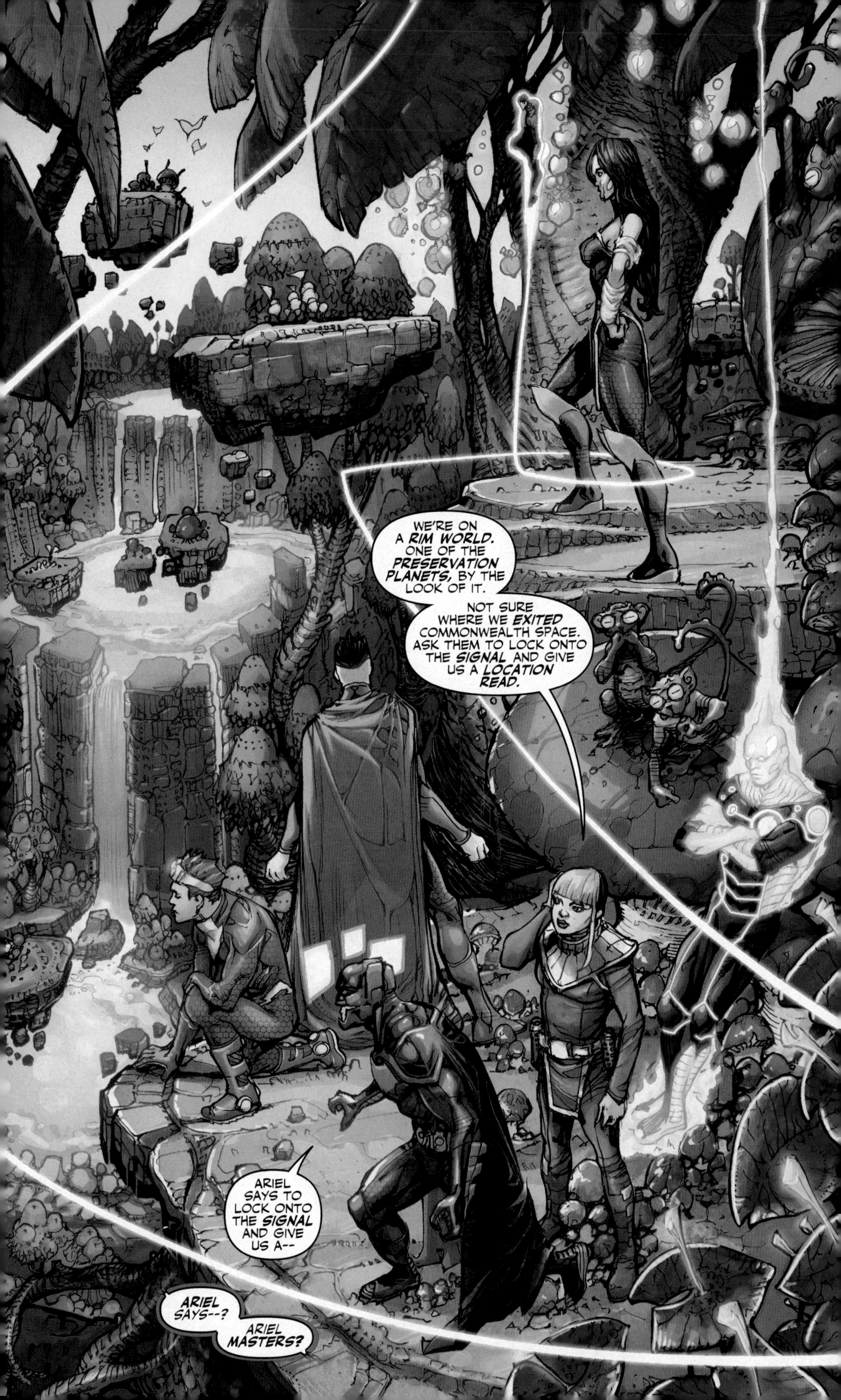

WE'RE ON A RIM WORLD. ONE OF THE PRESERVATION PLANETS, BY THE LOOK OF IT.
NOT SURE WHERE WE EXITED COMMONWEALTH SPACE. ASK THEM TO LOCK ONTO THE SIGNAL AND GIVE US A LOCATION READ.
ARIEL SAYS TO LOCK ONTO THE SIGNAL AND GIVE US A--
ARIEL SAYS--?
ARIEL MASTERS?

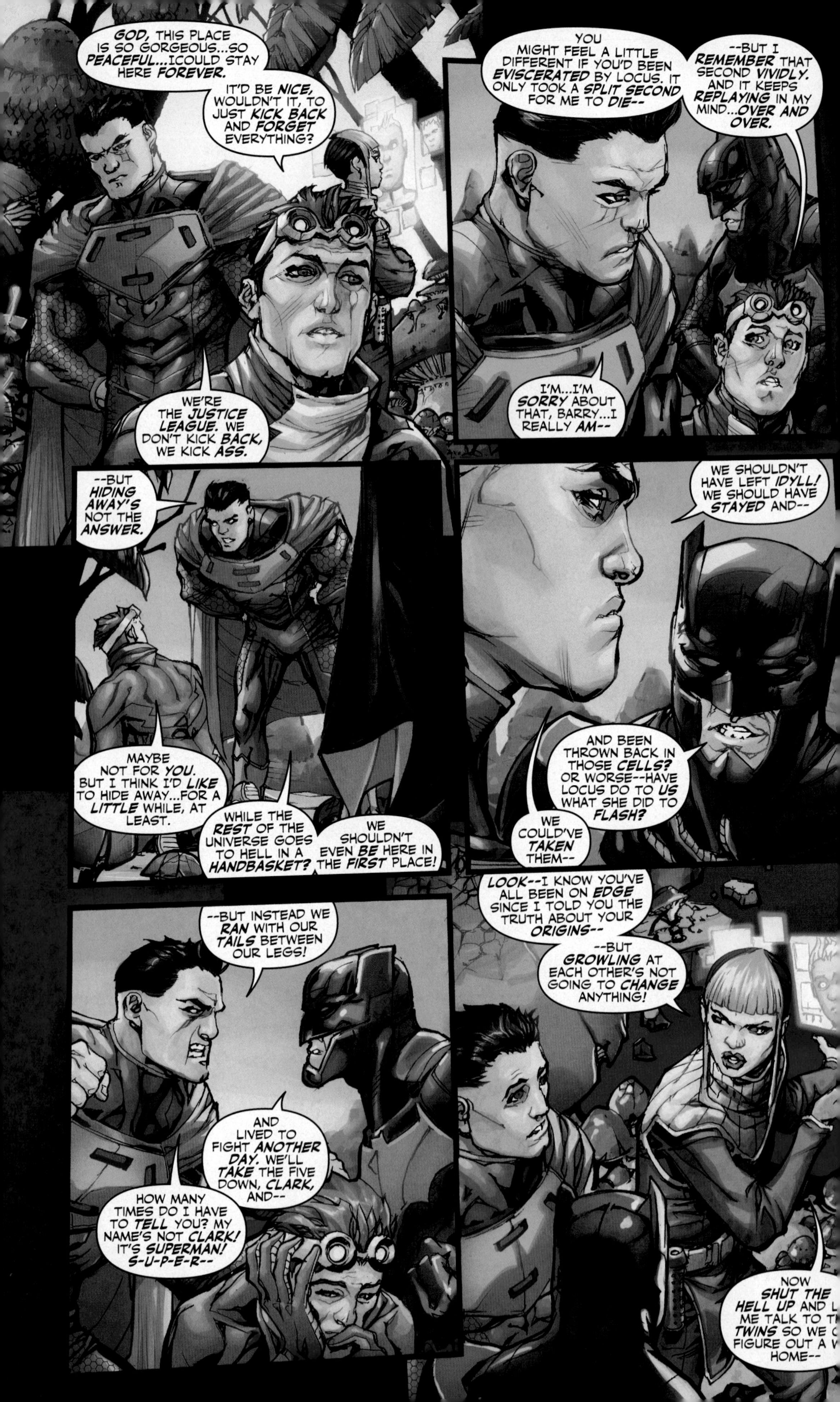
GOD, THIS PLACE IS SO GORGEOUS...SO PEACEFUL...ICOULD STAY HERE FOREVER.
IT'D BE NICE, WOULDN'T IT, TO JUST KICK BACK AND FORGET EVERYTHING?
WE'RE THE JUSTICE LEAGUE. WE DON'T KICK BACK, WE KICK ASS.
YOU MIGHT FEEL A LITTLE DIFFERENT IF YOU'D BEEN EVISCERATED BY LOCUS. IT ONLY TOOK A SPLIT SECOND FOR ME TO DIE--
--BUT I REMEMBER THAT SECOND VIVIDLY. AND IT KEEPS REPLAYING IN MY MIND...OVER AND OVER.
I'M...I'M SORRY ABOUT THAT, BARRY...I REALLY AM--
--BUT HIDING AWAY'S NOT THE ANSWER.
MAYBE NOT FOR YOU. BUT I THINK I'D LIKE TO HIDE AWAY...FOR A LITTLE WHILE, AT LEAST.
WHILE THE REST OF THE UNIVERSE GOES TO HELL IN A HANDBASKET?
WE SHOULDN'T EVEN BE HERE IN THE FIRST PLACE!
WE SHOULDN'T HAVE LEFT IDYLL! WE SHOULD HAVE STAYED AND--
WE COULD'VE TAKEN THEM--
AND BEEN THROWN BACK IN THOSE CELLS? OR WORSE--HAVE LOCUS DO TO US WHAT SHE DID TO FLASH?
--BUT INSTEAD WE RAN WITH OUR TAILS BETWEEN OUR LEGS!
AND LIVED TO FIGHT ANOTHER DAY. WE'LL TAKE THE FIVE DOWN, CLARK, AND--
HOW MANY TIMES DO I HAVE TO TELL YOU? MY NAME'S NOT CLARK! IT'S SUPERMAN! S-U-P-E-R--
LOOK--I KNOW YOU'VE ALL BEEN ON EDGE SINCE I TOLD YOU THE TRUTH ABOUT YOUR ORIGINS--
--BUT GROWLING AT EACH OTHER'S NOT GOING TO CHANGE ANYTHING!
NOW SHUT THE HELL UP AND L ME TALK TO T TWINS SO WE C FIGURE OUT A W HOME--

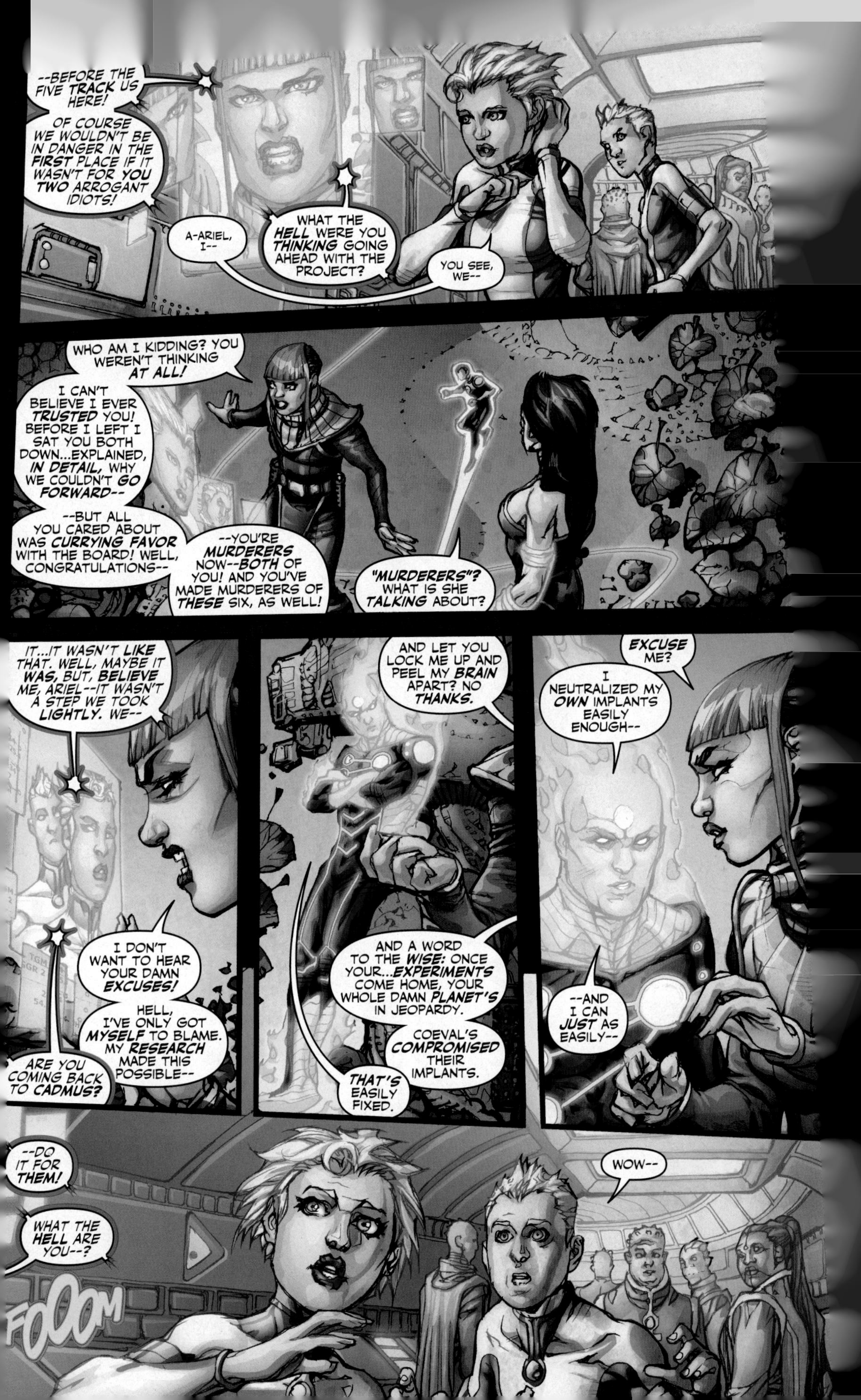
--BEFORE THE FIVE TRACK US HERE!
OF COURSE WE WOULDN'T BE IN DANGER IN THE FIRST PLACE IF IT WASN'T FOR YOU TWO ARROGANT IDIOTS!
A-ARIEL, I--
WHAT THE HELL WERE YOU THINKING GOING AHEAD WITH THE PROJECT?
YOU SEE, WE--
WHO AM I KIDDING? YOU WEREN'T THINKING AT ALL!
I CAN'T BELIEVE I EVER TRUSTED YOU! BEFORE I LEFT I SAT YOU BOTH DOWN...EXPLAINED, IN DETAIL, WHY WE COULDN'T GO FORWARD--
--BUT ALL YOU CARED ABOUT WAS CURRYING FAVOR WITH THE BOARD! WELL, CONGRATULATIONS--
--YOU'RE MURDERERS NOW--BOTH OF YOU! AND YOU'VE MADE MURDERERS OF THESE SIX, AS WELL!
"MURDERERS"? WHAT IS SHE TALKING ABOUT?
IT...IT WASN'T LIKE THAT. WELL, MAYBE IT WAS, BUT, BELIEVE ME, ARIEL--IT WASN'T A STEP WE TOOK LIGHTLY. WE--
I DON'T WANT TO HEAR YOUR DAMN EXCUSES!
HELL, I'VE ONLY GOT MYSELF TO BLAME. MY RESEARCH MADE THIS POSSIBLE--
ARE YOU COMING BACK TO CADMUS?
AND LET YOU LOCK ME UP AND PEEL MY BRAIN APART? NO THANKS.
AND A WORD TO THE WISE: ONCE YOUR...EXPERIMENTS COME HOME, YOUR WHOLE DAMN PLANET'S IN JEOPARDY.
COEVAL'S COMPROMISED THEIR IMPLANTS.
THAT'S EASILY FIXED.
EXCUSE ME?
I NEUTRALIZED MY OWN IMPLANTS EASILY ENOUGH--
--AND I CAN JUST AS EASILY--
--DO IT FOR THEM!
WHAT THE HELL ARE YOU--?
FOOOM
WOW--

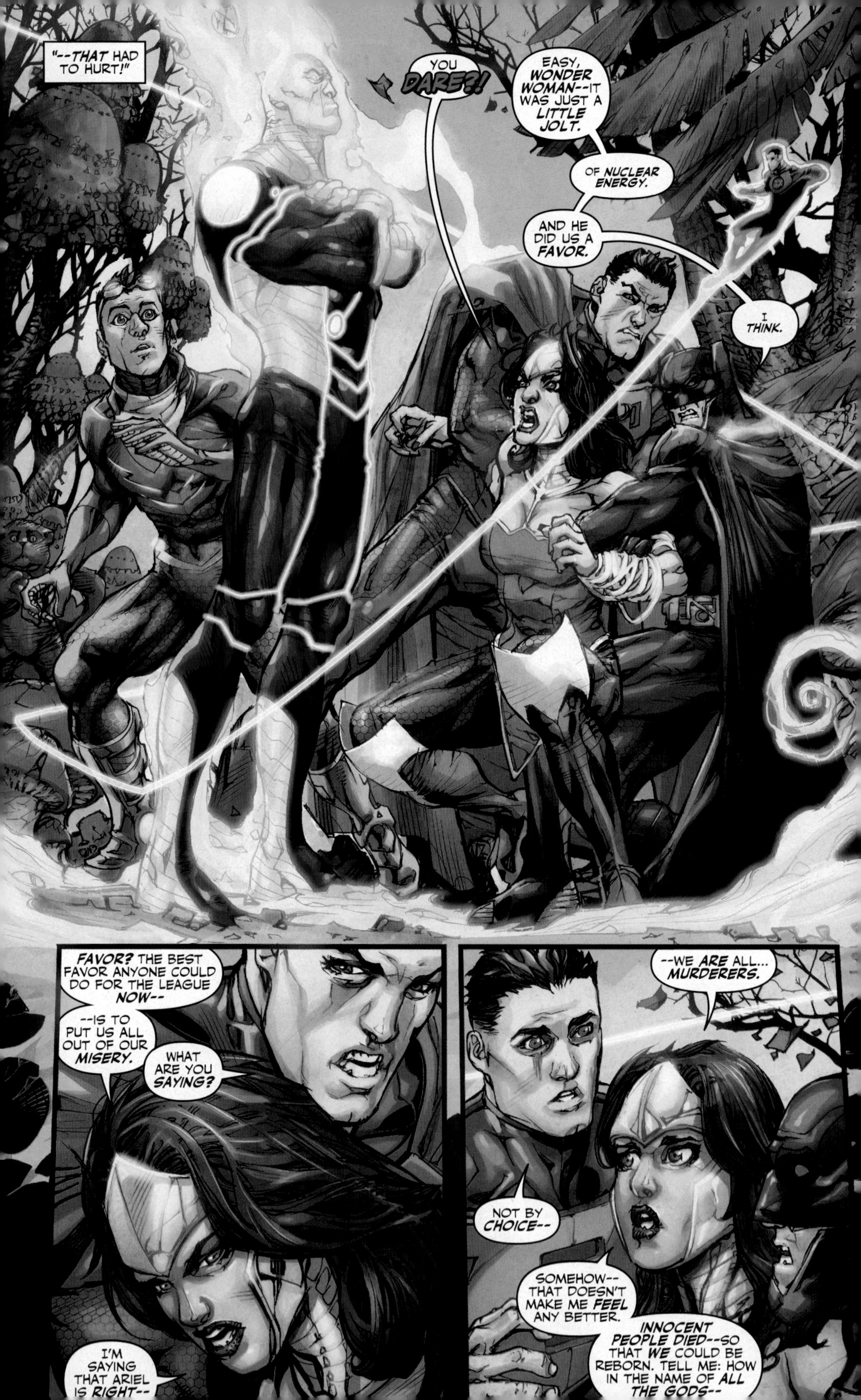
"--THAT HAD TO HURT!"
YOU DARE?!
EASY, WONDER WOMAN--IT WAS JUST A LITTLE JOLT.
OF NUCLEAR ENERGY.
AND HE DID US A FAVOR.
I THINK.
FAVOR? THE BEST FAVOR ANYONE COULD DO FOR THE LEAGUE NOW--
--IS TO PUT US ALL OUT OF OUR MISERY.
WHAT ARE YOU SAYING?
I'M SAYING THAT ARIEL IS RIGHT--
--WE ARE ALL... MURDERERS.
NOT BY CHOICE--
SOMEHOW--THAT DOESN'T MAKE ME FEEL ANY BETTER.
INNOCENT PEOPLE DIED--SO THAT WE COULD BE REBORN. TELL ME: HOW IN THE NAME OF ALL THE GODS--

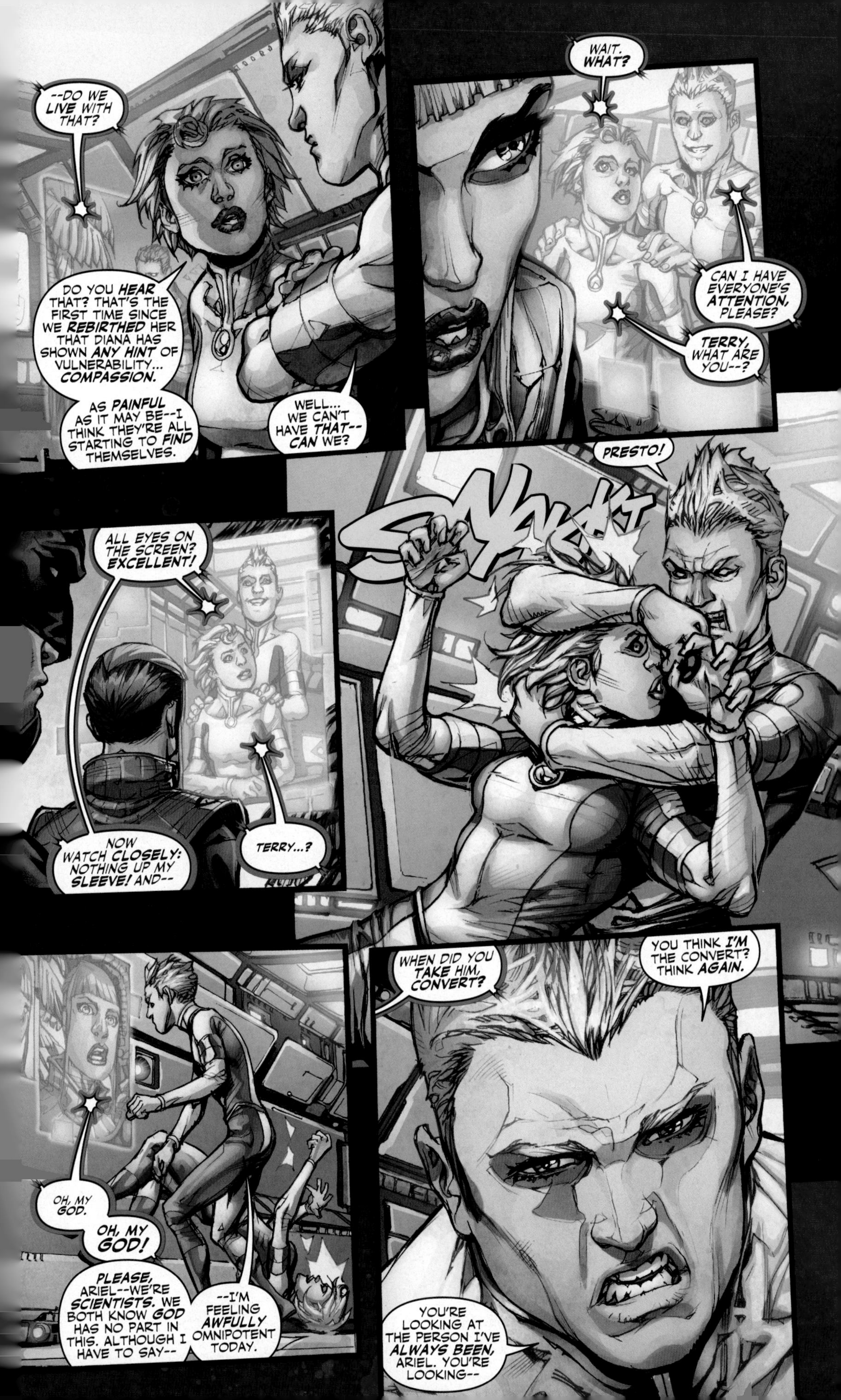
--DO WE LIVE WITH THAT?
DO YOU HEAR THAT? THAT'S THE FIRST TIME SINCE WE REBIRTHED HER THAT DIANA HAS SHOWN ANY HINT OF VULNERABILITY... COMPASSION.
AS PAINFUL AS IT MAY BE--I THINK THEY'RE ALL STARTING TO FIND THEMSELVES.
WELL... WE CAN'T HAVE THAT-- CAN WE?
WAIT. WHAT?
CAN I HAVE EVERYONE'S ATTENTION, PLEASE?
TERRY, WHAT ARE YOU--?
ALL EYES ON THE SCREEN? EXCELLENT!
NOW WATCH CLOSELY: NOTHING UP MY SLEEVE! AND--
TERRY...?
PRESTO!
SNAK!
OH, MY GOD.
OH, MY GOD!
PLEASE, ARIEL--WE'RE SCIENTISTS. WE BOTH KNOW GOD HAS NO PART IN THIS. ALTHOUGH I HAVE TO SAY--
--I'M FEELING AWFULLY OMNIPOTENT TODAY.
WHEN DID YOU TAKE HIM, CONVERT?
YOU THINK I'M THE CONVERT? THINK AGAIN.
YOU'RE LOOKING AT THE PERSON I'VE ALWAYS BEEN, ARIEL. YOU'RE LOOKING--

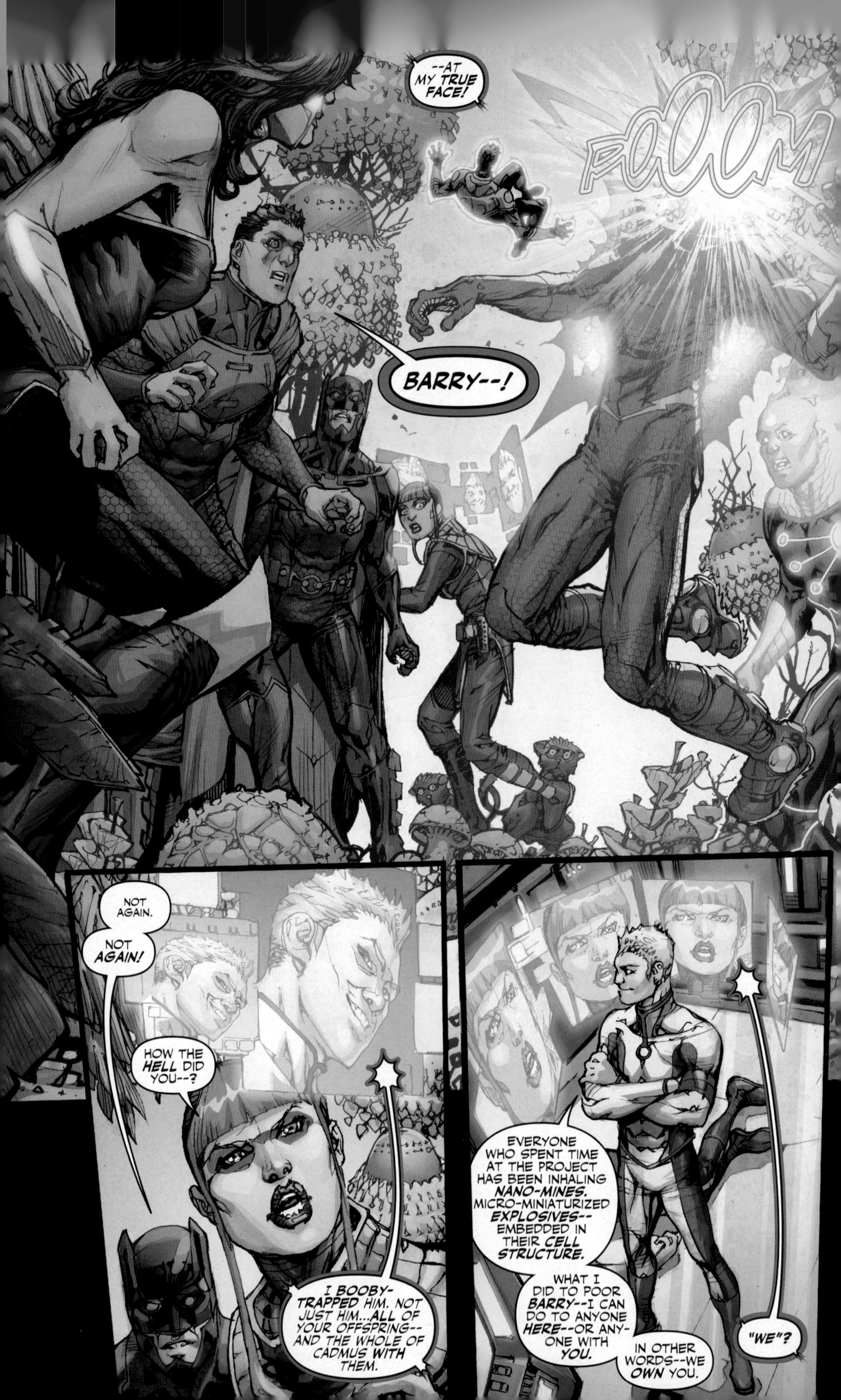

--AT MY TRUE FACE!
FOOOOM
BARRY--!
NOT AGAIN.
NOT AGAIN!
HOW THE HELL DID YOU--?
I BOOBY-TRAPPED HIM. NOT JUST HIM...ALL OF YOUR OFFSPRING--AND THE WHOLE OF CADMUS WITH THEM.
EVERYONE WHO SPENT TIME AT THE PROJECT HAS BEEN INHALING NANO-MINES. MICRO-MINIATURIZED EXPLOSIVES--EMBEDDED IN THEIR CELL STRUCTURE.
WHAT I DID TO POOR BARRY--I CAN DO TO ANYONE HERE--OR ANY-ONE WITH YOU.
IN OTHER WORDS--WE OWN YOU.
"WE"?

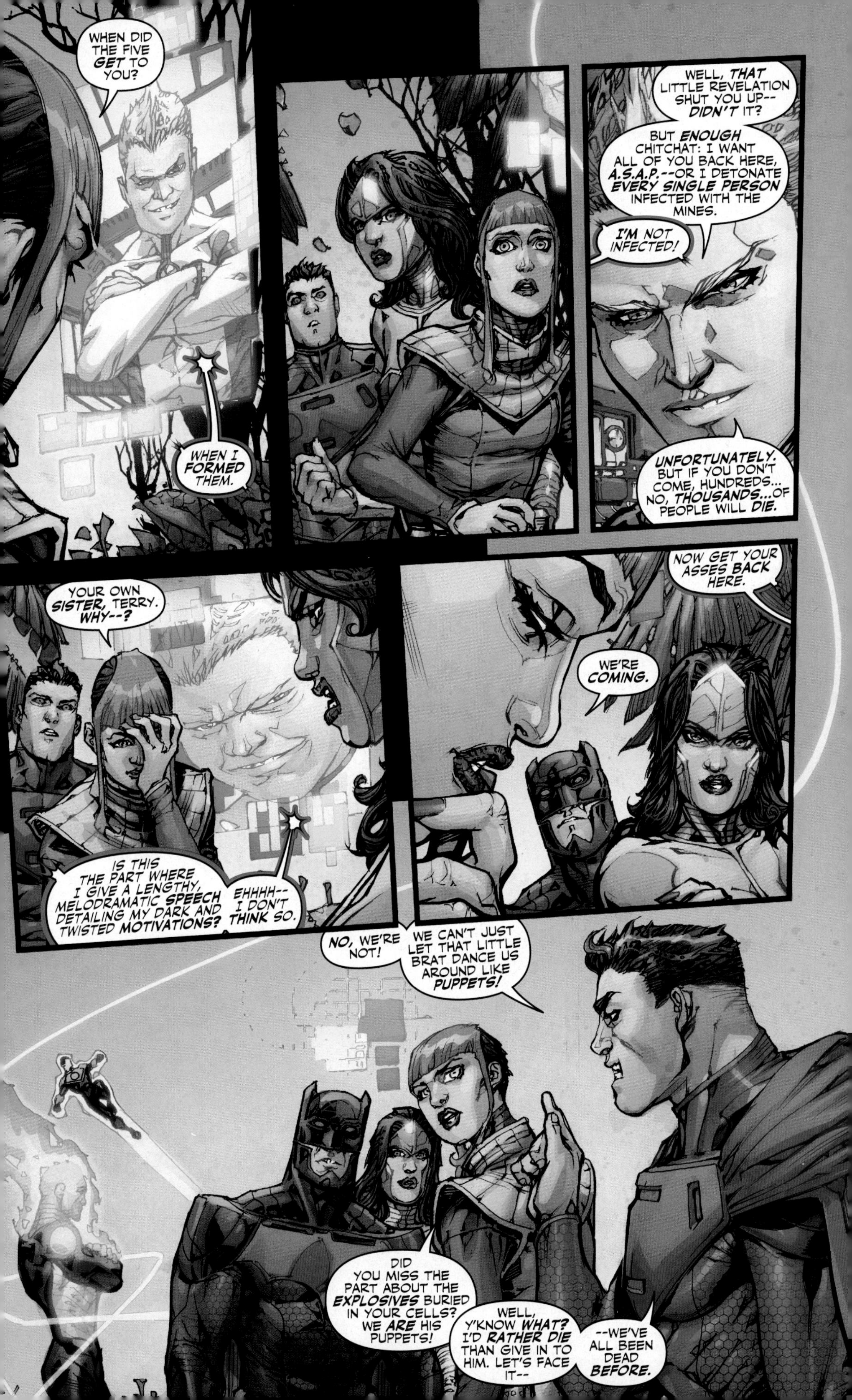
WHEN DID THE FIVE GET TO YOU?
WHEN I FORMED THEM.
WELL, THAT LITTLE REVELATION SHUT YOU UP-- DIDN'T IT?
BUT ENOUGH CHITCHAT: I WANT ALL OF YOU BACK HERE, A.S.A.P.--OR I DETONATE EVERY SINGLE PERSON INFECTED WITH THE MINES.
I'M NOT INFECTED!
UNFORTUNATELY. BUT IF YOU DON'T COME, HUNDREDS... NO, THOUSANDS...OF PEOPLE WILL DIE.
YOUR OWN SISTER, TERRY. WHY--?
IS THIS THE PART WHERE I GIVE A LENGTHY, MELODRAMATIC SPEECH DETAILING MY DARK AND TWISTED MOTIVATIONS?
EHHHH-- I DON'T THINK SO.
NOW GET YOUR ASSES BACK HERE.
WE'RE COMING.
NO, WE'RE NOT!
WE CAN'T JUST LET THAT LITTLE BRAT DANCE US AROUND LIKE PUPPETS!
DID YOU MISS THE PART ABOUT THE EXPLOSIVES BURIED IN YOUR CELLS? WE ARE HIS PUPPETS!
WELL, Y'KNOW WHAT? I'D RATHER DIE THAN GIVE IN TO HIM. LET'S FACE IT--
--WE'VE ALL BEEN DEAD BEFORE.

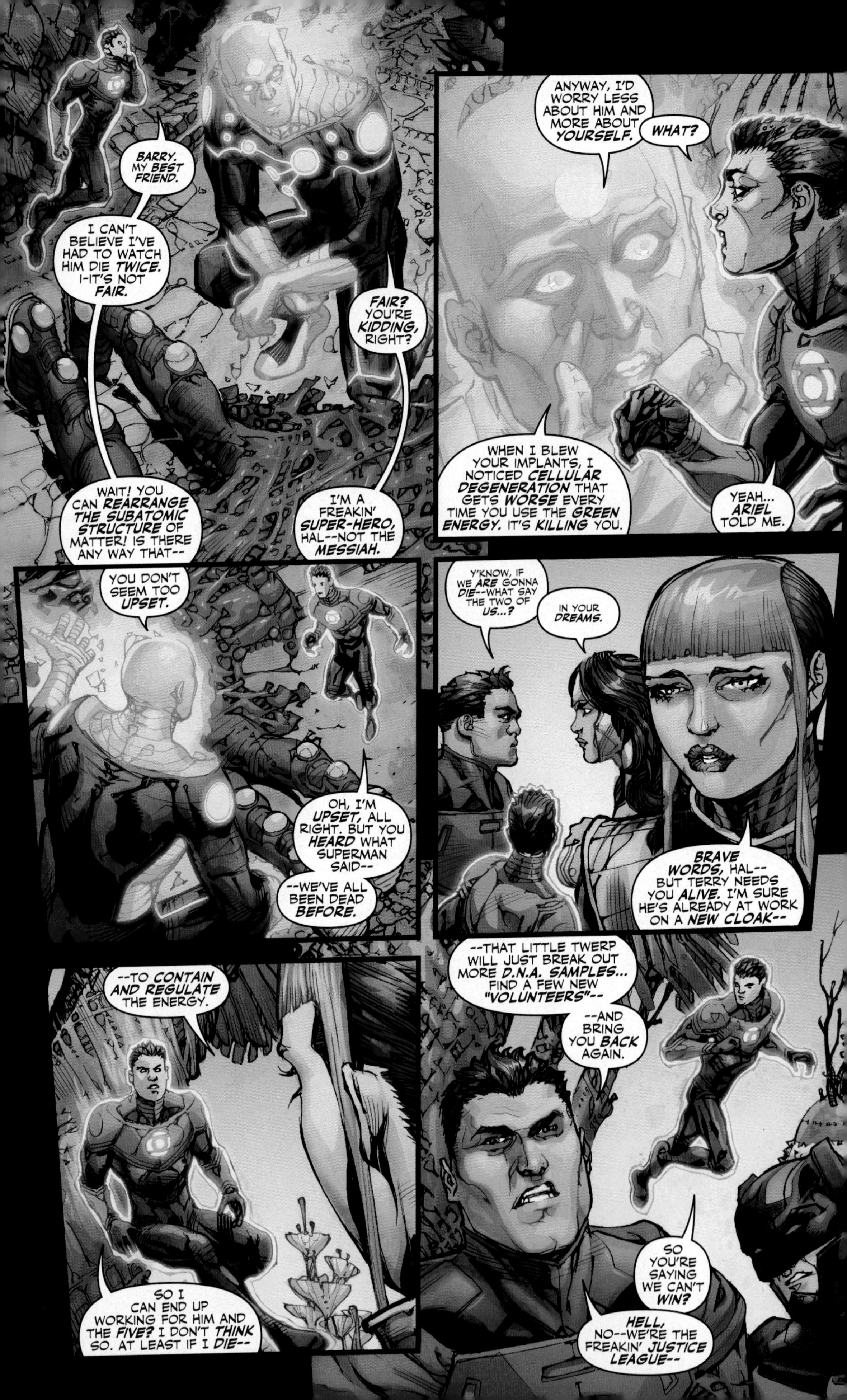
BARRY. MY BEST FRIEND.
I CAN'T BELIEVE I'VE HAD TO WATCH HIM DIE TWICE. I-IT'S NOT FAIR.
FAIR? YOU'RE KIDDING, RIGHT?
WAIT! YOU CAN REARRANGE THE SUBATOMIC STRUCTURE OF MATTER! IS THERE ANY WAY THAT--
I'M A FREAKIN' SUPER-HERO, HAL--NOT THE MESSIAH.
ANYWAY, I'D WORRY LESS ABOUT HIM AND MORE ABOUT YOURSELF.
WHAT?
WHEN I BLEW YOUR IMPLANTS, I NOTICED CELLULAR DEGENERATION THAT GETS WORSE EVERY TIME YOU USE THE GREEN ENERGY. IT'S KILLING YOU.
YEAH... ARIEL TOLD ME.
YOU DON'T SEEM TOO UPSET.
OH, I'M UPSET, ALL RIGHT. BUT YOU HEARD WHAT SUPERMAN SAID--
--WE'VE ALL BEEN DEAD BEFORE.
Y'KNOW, IF WE ARE GONNA DIE--WHAT SAY THE TWO OF US...?
IN YOUR DREAMS.
BRAVE WORDS, HAL--BUT TERRY NEEDS YOU ALIVE. I'M SURE HE'S ALREADY AT WORK ON A NEW CLOAK--
--TO CONTAIN AND REGULATE THE ENERGY.
SO I CAN END UP WORKING FOR HIM AND THE FIVE? I DON'T THINK SO. AT LEAST IF I DIE--
--THAT LITTLE TWERP WILL JUST BREAK OUT MORE D.N.A. SAMPLES... FIND A FEW NEW "VOLUNTEERS"--
--AND BRING YOU BACK AGAIN.
SO YOU'RE SAYING WE CAN'T WIN?
HELL, NO--WE'RE THE FREAKIN' JUSTICE LEAGUE--

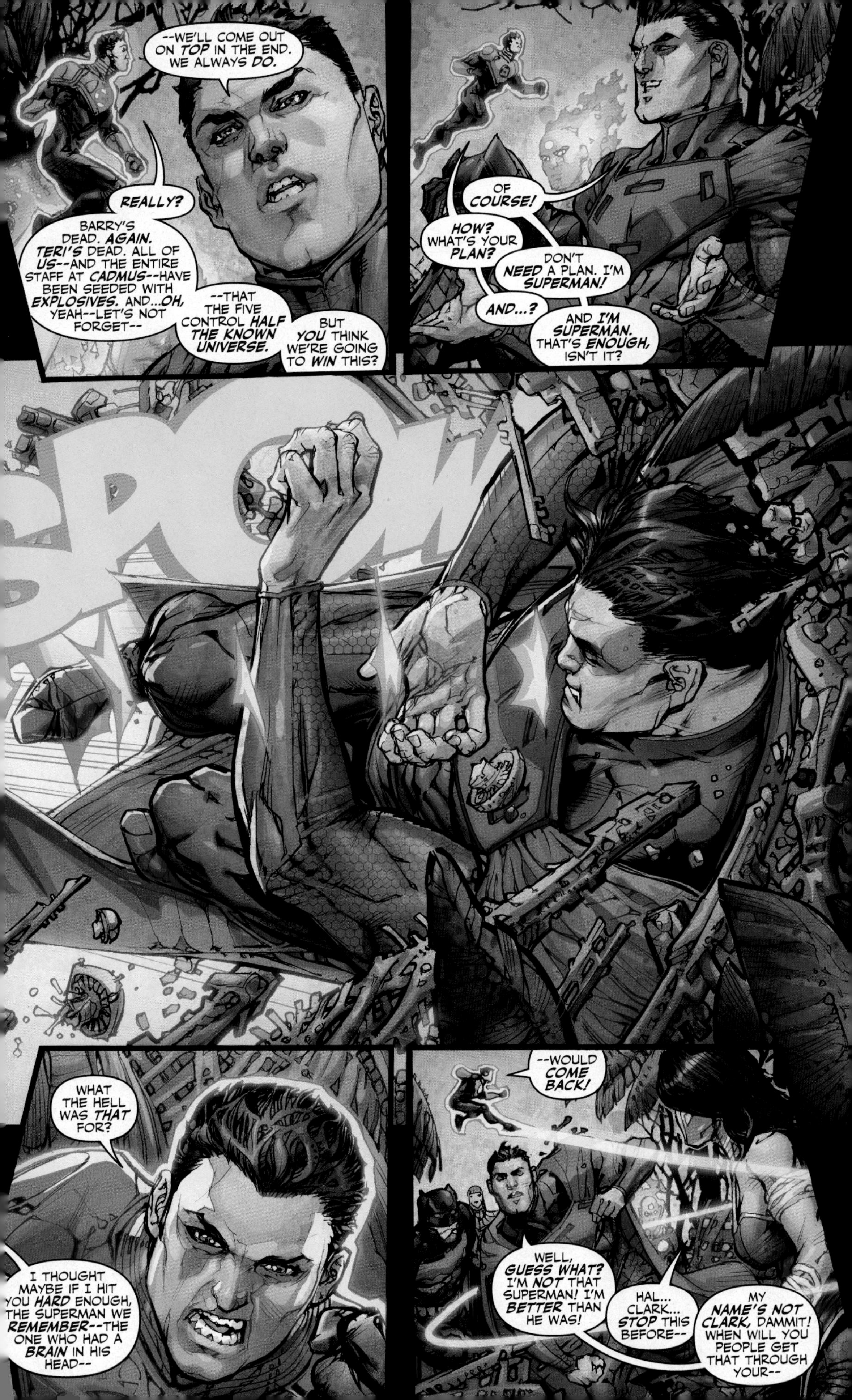
--WE'LL COME OUT ON TOP IN THE END. WE ALWAYS DO.
REALLY?
BARRY'S DEAD. AGAIN. TERI'S DEAD. ALL OF US--AND THE ENTIRE STAFF AT CADMUS--HAVE BEEN SEEDED WITH EXPLOSIVES. AND...OH, YEAH--LET'S NOT FORGET--
--THAT THE FIVE CONTROL HALF THE KNOWN UNIVERSE.
BUT YOU THINK WE'RE GOING TO WIN THIS?
OF COURSE!
HOW? WHAT'S YOUR PLAN?
DON'T NEED A PLAN. I'M SUPERMAN!
AND...?
AND I'M SUPERMAN. THAT'S ENOUGH, ISN'T IT?
WHAT THE HELL WAS THAT FOR?
I THOUGHT MAYBE IF I HIT YOU HARD ENOUGH, THE SUPERMAN WE REMEMBER--THE ONE WHO HAD A BRAIN IN HIS HEAD--
--WOULD COME BACK!
WELL, GUESS WHAT? I'M NOT THAT SUPERMAN! I'M BETTER THAN HE WAS!
HAL... CLARK... STOP THIS BEFORE--
MY NAME'S NOT CLARK, DAMMIT! WHEN WILL YOU PEOPLE GET THAT THROUGH YOUR--

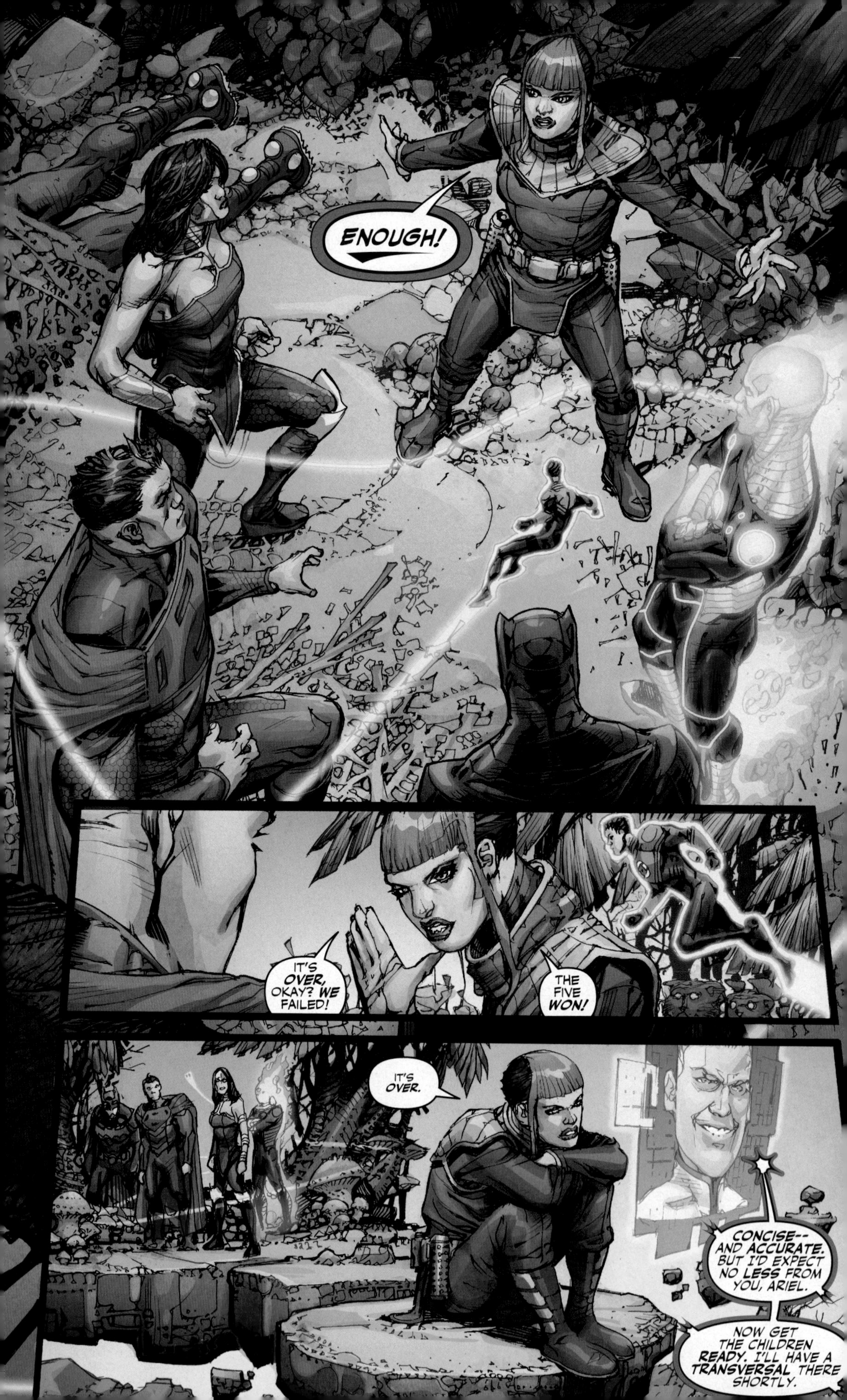
ENOUGH!
IT'S OVER, OKAY? WE FAILED!
THE FIVE WON!
IT'S OVER.
CONCISE-- AND ACCURATE. BUT I'D EXPECT NO LESS FROM YOU, ARIEL.
NOW GET THE CHILDREN READY. I'LL HAVE A TRANSVERSAL THERE SHORTLY.

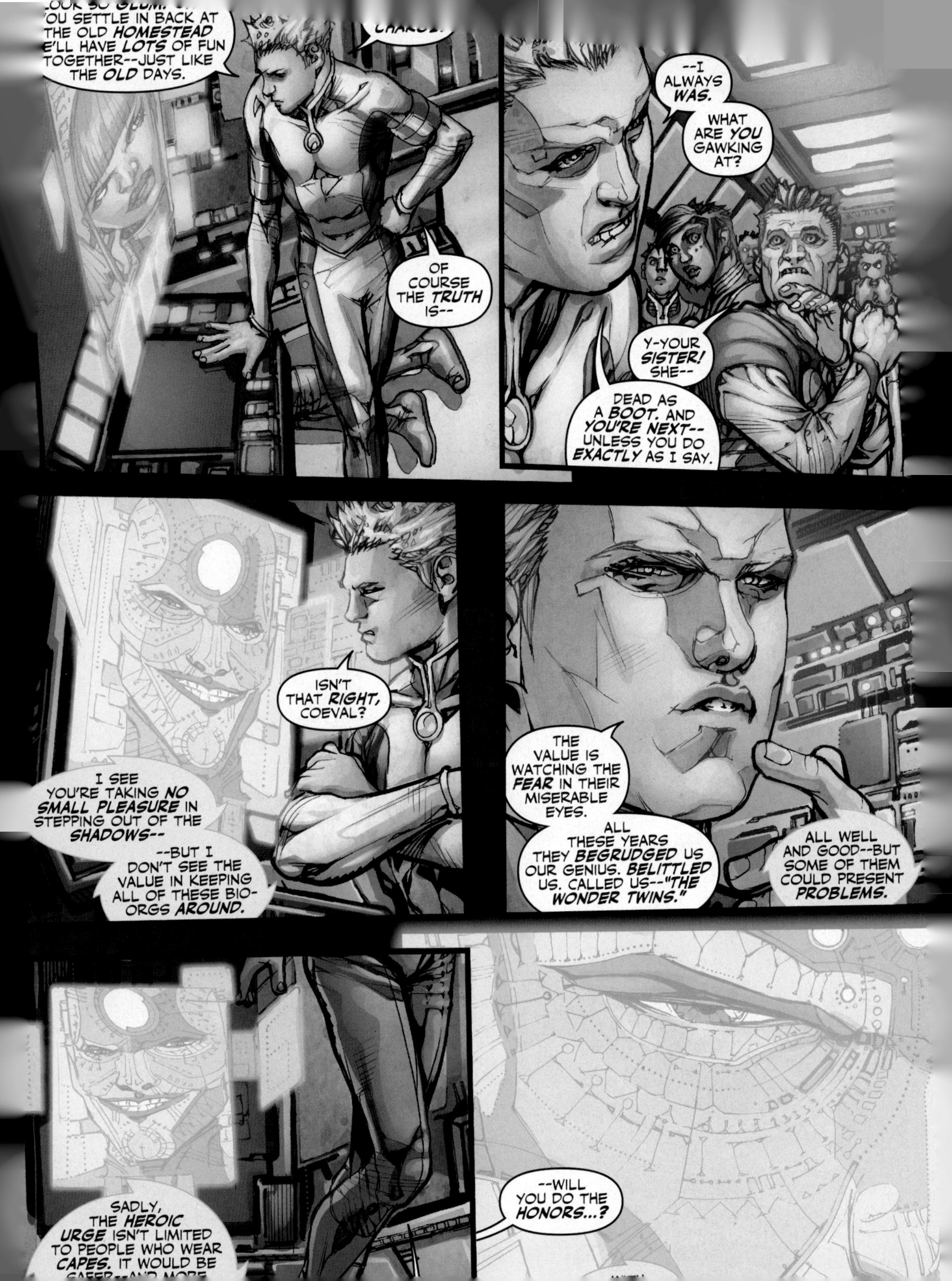
OU SETTLE IN BACK AT THE OLD HOMESTEAD E'LL HAVE LOTS OF FUN TOGETHER--JUST LIKE THE OLD DAYS.
OF COURSE THE TRUTH IS--
--I ALWAYS WAS.
WHAT ARE YOU GAWKING AT?
Y-YOUR SISTER! SHE--
DEAD AS A BOOT. AND YOU'RE NEXT-- UNLESS YOU DO EXACTLY AS I SAY.
ISN'T THAT RIGHT, COEVAL?
I SEE YOU'RE TAKING NO SMALL PLEASURE IN STEPPING OUT OF THE SHADOWS--
--BUT I DON'T SEE THE VALUE IN KEEPING ALL OF THESE BIO-ORGS AROUND.
THE VALUE IS WATCHING THE FEAR IN THEIR MISERABLE EYES.
ALL THESE YEARS THEY BEGRUDGED US OUR GENIUS. BELITTLED US. CALLED US--"THE WONDER TWINS."
ALL WELL AND GOOD--BUT SOME OF THEM COULD PRESENT PROBLEMS.
SADLY, THE HEROIC URGE ISN'T LIMITED TO PEOPLE WHO WEAR CAPES. IT WOULD BE
--WILL YOU DO THE HONORS...?

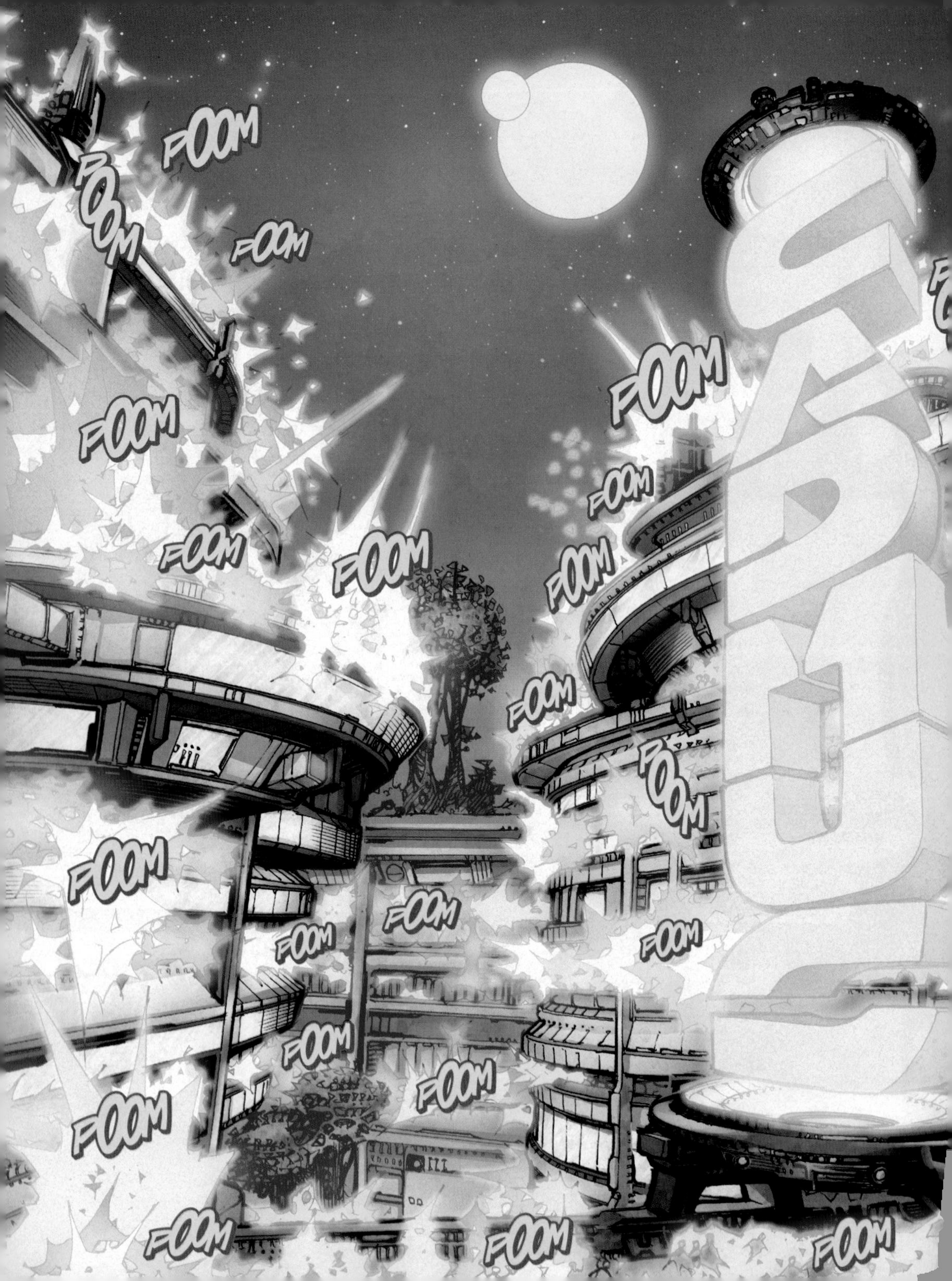
POOM
POOM
POOM
POOM
POOM
POOM
POOM
POOM
POOM
POOM
POOM
POOM
POOM
POOM
POOM
POOM
POOM
POOM
POOM
POOM
POOM

JUSTICE LEAGUE 3000 SKETCHBOOK
BY HOWARD PORTER

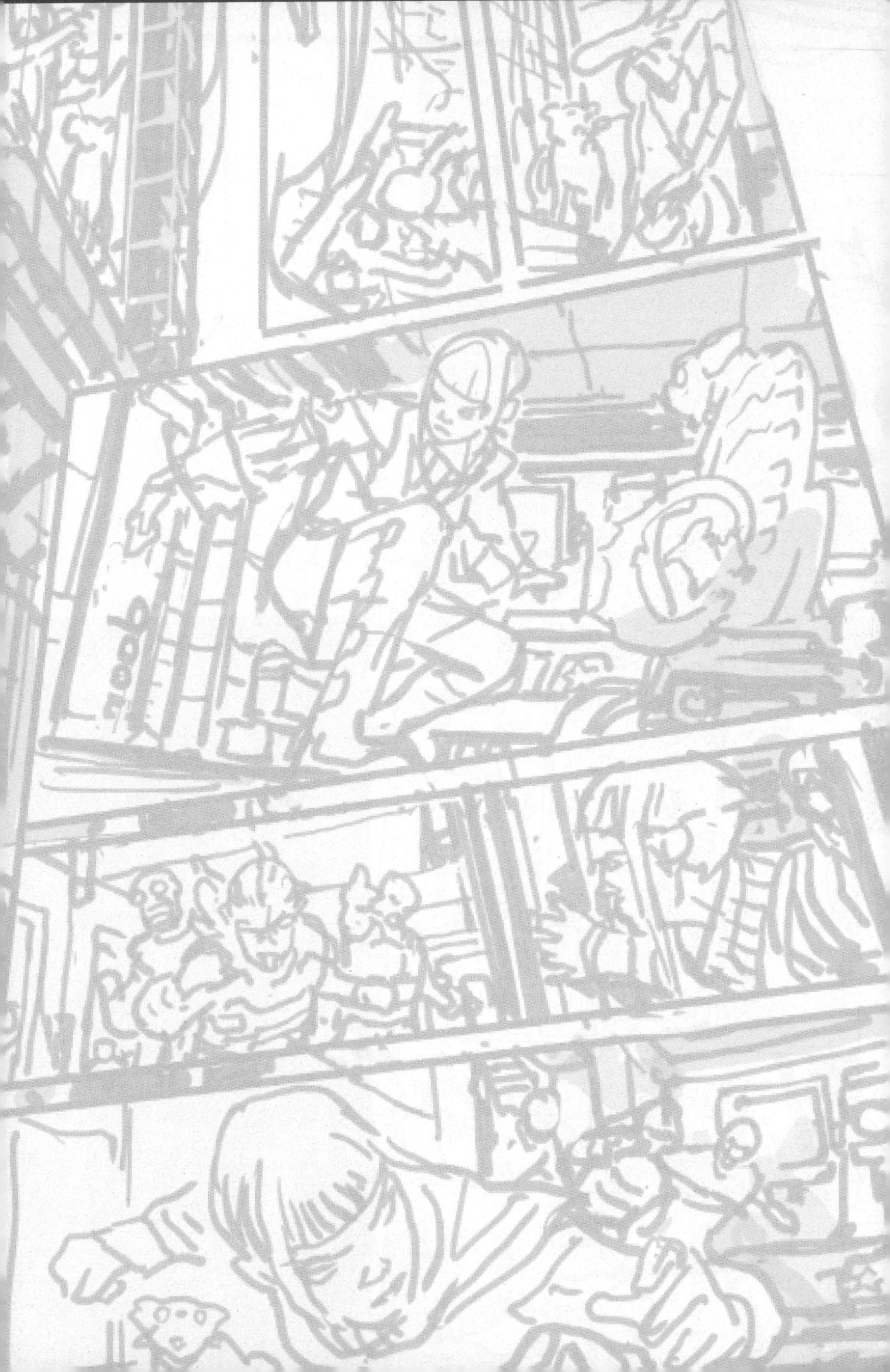

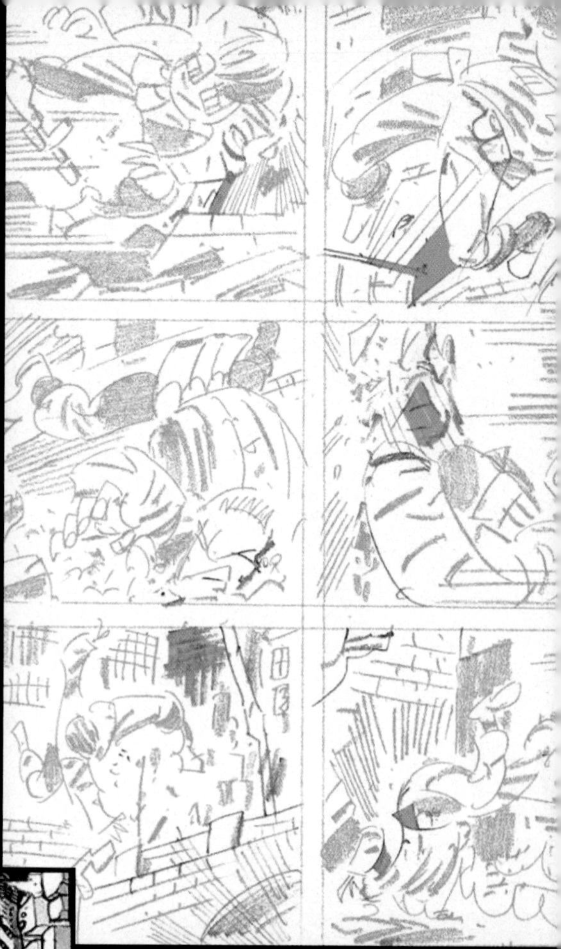

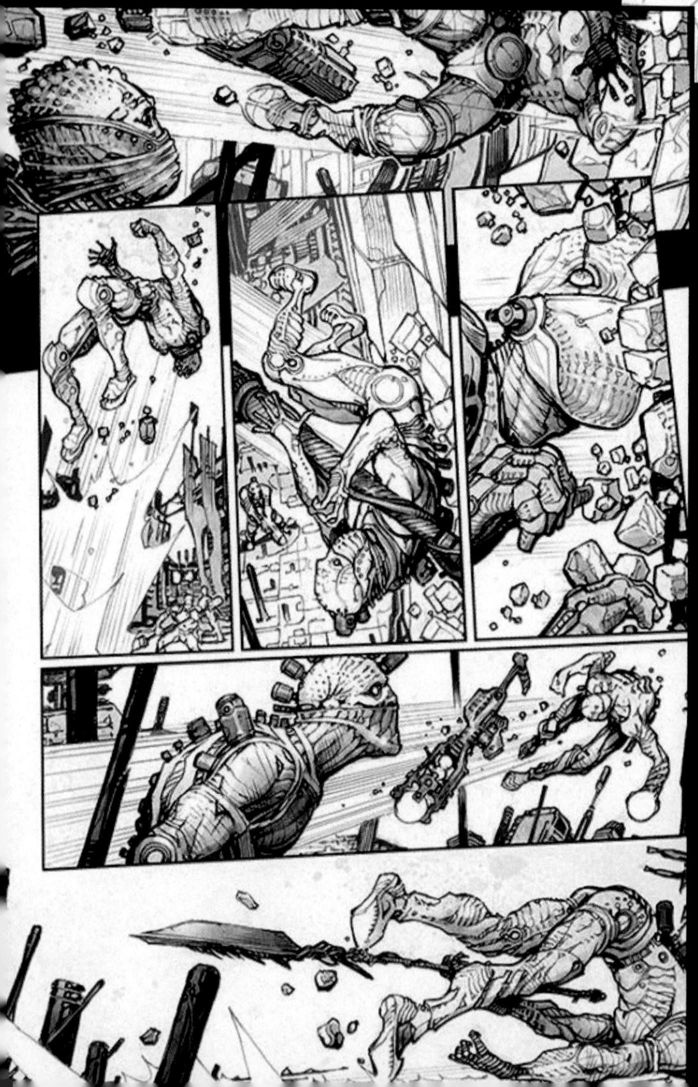

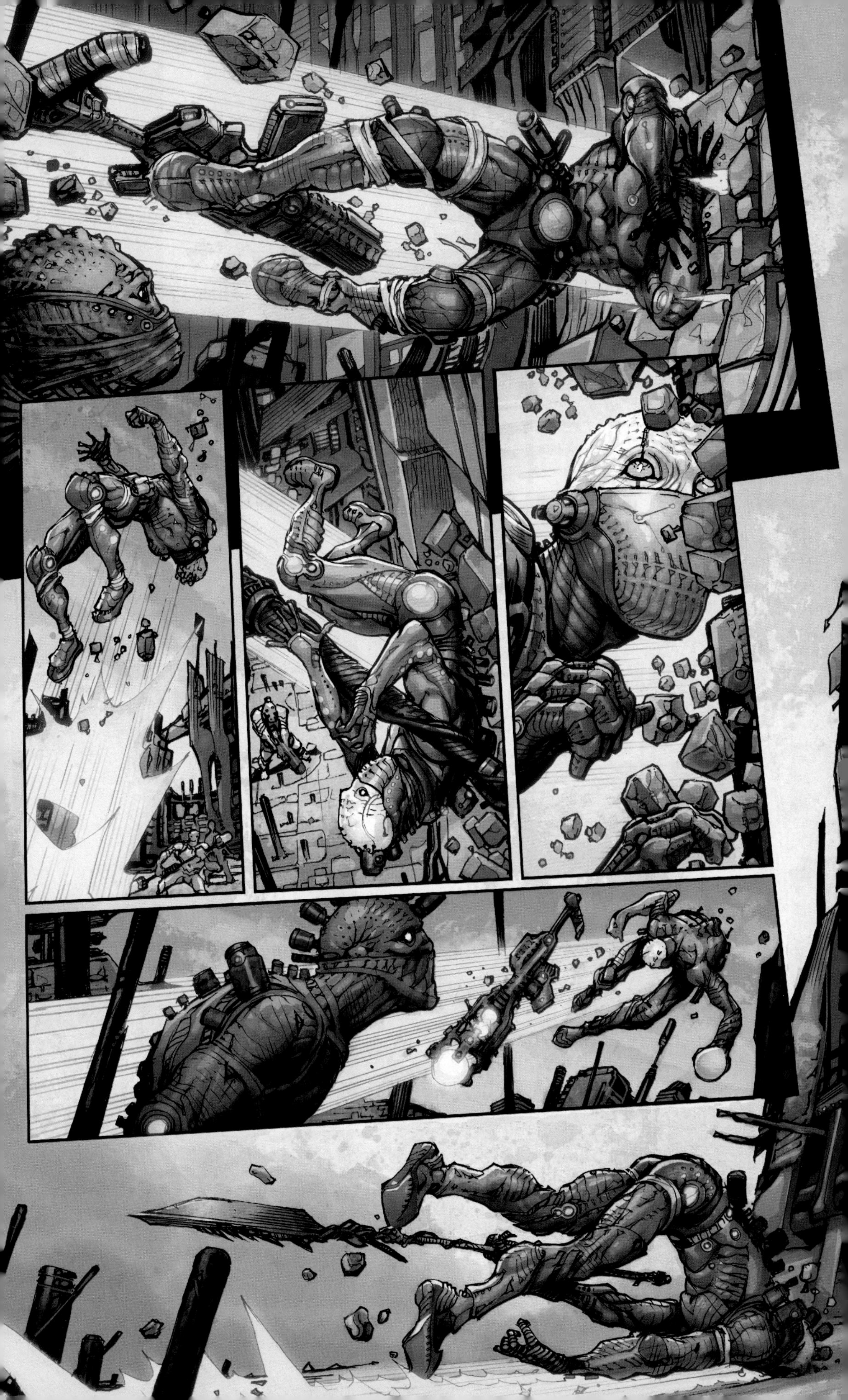

WOMAN IS NAKED BUT TASTEFULLY ANGLED/ SHADOWED
EVERYTHING IN ROOM LOOK JURY RIGGED
BLUE COLLAR STYL DRESS
APT HALLWAY
DRESSED TO BLEND IN
BACK INTO ROOM

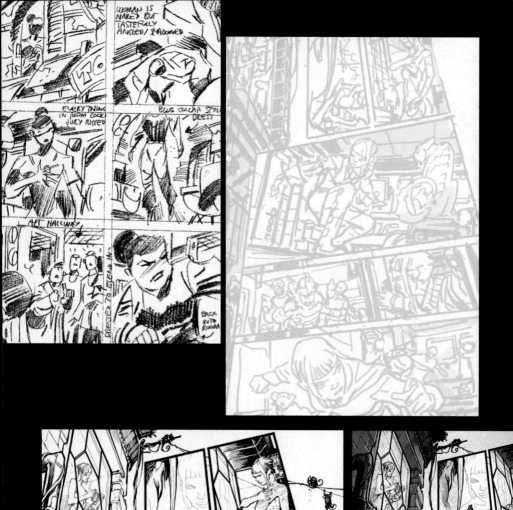

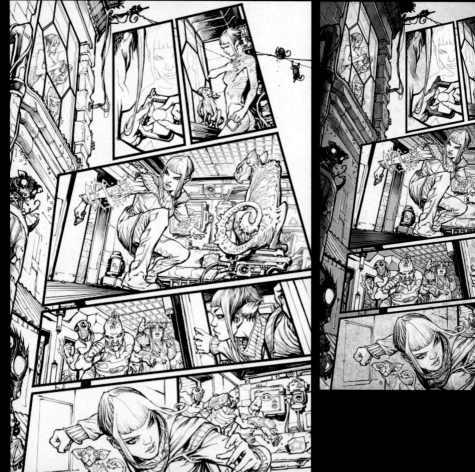

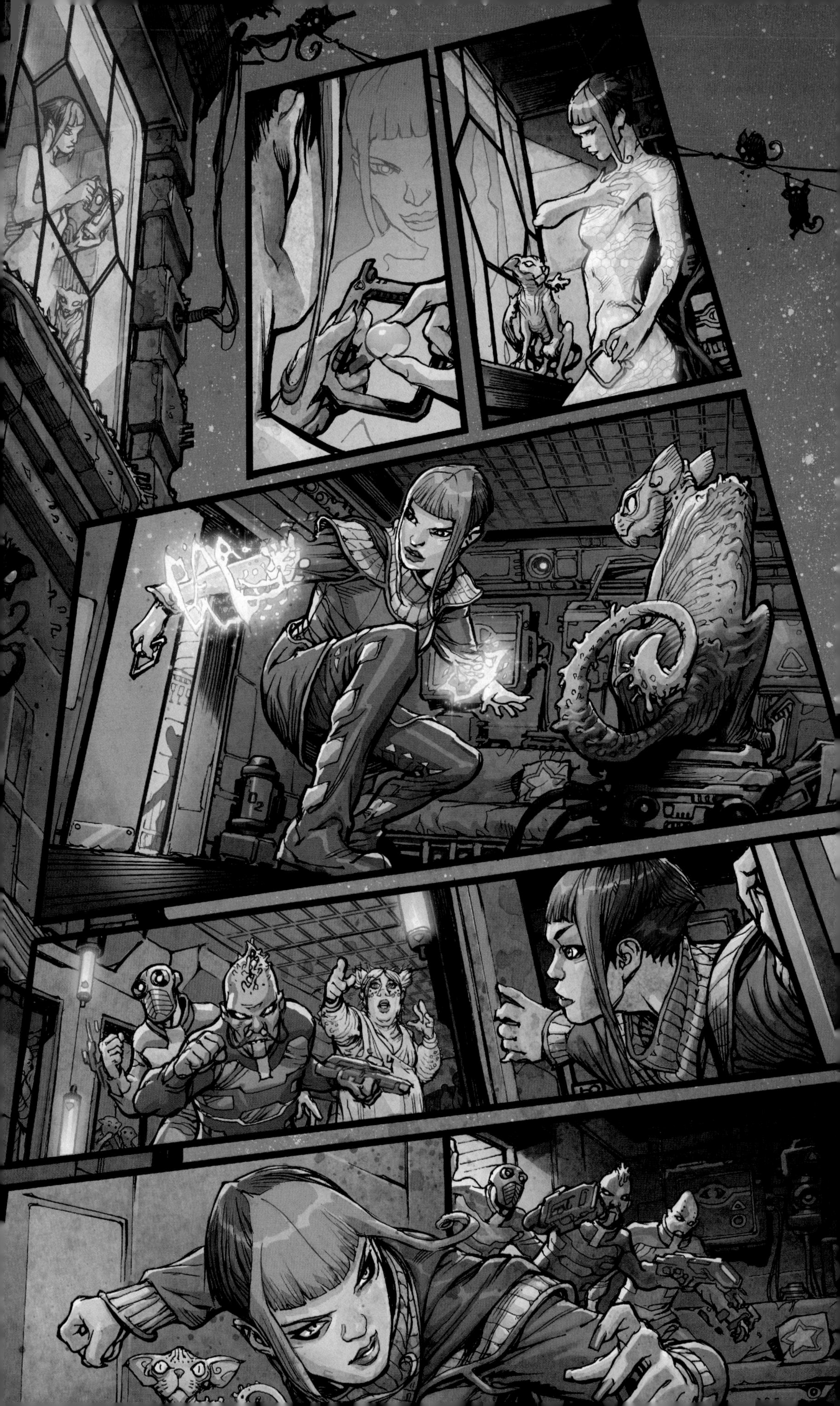

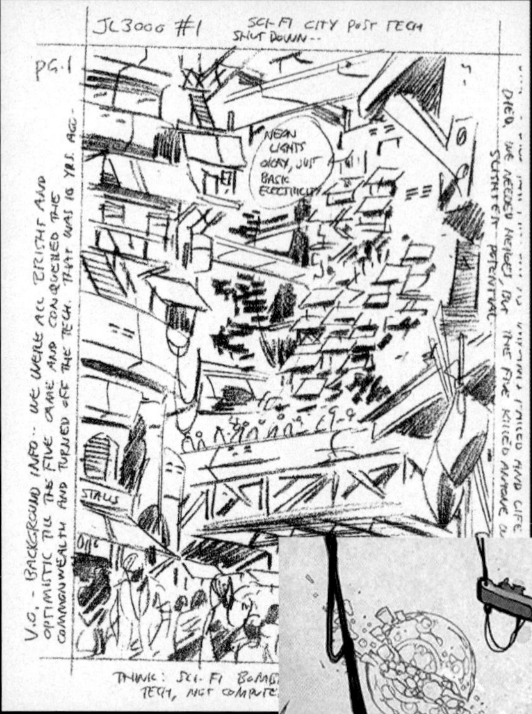
JL3000 #1
SCI-FI CITY POST TECH SHUT DOWN--
PG.1
NEON LIGHTS OKAY, JUST BASIC ELECTRICITY
STALLS
V.O. - BACKGROUND INFO - WE WERE ALL BRIGHT AND OPTIMISTIC TIL THE FIVE CAME AND CONQUERED THE COMMONWEALTH AND TURNED OFF THE TECH. THAT WAS 10 YRS AGO-
DIEGO, WE NEEDED HEIGHT, BUT
THE FIVE KILLED ANYONE
SCIENTIFIC POTENTIAL

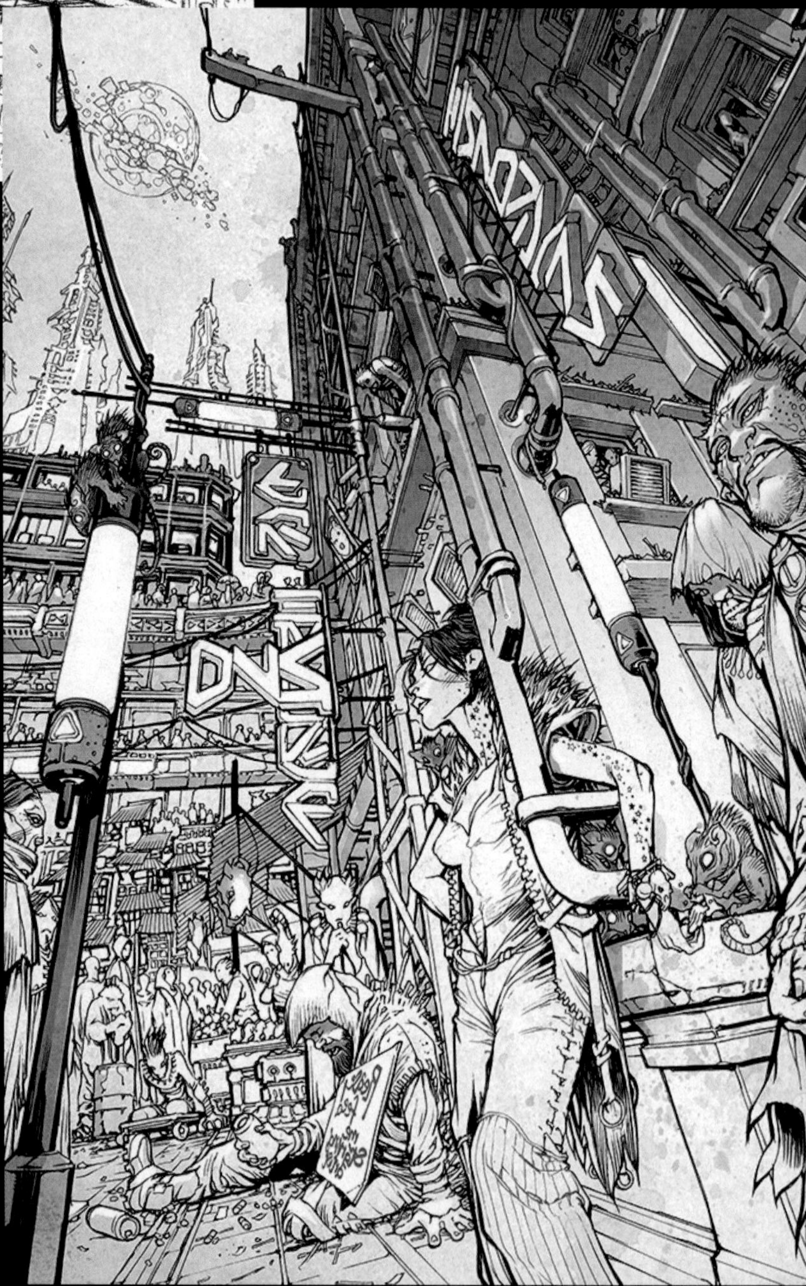

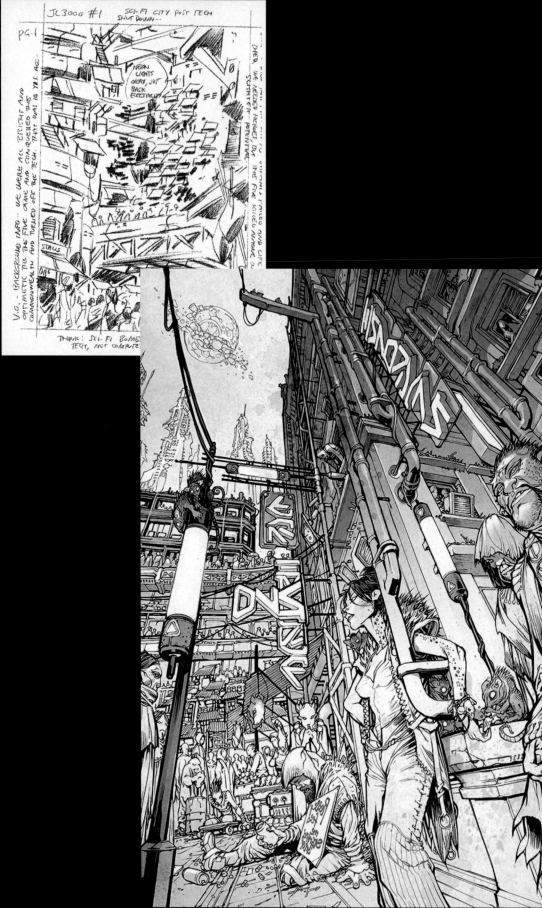

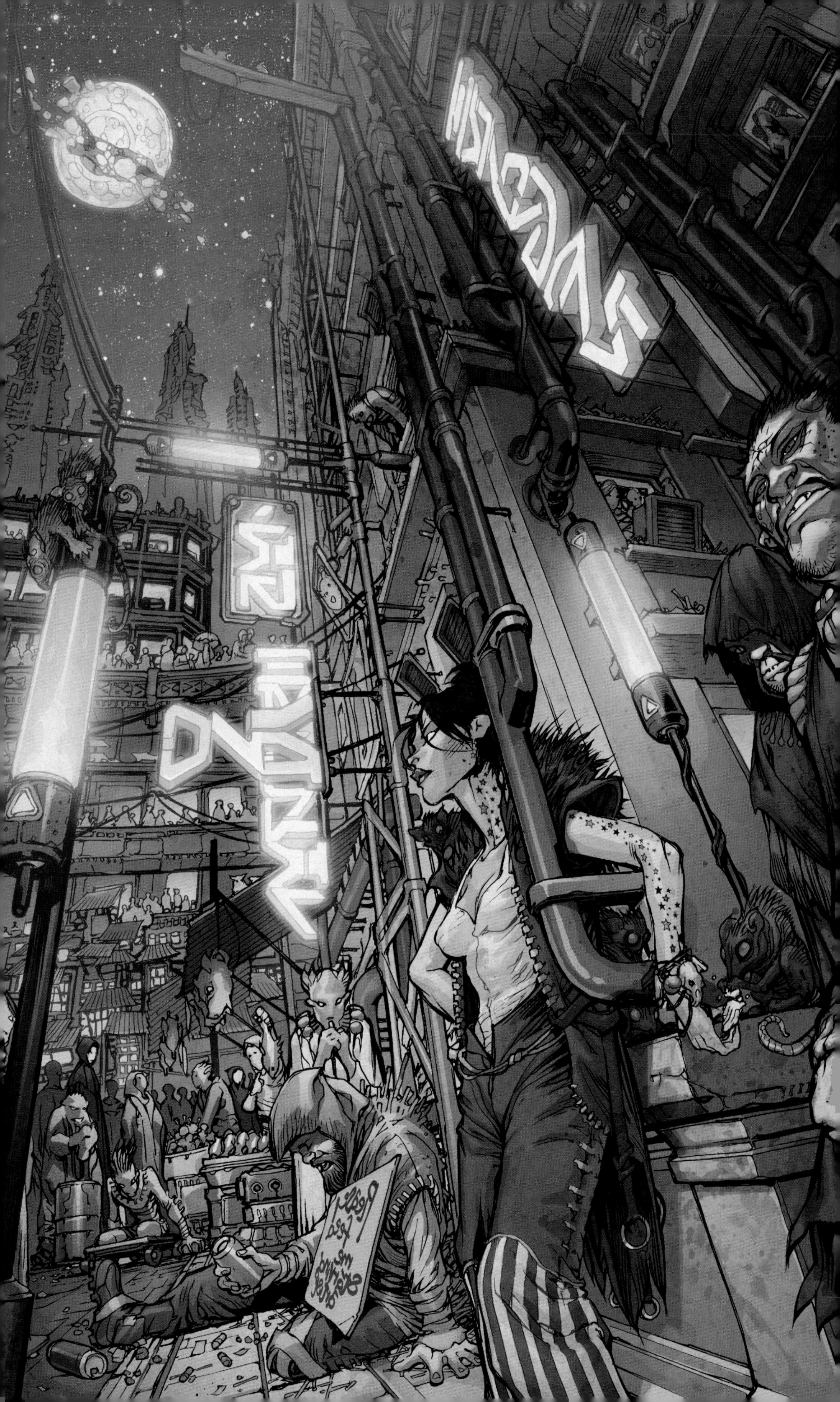

HOLO-FIELD BODY STOCKING® V7.2 - QUICK START GUIDE

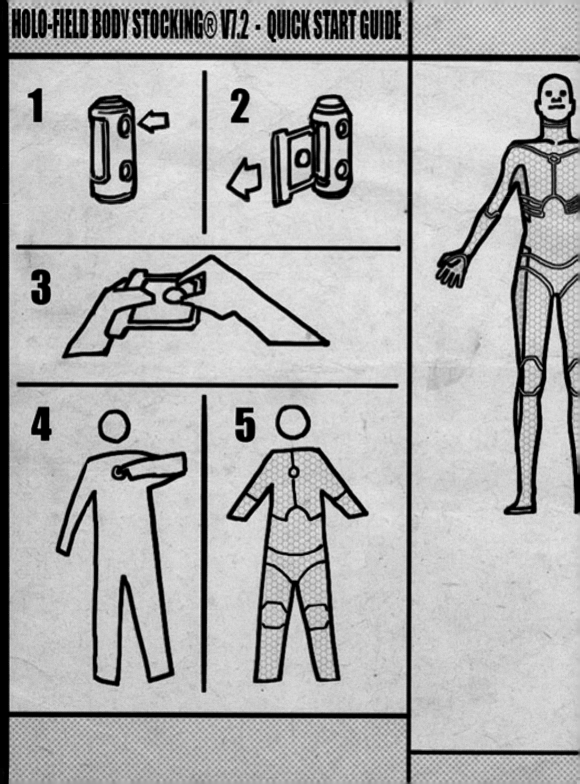

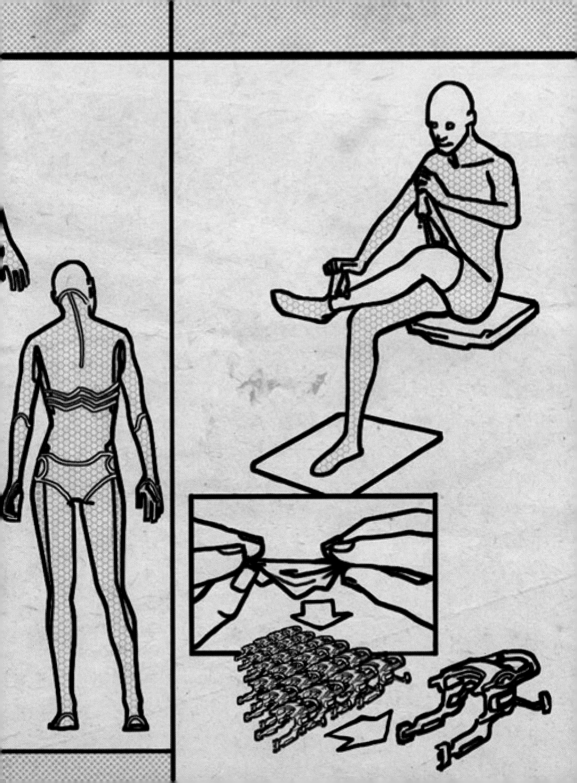

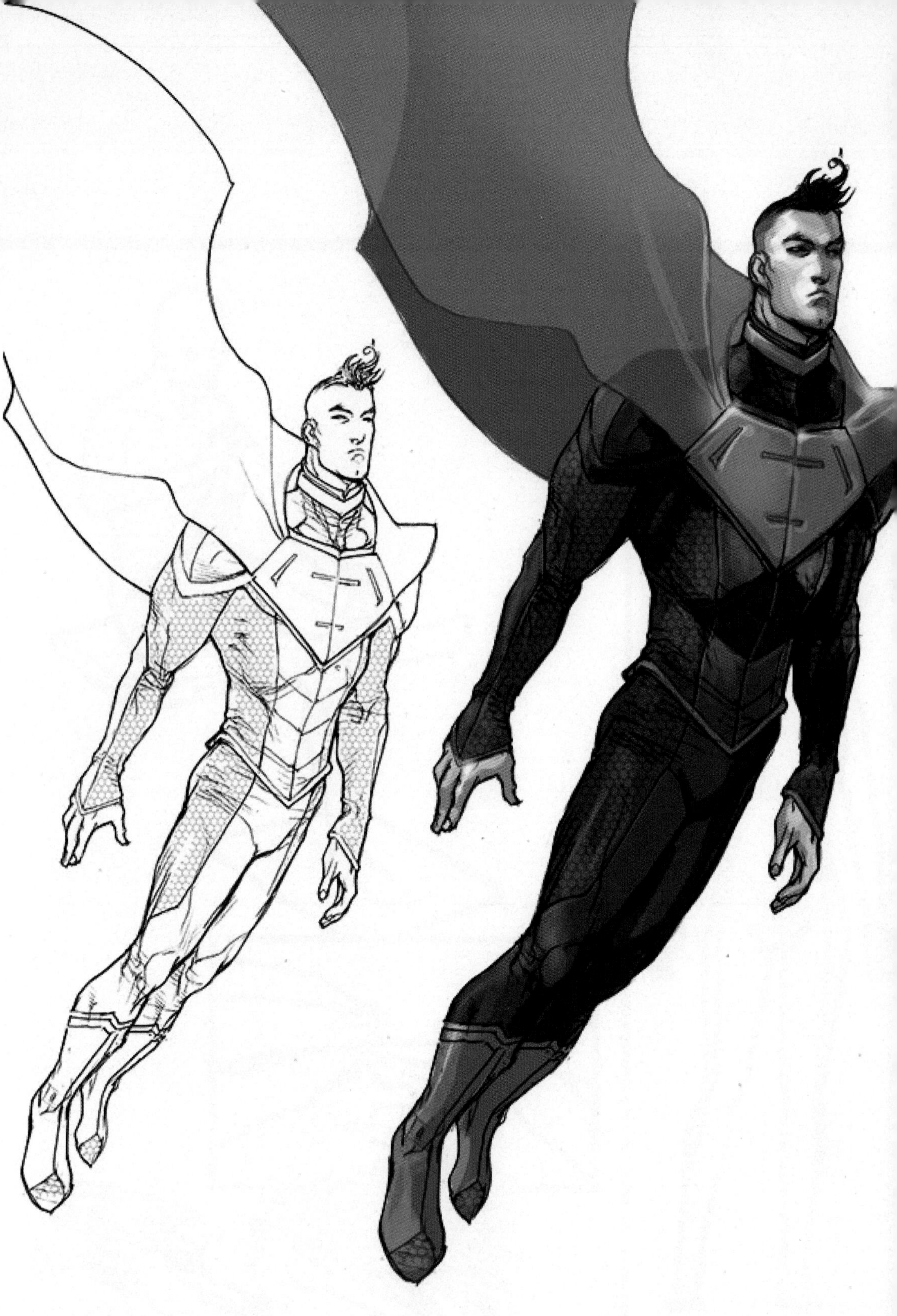

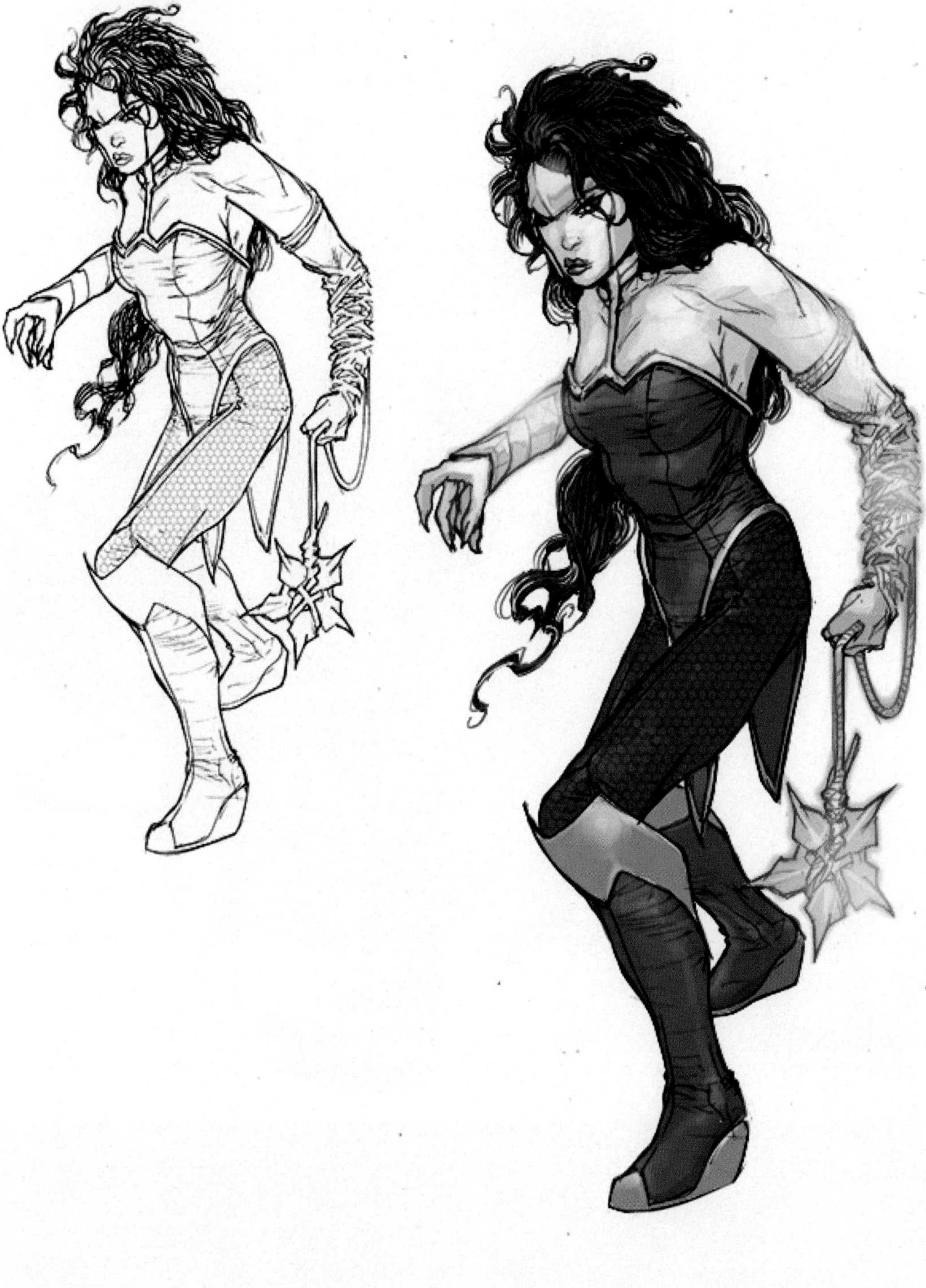

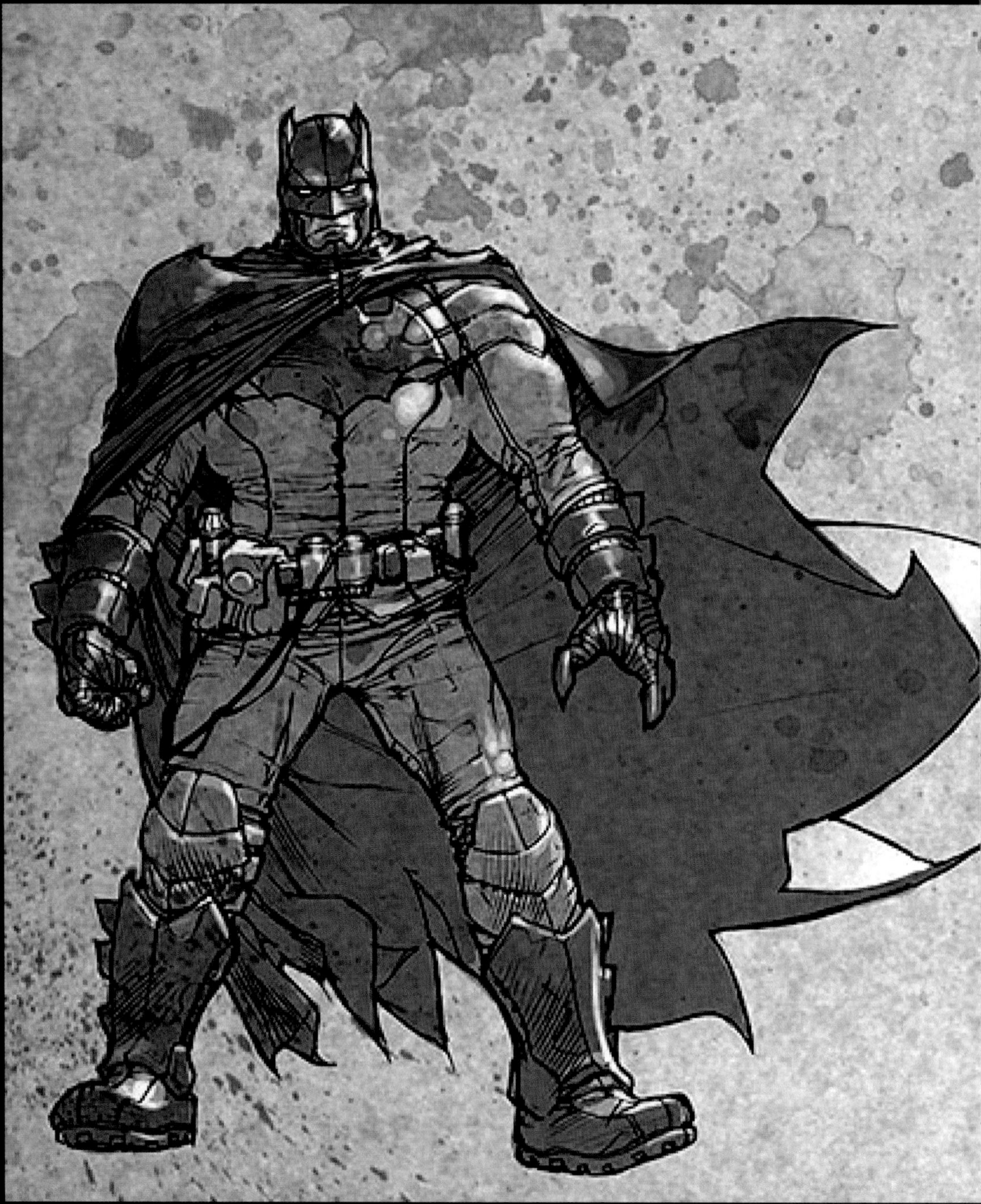

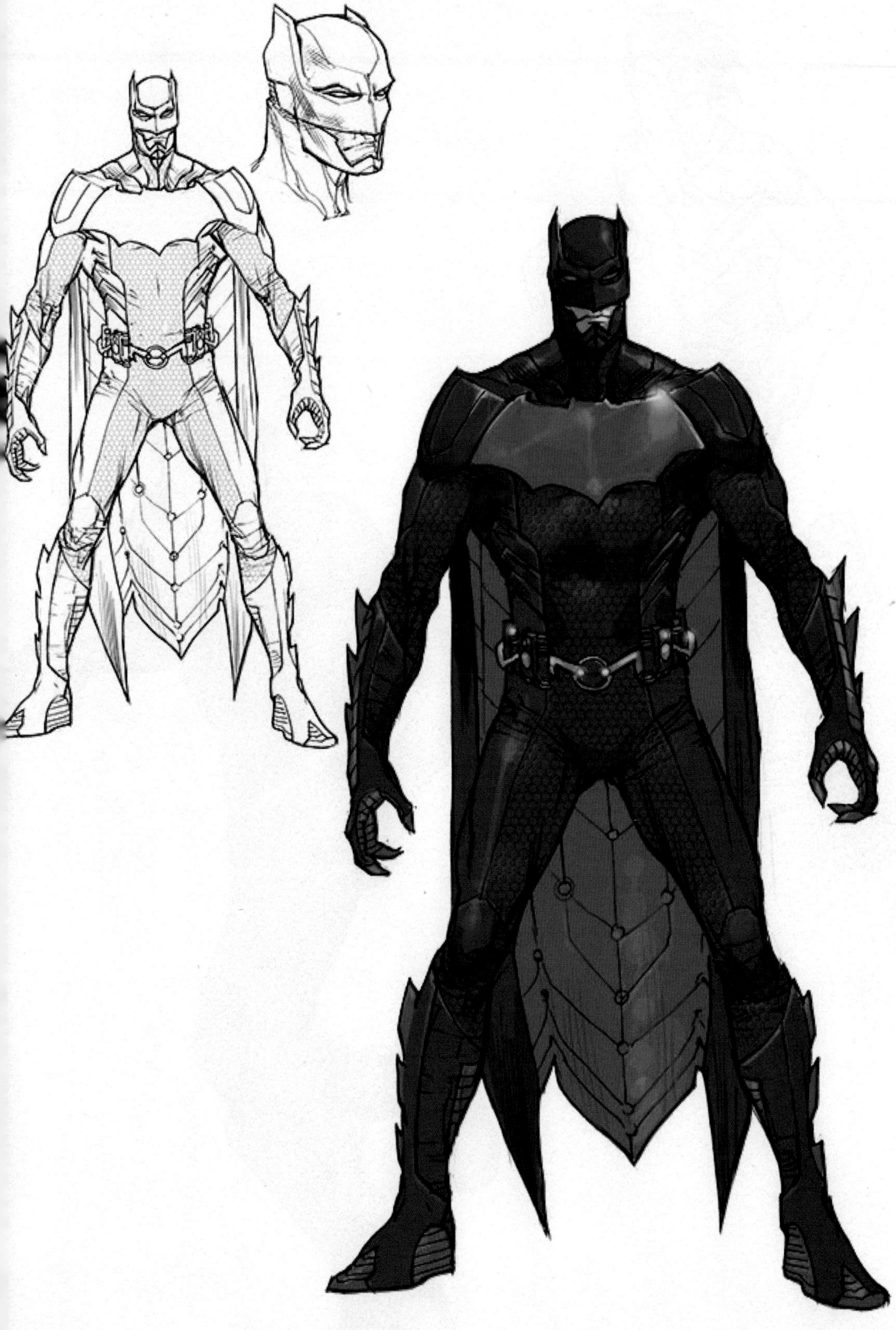

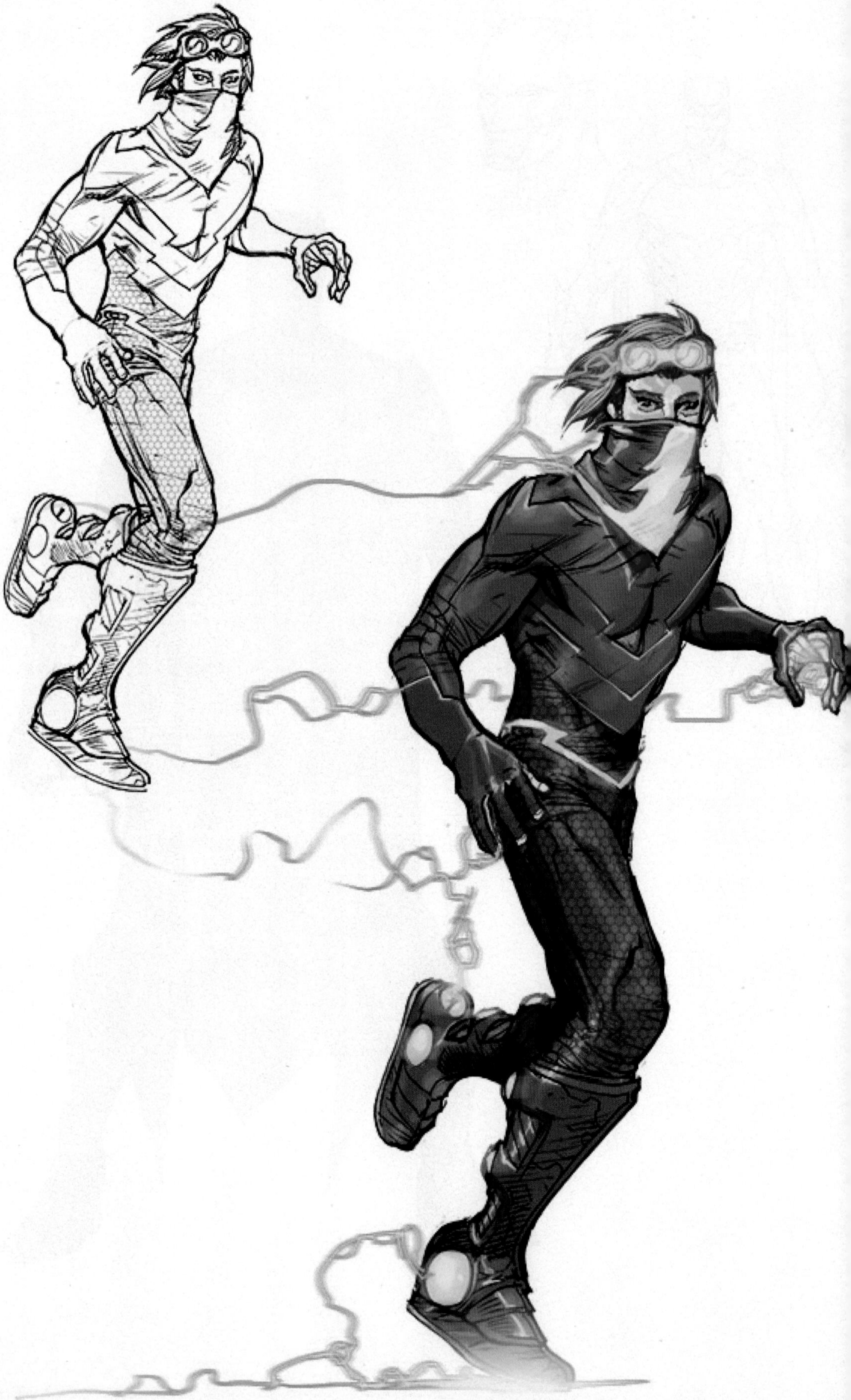

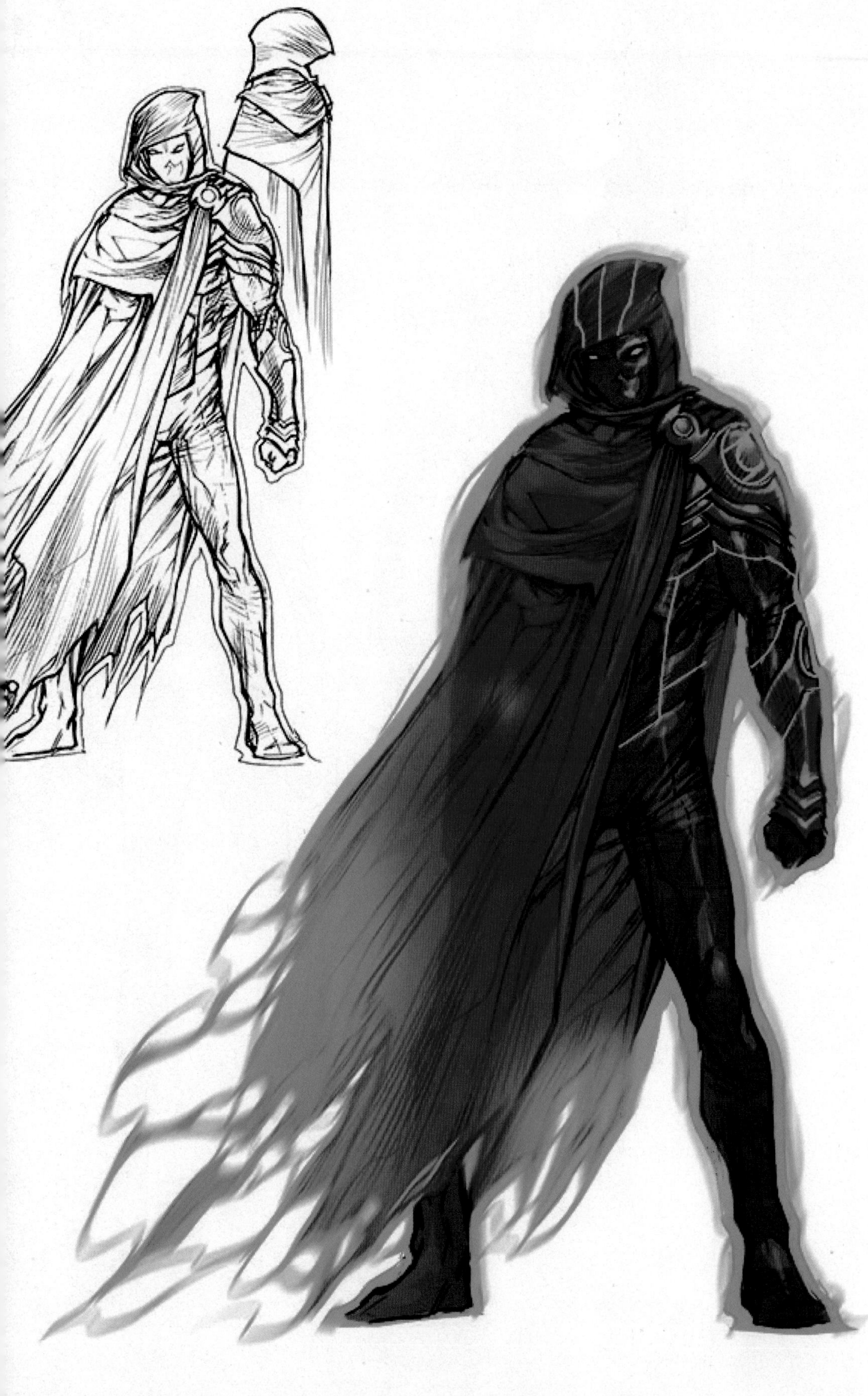

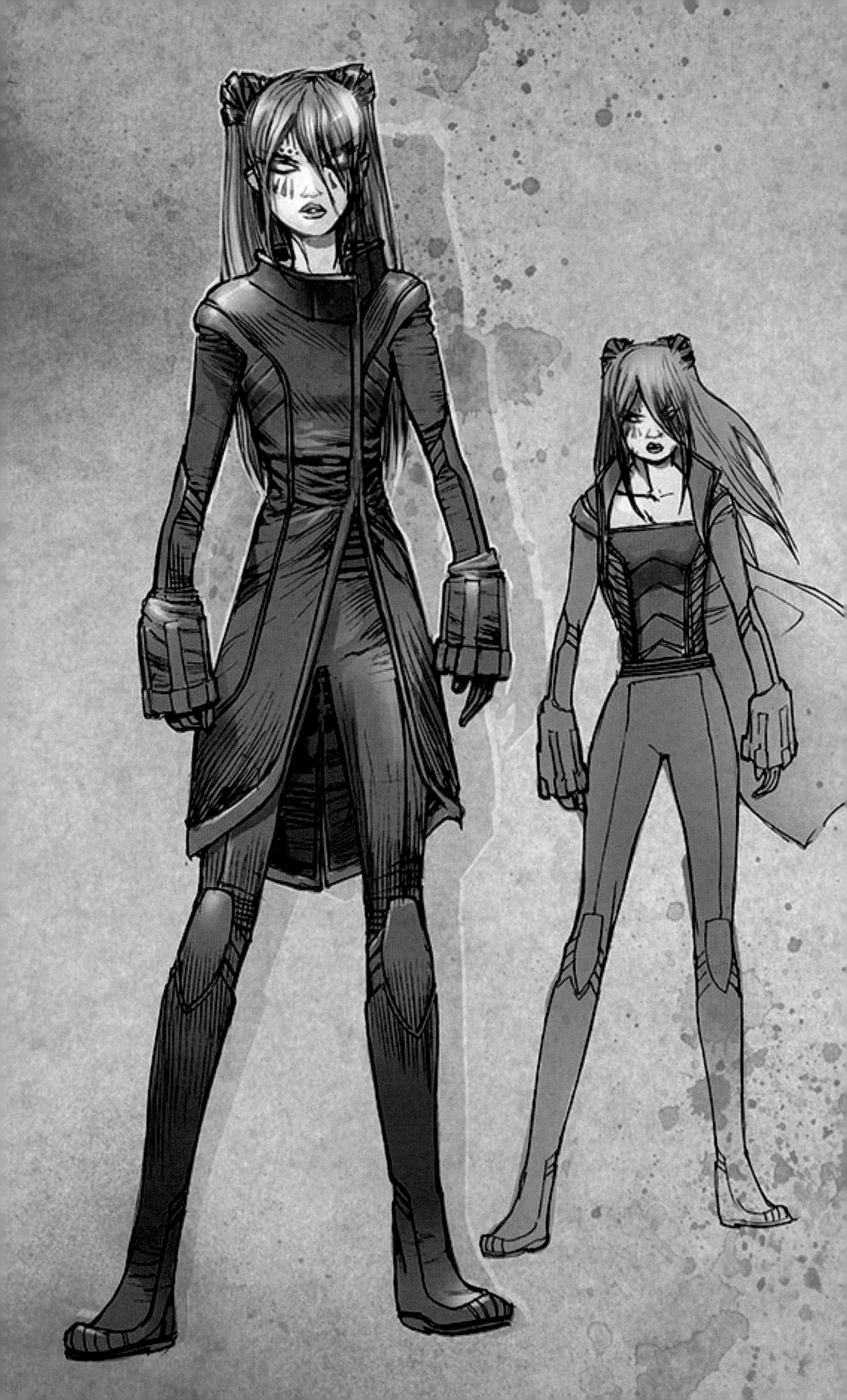

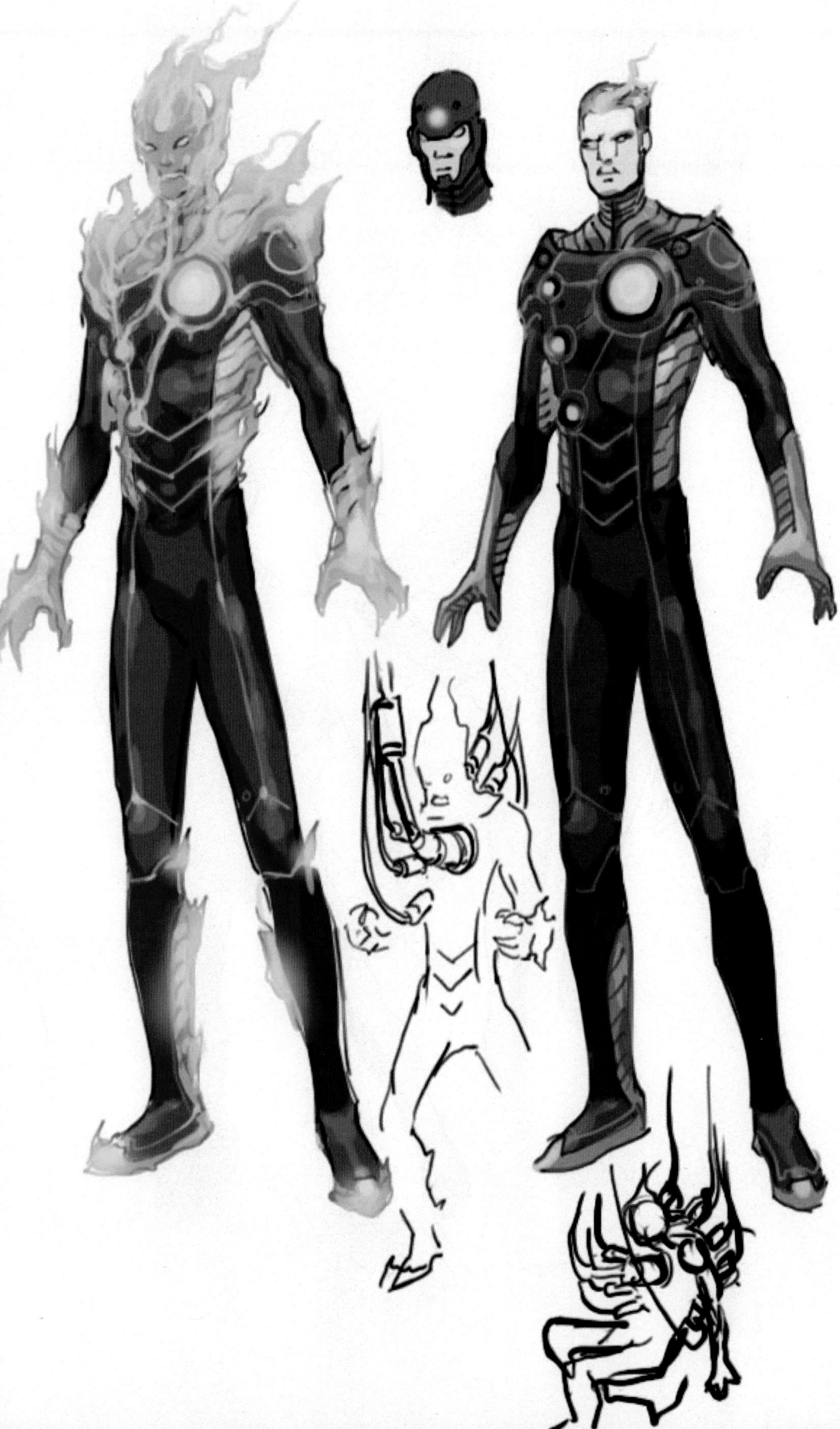

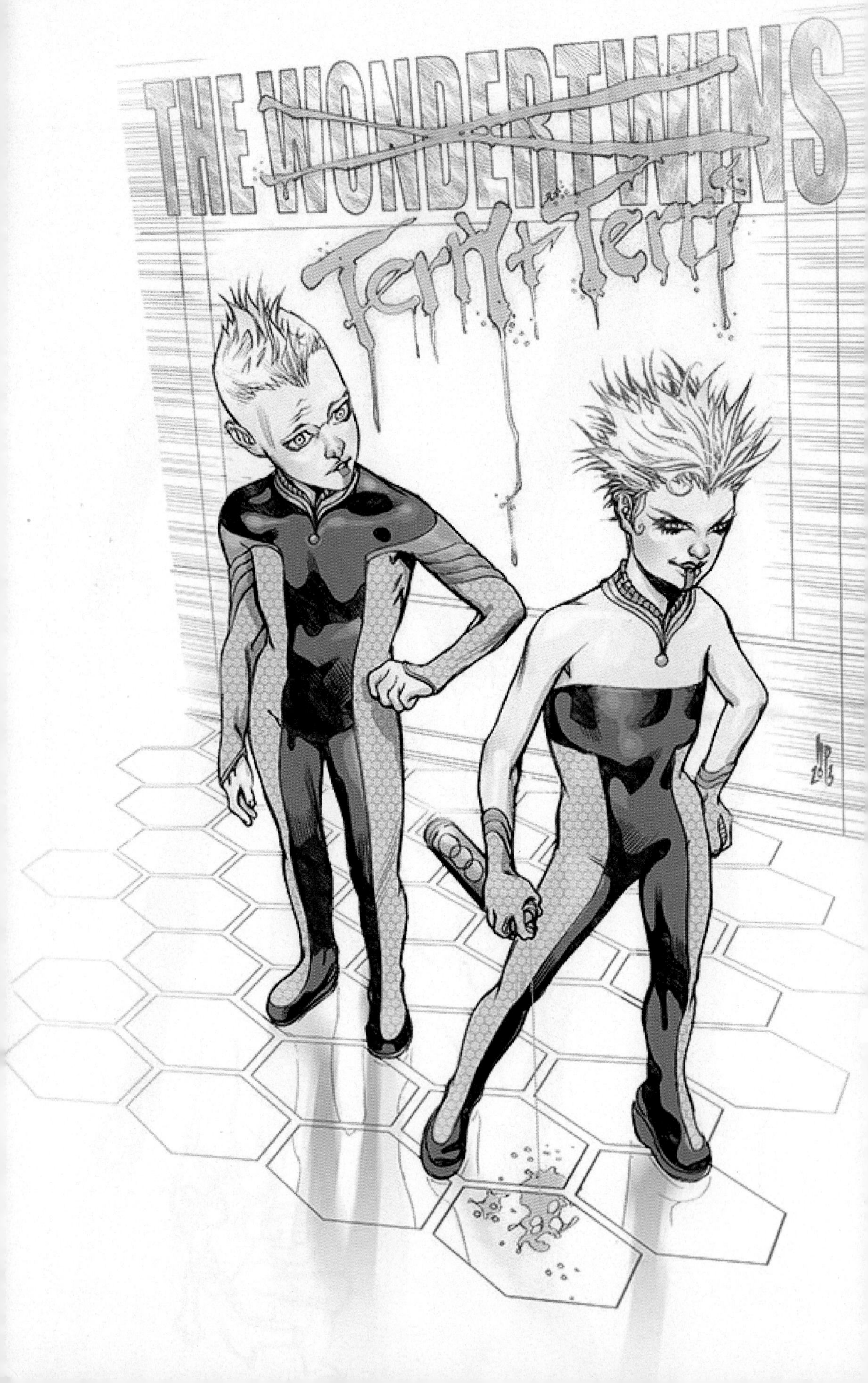
THE WONDERTWINS
Terry + Terry